CHARLES R. SWINDOLL

SWINDOLL'S
LIVING
INSIGHTS

NEW TESTAMENT COMMENTARY

MATTHEW 16-28

Tyndale House Publishers
Carol Stream, Illinois

Swindoll's Living Insights New Testament Commentary, Volume 1B

Visit Tyndale online at tyndale.com.

Insights on Matthew 16–28 copyright © 2020 by Charles R. Swindoll, Inc.

Designed by Nicole Grimes

Published in association with Yates & Yates, LLP (www.yates2.com).

The Library of Congress has catalogued the first volume as follows:
Names: Swindoll, Charles R., author.
Title: Insights on Matthew / Charles R. Swindoll.
Description: Carol Stream, Illinois : Tyndale House Publishers, Inc., 2020.
  | Series: Swindoll's living insights New Testament commentary | Includes
  bibliographical references. | Contents: Part 1: 1-15
Identifiers: LCCN 2019034800 (print) | LCCN 2019034801 (ebook) | ISBN
  9781414393827 (vol. 1 ; hardcover) | ISBN 9781414393971 (kindle edition)
  | ISBN 9781496410689 (epub) | ISBN 9781496410672 (epub)
Subjects: LCSH: Bible. Matthew—Commentaries.
Classification: LCC BS2575.53 .S95 2020 (print) | LCC BS2575.53 (ebook) |
  DDC 226.2/077—dc23
LC record available at https://lccn.loc.gov/2019034800
LC ebook record available at https://lccn.loc.gov/2019034801

ISBN 978-1-4964-3615-3   Hardcover

Printed in China
26 25 24 23 22 21 20
 7   6   5   4   3   2   1

CONTENTS

AUTHOR'S PREFACE

For more than sixty years I have loved the Bible. It was that love for the Scriptures, mixed with a clear call into the gospel ministry during my tour of duty in the Marine Corps, that resulted in my going to Dallas Theological Seminary to prepare for a lifetime of ministry. During those four great years I had the privilege of studying under outstanding men of God, who also loved God's Word. They not only held the inerrant Word of God in high esteem, they taught it carefully, preached it passionately, and modeled it consistently. A week never passes without my giving thanks to God for the grand heritage that has been mine to claim! I am forever indebted to those fine theologians and mentors, who cultivated in me a strong commitment to the understanding, exposition, and application of God's truth.

For more than fifty years I have been engaged in doing just that—*and how I love it!* I confess without hesitation that I am addicted to the examination and the proclamation of the Scriptures. Because of this, books have played a major role in my life for as long as I have been in ministry—especially those volumes that explain the truths and enhance my understanding of what God has written. Through these many years I have collected a large personal library, which has proven invaluable as I have sought to remain a faithful student of the Bible. To the end of my days, my major goal in life is to communicate the Word with accuracy, insight, clarity, and practicality. Without informative and reliable books to turn to, I would have "run dry" decades ago.

Among my favorite and most well-worn volumes are those that have enabled me to get a better grasp of the biblical text. Like most expositors, I am forever searching for literary tools that I can use to hone my gifts and sharpen my skills. For me, that means finding resources that make the complicated simple and easy to understand, that offer insightful comments and word pictures that enable me to see the relevance of sacred truth in light of my twenty-first-century world, and that drive those truths home to my heart in ways I do not easily forget. When I come across such books, they wind up in my hands as I devour them and then place them in my library for further reference . . . and, believe me, I often return to them. What a relief it is to have these resources to turn to when I lack fresh insight, or when I need just the right story or illustration, or when I get stuck in the tangled text and cannot find my way out. For the serious expositor, a library is essential. As a mentor of mine once said, "Where else can you have ten thousand professors at your fingertips?"

In recent years I have discovered there are not nearly enough resources like those I just described. It was such a discovery that prompted me to consider becoming a part of the answer instead of lamenting the problem. But the solution would result in a huge undertaking. A writing project that covers all of the books and letters of the New Testament seemed overwhelming and intimidating. A rush of relief came when I realized that during the past fifty-plus years I've taught and preached through most of the New Testament. In my files were folders filled with notes from those messages that were just lying there, waiting to be brought out of hiding, given a fresh and relevant touch in light of today's needs, and applied to fit into the lives of men and women who long for a fresh word from the Lord. *That did it!* I began to work on plans to turn all of those notes into this commentary on the New Testament.

I must express my gratitude to Mike Svigel for his tireless and devoted efforts, serving as my hands-on, day-to-day editor. He has done superb work as we have walked our way through the verses and chapters of all twenty-seven New Testament books. It has been a pleasure to see how he has taken my original material and helped me shape it into a style that remains true to the text of the Scriptures, at the same time interestingly and creatively developed, and all the while allowing my voice to come through in a natural and easy-to-read manner.

I need to add sincere words of appreciation to the congregations I have served in various parts of these United States for more than five decades. It has been my good fortune to be the recipient of their love, support, encouragement, patience, and frequent words of affirmation as I have fulfilled my calling to stand and deliver God's message year after year. The sheep from all those flocks have endeared themselves to this shepherd in more ways than I can put into words . . . and none more than those I currently serve with delight at Stonebriar Community Church in Frisco, Texas.

Finally, I must thank my wife, Cynthia, for her understanding of my addiction to studying, to preaching, and to writing. Never has she discouraged me from staying at it. Never has she failed to urge me in the pursuit of doing my very best. On the contrary, her affectionate support personally, and her own commitment to excellence in leading Insight for Living for more than three and a half decades, have combined to keep me faithful to my calling "in season and out of season." Without her devotion to me and apart from our mutual partnership throughout our lifetime of ministry together, Swindoll's Living Insights would never have been undertaken.

I am grateful that it has now found its way into your hands and, ultimately, onto the shelves of your library. My continued hope and prayer is that you will find these volumes helpful in your own study and personal application of the Bible. May they help you come to realize, as I have over these many years, that God's Word is as timeless as it is true.

The grass withers, the flower fades,
But the word of our God stands forever. (Isa. 40:8, NASB)

Chuck Swindoll
Frisco, Texas

THE STRONG'S
NUMBERING SYSTEM

Swindoll's Living Insights New Testament Commentary uses the Strong's word-study numbering system to give both newer and more advanced Bible students alike quicker, more convenient access to helpful original-language tools (e.g., concordances, lexicons, and theological dictionaries). The Strong's numbering system, made popular by the *Strong's Exhaustive Concordance of the Bible,* is used with the majority of biblical Greek and Hebrew reference works. Those who are unfamiliar with the ancient Hebrew, Aramaic, and Greek alphabets can quickly find information on a given word by looking up the appropriate index number. Advanced students will find the system helpful because it allows them to quickly find the lexical form of obscure conjugations and inflections.

When a Greek word is mentioned in the text, the Strong's number is included in square brackets after the Greek word. So in the example of the Greek word *agapē* [26], "love," the number is used with Greek tools keyed to the Strong's system.

On occasion, a Hebrew word is mentioned in the text. The Strong's Hebrew numbers are completely separate from the Greek numbers, so Hebrew numbers are prefixed with a letter "H." So, for example, the Hebrew word *kapporet* [H3727], "mercy seat," comes from *kopher* [H3722], "to ransom," "to secure favor through a gift."

INSIGHTS ON MATTHEW 16–28

As we step into the intensity of the second half of Matthew's Gospel, we see how Jesus fulfills—in an unexpected way—His destiny as the King, Israel's long-awaited Messiah. And by the end, we see how Jesus' mission turns into our mission, as we join with His initial followers in sharing the good news far and wide.

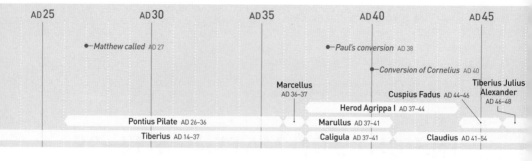

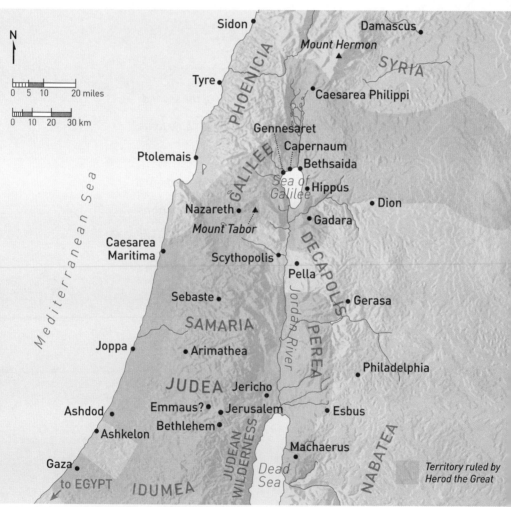

Map of Jesus' Life and Ministry. Matthew's story begins with the birth of Jesus in Bethlehem. It then traces Jesus' ministry throughout Galilee. After Jesus continued His ministry en route from Galilee to Judea, He was met with rejection in Jerusalem, ultimately resulting in His death.

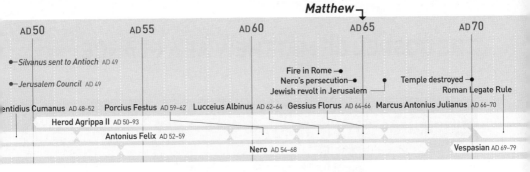

Matthew

AD 50   AD 55   AD 60   AD 65   AD 70

●—*Silvanus sent to Antioch* AD 49

●—*Jerusalem Council* AD 49

Fire in Rome —●
Nero's persecution —●
Jewish revolt in Jerusalem

Temple destroyed —●
Roman Legate Rule

entidius Cumanus AD 48–52   Porcius Festus AD 59–62   Lucceius Albinus AD 62–64   Gessius Florus AD 64–66   Marcus Antonius Julianus AD 66–70

Herod Agrippa II AD 50–93

Antonius Felix AD 52–59

Nero AD 54–68

Vespasian AD 69–79

MATTHEW

INTRODUCTION

From his remarkable perspective as one of the original twelve disciples, Matthew wrote his account of Jesus' birth, life, teachings, miracles, death, and resurrection to demonstrate to his intended Jewish readers that Jesus is the King, their long-awaited Messiah. Much of what that hated-tax-collector-turned-faithful-follower wrote came from his own eyewitness experiences. The rest was likely written on the basis of personal interactions with trustworthy sources: the other disciples, the mother and brothers of Jesus, and, of course, Jesus Himself. No doubt, Matthew knew the true story of Jesus' person and work as well as anybody in the first century.

But Matthew also knew the hardness of his readers' hearts. He knew that already during Jesus' ministry the Jewish leaders had rejected their Messiah with vehemence and violence. So, for the sake of his fellow Jewish believers, Matthew dealt with a question nagging many who had already become convinced that Jesus was the Messiah: "If Jesus really is the King, Israel's long-awaited Messiah, why don't we see the kingdom restored to Israel according to God's promises?"

One of Matthew's motivations in writing his Gospel was to report how Jesus had offered the kingdom to Israel and how the hard-hearted religious and political leaders of the nation had rejected Him (4:17; 16:13-28; 21:33-46). Yet in his Gospel—especially the second half—Matthew wanted to show that the fulfillment of a literal, earthly kingdom hasn't been set aside permanently; rather, it has been delayed until the future coming of the Son of Man in glory (19:28). In the meantime, the rejection of Jesus by Israel was allowing for the establishment of the church of baptized believers from all nations (16:18; 28:19-20).

Before we preview the course of this narrative of Israel's increasing

THE GOSPEL OF MATTHEW AT A GLANCE

SECTION	ANNOUNCEMENT AND ARRIVAL OF THE KING	PROCLAMATION AND RECEPTION OF THE KIN
PASSAGE	1:1–4:25	5:1–15:39
	Jesus' Credentials	Jesus' Message
THEMES	Birth Baptism Temptation	Miracles Discourses Parables
KEY TERMS	Baptize Christ Proclaim	Righteousness Authority Blessed Parable

POSITION AND REJECTION OF THE KING	PASSION AND TRIUMPH OF THE KING
16:1–25:46	26:1–28:20
Jesus' Suffering	Jesus' Victory
Opposition Rejection Second Coming	Passover and Arrest Suffering and Death Resurrection Ascension
Tribulation Woe Stumble	Hand Over Suffer

rejection of their Messiah, let's briefly review the overall shape of the Gospel and where we are in the plotline leading up to Matthew 16 through 28.

THE STORY THUS FAR

Matthew develops his plot in two distinct parts: Chapters 1 through 15 address the *identity of the King*, while chapters 16 through 28 address the *destiny and victory of the King*. Between these two sections we observe a shift from Jesus teaching the vast multitudes (Matt. 1–15) to Jesus narrowing His focus to be on teaching His closest disciples (Matt. 16–28). In the first half, Jesus' popularity among the people increases because of astonishing miracles and provocative teaching; in the second half, the hostility against Jesus rises to a feverish pitch. Geographically, the first fifteen chapters emphasize Jesus' ministry in the regions around the Sea of Galilee, while the second half increasingly focuses on His ministry in Judea and especially in Jerusalem—the center of religious and political power in Israel.

In the previous half volume, covering Matthew 1 through 15, we first explored the *Announcement and Arrival of the King* (1:1–4:25). These opening chapters developed Jesus' credentials as the long-awaited Messiah. Not only did He have the right genealogy to qualify as the messianic Son of David (1:1-17), but He also fulfilled numerous Old Testament prophecies and types that foretold or foreshadowed His birth and childhood (1:18–2:23). His baptism exhibited His consecration and commissioning, marking the point when He took the baton from John the Baptizer, who had been sent to announce the coming of the Messiah (3:1-17). Furthermore, as the Messiah-King, Jesus passed Satan's tests, demonstrating not only His identity as a perfect man with an impeccable nature but also His divine power (4:1-11). And prior to an official public launch of His ministry, Jesus began calling disciples to accompany Him, learn from Him, and assist Him in His work (4:12-25).

Next, we witnessed the *Proclamation and Reception of the King* (5:1–15:39). In these eleven chapters, Matthew recounted Jesus' teaching, preaching, and miracles, all in anticipation of His messianic kingdom. This section includes the famous "Sermon on the Mount" (5:1-7:29), accounts of numerous miracles that demonstrated Jesus' divine power and authority (8:1–9:38), and discourses on practical, moral, and spiritual themes amid growing controversy (10:1–12:50). We saw that not everyone was thrilled, however, about the advent of this Messiah, and Jesus switched from clear teaching and preaching about the kingdom of God to the use of parables for the purpose of veiling the mysteries of the kingdom to those who rejected His authority (13:1-58). As astonishing as it seems, the clear demonstration of His miraculous power was met with increasing resistance to His masterful preaching (14:1–15:39).

THE PLOT THICKENS

There's an old saying: "Politics makes strange bedfellows." Find the right cause, and two otherwise warring factions will set their differences aside and fight side by side against a common enemy instead of face to face against each other. For example, regardless of their differences on other matters, opposing political parties often join together in times of war to defeat a foreign enemy.

In Matthew 16 through 28, this aphorism proves true. We see startling, unexpected alliances forming against a shared enemy. Warring factions of Pharisees and Sadducees temporarily set aside their differences to eliminate a common threat. Generally, the Pharisees and Sadducees were on different ends of the theological spectrum. While the Pharisees believed in the sovereignty of God and in predestination regarding many matters, the Sadducees rejected the notion of predestination altogether in favor of a strong view of human free will.[1] While the Pharisees had adopted a complex system of oral traditions in addition to the written Law of Moses, the Sadducees accepted no teaching or tradition beyond what could be found in the five books of Moses (Genesis through Deuteronomy). Additionally, the Pharisees believed in angels, spirits, and life after death, while the Sadducees tended to reject such elements of the spiritual realm.

Despite these stark differences, the Pharisees and Sadducees banded together in their opposition to Jesus of Nazareth. That unprecedented alliance between sworn theological adversaries, between the right and the left, between the conservatives and the liberals, between the populists and the elitists, demonstrates the shared depth of their utter hatred for Jesus. While doctrinally Jesus stood much closer to the basic theology of the Pharisees, practically He rejected their hyper-legalistic applications of the Law to every aspect of life, which stemmed from the misguided interpretations of the rabbis. The Sadducees, on the other hand, would have felt their political and social power threatened by the growing belief among the masses in Jesus as none other than their King, Israel's long-awaited Messiah. So, for different reasons, the Pharisees and Sadducees saw Jesus and His disciples as a common enemy. Thus, they found themselves on the same team in opposition to Him, forging an alliance in hatred and hardness of heart.

As the curtain opens on the second half of the Gospel of Matthew, this sudden, unexpected alliance takes center stage. In the end, this coalition between Pharisees and Sadducees would lead not to the preservation of their ideologies but ultimately to their destruction.

PREVIEW OF THINGS TO COME

The second half of the Gospel of Matthew, chapters 16 through 28, chronicles the *destiny and victory of the King*. It can be divided into two parts.

Opposition and Rejection of the King (16:1–25:46). The beginning of Matthew 16 sets the tone of the chapters that follow: "The Pharisees and Sadducees came . . . testing Jesus" (16:1). From this point on, the religious leaders hound His every move while Jesus continues to prepare His disciples for the events that will transpire in the final days of His earthly ministry (16:1-28). A handful of Jesus' disciples witness His glorious Transfiguration, a brief but powerful glimpse of His glory and coming kingdom (17:1-13). Determined to carry out His ministry, Jesus continues to heal and to teach vital lessons about discipleship (17:14–18:35).

Slowly, His ministry takes Him closer to Jerusalem, further drawing the attention of the religious leaders bent on cornering Him with a basis for arrest. Meanwhile, Jesus continues to preach undeterred (19:1–20:34). Eventually Jesus arrives in Jerusalem, welcomed with praises from the masses but with increasing resistance from the leaders, which He answers with increased condemnation (21:1–23:36). This culminates in a lament over Jerusalem itself for its rejection of the Messiah (23:37-39), followed by a lengthy teaching concerning the end of the age, when the kingdom of the Messiah will be set up on the earth (24:1–25:46).

Passion and Triumph of the King (26:1–28:20). The last three chapters of Matthew's Gospel recount how the plot of the Jewish leaders to kill Jesus comes to fruition (26:1-16). After celebrating His last Passover with His disciples and instituting the Lord's Supper (26:17-35), Jesus is betrayed and arrested (26:36-56). He is unjustly tried by the leaders in Jerusalem, while His own disciples abandon Him (26:57–27:26). Then, in keeping with the Old Testament prophecies—as Jesus foretold—the Roman government, with the urging of the Jewish leaders, crucifies the rightful King of Israel, the long-awaited Messiah (27:27-56). Following His death, He is buried (27:57-66).

But, just as Jesus and the prophets of old had prophesied, He is raised on the third day, stepping out of the tomb in a miraculous, bodily resurrection, victorious over death (28:1-10). At the same time, those who had plotted against Him continue to conspire against the good news of His resurrection (28:11-15). Having risen victorious, the Lord Jesus meets with His disciples in Galilee to give them a new mission—one He has been preparing them for over the last three years: "Go therefore and make disciples of all the nations, baptizing them in the name of the Father and the Son and the Holy Spirit, teaching them to observe all that I commanded you; and lo, I am with you always, even to the end of the age" (28:19-20).

As we step into the intensity of the second half of Matthew's Gospel, we see how Jesus fulfills—in an unexpected way—His destiny as the King, Israel's long-awaited Messiah. And by the end, we see how Jesus' mission turns into our mission, as we join with His initial followers in sharing the good news far and wide.

OPPOSITION AND REJECTION OF THE KING (MATTHEW 16:1-25:46)

Convinced by His miraculous signs and His powerful preaching, Jesus' closest disciples had no doubts about who He was: the King, their long-awaited Messiah. And more than that, the Spirit had opened their eyes to a deeper truth: Jesus was not just a great teacher, a gifted prophet, and the rightful king; He was also "the Son of the living God" (16:16). While this profound truth would be further illuminated by Jesus' glorious transformation (17:1-13), it would appear to be contradicted by His disturbing predictions of His own betrayal, suffering, and death (16:21-23).

This section, which I'm calling *Opposition and Rejection of the King* (16:1-25:46), is characterized by these two contrasting themes in the life and ministry of Jesus—increased proof of His identity as the long-awaited Messiah and increased hostility against Him by those who had everything to lose at the coming of the King. The religious leaders' hypocrisy and false teachings would be exposed by the incarnation of Truth itself. The corrupt priesthood would be toppled and replaced by the eternal High Priest. The illegitimate king over Judea and the Gentile rulers would be dethroned by the rightful Heir of the house of David and Ruler of heaven and earth.

As such, the opposition builds to a climax as the scribes and Pharisees, priests and Sadducees, governors and rulers band together to do away with public enemy number one—Jesus, a mere "carpenter's son" from Nazareth (13:55).

KEY TERMS IN MATTHEW 16:1-25:46

thlipsis (θλῖψις) [2347] "affliction," "tribulation"
The Greek word *thlipsis* can refer to the coming Great Tribulation of the end times, leading up to Christ's physical return as King (24:21, 29-31), but more commonly it refers to the general trials and persecutions

experienced by Christians of every age (13:21; 24:9; John 16:33; Rom. 5:3). It could be that the ambiguity in how this term was used caused confusion among the Thessalonian believers, who may have believed the normal afflictions they were experiencing (1 Thes. 3:3-4; 2 Thes. 1:4-8) indicated that they were in the middle of the end-times Tribulation (Mark 13:19; Rev. 7:13-14).

ouai (οὐαί) [3759] "alas," "woe"

Loud wailing during times of deep sorrow was common in the ancient world. In fact, funerals of the rich were sometimes accompanied by professional mourners, often to increase the perception of grief at the loss of a person who may have had more enemies than allies. The exclamation *ouai!* intends to mimic a cry of anguish. As opposition to Jesus intensified, Jesus' words of lament for His critics also increased, finding their climax in His repeated "woes" against the scribes and Pharisees for their hypocrisy (23:13, 14, 15, 16, 23, 25, 27, 29). These were not just cries of anguish for their stubborn, wicked hearts, but also of sorrow for the judgments they and their followers would suffer because of their rejection of the Messiah.

skandalizō (σκανδαλίζω) [4624] "to cause to stumble"
skandalon (σκάνδαλον) [4625] "cause of stumbling"

In English, the noun "scandal" and the related verb "scandalize" refer to the effect of an action of questionable morality that leads to a bad reputation, public anger or shame, or shock. However, in the New Testament, the Greek term from which we get "scandal" refers to "an action or circumstance that leads one to act contrary to a proper course of action or set of beliefs."[1] In Matthew's Gospel, Peter is famously called a *skandalon* for suggesting that Jesus should shirk His mission to suffer and die for sin (16:23). Jesus also warns against those people or things that cause us to stumble into temptation and sin (18:7-9).

Testy Critics and Dull Disciples
MATTHEW 16:1-12

NASB

¹The Pharisees and Sadducees came up, and testing Jesus, they asked Him to show them a ªsign from heaven. ²But He replied to them, "ªWhen it is evening, you say, 'It will be fair weather, for the sky is red.' ³And in the morning, 'There will be a storm today, for the sky is red and threatening.' Do you know how to discern the ªappearance of the sky,

NLT

¹One day the Pharisees and Sadducees came to test Jesus, demanding that he show them a miraculous sign from heaven to prove his authority. ²He replied, "You know the saying, 'Red sky at night means fair weather tomorrow; ³red sky in the morning means foul weather all day.' You know how to interpret the weather signs in the sky, but you don't know

NASB

but cannot *discern* the signs of the times? 4An evil and adulterous generation seeks after a ᵃsign; and a ᵃsign will not be given it, except the sign of Jonah." And He left them and went away.

5And the disciples came to the other side *of the sea,* but they had forgotten to bring *any* bread. 6And Jesus said to them, "Watch out and beware of the ᵃleaven of the Pharisees and Sadducees." 7They began to discuss *this* among themselves, saying, "*He said that* because we did not bring *any* bread." 8But Jesus, aware of this, said, "You men of little faith, why do you discuss among yourselves that you have no bread? 9Do you not yet understand or remember the five loaves of the five thousand, and how many baskets *full* you picked up? 10Or the seven loaves of the four thousand, and how many large baskets *full* you picked up? 11How is it that you do not understand that I did not speak to you concerning bread? But beware of the ᵃleaven of the Pharisees and Sadducees." 12Then they understood that He did not say to beware of the leaven of bread, but of the teaching of the Pharisees and Sadducees.

16:1 ᵃOr *attesting miracle* 16:2 ᵃEarly mss do not contain the rest of v 2 and v 3 16:3 ᵃLit *face* 16:4 ᵃOr *attesting miracle* 16:6 ᵃOr *yeast* 16:11 ᵃOr *yeast*

NLT

how to interpret the signs of the times!* 4Only an evil, adulterous generation would demand a miraculous sign, but the only sign I will give them is the sign of the prophet Jonah.*" Then Jesus left them and went away.

5Later, after they crossed to the other side of the lake, the disciples discovered they had forgotten to bring any bread. 6"Watch out!" Jesus warned them. "Beware of the yeast of the Pharisees and Sadducees."

7At this they began to argue with each other because they hadn't brought any bread. 8Jesus knew what they were saying, so he said, "You have so little faith! Why are you arguing with each other about having no bread? 9Don't you understand even yet? Don't you remember the 5,000 I fed with five loaves, and the baskets of leftovers you picked up? 10Or the 4,000 I fed with seven loaves, and the large baskets of leftovers you picked up? 11Why can't you understand that I'm not talking about bread? So again I say, 'Beware of the yeast of the Pharisees and Sadducees.'"

12Then at last they understood that he wasn't speaking about the yeast in bread, but about the deceptive teaching of the Pharisees and Sadducees.

16:2-3 Several manuscripts do not include any of the words in 16:2-3 after *He replied.* 16:4 Greek *the sign of Jonah.*

I've witnessed a lot of arguments over my lifetime of ministry. At times, it seems that the favorite indoor sport of some Christians is arguing. I'm convinced that some Christians aren't happy unless they have a theological question to bicker about or some church issue to debate. I've seen examples from the tragic to the ridiculous. Rarely do I see believers argue over essential doctrines of the Christian faith or clear matters of morality. Most often it's the same old discussions that Christians have debated for centuries—predestination or free will; who, when, and how to baptize; what style of worship a church should have; what the right order of end-times events is.

When you analyze these arguments, you find that most often everybody is talking and nobody is listening. Or, if they are listening, either they won't hear what's being said because their attitude is argumentative or they don't hear what's being said because they're self-absorbed. The result in these situations is not a conclusion to "agree to disagree" and to live in peace but an unceasing continuation of the argument with no progress being made by either side.

In the first century, Jesus had to deal with both categories of bad listeners. His critics were in the first category. They wouldn't hear because of their argumentative nature. They were testy. But His disciples were in the second category. They didn't hear because they were preoccupied with themselves. They were dull.

As we enter the story of Matthew 16:1-12, we find ourselves with the disciples in the village Matthew calls Magadan (15:39), probably another name for Magdala, the hometown of Mary Magdalene. Here we see how Jesus dealt with those testy critics and dull disciples . . . and how we can glean important, practical truths from those encounters.

— 16:1-4 —

Most twenty-first-century readers probably wouldn't think twice about the opening words of Matthew 16: "The Pharisees and Sadducees came" (16:1). But to first-century Jewish readers, linking the Pharisees and Sadducees together would have been like saying "the liberals and conservatives" or "the Calvinists and Arminians" or "the Catholics and Protestants." Under normal circumstances, the Pharisees and Sadducees were on opposite sides of most issues.

The term "Pharisee" most likely means "separated one."[2] Pharisees strove for a strict, traditional, orthodox approach to faith and practice within Judaism. While they tended to preserve theological positions that were in line with Scripture, their methods for maintaining purity had deteriorated into legalism and hypocrisy. They also believed that the traditional teachings they developed in the course of their study of the Scriptures were as authoritative as those Scriptures themselves. This led many to argue that these teachings had actually been passed down to the rabbis from Moses through oral tradition.[3] The Pharisees maintained a strong belief in the sovereignty of God and in predestination and also embraced beliefs in angelic beings, a spiritual dimension of humanity, the afterlife—and the rewards or punishments therein—and the resurrection of the body.

By contrast, the faction of the Sadducees rejected the doctrine of predestination and strongly emphasized human free will.[4] They also rejected the Pharisees' views of oral tradition and instead embraced doctrines and practices that could be established only on the basis of the Pentateuch—the five books of Moses. The Sadducees also denied the existence of angels, the continuation of the soul after death, and the resurrection of the body. Instead, they emphasized the blessings in *this* life for faithfulness to the covenant of Moses and stressed that the Law was vital for Israel to maintain its prosperity in the Promised Land and a place among the nations.[5]

Given the fact that the Pharisees and Sadducees usually stood toe to toe against each other, seeing them stand shoulder to shoulder in their cooperation against Jesus would have surprised Matthew's original, Jewish readers. Yet when it came to the growing popularity of that pesky preacher from Nazareth and the persuasive power of His miracles, the Pharisees and Sadducees were willing to set aside their differences and work together against Jesus.

Both groups wanted to get rid of Jesus, so they were continually putting Him to the test. I find the kind of demand they made in this scene quite revealing. They asked Jesus for "a sign from heaven" (16:1). Note that they didn't seem to question His power. He had been performing astonishing miracles for some time, and His reputation as a healer had spread far and wide. However, His critics constantly questioned the *source* of His power. Was it really from God? Or from Satan? Was it legitimately from heaven? Or from the lower parts of the earth?

The new alliance of critics pressed Jesus for some blazing, ear-shattering event similar to the splitting of the Red Sea or the appearance of the pillar of fire and smoke in the Exodus narrative. Without such a miraculous sign with clear heavenly origins, they would not believe and would refuse to accept His divine authority. However, based on their track record of unreasonable skepticism, I think that even if Jesus had performed some amazing sign on demand, their hardness of heart was such that they still would have rejected Him and refused to believe.

Jesus knew their hearts. He wasn't about to succumb to their cynical demands for miraculous signs. There was simply no way to win at their game, played by their rules, because the rules constantly changed. Jesus' answer reveals His great wisdom. His critics were weather-wise but spiritually foolish. He quoted a famous proverbial rule of thumb used to predict the weather (16:2-3). We have a similar saying today, which goes something like this:

A red sky at night is a sailor's delight,
But a red sky in the morning is a sailor's warning.

Jesus wasn't revealing the key to all meteorological predictions. His purpose was not to give them (or us) an infallible guide to make accurate weather forecasts. Rather, He was pointing out the inconsistency of His critics by applying rules of logic to the evidence. Generally speaking, the rhyme is true. Having observed the pattern of red skies in the evening or morning and having correlated such patterns with the likelihood of stormy weather, people had inductively concluded that a red sky at night meant fair weather was probable, while a red sky in the morning meant that stormy weather was likely.

By the same rules of induction, they should have also discerned "the signs of the times" (16:3). By "signs of the times," Jesus was probably referring to the many miraculous signs that had already repeatedly and clearly pointed to the fact that He was the long-awaited Messiah. Recall that when John the Baptizer had questioned whether Jesus was the "Expected One," Jesus had replied, "Go and report to John what you hear and see: the blind receive sight and the lame walk, the lepers are cleansed and the deaf hear, the dead are raised up, and the poor have the gospel preached to them" (11:3-5). Based on these clear signs of the coming of the messianic kingdom, anybody with a believing heart and a discerning mind should have been able to conclude that the Messiah was present. But even in light of these clear signs of the Messiah, the Pharisees and Sadducees had closed the eyes of their hearts and blocked their ears to discernment. Instead, they wallowed in hard-hearted unbelief.

Jesus then repeated the same stinging rebuke He had leveled against the scribes and Pharisees earlier (see 12:38-40). This time, He lashed out at the Pharisees and Sadducees. They were "an evil and adulterous generation" whom He would not indulge with a made-to-order sign. Rather, the only thing they would get to confirm Jesus' identity as the Messiah was "the sign of Jonah" (16:4). That is, just as Jonah was in the belly of the fish for three days, the Son of Man would be buried in the earth for three days (12:40). The Resurrection itself was the only sign they would be given, and even then, most would not believe.

Jesus' answer suggests that He was fed up with His critics. He had said enough and done enough to convince anyone who was open to the evidence and honest enough to accept it. All they wanted to do was nitpick and argue over what actually constituted a sign from heaven vs.

a sign from earth. But enough was enough. Instead of wasting His time with immovable critics, Jesus "left them and went away" (16:4).

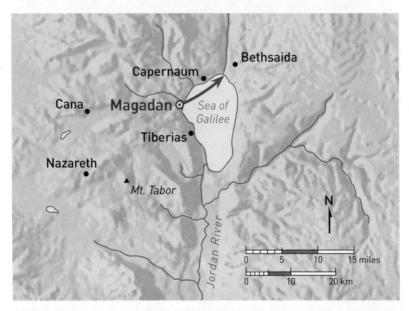

Magadan (also called Magdala) was on the western shore of the Sea of Galilee about 3 miles northwest of Tiberias. After refusing to give the Pharisees and Sadducees a "sign from heaven," Jesus boarded a boat and sailed to the northern end of the sea near Bethsaida.

— 16:5-12 —

Leaving behind the testy critics who had come down from Jerusalem to Magadan, Jesus and His disciples headed across to the other side of the Sea of Galilee, to the northern shore where the Jordan River flows into the lake. Later, He and His disciples would take the road that ran from the city of Bethsaida far north to the city of Caesarea Philippi (16:13; cf. Mark 8:22-27).

Presumably after learning that they were about to head on a long journey northward, the disciples commented that they had forgotten to bring bread for the journey (Matt. 16:5). Earlier, they had departed to Magadan hauling "seven large baskets full" of bread from the miracle of the feeding of the four thousand (15:37). Somewhere along the way, they had unloaded the bread, perhaps giving it to some of the followers in Magadan. In any case, they had failed to load enough for the trip.

While the disciples fretted over the bread, Jesus' mind was elsewhere. He had just dealt with testy critics who were stubborn of heart, unwilling to accept the evidence that had been placed before them.

Their impenetrable unbelief caused Him deep anguish, which He carried with Him across the lake. While Jesus was still stewing over the heated confrontation with the frowning critics, His dull disciples were worried about bread. Maybe they started pointing fingers, playing the blame game, fretting over what to do about the problem. Maybe some suggested rushing back across the lake or finding a place to grab some fresh supplies. But Jesus was preoccupied with something else. He was instead thinking about the wicked leaders, their diabolical plot to capture and kill Him, and their dangerous false teaching, which poisoned the people's minds. All the while, He was just hearing "bread, bread, bread, bread, bread" from His disciples.

Finally, Jesus cut in: "Watch out and beware of the leaven of the Pharisees and Sadducees" (16:6). I picture the disciples suddenly silent, only half listening. They were still thinking about bread as Jesus mentioned leaven, or yeast. Something about Pharisees and Sadducees. Did that have something to do with bread? They began arguing with themselves again about the lack of bread and how they apparently needed to avoid the kind of leavened bread that Pharisees and Sadducees ate . . . or something like that.

Clearly, the disciples were clueless. They were thinking with their stomachs while Jesus was concerned about spiritual things. So He intruded on their misguided conversation again, scolding them for their "little faith" (16:8). Had they totally forgotten that Jesus didn't need baskets full of bread to provide for their needs on the journey? Didn't they remember the miracles of the five loaves that fed the five thousand men and the seven loaves that fed the four thousand (16:8-10)? Hadn't He provided an overabundance of food for them and for everybody else? Why in the world were they concerned about food? Jesus could have said the word and filled their boat with bread until it sunk!

Jesus was perturbed that the dull disciples could only think of the emptiness of stomachs while He was concerned about the emptiness of souls. Their conversation should have been about the Pharisees and Sadducees, the growing opposition to the preaching of Jesus, the stubbornness of the critics' hearts, and the danger that they posed to the easily swayed masses. The disciples' preoccupation with earthly things had desensitized them regarding spiritual things.

Jesus finally spelled it out for His disciples. He wasn't speaking about literal bread and literal yeast, but about the poisonous corruption of the Pharisees and the Sadducees—that is, their teaching (16:11-12). So devoted were Jesus' critics to taking Him down and crushing His following that they were willing to explain away even the most obvious proof of who He was. This kind of skepticism and cynicism was contagious, and it was going to become widespread (see Mark 8:15).

I can imagine that the disciples felt a little stupid, not because they had failed to catch Jesus' figure of speech but because they had been so worried about finding physical bread while Jesus was concerned about those who rejected the Bread of Life. Slowly but surely, though, the disciples were coming around.

APPLICATION: MATTHEW 16:1-12

Dull or Deep?

I'm sorry to say that far too many of us fit quite comfortably in the garb of the skeptical Pharisees and Sadducees or in the sandals of the worldly-minded disciples.

For a moment, put on the garb of the testy critics. You're wearing those robes and looking all important with your questions, searching for more evidence, demanding more proof. You're determined that you'll only believe after God meets the burden of proof and your own personal standard of evidence. But then, just as God shows Himself to be real, the bar for passing your standard of "a sign from heaven" is raised. This is a typical pattern of the hard-hearted, unbelieving skeptic. Honestly, in such a case, there's not much that can be done.

Jesus walked away from people like that, which can be a lesson for us. There are times when we've said and done all we can do with people who are hardened to the gospel. We've spoken to them about Jesus, answered their questions, responded to their objections, and given them a defense of our faith, only to hear more arguments. When we realize that we're dealing with people who won't accept the truth, we're wasting our time pushing harder or talking louder. Instead, we may simply need to walk away and leave them in God's hands. Continue to pray, to be a friend to them, and to be open if God does a work in their lives, having a sincere desire to really listen and being ready to lead them back if the opportunity presents itself. But until then, there's not much that can be done.

Now walk in the sandals of the dull disciples. You're supersaturated with spiritual things—a study Bible, a great church family, Christian books and music. But as you listen to the sermons or sing the messages or read the words or pray the prayers, they pass right through you. You've heard the gospel so much that it no longer makes an impact on your life. As the pastor preaches, you're thinking about what's for lunch or dinner. As you pray, your mind wanders to the next thing on the calendar. Though your eyes are wide open and your ears unstopped, you need to wake up and listen, to see spiritual things and hear spiritual words, the stuff beyond the everyday busyness of life.

I love these lines from Elizabeth Barrett Browning:

> Earth's crammed with heaven,
> And every common bush afire with God;
> But only he who sees, takes off his shoes,
> The rest sit round it, and pluck blackberries.[6]

Are you sitting around plucking blackberries, preoccupied with your next meal? Your next slice of bread? Your next career move? Your next car? All your creature comforts? Then you're probably missing the spiritual lessons of life that God is trying to teach you in order to deepen you.

I like to think the disciples were ashamed at their small-mindedness, their shallow thinking, their failure to grasp the simple analogy Jesus had used to redirect their thoughts and words to vital spiritual things. Let's not be that way. Let's not be dull disciples, but deep disciples.

Answering Life's Ultimate Question
MATTHEW 16:13-20

NASB

13 Now when Jesus came into the district of Caesarea Philippi, He was asking His disciples, "Who do people say that the Son of Man is?" 14 And they said, "Some *say* John the Baptist; and others, ªElijah; but still others, ᵇJeremiah, or one of the prophets." 15 He said to them, "But who do you say that I am?" 16 Simon Peter answered, "You are ªthe Christ,

NLT

13 When Jesus came to the region of Caesarea Philippi, he asked his disciples, "Who do people say that the Son of Man is?"*

14 "Well," they replied, "some say John the Baptist, some say Elijah, and others say Jeremiah or one of the other prophets."

15 Then he asked them, "But who do you say I am?"

16 Simon Peter answered, "You are the Messiah,* the Son of the living God."

NASB

the Son of the living God." ¹⁷And Jesus said to him, "Blessed are you, Simon ᵃBarjona, because flesh and blood did not reveal *this* to you, but My Father who is in heaven. ¹⁸I also say to you that you are ᵃPeter, and upon this ᵇrock I will build My church; and the gates of Hades will not overpower it. ¹⁹I will give you the keys of the kingdom of heaven; and whatever you bind on earth ᵃshall have been bound in heaven, and whatever you loose on earth ᵇshall have been loosed in heaven." ²⁰Then He ᵃwarned the disciples that they should tell no one that He was ᵇthe Christ.

16:14 ᵃGr *Elias* ᵇGr *Jeremias* 16:16 ᵃI.e. the Messiah 16:17 ᵃI.e. son of Jonah 16:18 ᵃGr *Petros*, a stone ᵇGr *petra*, large rock; bed-rock 16:19 ᵃGr *estai dedemenon*, fut. pft. pass. ᵇGr *estai lelumenon*, fut. pft. pass. 16:20 ᵃOr *strictly admonished* ᵇI.e. the Messiah

NLT

¹⁷Jesus replied, "You are blessed, Simon son of John,* because my Father in heaven has revealed this to you. You did not learn this from any human being. ¹⁸Now I say to you that you are Peter (which means 'rock'),* and upon this rock I will build my church, and all the powers of hell* will not conquer it. ¹⁹And I will give you the keys of the Kingdom of Heaven. Whatever you forbid* on earth will be forbidden in heaven, and whatever you permit* on earth will be permitted in heaven." ²⁰Then he sternly warned the disciples not to tell anyone that he was the Messiah.

16:13 "Son of Man" is a title Jesus used for himself. 16:16 Or *the Christ. Messiah* (a Hebrew term) and *Christ* (a Greek term) both mean "anointed one." 16:17 Greek *Simon bar-Jonah*; see John 1:42; 21:15-17. 16:18a Greek *that you are Peter*. 16:18b Greek *and the gates of Hades*. 16:19a Or *bind*, or *lock*. 16:19b Or *loose*, or *open*.

All of us have taken classes that have climaxed in a final exam. Quite often, that exam makes up the single most important grade in the course. Well-prepared exams help both the student and the teacher determine whether the teacher accomplished what he or she set out to teach and whether the student grasped the important points. It's not uncommon for the final exam to have only a few questions, but these questions are probing and strategic, addressing the core matters of the course.

Day after day for many months, Jesus had been training His disciples. Moment by moment they heard His teaching, observed His actions, witnessed His miracles, and got to know Him up close and personal. He invited them into His world, allowing them to observe His methods of ministry and, hopefully, to learn His ways. Finally, the day came for their final exam, which consisted of one crucial question. In fact, it's life's ultimate question for all people. How we answer this question will have everything to do with our eternal destiny.

— 16:13-14 —

Jesus knew that the end of His earthly ministry was fast approaching. He also knew that He needed all the time He could get with His disciples. He had so much to say to them and so much to teach them, even though there were many things they couldn't bear to hear or to understand. With the increased ferocity of His critics, who were plotting to take His life, and with the constant presence of crowds following Him and His disciples around, Jesus withdrew from the hubbub of activity around the Sea of Galilee, and He led His disciples north to a region around the source of the Jordan River, near a city known as Caesarea Philippi. A mostly non-Jewish city, Caesarea Philippi served as a quiet retreat where Jesus could have some alone time with His closest followers without constant intrusions.

To this day, at the ruins of Caesarea Philippi, a visitor can discern the remains of a region infested with idolatry. Several niches are carved into the side of a looming cliff where statues of deities were once enshrined. And several foundations of temples can be discerned along the same cliff in the upper city, like a strip mall of paganism. It was in the vicinity of this polytheistic, pagan city that Jesus asked, "Who do people say that the Son of Man is?" (16:13).

The question regarded the popular buzz about Jesus' identity. What were *they* saying? As people heard the teaching and saw the miracles, then talked among themselves in the public square, what was the word on the street? Of course, this wasn't the core question. He didn't drag the disciples all the way to the beginning of the Jordan River to ask them *that* question. Jesus wasn't a premodern equivalent to a modern social media addict desperate for attention, always worried about what other people thought of Him. Rather, the question was His way of leading His disciples to understand exactly what life's ultimate question is.

The disciples dutifully reported what they had heard

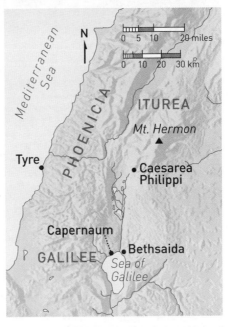

After discussing the dangerous teaching of the Pharisees and Sadducees, Jesus and His disciples traveled north to the largely non-Jewish area of Caesarea Philippi.

21

CAESAREA PHILIPPI

MATTHEW 16:13

Not to be confused with Herod the Great's port city, Caesarea Maritima ("Caesarea by the Sea"), Caesarea Philippi was situated about 25 miles north of the Sea of Galilee at the base of Mount Hermon. Caesar Augustus had given the city to Herod the Great as a reward for his loyalty. To show his gratitude, Herod constructed a large temple of white stone in Caesar's honor. When Herod died, his son Philip the Tetrarch made the city his main residence, beautifying and enlarging it. As such, it became known as Caesarea Philippi—that is, "Philip's Caesarea."

At the base of a cliff in the upper city, an underground spring bubbled up from a cave, becoming a gushing tributary of the Jordan River. In Old Testament times, pagans had gathered on this site to worship Baal. Hence, this location was referred to as Baal-gad or Baal-hermon (see Josh. 11:17; Judg. 3:3; 1 Chr. 5:23). Later, the Greeks dedicated a temple there to the god Pan.[7] Today, the site is known as Banias, the Arabic version of Panias, or "place of Pan."

Public Domain/Wikimedia Commons

The ruins of **Caesarea Philippi** include the foundations of several temples, which had niches for idols.

being murmured among the crowds. Some were saying that Jesus was John the Baptist . . . or Elijah . . . or Jeremiah . . . or some other prophet. I find it interesting that all these options required somebody either to come back from the dead, or in the case of Elijah, to return from his ascent to heaven (2 Kgs. 2:11). Stanley Toussaint observes, "Their thinking bore testimony to the supernatural character of Jesus, but they failed to identify Him as the Messiah."[8]

— 16:15-16 —

After hearing the various answers tossed around in the public square, Jesus dug deeper. I can imagine Him nodding knowingly as the disciples listed off the top few contenders. Then, perhaps pointing at them, He said, "But who do you say that I am?" (16:15). The Greek word for "you" here is plural. Jesus was addressing all the disciples. If Jesus were in Texas, He would have used "y'all." The word is also brought to the very front of the statement in the original Greek text, indicating that Jesus was emphasizing it: "But YOU, who do YOU say that I am?"

This is it—the all-important question. If they got this one wrong, nothing else would matter. Jesus knew He didn't have much more time to be with them. He wanted to make sure that His closest disciples, who would be carrying on the preaching of the gospel after His departure, had a clear idea of His identity. It was the key to understanding everything—His teachings, His actions, and especially what He was going to accomplish in Jerusalem during the last few days of His public ministry. Without a right understanding of who Jesus is, there can't be a right understanding of what He has done.

I can imagine a brief period of silence as all the disciples' eyes were on Him. They no doubt felt the weight of this question. They knew the other identifications—the ones from the crowd—were wrong. And they knew that they of all people should get it right. Yet the text records that it was Simon Peter alone who spoke up. Was he speaking as a representative of the group, presenting the consensus they all had held? Or were the rest reluctant to give their opinions, unsure of their answers? Were some of them still dull of hearing?

In any case, Simon Peter answered, "You are the Christ, the Son of the living God" (16:16). This confession of faith is too vital to race over. We need to break it down and think about it carefully. The word "Christ" (Greek *Christos* [5547]) is a translation of the Hebrew word *mashiach* [H4899], from which we get the English word "messiah." The Hebrew term means "anointed one." In the Old Testament, an anointing ceremony, in which olive oil was used, was performed to consecrate prophets (1 Kgs. 19:16), priests (Exod. 28:41), and kings (1 Sam. 10:1). But while Israel had many anointed prophets, priests, and kings throughout its history, all of these were seen as anticipating the ultimate Prophet, Priest, and King—the Messiah, or Christ.

Along with his confession that Jesus was the long-awaited Messiah, Peter also confessed that Jesus was the "Son of the living God." This title probably comes from Psalm 2, a messianic psalm that the disciples would have been very familiar with:

> "I will surely tell of the decree of the LORD:
> He said to Me, 'You are My Son,
> Today I have begotten You.'" (Ps. 2:7)

That the Messiah, or anointed King, would be the Son of God, installed as His regent, was a common idea at the time. In fact, Psalm 89 says this concerning King David:

> "He will cry to Me, 'You are my Father,
> My God, and the rock of my salvation.'
> I also shall make him My firstborn,
> The highest of the kings of the earth.
> My lovingkindness I will keep for him forever,
> And My covenant shall be confirmed to him.
> So I will establish his descendants forever
> And his throne as the days of heaven." (Ps. 89:26-29)

Peter also clarified that Jesus was the Son of the "living God" (Matt. 16:16). This phrase is common in the Old Testament (Deut. 5:26; Josh. 3:10; 1 Sam. 17:26). And it is used to contrast the true, living (that is, *real*) God from false gods (Acts 14:15). R. T. France suggests, "The adjective *living* . . . may perhaps have been included to contrast the one true God with the local deities (Caesarea Philippi was a centre of the worship of Pan)."[9]

I appreciate two things about Peter's answer to Jesus' ultimate question. First, though Peter was in way over his head theologically, he didn't hesitate to state the truth. I'm not sure Peter was fully aware of what it meant that Jesus was the Messiah. Surely he understood its implications for Jesus' kingship in relation to being the descendant of David, but whether Peter knew that Jesus was also the anointed Prophet and the anointed, eternal High Priest, we can't be sure. And when Peter called Jesus the "Son of the living God," did he have a full knowledge of Jesus' divine sonship as the second person of the Trinity, co-eternal with the Father? Certainly Peter understood that Jesus was greater than any human he had ever met, that He had been sent by God, and that He was the Son of God in the sense that He was the descendant of David destined to be enthroned as the Messiah. But it may very well be that Peter spoke more than he knew when he confessed Jesus as the Christ, the Son of God.

Second, Peter wasn't afraid to risk himself in front of his peers. Remember, due either to uncertainty or to fear, the rest of the disciples kept quiet. Perhaps they were waiting for somebody else to venture an opinion, and then they would read Jesus' body language or wait for His response before either agreeing or disagreeing. For whatever reason, they played it safe and said nothing. But not Peter. Even though he was operating way above his pay grade, he went for broke and said what was on his heart.

— 16:17-20 —

Jesus' response to Peter's confession of faith included a blessing (16:17), a naming (16:18), two promises (16:18-19), and a strong warning (16:20). Let's look at each of these.

A blessing (16:17). Peter had obviously spoken the truth. Jesus praised him for his confession by instantly blessing him, calling him by his full legal name: "Simon Barjona," that is, "Simon, son of Jonah." But the Lord also pointed out that Simon's understanding of His identity hadn't come from careful observation and the interpretation of data. He wasn't any smarter or holier than the rest of the disciples. This truth of Jesus' identity had not been revealed by "flesh and blood," but by the heavenly Father Himself. This means that Peter's insight was given by divine revelation, not human perception. Earlier Jesus had taught, "All things have been handed over to Me by My Father; and no one knows the Son except the Father; nor does anyone know the Father except the Son, and anyone to whom the Son wills to reveal Him" (11:27). The Gospel of John records a similar thought: "No one can come to Me unless it has been granted him from the Father" (John 6:65). Likewise, the apostle Paul wrote, "No one can say, 'Jesus is Lord,' except by the Holy Spirit" (1 Cor. 12:3). To know Jesus rightly is a gift from God.

A naming (Matt. 16:18). This isn't quite the first time Jesus called Simon by the Aramaic name Cephas, translated into Greek as Petros. The Gospel of John records that at their very first meeting, Jesus said to Simon, "'You are Simon the son of John; you shall be called Cephas' (which is translated Peter)" (John 1:42). However, there Jesus stated this detail in the future tense—"You shall be called"—while in Matthew 16:18 Jesus states it as a present fact—"You are Peter." I take it,

WAS PETER THE FIRST POPE?

MATTHEW 16:18-19

The Roman Catholic Church has traditionally viewed Peter as the first pope, thus connecting the line of papal succession to apostolic authority. But does the New Testament suggest that Jesus intended for Peter to be the singular head of a universal church? The coupling of Peter's position of leadership and influence among the Twelve and his unique renaming relayed in Matthew 16:18-19 has understandably led to this sort of conclusion.

Statue of St. Peter in front of St. Peter's Basilica in the Vatican

This issue deserves a closer look. We need not conclude from this passage that Jesus gave Peter special authority to become the singular foundation upon which the universal church was established. Yes, it's true that Jesus renamed Simon "Rock" because of his confession about Christ. However, Matthew uses the Greek masculine noun *Petros* [4074] when referring to the disciple's new name, while for the "rock" upon which the church would be built, he uses the feminine *petra* [4073], a more ambiguous term. It may be that the underlying Aramaic words were the same, but Matthew makes it clear to his readers that Jesus had a different "rock" in mind than Peter himself—presumably either Jesus or the confession Peter had uttered. Furthermore, although the authority of "binding and loosing" is addressed to Peter as the singular subject in 16:19, this same authority is also given to all disciples in 18:18 (cf. John 20:23). Finally, Peter himself used the term *petra* to refer to Christ, the "rock of offense" (1 Pet. 2:8), whom he regarded as the "corner stone" of the church (1 Pet. 2:4-8).

Although Peter was certainly a great leader in the first-century church, it does not seem to be suggested in the New Testament that Peter had unique authority over all the other apostles. The notion that Peter's leadership in Rome (and that of his presumed successors) should have primacy over the entire church developed under later papal authorities. This idea was not the viewpoint of the earliest church fathers and has not been accepted by either the Eastern Orthodox Church or the Protestant Church. While the conferring of this designation as "first pope" has a long history within the Roman Catholic Church, it does not stem from the early church itself nor from the words of Jesus.

then, that in this moment at Caesarea Philippi, Simon fulfilled the sole requirement necessary to become what He was meant to be: Cephas (or Peter). That requirement continues to be the foundation stone of the Christian faith—the confession of Jesus as the Christ, the Son of the living God (John 20:31).

Two promises (Matt. 16:18-19). Both promises in this passage relate to the future. The first is "Upon this rock I will build My church" (16:18). Upon which "rock"? It is unlikely that Jesus was referring to Peter himself as the "rock" upon which the church would be built. If Jesus had intended to teach that the church would be built on Peter (a notion expressed in the Roman Catholic Church teaching that Peter was the first in a line of popes), He could have easily made that crystal clear by saying, "On you, Peter, I will build My church." Instead, He used the pronoun "this," which would be a strange way of pointing out the person to whom He was speaking. (For more on this topic, see the feature "Was Peter the First Pope?" on the facing page.)

To paraphrase, Jesus was saying something like, "You are 'Rocky,' and upon this rock I will build my church." Jesus was employing a wordplay, or a kind of pun. It seems best to see the "rock" upon which the church is built as Peter's solid confession of faith. Because of its heavenly, divine origin, it would serve as a firm foundation to be built upon. The church, the body of believers in Jesus Christ, baptized by the Holy Spirit and sealed for redemption, was established on earth at Pentecost (Acts 2:1-4) and will continue under God's protection until the resurrection and rapture of those "in Christ" (1 Thes. 4:16-17). (For more information, see the feature "When Did the Church Begin?" on page 30).

So firm was this foundation that not even the "gates of Hades" would be able to overpower it (Matt. 16:18). The expression "gates of Hades" in the Septuagint (the Greek translation of the Hebrew Bible) translates the Hebrew "gates of Sheol," an expression denoting the place of the dead, as in Isaiah 38:10: "'In the middle of my life I am to enter the gates of Sheol; I am to be deprived of the rest of my years.'" We also see the phrase appear in intertestamental literature, as in Wisdom of Solomon 16:13: "For thou hast power over life and death; thou dost lead men down to the gates of Hades and back again" (RSV). What this statement in Matthew means, simply put, is that nothing will stop the building of Christ's church—not even the powers of death and hell, Satan, or sinners. A. T. Robertson notes, "Christ's church will prevail and survive because He will burst the gates of Hades and come forth conqueror. He will ever live and be the guarantor of the perpetuity of His people or church."[10]

The second promise is "I will give you the keys of the kingdom of heaven" (Matt. 16:19). I understand this, too, as relating to the timing of the establishment of the church at Pentecost and referring primarily to Peter's authority on earth to open up membership in the physical, visible, earthly community that would become known as the church, in keeping with God's heavenly initiative. Let me explain. The "doors" of the church would be unlocked when Peter invited believing, repentant Jews into the fold on Pentecost:

> Peter said to them, "Repent, and each of you be baptized in the name of Jesus Christ for the forgiveness of your sins; and you will receive the gift of the Holy Spirit. For the promise is for you and your children and for all who are far off, as many as the Lord our God will call to Himself." And with many other words he solemnly testified and kept on exhorting them, saying, "Be saved from this perverse generation!" So then, those who had received his word were baptized; and that day there were added about three thousand souls. (Acts 2:38-41)

Next, Peter would unlock the "doors" of the church for the Samaritans, a group of people descended from the mixture of Israelites and Gentiles following the Exile. Philip had preached the gospel in Samaria, and many had believed and were baptized. The book of Acts records Peter's involvement from that point:

> Now when the apostles in Jerusalem heard that Samaria had received the word of God, they sent them Peter and John, who came down and prayed for them that they might receive the Holy Spirit.

For He had not yet fallen upon any of them; they had simply been baptized in the name of the Lord Jesus. Then they began laying their hands on them, and they were receiving the Holy Spirit. (Acts 8:14-17)

Finally, Peter would unlock the "doors" of the church to the Gentiles when he ordered the Roman centurion Cornelius and other Gentile believers in Jesus to be baptized: "Then Peter answered, 'Surely no one can refuse the water for these to be baptized who have received the Holy Spirit just as we did, can he?' And he ordered them to be baptized in the name of Jesus Christ" (Acts 10:46-48).

But what about the second part of the promise: "Whatever you bind on earth shall have been bound in heaven, and whatever you loose on earth shall have been loosed in heaven" (Matt. 16:19)? By ignoring the grammatical elements of the Greek verbs used here and by relying on a faulty Latin translation in the Vulgate, it has been mistakenly taught by the Roman Catholic Church that Jesus gave Peter special authority to "bind and loose" in the sense of forgiving sins and withholding forgiveness—and that this earthly act would have heavenly effects. However, there are a couple of problems with that interpretation. First, the same promise is repeated almost exactly in Matthew 18:18 regarding church discipline, and there is an important difference: There the second person *plural* form of the pronoun *you* is used in reference to the gathered church. This means that whatever the "binding and loosing" authority describes, it is not limited to Peter alone or to his individual successors, but to the church as a whole. Jesus gave a similar authority to all of the disciples equally in John 20:22-23, when He breathed on them and said, "Receive the Holy Spirit. If you forgive the sins of any, their sins have been forgiven them; if you retain the sins of any, they have been retained."

Reading all these passages together, we can draw the following conclusions. Peter as well as the rest of the disciples were granted special spiritual authority—the same authority granted to all believers who gather as the church in the name of Jesus. All redeemed men and women are indwelled by the Spirit, and the gathered church is itself the temple of the Holy Spirit (1 Cor. 3:16; 6:19; Eph. 2:19-22). The Lord commissions and empowers believers to proclaim His message of forgiveness, to baptize, and, as a church body, to grant membership and dismiss from membership as acts of maintaining church order and discipline.

A second problem with the aforementioned interpretation is that the phrases rendered "shall have been bound/loosed" and "have been forgiven/retained" (Matt. 16:19; 18:18; John 20:23) in the NASB are in

WHEN DID THE CHURCH BEGIN?

MATTHEW 16:18

If you begin reading through the New Testament at Matthew, the first mention of the word "church" (ekklēsia [1577]) comes at Matthew 16:18. It appears again at 18:17, but never in the Gospels of Mark, Luke, or John. The term ekklēsia then jumps off the pages of the book of Acts (e.g., Acts 5:11; 7:38) and appears frequently throughout the rest of the New Testament as the technical term for the new community of disciples of Jesus Christ.

Theologians have answered the question "When did the church begin?" in a number of ways. Some have suggested that the church consists of all the people of God from Adam to the end of time.[11] Others see the church as beginning with the call of Abraham, because he was the first recipient of the unique covenant promises that became the root of all future covenants.[12]

However, based on Matthew 16:18 and a few other New Testament passages, it seems best to see the church as beginning at Pentecost with the promised baptism of the Holy Spirit. Jesus said in Matthew 16:18, "I will build My church." The verb meaning "to build," oikodomeō [3618], is in the future tense, pointing to an activity that Christ had not yet begun at the time He was speaking to Peter. In Ephesians 2:20, Paul says that the church is "built on the foundation of the apostles and prophets, Christ Jesus Himself being the corner stone." The verb is the same—a form of oikodomeō. But here Paul uses the aorist tense, indicating something that occurred in the past. This suggests that sometime between Jesus' ministry and Paul's ministry the church was established.

This leaves us with really only one option for the timing of the founding of the church. Jesus said in Acts 1:5 that the disciples would be "baptized with the Holy Spirit" shortly after His ascension. This baptism of the Holy Spirit is the means by which believers are incorporated into the body of Christ (1 Cor. 12:12-13). And because this baptism of the Spirit didn't occur until Pentecost (Acts 2:1-4), we can mark Pentecost as the point when Christ began to fulfill His promise to Peter that "I will build My church" (Matt. 16:18).

From Pentecost onward, the forces of wickedness have been trying to destroy the church and its proclamation of the truth. Whether by attacks from outside in the form of persecution or attacks from within in the form of destructive false teaching by heretics, Satan has tried with all his might to tear down Christ's building project or to destroy its foundation. However, after two millennia, Christ's promise still stands: "The gates of Hades will not overpower it" (16:18).

the passive voice, indicating that the action is taken by God (referred to by commentators as the "divine passive"). Furthermore, the tenses of these verbs convey the notion of ongoing results stemming from a *completed* action. The true believers have already been forgiven of their sins by God in heaven; they have already been accepted into the heavenly family and baptized by the Holy Spirit if they are truly saved. If any respond with belief to the preaching of the gospel, Peter, the disciples, and the church as a whole would have authority to pronounce on earth what is true in heaven.

A strong warning (Matt. 16:20). Jesus concluded His response to Peter's bold confession of faith that Jesus is "the Christ, the Son of the living God" (16:16) with a somewhat surprising warning. He told all the disciples to "tell no one that He was the Christ" (16:20). Why would He say that? Why not tell them to proclaim the truth of His messiahship far and wide?

The fact is that most Jews in the first century had a very different picture of the person and work of the Messiah. If they were to say, "Jesus is the Messiah," they would have thought of Him as a political revolutionary and military leader who would wage the final war of the Lord against Rome and the other enemies of Israel and restore the kingdom. Nobody was expecting a suffering Messiah who would die and rise again, ascend to heaven to serve as a heavenly High Priest, and then return as Judge and King centuries later. The people's expectations were so misguided that if the disciples had publicly announced that Jesus was the long-awaited Messiah at that time, it could have created chaos—especially when Jesus headed for the Cross.

So, for the meantime, Jesus' identity was kept quiet. His disciples knew who He was—the Christ, the Son of the living God. But even they still had a lot to learn about what He had come to accomplish.

APPLICATION: MATTHEW 16:13-20

The All-Important Question

People today have all sorts of opinions about who Jesus was. Many say He was just a great moral teacher, like Confucius or Buddha. Others think He was a radical religious or social reformer like Martin Luther or Martin Luther King, Jr. Still others think He was just a peasant rabbi whose teachings were misinterpreted or misrepresented by His followers. Or that He was a wild-eyed apocalyptic preacher whose predictions about the end of the world failed to come to pass. Or a political figure whose revolt got Him killed. Or a mild-mannered sage who was at the wrong place at the wrong time and happened to get Himself executed. The devotees of some religions think He was a great prophet but not the greatest prophet. Others say He was just an incarnation of the archangel Michael, or the first created being, not God the Son.

Yet many believe what Peter and the other disciples believed and what the New Testament teaches: that Jesus was and is the God-man—the eternal Son of God who became human, lived a sinless life, died as a perfect substitute for our sins, rose miraculously and victoriously from the dead, ascended into heaven to intercede for us as our High Priest, and will come again as our Judge and King. That's the Jesus I accepted at a young age and the Jesus I've served for the rest of my life.

What about you? Who do you say Jesus is? And do your words and actions, life choices and priorities, passions and pursuits show it? Can you explain to others why you believe what you believe about Christ's person and work? Can you lead others to find the right answer to life's ultimate question? There is no more important question than Jesus' question to the disciples that day while surrounded by worshipers of false gods and countless idols: "Who do you say that I am?"

Three "Nevers" to Never Forget
MATTHEW 16:21-28

NASB

21 From that time ᵃJesus began to show His disciples that He must go to Jerusalem, and suffer many things from the elders and chief priests and scribes, and be killed, and be raised up on the third day. 22 Peter took Him aside and began to rebuke Him, saying, "ᵃGod forbid *it*, Lord! This shall

NLT

21 From then on Jesus* began to tell his disciples plainly that it was necessary for him to go to Jerusalem, and that he would suffer many terrible things at the hands of the elders, the leading priests, and the teachers of religious law. He would be killed, but on the third day he would be raised from the dead.

22 But Peter took him aside and began to reprimand him* for saying such things. "Heaven forbid, Lord," he said. "This will never happen to you!"

never ᵇhappen to You." ²³But He turned and said to Peter, "Get behind Me, Satan! You are a stumbling block to Me; for you are not setting your mind on ªGod's interests, but man's."

²⁴Then Jesus said to His disciples, "If anyone wishes to come after Me, he must deny himself, and take up his cross and follow Me. ²⁵For whoever wishes to save his ªlife will lose it; but whoever loses his ªlife for My sake will find it. ²⁶For what will it profit a man if he gains the whole world and forfeits his soul? Or what will a man give in exchange for his soul? ²⁷For the Son of Man is going to come in the glory of His Father with His angels, and WILL THEN ªREPAY EVERY MAN ACCORDING TO HIS ᵇDEEDS.

²⁸"Truly I say to you, there are some of those who are standing here who will not taste death until they see the Son of Man coming in His kingdom."

16:21 ªTwo early mss read *Jesus Christ* 16:22 ªLit (God be) *merciful to You* ᵇLit *be* 16:23 ªLit *the things of God* 16:25 ªOr *soul* 16:27 ªOr *recompense* ᵇLit *doing*

²³Jesus turned to Peter and said, "Get away from me, Satan! You are a dangerous trap to me. You are seeing things merely from a human point of view, not from God's."

²⁴Then Jesus said to his disciples, "If any of you wants to be my follower, you must give up your own way, take up your cross, and follow me. ²⁵If you try to hang on to your life, you will lose it. But if you give up your life for my sake, you will save it. ²⁶And what do you benefit if you gain the whole world but lose your own soul?* Is anything worth more than your soul? ²⁷For the Son of Man will come with his angels in the glory of his Father and will judge all people according to their deeds. ²⁸And I tell you the truth, some standing here right now will not die before they see the Son of Man coming in his Kingdom."

16:21 Some manuscripts read *Jesus the Messiah.* 16:22 Or *began to correct him.* 16:26 Or *your self?* also in 16:26b.

Over and over again, Jesus challenges people's expectations. It never ceases to amaze me how distorted or completely broken many people's opinions are about who Jesus is, what He came to do, and how He feels about our personal attitudes and actions. The name of Jesus is often invoked to defend some religious, social, or political cause. He's often cited in support of some half-baked ideology, philosophy, or theology. And a lot of people today readily accept a domesticated version of Jesus that confirms their prejudices, fits their worldviews, or leaves their comfortable lives untouched.

The people in Jesus' day were no different. They had notions of the coming Messiah that were selective, self-serving, distorted, or simply false. Many expected the Messiah to suddenly appear, overthrow the Roman Empire with a fury of fire from heaven, and weed out the wicked from the world with an army of avenging angels. Beyond this, the Messiah would immediately destroy Satan and his demonic forces once and for all, consign the wicked to everlasting fire, and usher the righteous into God's eternal kingdom.

Jesus of Nazareth, with His ragtag band of outcasts, wasn't what most Jews had in mind for the Messiah. But the dullness that accompanied faulty expectations wasn't limited to just the crowds of rubberneckers and hangers-on who hoped to catch a few miracles or hear a scathing rebuke of the Pharisees. The disciples themselves, who fully embraced who Jesus was, "the Christ, the Son of the living God" (16:16), still had a long way to go before they could accept what He had come to do: "suffer . . . and be killed, and be raised up on the third day" (16:21).

— 16:21 —

Peter's profound profession of faith in Jesus as "the Christ, the Son of the living God" (16:16) no doubt received a round of "amens" and affirming nods from the other eleven disciples. Maybe a quiet "Aww, he beat me to it" could be heard from the back. I'm sure they knew it to be true—or at least hoped it was. Who else could He be but the King, the long-awaited Messiah? Though Peter was the only one to speak up, he surely spoke for the rest of the Twelve.

But even though the disciples likely had a clearer understanding of what it meant for Jesus to be the Messiah and Son of God than did the average crowd member or the above-average Pharisee or Sadducee, they were still very much in the dark regarding the exact mission of Jesus. Slowly but surely, Jesus was going to dissipate the fog and reveal what was going to happen to Him in the coming weeks.

So, immediately on the heels of Peter's confession and Jesus' warning not to broadcast the fact that He was the Messiah, Jesus stated plainly the reason for His coming to earth. It wasn't to defeat and dethrone the Jewish elders, chief priests, and scribes, but to suffer humiliation and persecution at their hands. It wasn't to conquer the Roman Empire and replace it with His eternal kingdom, but to conquer death and sin by dying in the place of sinners and rising again victorious. All of this would happen in the near future when He would go up to Jerusalem.

The idea that the Messiah, Son of the living God, would go to Jerusalem to be killed was so unexpected, so foreign, and so distasteful to the disciples that I wonder if they even heard the words "and be raised up on the third day" (16:21). Despite the fact that it didn't make sense to them, it was the plain truth. This was God's plan. This truth introduces the first of three "nevers" we must never forget: *We must never think that just because something is unexpected, it's unacceptable.*

— 16:22-23 —

As soon as Jesus calmly and quietly explained to His disciples what would befall Him in Jerusalem at the hands of their enemies, Peter responded. This time he took Jesus aside, away from the rest of the disciples, and actually began to scold Him! The Greek word translated "rebuke," *epitimaō* [2008], means "to express strong disapproval of someone" or even to "warn in order to prevent an action or bring one to an end."[13]

Peter was flabbergasted that Jesus would even think something like that! Peter knew that the Messiah wasn't supposed to be killed by His enemies; the Messiah was supposed to conquer them. And the Messiah wasn't supposed to get arrested and be mistreated by His opponents; the Messiah was supposed to exercise judgment against them. With these sure facts in hand, Peter took Jesus aside and corrected His faulty understanding of what the Messiah was supposed to do.

Oh, how quickly our fortunes can change! A high roller can go from winning the house to losing everything with one foolish gamble. A politician running for office can go from being a shoo-in to being *persona non grata* with one scandalous misstep. A star athlete can go from MVP to unemployed with a career-ending injury. And the spokesman of the twelve disciples can go from God-inspired confessor (16:16) to Satan-inspired tempter (16:23) in less than eight verses! How did this happen? Peter allowed a human viewpoint to take control, and when he did, he placed himself in the position of being God's counselor. He actually said to the Lord of all, "God forbid it, Lord! This shall never happen to You" (16:22). What presumption!

Jesus' rebuke would have felt like a smack in the face. In fact, the text indicates that Jesus didn't even let Peter unload his whole case against God's plan. It says that Peter "*began* to rebuke" (emphasis mine), suggesting that Jesus literally interrupted Peter's words and stopped him from digging himself deeper into the pit of verbal stupidity. Jesus physically got into Peter's face and said, "Get behind Me, Satan!" (16:22-23). Ouch! Without realizing it, Peter was actually taking on the role of the adversary by doing what Satan does—tempting people to take a course of action directly contrary to God's will. What's worse, Peter did so by invoking God Himself—"God forbid!"

Peter got himself into that mess because his mind was set not on God's interests, but on man's. He had allowed himself to revert to his old ways of thinking, according to "flesh and blood" rather than according to the "Father who is in heaven" (cf. 16:17). One moment he was soaring on the wings of eagles with heavenly insight, the next moment he was pecking at the ground with the chickens. This leads us to the second of the three "nevers" we must never forget: *We must never think that the Lord should alter His plan to fit our preferences.*

— 16:24-26 —

I'm not sure how (or if) I'd recover from a stinging censure from the Lord like the one Peter got slapped with when Jesus called him Satan and rebuked him for gross worldliness. I can imagine Peter's eyes shifting from side to side to make sure none of the eleven other disciples overheard the Lord's reproof. Whew! Nobody did. The exchange had only been between Jesus and Peter. How merciful was the Lord in not exposing Peter's foolishness to the entire Twelve!

Jesus then turned away from Peter, raised His voice, and addressed all the disciples with additional difficult teaching. He took the opportunity, while they were still ruminating on the fact that He had predicted His own suffering and death in Jerusalem, to unpack what was involved in truly being one of His followers. Since living right starts with thinking straight, here's what it would take: *being willing to die with Him* (16:24).

The admonition in 16:24-25 is similar to a charge Jesus gave earlier, recorded in Matthew 10:

MATTHEW 10	MATTHEW 16
"And he who does not take his cross and follow after Me is not worthy of Me." (10:38)	"If anyone wishes to come after Me, he must deny himself, and take up his cross and follow Me." (16:24)
"He who has found his life will lose it, and he who has lost his life for My sake will find it." (10:39)	"For whoever wishes to save his life will lose it; but whoever loses his life for My sake will find it." (16:25)

At the time, when Jesus first urged His followers to take up their crosses and follow Him (10:38), the disciples didn't have in mind that Jesus was going to literally take up a cross and literally lose His life. That idea was far from them. They probably thought more in the abstract, that Jesus was calling for a general willingness to give up everything for the sake of the ministry, even their own lives if necessary. But with the revelation that Jesus would "go to Jerusalem, and suffer many things from the elders and chief priests and scribes, and be killed" (16:21), the abstract and general had become concrete and particular. Even the mode of death was revealed: the cross. One commentator notes, "Crucifixion was the worst kind of punishment then known; hence the phrase, *to take his cross*, signifies the voluntary readiness to suffer the utmost in this world for Christ."[14]

I like how Kent Hughes describes the meaning of taking up our cross and following Christ:

> What are our crosses? They are not simply trials or hardships. It is typical to think of a nutty boss or an unfair teacher or a bossy mother-in-law as our "cross." But they are not. . . . A cross comes from specifically walking in Christ's steps, embracing his life. It comes from bearing disdain because we are embracing the narrow way of the Cross. . . . It comes from living out the business and sexual ethics of Christ in the marketplace and world. It comes from embracing weakness instead of power. It comes from extending oneself in difficult circumstances for the sake of the gospel.[15]

I'll bet you could hear a few gulps or even a couple of gasps from the disciples at hearing those words. Certainly, there were no more butt-ins from Peter, and none of the other disciples would try to push their own preferences or conditions on the cost of discipleship Christ was spelling out. They knew better than that.

Yet Jesus encouraged them that though the demand for discipleship was high, the rewards were inestimable. Yes, those who gripped their lives with white knuckles would lose them in the end. And if they didn't surrender their souls to Christ, everything they held onto would be lost forever. But those who let go in self-denial and opened themselves up to whatever God had for them would be rewarded beyond imagination (16:25). This reward wouldn't necessarily come in *this* life, however. A person could gain the "whole world" yet forfeit his or her soul. What person, when faced with an eternity of damnation, would not wish to have given up everything previously held dear on earth for the joys of heaven? That's the argument Jesus was making as He urged the disciples to a life of total abandon when it came to following Him. This brings us to our third and final "never" we must never forget: *We must never think that being a close follower of Jesus can happen without self-denial.*

— 16:27-28 —

I began this section by pointing out some of the errant views people had about the Messiah at the time of Jesus. Most of these views centered on the notion that the Messiah would be a warrior-king who would immediately overcome the enemies of Israel, subdue all other nations, and establish a kingdom on this earth. This coming of the kingdom of heaven would be glorious, with an army of angels attending the Messiah's advent. He would arrive as Judge and King, destroying all enemies spiritual and physical, including Satan and his demons. The wicked would be punished and the righteous would be rewarded.

The problem with this view of the Messiah's coming is not that it was wrong, but that it was incomplete. Indeed, the Messiah *would* rule as Judge and reign as King. There *would* be reward for the righteous. And there *would* be a glorious, eternal kingdom. Jesus' startling revelation to His disciples that the Son of Man would suffer, die, and rise again was not intended to cancel out or replace the expectation of the Son of Man coming in glory with His angels to establish the kingdom and to repay the righteous with rewards and the wicked with punishment (16:27-28). Rather, Jesus' teaching clarified that the same Messiah who would one day wear the crown would also bear the cross; in fact, without the cross, there would be no crown.

So Jesus concluded His teaching concerning His own suffering, death, and resurrection—and His calling to follow Him in that pattern of selfless abandon—with a reminder that He would ultimately fulfill the Jewish expectation of the messianic Judge and King. Because He would "be raised up on the third day" (16:21), the Son of Man would be in a position of victory to one day "come in the glory of His Father with His angels" and "then repay every man according to his deeds" (16:27).

Jesus then left them with the mysterious promise that some of the disciples standing there would not die "until they see the Son of Man coming in His kingdom" (16:28). By this statement, Jesus didn't mean that some of His disciples would live throughout the church age to witness the Second Coming. Nor did He intend to communicate that the return of Christ was just a spiritual, nonliteral event that would take place sometime in the first century while a few of the disciples were still alive. Rather, the meaning of the words will become clear in the very next chapter, when Jesus is miraculously transfigured in the presence of some of the disciples as a foretaste of the advent of His glorious kingdom on earth (17:1-8).

APPLICATION: MATTHEW 16:21-28

Staying Attuned to the Three "Nevers"

Living right begins with thinking straight. And the only way that can happen is to think like God thinks, which goes completely against our nature. In fact, God Himself said, "My thoughts are not your thoughts, nor are your ways My ways" (Isa. 55:8). In light of this fact, I'd like us to review and ponder the "three 'nevers' to never forget" that we saw in our study of this passage.

First, *never think that just because something is unexpected, it's unacceptable.* Often throughout life we come face to face with what we never anticipated. We don't see it coming. We have everything planned, settled, and proceeding smoothly until out of the blue our neat, comfortable little world is invaded by the unexpected. Maybe it's a diagnosis we never thought we'd hear. Or a relationship we thought was solid that suddenly turns sour. Or a relocation we didn't anticipate, or a job loss we didn't see coming. Even if the sudden, unexpected change isn't negative, it can still be shocking and disorienting. An unexpected pregnancy, a surprise promotion, a totally new ministry opportunity. If we're riveted to a human viewpoint, we'll fight the unexpected, resist it, resent it, and refuse to accept it. Yet we need to be open to the sudden right or left turns—or total reversals—that God may orchestrate in our lives. Never think that just because something is unexpected, it's unacceptable.

Second, *never think that the Lord should alter His plan to fit your preferences.* Regardless of how long we've walked with the Lord, or how important our role in ministry may be, or how strange His plan may seem to us, when He makes His will known, there's only one appropriate response: obedience. God's plan isn't to be questioned, renegotiated, or tweaked to fit our own preferences. We do what He places before us—when He wants and how He wants. This means altering *our* thinking to fit with *His* thinking, not pleading with Him to change His plan to conform to ours.

Third, *never think that being a close follower of Jesus can happen without self-denial.* "It's not about me" is the exact opposite of how the vast majority of our world thinks. This explains why people are so important in their own minds and why a spirit of entitlement is so pervasive in our culture. As we weigh the cost of true discipleship against what the world has to offer, we would do well to remember the immortal words of Jim Elliot, who gave his life in martyrdom as a missionary to natives of Ecuador: "He is no fool who gives what he cannot keep to gain that which he cannot lose."[16] Are you grasping onto the temporary things of this world, which are impossible to keep, and forsaking the things of eternity, which can never be lost?

We would do well to never forget these things. And as we take them to heart, we'll learn how to think straight about Jesus and about our relationship with Him and what He wants to do in our lives. As we do, we'll have "the mind of Christ" (1 Cor. 2:16).

A Terrifying Glimpse of Glory
MATTHEW 17:1-13

NASB

[1] Six days later Jesus took with Him Peter and [a]James and John his brother, and led them up on a high mountain by themselves. [2] And He was transfigured before them; and His face shone like the sun, and His garments became as white as light. [3] And behold, Moses and Elijah appeared to them, talking with Him. [4] Peter said to Jesus, "Lord, it is good for us to be here; if You wish, I will make three [a]tabernacles here, one for You, and one for Moses, and one for Elijah." [5] While he was still speaking, a bright cloud overshadowed them, and behold, a voice out of the cloud said, "This is My beloved Son, with whom I am well-pleased; listen to Him!" [6] When the disciples heard *this*, they fell [a]face down to the ground and were terrified. [7] And Jesus came to *them* and touched them and said, "Get up, and do not be afraid." [8] And lifting up their eyes, they saw no one except Jesus Himself alone.

[9] As they were coming down from the mountain, Jesus commanded them, saying, "Tell the vision to no

NLT

[1] Six days later Jesus took Peter and the two brothers, James and John, and led them up a high mountain to be alone. [2] As the men watched, Jesus' appearance was transformed so that his face shone like the sun, and his clothes became as white as light. [3] Suddenly, Moses and Elijah appeared and began talking with Jesus.

[4] Peter exclaimed, "Lord, it's wonderful for us to be here! If you want, I'll make three shelters as memorials*—one for you, one for Moses, and one for Elijah."

[5] But even as he spoke, a bright cloud overshadowed them, and a voice from the cloud said, "This is my dearly loved Son, who brings me great joy. Listen to him." [6] The disciples were terrified and fell face down on the ground.

[7] Then Jesus came over and touched them. "Get up," he said. "Don't be afraid." [8] And when they looked up, Moses and Elijah were gone, and they saw only Jesus.

[9] As they went back down the mountain, Jesus commanded them, "Don't tell anyone what you have

one until the Son of Man has risen from the dead." [10]And His disciples asked Him, "Why then do the scribes say that Elijah must come first?" [11]And He answered and said, "Elijah is coming and will restore all things; [12]but I say to you that Elijah already came, and they did not recognize him, but did [a]to him whatever they wished. So also the Son of Man is going to suffer [b]at their hands." [13]Then the disciples understood that He had spoken to them about John the Baptist.

17:1 [a]Or *Jacob*   17:4 [a]Or *sacred tents*   17:6 [a]Lit *on their faces*   17:12 [a]Lit *in him; or in his case*   [b]Lit *by them*

seen until the Son of Man* has been raised from the dead."

[10]Then his disciples asked him, "Why do the teachers of religious law insist that Elijah must return before the Messiah comes?*"

[11]Jesus replied, "Elijah is indeed coming first to get everything ready. [12]But I tell you, Elijah has already come, but he wasn't recognized, and they chose to abuse him. And in the same way they will also make the Son of Man suffer." [13]Then the disciples realized he was talking about John the Baptist.

17:4 Greek *three tabernacles.*   17:9 "Son of Man" is a title Jesus used for himself.   17:10 Greek *that Elijah must come first?*

Too much casual familiarity with the things of God can cause us to lose our awe of Him. The fact that you're reading this indicates that you probably have countless resources about God at your fingertips—resources about His nature, character, works, and ways. Chances are good that this isn't the only resource in your library. The more we hear and read about the things of the Lord, the easier it becomes to lose a healthy fear of Him in the flood of familiarity.

The way we use our words doesn't help. We say we "love" God . . . but we also say we "love" everything from Thai food to country music. And so much around us is referred to as "awesome"—from cars to cans of soda—that the only truly awesome One no longer seems that awesome. High and holy things have now become commonplace. And as a result, we've lost a clear sense of the greatness and glory of the Lord.

The saying goes, "Familiarity breeds contempt." When it comes to believers and the things of God, *contempt* is a bit too strong. But the principle remains. Familiarity can certainly lead to ho hums at the hearing of the gospel, shoulder shrugs at profound theology, and even a been-there-done-that attitude toward living the Christian life.

I often wonder whether this happened to the disciples. After all, they were just as human as you and me. Just as fallen, frail, and fickle. Just as susceptible to the desensitizing that comes from an overexposure to the amazing and miraculous. Yes, the disciples had seen and heard it all as they followed in the footsteps of Jesus. But could they have been growing numb to the fact that they were in the presence of Awesomeness Incarnate?

If so, a few of them would soon experience a terrifying glimpse of glory that would snap them out of their stupor.

— 17:1-3 —

After Peter's confession of faith in the Lord as the long-awaited Messiah and the Son of God, Jesus had surprisingly predicted that He would "be killed, and be raised up on the third day" (16:21). Such events were not usually associated with the anticipated coming of the victorious Messiah-King. But then Jesus also affirmed something that would have been more familiar to His disciples: He would later "come in the glory of His Father with His angels" (16:27). As a matter of fact, Jesus promised that some of those very disciples standing there would "not taste death until they see the Son of Man coming in His kingdom" (16:28).

We know that all of the disciples died by the end of the first century. None of them lived to witness the glorious second coming of Christ as Judge and King, which even now awaits a future fulfillment. So, what could Jesus have meant by His promise that some would see the Son of Man coming in His kingdom? As I understand it, in its most immediate sense, Jesus had in mind what would transpire six days later—His unique and awesome Transfiguration, bathed in glory, in which he would appear in a similar way as He will when He comes again "in the glory of His father" (16:27). This event, which provided a foretaste of the coming kingdom, would be witnessed not by all the disciples, but by a select few: Peter, James, and John.

Both Matthew and Mark report that "six days" after the events in Caesarea Philippi recorded at the end of Matthew 16, Jesus took Peter, James, and John (the brother of James) to "a high mountain" (17:1; Mark 9:2). Luke's Gospel, probably including partial days on either end of the full six days, uses a less precise number—"some eight days after" (Luke 9:28). In any case, the event occurred about a week later.

Which "high mountain" did they climb? Some interpreters have attempted to identify it as Mount Tabor, located clear on the other side of the Sea of Galilee. Granted, the span of a week between the events of Matthew 16 and the Transfiguration would have been enough time to walk the approximately 60-mile route from Caesarea Philippi to Mount Tabor.[17] But we should recall that the disciples had arrived in the region of Caesarea Philippi after the long walk from the Sea of Galilee for the purpose of a little break from the crowds. A route back south to Mount

COMING(S) OF THE KINGDOM?

MATTHEW 17:1-13

Matthew, Mark, and Luke all record Jesus' promise: Some of the disciples standing with Him would not die "until they see the Son of Man coming in His kingdom" (16:28), or "until they see the kingdom of God" (Luke 9:27), or "until they see the kingdom of God after it has come with power" (Mark 9:1). All these variations of Jesus' prophecy relate to the coming of the kingdom in power, centered on the presence of Christ. For centuries interpreters have scratched their heads—and commentators have written many words—trying to understand what Jesus meant by this promise. Most have seen some kind of connection between what Jesus said and what He showed three of His disciples in the very next account that follows in all three Gospels—the Transfiguration (Matt. 17:1-8; Mark 9:2-8; Luke 9:28-36). But does this mean that after that brief glimpse of glory, the coming of Christ's kingdom was fulfilled?

We can better understand the significance of Jesus' promise as well as the event of the Transfiguration when we understand a little about the nature of the coming of Christ's kingdom. The Bible presents the coming kingdom of God not as one simple thing but as a complex concept. In the most general sense, "God's kingdom" refers to His eternal, sovereign rule over heaven and earth—things visible and invisible (Ps. 145:11-13; Dan. 4:3). In that sense, nothing ever was, is, or will be outside of God's kingdom.

More specifically in the New Testament, the arrival of the promised Messiah—God in the flesh—revealed the coming of the kingdom of God in a new way, though His heavenly power and glory were mostly veiled to those who saw Him (John 1:10). Later, after the resurrection and ascension of Christ, the coming of the Holy Spirit at Pentecost (Acts 2) would hail the coming of a mysterious form of the kingdom manifested through the righteousness and power of the church (Rom. 14:17; 1 Cor. 4:20). During this time, Christ would reign in the lives of believers through the Spirit (John 3:3-5; see also John 18:36). Ultimately, though, all these forms of the kingdom of God anticipate the eternal reign of Christ that will begin at His second coming, expand through the Millennium (Rev. 20:1-6), and continue into eternity (Rev. 20:7–22:5). At that time the eternal reign of God and the earthly reign of the Messiah will unite.

So, what did Jesus mean when He said that some of the disciples would not taste death until they saw the Son of Man coming in His kingdom? And how does this relate to the Transfiguration? First, I don't think the Transfiguration completely fulfills the prophecy of the coming kingdom, as if there's to be no future fulfillment of the coming of Christ in glory. That would be a pretty stingy fulfillment of an enormous promise. As glorious as it was, the Transfiguration alone couldn't be the be-all and end-all of kingdom expectations. Second, I don't think we're required to choose one fulfillment in exclusion of all the others. That is, interpreting this way is more in keeping with the way biblical prophecy works, in terms of near and far fulfillments.[18]

In the immediate context, the glorious Transfiguration partially fulfilled Christ's promise that some would see the coming of the kingdom of God in glory, as a brief snapshot or foretaste. However, it was more than just a symbolic representation. At that moment, on that mountain, heaven and earth touched, Jesus was glorified, Old Testament saints appeared, and the glory of the Father descended upon the mountain. These were all real manifestations of what the kingdom of God will be like in the future. But it didn't last. Though real, it was only a temporary glimpse.

A second, fuller revelation of the kingdom came after the resurrection and ascension of Christ and the coming of the Holy Spirit at Pentecost—which most of those standing with Christ experienced (Judas alone was excluded). But even that wasn't the fullness of the kingdom. It, too, was a foretaste. Most (not James, who was martyred early) witnessed the advancement of the kingdom through the preaching of the gospel around the known world. And John saw an unprecedented preview of the kingdom of God when He witnessed the visions recorded in the book of Revelation. Even still, the full manifestation of the kingdom remains future.

Though the Transfiguration scene wasn't the full arrival of the kingdom of God on earth, it does reveal an important theological truth: The kingdom of God is always near—ready at any moment to break through the thin fabric separating earth from heaven, this present age from the age to come. The Transfiguration became a prophetic type of the future manifestations of the kingdom and revealed just how near the kingdom really is. It could literally appear on earth at any moment!

Tabor would have brought them straight through territory where Jesus held celebrity status, to a mountain that was occupied by a settlement in the first century.[19] It seems more likely that the men rested for a week in the region of Caesarea Philippi and then Jesus took Peter, James, and John up Mount Hermon by themselves (17:1).

What happened next was nothing less than awesome. Jesus, the God-man, had been living, in terms of His appearance, as an ordinary human for over thirty years, veiling His divine glory. Don't let the ancient artwork and icons fool you: Jesus didn't walk around with a glowing halo floating around His head. Nobody would have pegged Him as anything other than just a normal guy—at least with respect to His appearance. Philippians 2:6-8 describes from a theological perspective what everybody witnessed every day at the practical level: Although

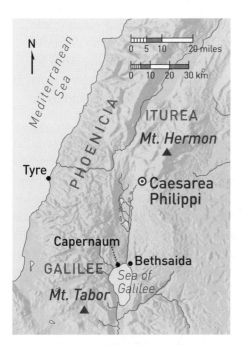

Though some have identified the location of the Transfiguration as Mount Tabor, southwest of the Sea of Galilee, the more likely location is Mount Hermon, near Caesarea Philippi.

before the Incarnation God the Son existed in resplendence and magnificence "in the form of God," He "emptied Himself" of that manifestation of heavenly glory. He took "the form of a bondservant" and appeared "in the likeness of men" such that all those around Him found Him "in appearance as a man." Though Jesus displayed His authority and power through teaching and miracles, He continued to cloak His visible glory from others throughout His earthly ministry . . . until that day on the mountain. That event proved to Peter, James, and John that during every moment of Jesus' human life, He was simultaneously fully divine. That truth of the Incarnation would become the backbone of a body of doctrine related to the person and work of Christ.

In fact, some three decades later, in the AD 60s, Peter himself would reflect on that glimpse of glory:

> For we did not follow cleverly devised tales when we made known to you the power and coming of our Lord Jesus Christ, but we were eyewitnesses of His majesty. For when He received honor and glory from God the Father, such an utterance as this was made to Him by the Majestic Glory, "This is My beloved Son with whom I am well-pleased"—and we ourselves heard this utterance made from heaven when we were with Him on the holy mountain. (2 Pet. 1:16-18)

And six decades after the Transfiguration, in the AD 90s, John reflected,

> In the beginning was the Word, and the Word was with God, and the Word was God. He was in the beginning with God. All things came into being through Him, and apart from Him nothing

> came into being that has come into being. In Him was life, and the life was the Light of men. The Light shines in the darkness, and the darkness did not comprehend it. . . . And the Word became flesh, and dwelt among us, and we saw His glory, glory as of the only begotten from the Father, full of grace and truth. (John 1:1-5, 14)

These profound theological conclusions were drawn from the profound experiences Peter and John had (see 1 Jn. 1:1-3).

Matthew's words are succinct: Jesus was "transfigured before them" (Matt. 17:2). The Greek term translated "transfigured" has become one of our English words: "metamorphosis." The Greek verb *metamorphoō* [3339] means "to change in a manner visible to others."[20] This doesn't mean that Jesus' inward essence changed but rather that His outward appearance was transformed. What changed? His face "shone like the sun" and His clothing "became as white as light." I see no reason to interpret this as anything other than literal. Jesus wasn't just glowing, He was shining! People can stare all night at the moon and suffer no harm because the moon merely reflects rays of the true source of light, the sun. But if you look directly at the sun for more than a few seconds, its brilliance will blind you, because the sun is the source itself. In the same way, Jesus isn't merely a reflector of God's glory—He is the source of divine glory as the second person of the Trinity. This was the greatest, most evident confirmation of Jesus' deity thus far in His earthly life. And His disciples would never forget it.

But that wasn't all. Remember, this wasn't just a manifestation of Christ's divine nature; it was also a foretaste of His coming kingdom, when heaven itself would break into the earthly realm. Suddenly two more figures joined the group: Moses and Elijah. If you were to ask me how the disciples knew it was Moses and Elijah, I couldn't tell you. Matthew simply notes that Moses and Elijah were talking with Jesus (17:3). Luke indicates that the conversation concerned "His departure which He was about to accomplish at Jerusalem" (Luke 9:30-31). It is quite possible that their identities were given during that conversation, which was never recorded in any of the Gospels.

What is the significance of these two figures—Moses and Elijah— appearing with Jesus? Commentators have given several suggestions, but I think the best explanation is that they serve as personal representatives of the Law and the Prophets—both of which pointed to and anticipated the coming of the Messiah.[21]

"What Is Glory?"

MATTHEW 17:2

As a teenager, I didn't know what "glory" meant. That was a problem, because I'd just sung about it for over an hour in George Frideric Handel's magnificent oratorio Messiah. My mother sang beautiful soprano. My sister had a lovely contralto voice; my brother, a strong bass. And I pitched in a little tenor. We had gone through the process of trying out for the choir that sang Messiah every year, and we had all made it.

If you know the piece, you know that it begins with a lyrical tenor recitative, "Comfort ye, comfort ye My people. . . . Speak ye comfortably to Jerusalem." The lyrics come directly out of Isaiah 40:1-2. Then it moves on to the aria: "Ev'ry valley shall be exalted, and ev'ry mountain and hill made low; the crooked straight and the rough places plain" (see Isa. 40:4). It's a beautiful beginning to this magnum opus of Handel.

Then the conductor, Dr. Walter Jenkins, had the choir stand. And there I stood, a mere teenager beside real singers—many of them professionals. The conductor began as he brought the baton down, "And the glory, the glory of the Lord shall be revealed!" I'll never forget it. I'd never sung in a group like that. I got real quiet and just mouthed the words so I could hear the choir singing. To be honest, I couldn't hold back the tears.

The glory. The glory of the Lord. But what was glory? I didn't know what the word meant. On the way home, as my dad drove us through Houston on a cold, rainy winter evening in December, I was sitting in the middle of the back seat of our '47 Chevy pondering those lyrics. It was nagging me, so I finally asked, "Dad, what is glory?"

And he immediately used the famous fatherly words, "Ask your mother." After all, he was driving and couldn't address such a weighty issue.

So I said, "Mom, what is glory?"

(continued on next page)

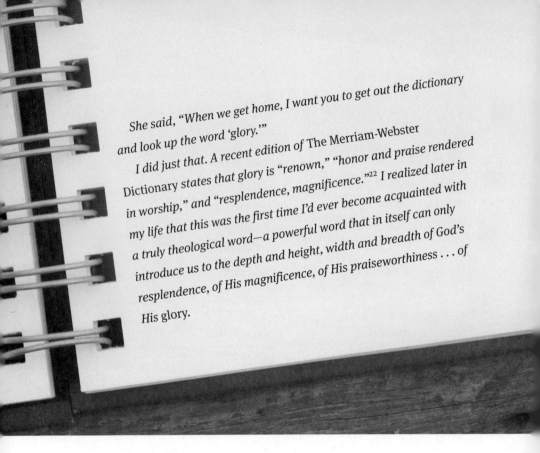

She said, "When we get home, I want you to get out the dictionary and look up the word 'glory.'"

I did just that. A recent edition of The Merriam-Webster Dictionary states that glory is "renown," "honor and praise rendered in worship," and "resplendence, magnificence."[22] I realized later in my life that this was the first time I'd ever become acquainted with a truly theological word—a powerful word that in itself can only introduce us to the depth and height, width and breadth of God's resplendence, of His magnificence, of His praiseworthiness . . . of His glory.

— 17:4-8 —

There they stood on the mountain, Jesus emanating the light of divine glory while Moses and Elijah conversed with Him. Luke's Gospel tells us that prior to the Transfiguration, Jesus had been praying on the high mountain, and the three disciples had dozed off (Luke 9:28, 32). When they awoke to witness the brilliant light and visitors from the heavenly realm, they were clearly dumbfounded. But that didn't stop Peter from blurting out the first thing to pop into his head: "Lord, it is good for us to be here; if You wish, I will make three tabernacles here, one for You, and one for Moses, and one for Elijah" (Matt. 17:4).

Why Peter uttered those words is not easy to discern. Luke notes that Peter spoke "not realizing what he was saying" (Luke 9:33). And Mark adds the detail that Peter didn't know how to respond to the situation because they were "terrified" (Mark 9:6). Some think that perhaps the Feast of Tabernacles (or Booths) was near (cf. John 7:2), and Peter meant that all of them could keep the feast on the mountain, which would have required them to build small dwellings to sleep in.[23] Richard Gardner's estimation is more optimistic: "Peter wants this moment to last forever."[24] Whatever the case, it seems clear that Peter would have been better off to just maintain reverent silence in the face of such a dazzling display of awesome glory. One of the most helpful pieces of advice I've ever heard could have done Peter well that night: "Never miss an opportunity to shut up!"

Needless to say, Jesus, Moses, and Elijah didn't take Peter up on his rash offer. In fact, the divine presence took control of that awkward moment with an awesome intervention (cf. Deut. 5:22). While the rambling words were still spilling from Peter's mouth, a bright cloud rolled over the disciples, and out of that cloud boomed the voice of God the Father: "This is My beloved Son, with whom I am well-pleased; listen to Him!" (Matt. 17:5). This wasn't the first time the voice of God the Father testified concerning Jesus. After Jesus' baptism in the Jordan, the heavens opened and a voice said, "This is My beloved Son, in whom I am well-pleased" (3:17). The only difference between these two statements from the Father is the addition of the imperative on the Mount of Transfiguration: "Listen to Him!" (17:5). What an appropriate admonition at a moment when Peter was speaking nonsense.

Finally, they got it. With those words of God the Father echoing in their ears, they face-planted onto the ground in reverent awe. Matthew says at this point that they were "terrified" (17:6). Silence followed. That was the right response. No awkward words spoken with little thought. No leaping forward to build booths. No thoughts about how great it was to be there and to see those things. But total silence and absolute awe.

With the disciples in their prone position, trembling in fear, Jesus reached out His comforting hand, graciously touched them, and said, "Get up, and do not be afraid" (17:7). As they lifted their heads, they saw only Jesus (17:8). Moses and Elijah, as well as the cloud of the Father's presence, had vanished. Jesus' glorious transformation had apparently also waned. They had witnessed a terrifying glimpse of glory. The heavenly kingdom in all its brilliance had truly—but briefly—burst into the earthly realm. One day, when Jesus returns as Judge and King, that otherworldly glory that transforms the present world will remain forever (Rev. 21:3-4).

— 17:9-13 —

Try to imagine how preoccupied—and at the same time overwhelmed—Peter, James, and John were when they began their journey back down the mountain toward Caesarea Philippi. They had likely experienced nearly a week of rest and relaxation. Then Jesus asked them to join Him in a steep climb up the side of the snowcapped Mount Hermon to pray. There, out of the blue, they experienced in the flesh the sight, sound, and terrifying awe of the glorious Transfiguration of the Son of God—as well as the unexpected and unbelievable cameo appearances of Moses and Elijah.

I'm sure as they began their descent of the mountain toward the rest of the disciples waiting below, they couldn't contain their eagerness to wow their friends with their experience of the Transfiguration. But Jesus put the brakes on that right away. On their way down, Jesus instructed them not to tell anyone what they had seen "until the Son of Man has risen from the dead" (17:9). Mark's account records that they didn't quite understand what Jesus meant by His reference to the resurrection of the Son of Man (Mark 9:10). I can imagine them pondering, *Is He referring to Himself? To all humanity in the general resurrection? How will we know when it's happened?*

In their discussions, somebody mentioned that Elijah had to come before the coming of the Messiah. This expectation was based on a prophecy of Malachi, which stated, "Behold, I am going to send you Elijah the prophet before the coming of the great and terrible day of the Lord. He will restore the hearts of the fathers to their children and the hearts of the children to their fathers, so that I will not come and smite the land with a curse" (Mal. 4:5-6). Hadn't Elijah appeared just a moment ago? Why would Jesus die and rise again if Elijah had arrived to restore godliness in Israel? In R. T. France's words, "Altogether, their eschatological time-table is confused!"[25]

In this bewildered state, the disciples asked Jesus for clarification: Was it right to expect Elijah to come first—that is, before the Day of the Lord, the Final Judgment, the resurrection of the dead, and the beginning of the messianic age? Jesus responded by affirming the teaching of the scribes and the words of the prophet Malachi: "Elijah is coming and will restore all things" (Matt. 17:11). However, Jesus added an important layer to the incomplete teaching of the scribes: A prophet in the spirit of Elijah had already come in the person and ministry of John the Baptizer (17:12). Like the Elijah prophesied in Malachi, John had come to call for repentance and to restore the spiritual condition of Israel. Yet they rejected him. He was eventually arrested by the illegitimate "king of the Jews," Herod, who'd had him killed.

Earlier, Jesus had said that if the critics and scoffers among the Jews would have accepted the truth that Jesus was the long-awaited Messiah, the coming King of Israel—"if you are willing to accept it" (11:14)—then John the Baptizer would have fulfilled their expectation of a prophet coming in the spirit and power of Elijah. Regarding their faulty perspective, Stanley Toussaint notes, "Since John did not accomplish this, the coming of Elijah is still future. One can logically conclude, therefore, that the coming of the kingdom is also postponed and future."[26]

So, Elijah had come, in a prophetic sense, in the person of John the Baptizer. The disciples understood this (17:13). John's ministry of preparation for the Messiah had been rejected; for the most part, the people of Israel did not repent and turn to the Lord. Therefore, the Son of Man—Jesus—would also suffer the same kind of rejection and treatment by the same people (17:12). Just as Jesus had begun teaching them already in Caesarea Philippi, the Son of Man would "suffer many things from the elders and chief priests and scribes, and be killed, and be raised up on the third day" (16:21).

But does this mean that the coming of Elijah—or another prophet in the spirit and power of Elijah—was forever set aside? The vision on the Mount of Transfiguration seems to have kept the hope alive that the coming of a literal Elijah was still a real possibility. And Jesus' words in Matthew 17:11—"Elijah is coming and will restore all things"—points to something yet future from Jesus' perspective. This has led some to expect a future coming of Elijah (or a prophet similar to Elijah) prior to the second coming of Christ who will call Israel to repentance and bring about a massive revival during the end times. In addition, many relate this coming of Elijah to the ministry of the two witnesses in Revelation 11:3-14. In fact, some have identified these witnesses as Moses and Elijah. After all, they've already made an appearance: during Jesus' Transfiguration, discussing Christ's mission in Jerusalem (Luke 9:30-31). Others have identified the two witnesses as Enoch and Elijah, the two people in the Old Testament who departed this world without experiencing physical death (see Gen. 5:24 and Heb. 11:5; 2 Kgs. 2:11-12).

The book of Revelation gives very few specifics about the identity of the two witnesses. What we know is that they will be given authority to prophesy for three and a half years, during which time they will be protected from harm and given special power to call down plagues and judgments on their wicked adversaries (Rev. 11:3-6). Because the symbols of the two olive trees and two lampstands in Revelation 11:4 correspond to the symbols representing Zerubbabel and Joshua in Zechariah 3-4, it may be that the testimony of the two witnesses will somehow relate to the rebuilding of the temple in Jerusalem as mentioned in Revelation 11:1-2. Most importantly, their miraculous authority will be similar to that of Moses, Elijah, and other Old Testament prophets, demonstrating the crucial nature of their ministry during the future Tribulation period. It seems likely to me that the two figures, who will seemingly come in the spirit of Moses and Elijah, will serve to fulfill the prophecy of Malachi 4, just as John the Baptizer would have fulfilled that prophecy had Israel accepted him.

APPLICATION: MATTHEW 17:1-13

Tackling Three Horrible Habits

The astonishing account of Jesus' Transfiguration has deep theological implications for understanding the person of Christ—His true deity embodied in true humanity. And it has powerful implications regarding the work of Christ because it provides a brief glimpse of His future coming in glory. I think we've adequately explored these aspects of this profound experience in the comments above. As we move toward application, I'd like us to put ourselves in the place of the three privileged disciples who witnessed the Transfiguration. As we do, I want us to tackle three horrible habits that have become common in our time: moving too fast, talking too much, and reacting too quickly.

First, *if you move too fast, you'll stay too shallow.* Like a speedboat skipping across the surface of the water, it's impossible to go deep when you're moving as fast as you can through life. In my experience, God doesn't hurry to catch up with us; we slow down to walk with Him. The Lord wants us to go deeper. He wants us to think more deeply. He wants us to be men and women who think His thoughts, and that doesn't come by skimming the surface of the Bible, or rushing through our quiet times, or hurrying through our prayer lists. Experiences like the Transfiguration require decades—not minutes—of meditation and reflection. Some thirty years later, Peter was still pondering its implications, and so was John in the twilight years of his life. So slow down to go deep.

Second, *if you talk too much, you'll listen too little.* The result will be that you grasp far less than you could. Do you know what it's like to sit through a play when the person next to you keeps talking, commenting on everything, asking questions, and jabbering through the whole performance? They (and you) miss details important for making sense of the story. The Christian life is the same way. We need to learn to be quiet. Eventually the disciples on the Mount of Transfiguration realized that. They closed their mouths and embraced the awesomeness of the experience. We need to learn that too. Talk less. Listen more. When I lead groups of pilgrims to Israel, I often begin the journey with an opening devotion in which I urge them to "walk a little slower, talk a little less, think a little deeper, write a little more, and let the wonder in." All those things go together. And they can all be ruined if we don't learn to listen. So talk less to hear more.

Third, *if you react too quickly, you'll miss the rewards of waiting patiently.* Our tendency in our fast-paced lifestyle is to react thoughtlessly and rashly. How many times have you, like Peter, blurted out the first thing on your mind and then regretted it later? I have to admit that I've done that more than I wish. Of course, there are emergency situations and brief occasions that require immediate action. But most of the time, urgency is imagined. We need to learn to stop, take a deep breath, take in a situation or experience, ponder it, and then respond carefully rather than react quickly. Prudence is a virtue too often lost in our modern world. Let's be people who retrieve it and live it. Take time to respond wisely.

Micro-Faith and Mega-Obstacles
MATTHEW 17:14-21

NASB

14When they came to the crowd, a man came up to Jesus, falling on his knees before Him and saying, 15"aLord, have mercy on my son, for he is a blunatic and is very ill; for he often falls into the fire and often into the water. 16I brought him to Your disciples, and they could not cure him." 17And Jesus answered and said, "You unbelieving and perverted generation, how long shall I be with you? How long shall I put up with you? Bring him here to Me." 18And Jesus rebuked him, and the demon came out of him, and the boy was cured aat once.

19Then the disciples came to Jesus privately and said, "Why could we

NLT

14At the foot of the mountain, a large crowd was waiting for them. A man came and knelt before Jesus and said, 15"Lord, have mercy on my son. He has seizures and suffers terribly. He often falls into the fire or into the water. 16So I brought him to your disciples, but they couldn't heal him."

17Jesus said, "You faithless and corrupt people! How long must I be with you? How long must I put up with you? Bring the boy here to me." 18Then Jesus rebuked the demon in the boy, and it left him. From that moment the boy was well.

19Afterward the disciples asked Jesus privately, "Why couldn't we cast out that demon?"

NASB

not drive it out?" **20**And He said to them, "Because of the littleness of your faith; for truly I say to you, if you have faith ᵃthe size of a mustard seed, you will say to this mountain, 'Move from here to there,' and it will move; and nothing will be impossible to you. **21**[ᵃBut this kind does not go out except by prayer and fasting."]

17:15 ᵃOr *Sir* ᵇOr *moonstruck; Gr seleniazo*
17:18 ᵃLit *from that hour*   17:20 ᵃLit *as*
17:21 ᵃEarly mss do not contain this v

NLT

20"You don't have enough faith," Jesus told them. "I tell you the truth, if you had faith even as small as a mustard seed, you could say to this mountain, 'Move from here to there,' and it would move. Nothing would be impossible.*"

17:20 Some manuscripts add verse 21, *But this kind of demon won't leave except by prayer and fasting.* Compare Mark 9:29.

Anybody who has had a child suffering from a serious injury or chronic illness—whether physical or mental—can relate to the next scene described in Matthew's Gospel. The child in this story was a danger to himself and to others. His condition would be described as acute. The situation couldn't go on the way it was for much longer before the boy would lose his life. What an agonizing predicament! What raw reality and real-world suffering! And what a contrast with the vision of Jesus' Transfiguration on the mountain just hours before!

Anytime we read an account in Scripture, we need to keep its context in mind—its literary, historical, and geographical context. Often the author intentionally places particular narratives side by side to draw comparisons and contrasts. This story of a boy suffering from demonic attacks follows right on the heels of a powerful portrayal of Jesus' glory. While the glorious vision took place on a mountaintop, the encounter with the forces of wickedness takes place in a valley. From the ecstasy of heavenly brilliance, Jesus and His three disciples descend into the misery of earthly suffering.

To complicate things, Jesus finds Himself back in the midst of an agitated crowd, egged on by rascally critics who were centered on a desperate and dejected family and confused and disconcerted disciples. Not until Jesus steps into the situation is there relief—immediate and permanent. Flowing from this dramatic scene are some important, surprising, and unforgettable lessons about faith.

— 17:14-18 —

To get a full understanding of the events described in this passage, we need to retrieve a few details from the Gospels of Mark and Luke. After the incredible experience of the Transfiguration, Jesus and the three disciples reached the bottom of the mountain the next day (Luke 9:37)—most likely returning to Caesarea Philippi. There they found the rest of the disciples, who had not joined Jesus, Peter, James, and John on the mountain (Mark 9:14). However, the disciples weren't alone, twiddling their thumbs or snoozing quietly in hammocks. Around them a large crowd had formed (Matt. 17:14; Mark 9:14; Luke 9:37).

Where had the crowd come from? Read together, the three accounts give us a good idea of what had happened. While Jesus and His three disciples had gone up the mountain, the rest of the disciples had encountered a man who had a son suffering from a severe physical, mental, and spiritual plight. Matthew describes him as a "lunatic" (Matt. 17:15), which is a translation of the Greek verb *selēniazomai* [4583]. The English term "lunatic" is derived from the Latin word for "moon" (*luna*). The related Greek noun *selēnē* [4582] also means "moon." Literally, the boy was "moonstruck." One lexicon explains: "In the ancient world epileptic seizure was associated with transcendent powers of the moon."[27] All three accounts indicate that the boy's condition resulted from demonic attacks. The symptoms were complex:

- He was mute but able to scream (Mark 9:17; Luke 9:39).
- He was being slammed to the ground and would become stiff (Mark 9:18; Luke 9:42).
- He would foam at the mouth and grind his teeth (Mark 9:18, 20; Luke 9:39).
- He would convulse and roll on the ground (Mark 9:20; Luke 9:39, 42).
- He was being thrown into fire and water (Matt. 17:15; Mark 9:22).
- He was being physically injured after each attack (Luke 9:39).

I can't imagine how much that boy's family suffered! Somehow, the father had learned that Jesus of Nazareth was in town and that He had a reputation for working miracles. He attempted to bring the boy to Jesus but found only the nine remaining disciples awaiting His return from the mountain. Rather than waiting for Jesus to return, the disciples took it upon themselves to cast out the demon and heal the boy (Matt. 17:16). Apparently, their attempts at delivering the boy from his demonic attacks had failed.

In the aftermath of their inability to drive the demon out of the boy, a large crowd had gathered, and among them were "scribes arguing with them" (Mark 9:14). We can imagine that when the disciples failed to perform miracles like Jesus, the scribes took advantage of that fact to criticize them and perhaps denounce them as deceivers. While the scribes accused the disciples (and, by extension, their Master) of fraud, the father of the boy must have become increasingly distressed in his desperation. The boy himself continued to suffer from his demon-induced insanity as the crowd became worked up by the ensuing controversy.

Then Jesus arrived.

Immediately, the father of the afflicted boy rushed to Jesus and dropped to his knees (Matt. 17:14). He was obviously unconcerned with the theological debate occurring between the scribes, the disciples, and the crowd. And the failure of the disciples to cast the demon out of the boy had not deterred his confidence that Jesus Himself would be able to help. He pleaded for mercy from Jesus, described his son's condition, and explained that the disciples were unable to cure his boy (17:15-16).

At first glance, it looks like Jesus was frustrated and fed up with the disciples who were unable to drive the demon out of the boy. Jesus' reaction to the father's plea reveals irritation: "You unbelieving and perverted generation, how long shall I be with you? How long shall I put up with you?" (17:17). But remember that Jesus was standing amid a crowd of onlookers, a handful of scribes criticizing the disciples, and the disciples themselves, who were unable to explain their failure. In light of this, it seems more likely that Jesus directed His words of rebuke not at the disciples specifically, but to all humanity. He indicted the father of the boy, His own disciples, the watching crowd, and all people throughout history. In the Garden, humanity experienced an estrangement from God that perverted God's world order and made all people helpless before sin, sickness, and spiritual wickedness. Without the power of God intervening for us, we remain powerless in the face of the devil's might.

But Jesus wasn't bound by the shackles of unbelief and perversion. He turned to the father of the boy and said, "Bring him here to Me" (17:17). Mark's Gospel indicates that when the boy was brought to Jesus, he immediately went into one of his convulsions, rolling on the ground and foaming at the mouth (Mark 9:20). The crowd began to swell as more and more people arrived to see the conclusion of this dramatic encounter. Would Jesus be able to help the boy? Or would His words be no more effective than those of His disciples? I suspect that a hush fell on the crowd, so the only thing people could hear was the boy screaming.

Matthew's Gospel tells us that Jesus "rebuked him" (Matt. 17:18). Mark relays Jesus' actual words: "You deaf and mute spirit, I command you, come out of him and do not enter him again" (Mark 9:25). Matthew then notes that the demon left the boy and that he was immediately cured of all his symptoms (Matt. 17:18). I can picture gasps of surprise, outbursts of joy, and murmuring from the crowd when they saw the ease with which Jesus simply ordered the demon away. I'm sure the father cried tears of joy as he embraced his son, who had been returned to him safe and sound. I'm sure the disciples stood there bewildered, still wondering why their own attempts at commanding the demon had failed. And I'm certain the skeptical scribes who had been arguing with the disciples grew red-faced with embarrassment and anger as the crowd suddenly shifted allegiance to Jesus, despite the earlier failure of the disciples.

— 17:19-21 —

But why hadn't the demon departed earlier, when the disciples had tried to rebuke it themselves before Jesus, Peter, James, and John arrived? That profound theological and practical question obviously nagged the disciples. They were so troubled by it that they came to Jesus privately—far from the watchful eyes of the crowd or the prying ears of the scribes—and asked Him what they had done wrong (17:19). Earlier, after all, Jesus Himself had given them authority to "heal the sick, raise the dead, cleanse the lepers, cast out demons" (10:8). Had their power waned? Had their authority expired?

Luke's Gospel doesn't record that private conversation. And Mark's account simply relays Jesus' explanation that "this kind cannot come out by anything but prayer" (Mark 9:29; cf. Matt. 17:21).[28] Matthew adds another layer of depth to Jesus' explanation. Their failure to cast out the demon was due to their "littleness of . . . faith" (17:20). Jesus assured them that if they had faith even the size of a mustard seed, nothing would be impossible for them. In fact, He even pointed to the northeast at the snowcapped Mount Hermon from which He had just descended and insisted that with mustard-seed-sized faith they would be able to command that very mountain to move, and it would obey them.

Jesus was undoubtedly using hyperbole to drive home His point of the importance and power of faith. He used one of the smallest things in the world—a mustard seed—to condemn the relatively tiny faith of the disciples. If such small faith had the potential to move Mount Hermon—the biggest thing on the horizon—then the disciples' faith must have been microscopic! Far from comforting, this scolding would have discouraged and shamed the disciples even more.

Mustard Seed: © David Turner/Wikimedia Commons;
Mt. Hermon: © Beivushtang at English Wikipedia

Actual size

Jesus admonished the disciples that if they had faith even the size of a **mustard seed**, they could cause a mountain to move. He likely made this statement near the base of **Mount Hermon**, the highest peak in Israel.

To understand Jesus' rebuke of the disciples' little faith and its relationship to driving out the demon with prayer, we need to consider the entire context—including the event of the Transfiguration that only Peter, James, and John had witnessed. Those three disciples returned from their "mountaintop experience" with an insight into Jesus' identity, glory, and power that the others had not experienced. So, while the nine remaining disciples did have an understanding of who Jesus was, they likely did not have a particularly complete understanding. They still had more to learn.

Also, they were operating outside of Jesus' presence and without His explicit commissioning. Unlike the earlier sending out of the disciples with unique authority over sickness and demons (10:8), this time they were acting on their own. Perhaps they doubted whether they had the authority to do so. Besides this, they were operating under the watchful eyes of the scribes and the doubtful eyes of the crowd. It's amazing how the skepticism of the masses can cause our own faith to wane. Finally, the case of the boy afflicted by the demon may have been more severe than any they had ever experienced. Perhaps they wondered whether the authority given to them by Jesus could handle such a difficult demon.

Had the disciples fully grasped who Jesus was and what His power could accomplish, they probably would have opted to pray. They had clearly not yet learned the truth that Jesus would teach them later: "Whatever you ask in My name, that will I do, so that the Father may be glorified in the Son. If you ask Me anything in My name, I will do it" (John 14:13-14). Also, they had not yet received the fullness of the Holy Spirit, who would indwell them, empower them, and enable them to carry out these works in Jesus' name by faith.

In short, the disciples had forgotten their complete and permanent dependence on Jesus Christ. Their ability to perform miracles was dependent upon Jesus' omnipotence, not their diligence. In a sense, then, it wasn't a problem of not having *enough* faith, as if they needed to just close their eyes, make tight fists, and will more power into their lives. No, even mustard-seed faith would move Mount Hermon. *True* faith is what they needed—the kind of faith that turns from self-confidence to confidence in the power of Jesus Christ alone. With His power, nothing is impossible.

APPLICATION: MATTHEW 17:14-21

Shining the Light of the Mountain in the Darkness of the Valley

Mountaintop moments are designed to change our perception, not our address. Periodically throughout life, God pulls us aside to slow us down, get our attention, teach us something deeper about Him, and remind us that He alone is God. We often call these "spiritual high points" or "mountaintop experiences." They can occur alone or with others, in moments of worship or periods of reflection. God can meet us while we're lying on a hospital bed or attending a church retreat. He can reveal His glory while we're going through times of testing, while we're sitting in a classroom, or while we're driving in a car. These experiences are clarifying, reassuring, and essential to prepare us for what lies ahead. But we can't live there. After the mountaintop experiences end, we need to descend the slopes back to "normal" life—back to the valley of restless crowds and relentless critics.

As I reflect on the stunning contrast between the disciples' literally illuminating mountaintop experience and the sudden challenges they faced in the dark valley below, a few practical thoughts come to mind, each beginning with the word *never*.

First, *never forget what the Lord taught you in the mountaintop experience.* Take the light He shined in that moment into the valley below. Let it illuminate your life. Don't leave what you learned there on the summit of spiritual experience. I like to write my insights down as a reminder of what the Lord has shown me. There are certain times and places in my life I can go back to and remember how the Lord broke through and revealed His character and power to me in unique ways. I've never forgotten these insights, and they've been foundational for much of my ministry. It's amazing how experiences like that can change our perspectives. Don't forget them. Take them with you as constant reminders of who God is and what He can do. You'll need that perspective in the valley below.

Second, *never allow earthly obstacles to eclipse divine truth.* There are principles in the Bible that are always true, always reliable. They are proven over and over in your own life. Don't let the severity of the plight, the impossibility of the situation, or the size of the problem overwhelm you. When faced with such a complex case as the demonized boy, the disciples forgot all the impossible challenges that Jesus had already overcome. They thought, *Nope, this one's just too hard.* Instead, they could have realized that when it comes to the power of God, the size of the obstacle is utterly irrelevant. Again, don't forget what God has shown you in your mountaintop experiences. Shine that light into the gloom of your situation, then walk through it. Throughout life we will be faced with great opportunities disguised as impossible situations. Don't be intimidated by them. Don't back down. Remember divine truth and trust God.

Finally, *never think previous failures mean something can't be done.* We all look back on things we've done wrong or areas where we've failed as evidence that we can't take the next difficult step or face the next daunting challenge. False! Past failures prove nothing except that you are a fallen, frail human being who needs to get over yourself and trust God entirely. Faith will drive out our fear of failure. The disciples could have continued to obsess over their failure to drive out the demon; instead, they went straight to Jesus to find out what went wrong. And the rest of the New Testament shows that they didn't quit. They let their failure motivate them toward a deeper relationship with Christ and a better understanding of the life of faith.

Death and Taxes
MATTHEW 17:22-27

NASB

22 And while they were gathering together in Galilee, Jesus said to them, "The Son of Man is going to be ªdelivered into the hands of men; 23 and they will kill Him, and He will be raised on the third day." And they were deeply grieved.

NLT

22 After they gathered again in Galilee, Jesus told them, "The Son of Man is going to be betrayed into the hands of his enemies. 23 He will be killed, but on the third day he will be raised from the dead." And the disciples were filled with grief.

²⁴When they came to Capernaum, those who collected the ªtwo-drachma *tax* came to Peter and said, "Does your teacher not pay the ªtwo-drachma *tax?*" ²⁵He said, "Yes." And when he came into the house, Jesus spoke to him first, saying, "What do you think, Simon? From whom do the kings of the earth collect customs or poll-tax, from their sons or from strangers?" ²⁶When Peter said, "From strangers," Jesus said to him, "Then the sons are ªexempt. ²⁷However, so that we do not ªoffend them, go to the sea and throw in a hook, and take the first fish that comes up; and when you open its mouth, you will find ᵇa shekel. Take that and give it to them for you and Me."

17:22 ªOr *betrayed* **17:24** ªEquivalent to two denarii or two days' wages, paid as a temple tax **17:26** ªOr *free* **17:27** ªLit *cause them to stumble* ᵇLit *standard coin,* which was a shekel

²⁴On their arrival in Capernaum, the collectors of the Temple tax* came to Peter and asked him, "Doesn't your teacher pay the Temple tax?"

²⁵"Yes, he does," Peter replied. Then he went into the house.

But before he had a chance to speak, Jesus asked him, "What do you think, Peter?* Do kings tax their own people or the people they have conquered?*"

²⁶"They tax the people they have conquered," Peter replied.

"Well, then," Jesus said, "the citizens are free! ²⁷However, we don't want to offend them, so go down to the lake and throw in a line. Open the mouth of the first fish you catch, and you will find a large silver coin.* Take it and pay the tax for both of us."

17:24 Greek *the two-drachma [tax];* also in 17:24b. See Exod 30:13-16; Neh 10:32-33. **17:25a** Greek *Simon?* **17:25b** Greek *their sons or others?* **17:27** Greek *a stater* [a Greek coin equivalent to four drachmas].

Jesus and His disciples were inseparable. This became all the more obvious as Jesus entered the final six months of His public ministry. As the Cross loomed larger on the horizon, He spent less time with the multitudes and more time with those who were dedicated to following Him—the men and women who were His faithful disciples—and especially with the Twelve who had received the special calling, and even more particularly, with the three who had been privy to certain astonishing miracles.

However, what He often wanted to talk to them about was not what they wanted to hear. As conflict with critics intensified and the disciples could sense increasing unrest among the crowds, they likely envisioned an ultimate showdown between the hypocritical teachers and crooked rulers on one side and the Son of God in the flesh and His wonder-working disciples on the other. Yet Jesus kept on talking about His arrest, suffering, and death. The last thing the disciples wanted to think about was His dying and leaving them to carry on without Him. In their minds, that scenario didn't make any sense.

This may seem inexplicable until we begin to think about how we respond to unwelcome news. When given a terminal diagnosis, our first step is frequently to disbelieve—to deny the facts, attack the messenger, and seek a second and third opinion. Likewise, when faced with the tragic news of a loved one's death, our first reaction is often to deny it, shut out the truth, and hold on a little longer to the hope that maybe, just maybe, we heard the news wrong or there has been some terrible mistake.

But Jesus' task was to push through the denial in advance of the betrayal. He wanted to prepare His disciples for life after He had departed from them. So, in spite of the difficulty the Twelve had in struggling through these repeated reminders, Jesus faithfully, frequently, and abruptly brought up the subject none of them wanted to face. At the same time, He continued to prepare them in other ways—performing miracles, teaching deeper spiritual truths, and setting an example for them to follow.

— 17:22-23 —

Having spent over a week in the region of Caesarea Philippi in the shadows of Mount Hermon, Jesus and the disciples again made their way back to Galilee. In that familiar territory and with familiar faces in the crowds—both friends and foes—they no doubt began to feel the increasing tension of scowling critics and scoffing skeptics. In this atmosphere, Jesus spoke directly concerning His coming passion.

While Jesus had already revealed to them that He would suffer, die, and rise again (16:21; 17:12), now He added an additional detail: He would be "delivered into the hands of men" (17:22). The Greek word translated "delivered" is *paradidōmi* [3860], which means to "hand over, turn over, give up a person."[29] Had the disciples put some thought into the statement at the time, immediately the question would have come up—"By whom is the Son of Man going to be handed over?" Clearly, He would be handed over to those who would torture and kill Him, but who would betray Him in such a way? Perhaps they would have recognized that Jesus was revealing for the first time an "inside job," in which one of their own would betray Him.

But they didn't think that deeply. In fact, it doesn't seem that they paid attention to anything but "they will kill Him" (17:23). Their response seemed to dwell strictly on the fact of Jesus' death, because "they were deeply grieved." Often when strong emotions overtake us, it's hard to hear correctly or to think clearly. The disciples didn't ask about the treachery involved in His arrest, or the miracle involved in His being "raised on the third day."

JESUS' PREDICTIONS OF HIS PASSION IN MATTHEW

As the end of His earthly ministry approached, Jesus predicted His own suffering, death, and resurrection more frequently. In the following list, note the increasing clarity of His statements:

- "He who does not take his cross and follow after Me is not worthy of Me." (10:38)
- From that time Jesus began to show His disciples that He must go to Jerusalem, and suffer many things from the elders and chief priests and scribes, and be killed, and be raised up on the third day. (16:21)
- Then Jesus said to His disciples, "If anyone wishes to come after Me, he must deny himself, and take up his cross and follow Me." (16:24)
- "But I say to you that Elijah already came, and they did not recognize him, but did to him whatever they wished. So also the Son of Man is going to suffer at their hands." (17:12)
- And while they were gathering together in Galilee, Jesus said to them, "The Son of Man is going to be delivered into the hands of men; and they will kill Him, and He will be raised on the third day." (17:22-23)
- "Behold, we are going up to Jerusalem; and the Son of Man will be delivered to the chief priests and scribes, and they will condemn Him to death, and will hand Him over to the Gentiles to mock and scourge and crucify Him, and on the third day He will be raised up." (20:18-19)
- "The Son of Man did not come to be served, but to serve, and to give His life a ransom for many." (20:28)
- "But when the vine-growers saw the son, they said among themselves, 'This is the heir; come, let us kill him and seize his inheritance.' They took him, and threw him out of the vineyard and killed him." (21:38-39)
- "You know that after two days the Passover is coming, and the Son of Man is to be handed over for crucifixion." (26:2)
- "Why do you bother the woman? For she has done a good deed to Me. . . . For when she poured this perfume on My body, she did it to prepare Me for burial." (26:10, 12)

Luke's Gospel fills in a little more detail about the disciples' state of mind: "They did not understand this statement, and it was concealed from them so that they would not perceive it; and they were afraid to ask Him about this statement" (Luke 9:45). Jesus didn't dwell on the subject. He had said all He wanted to say at that moment. He was planting seeds for later, allowing the words to sink in.

— 17:24-27 —

As the saying goes, two things in life are certain: death and taxes. Jesus had just prophesied that He would die, which confused and disturbed the disciples (17:23). Now the question of paying taxes came up.

It clearly wasn't something that was on their minds. In fact, the issue hit them suddenly as they were finally making it back to their home base of Capernaum. The tax collectors themselves approached Peter, bringing a question that, in its linguistic form, expected a positive answer: "Does your teacher not pay the two-drachma tax?" (17:24). Why did they go to Peter? Why not to Jesus Himself? William Barclay notes, "There is little doubt that the question was asked with malicious intent and that the hope was that Jesus would refuse to pay; for, if he refused, the orthodox would have grounds for making an accusation against him."[30] Here we see the opponents of Jesus trying to snare Him any way they could. If outright, face-to-face confrontation simply ended in embarrassment, they would try to take Jesus down through less direct means.

The problem was that at the time the temple tax wasn't actually obligatory, either by Roman law or by a literal reading of the Law of Moses.[31] It was merely customary and voluntary.[32] At the time of Jesus, the temple tax was more a test of one's loyalty to the temple in Jerusalem and of patriotism toward Israel. As such, this wasn't a test of Jesus' fidelity to the Law of Moses but to the religious and political culture of the time. Would Jesus conform to cultural expectations? Or would He defy the man-made social rules and take a path of independence?

Without hesitation, Peter responded with a yes on behalf of Jesus (17:25). His defense of Jesus' willingness to pay the tax probably wasn't rash or out of line. Because the tax was paid annually, it is likely that Peter knew Jesus had paid it in the past. However, it seems that neither Peter nor Jesus had any money at the moment to actually pay the tax. Regardless, Matthew makes it clear that Jesus was in a house (presumably Peter's) in Capernaum, while Peter had the conversation with the tax collectors outside. Jesus either overheard the brief conversation or was aware of it through supernatural means.

When Peter came indoors, Jesus took the opportunity to explain His position on the temple tax. Peter (and others) may have wondered why Jesus, the Son of God, condescended to pay a tax for the temple that was neither prescribed by Scripture nor required by Roman law. What a perfect teaching moment for Jesus to mentor Peter and the rest of the disciples regarding the surrender of personal rights for the sake of a higher purpose.

Jesus began by posing a question about taxation in general: Do the world's kings exact taxes from their sons, or from strangers (17:25)? The answer is obvious: Kings don't tax their own children. In fact, a

THE TEMPLE TAX

MATTHEW 17:24

The "two-drachma tax" referred to in Matthew 17:24 was the annual tax that was expected to be paid for the upkeep of the temple. A. T. Robertson notes, "Every Jewish man twenty years of age and over was expected to pay it for the maintenance of the temple. But it was not a compulsory tax like that collected by the publicans for the government."[33]

Though some may have tried to provide a biblical basis for the tax by appealing to Exodus 30:11-16, that passage apparently doesn't establish a regular, annual payment, but a one-time contribution following a census at the time of Moses, collected for the ministry of the tabernacle. Because of this, the temple tax in Jesus' day was controversial. R. T. France notes, "The Sadducees disapproved of the tax, and the men of Qumran paid it only once in a lifetime."[34]

The Jewish historian Josephus records that after the destruction of the temple in AD 70, the Roman emperor "laid a tribute upon the Jews wheresoever they were and enjoined every one of them to bring two drachmae every year into the Capitol, as they used to pay the same to the Temple at Jerusalem."[35] By "the Capitol," Josephus was referring to the temple of Jupiter Capitolinus in Rome.[36] As such, the same tax that in Jesus' day had been looked upon as a mark of religious loyalty and patriotism would in the late first century be frowned upon as a sign of religious betrayal and treachery.

king's family benefits from the collection of taxes. Furthermore, a king is the ultimate authority—the one who determines who pays taxes in his realm. Thus, children of a king are exempt (17:26).

The logical and practical conclusion, therefore, would be that Jesus should not have to pay the temple tax. After all, Jesus is the Son of God. The temple is dedicated to God and to His service. As such, Jesus should be exempt from the temple tax, just as the sons of earthly kings are exempt from civil taxes. And to follow the reasoning to its logical conclusion: Because Jesus' disciples were His spiritual family (12:49-50), they also should be exempt from the temple tax.

Yet Jesus paid the temple tax. Why? Was it because He was in full support of the tax collectors' endeavors and believed the temple tax was obligatory and just? Was it because He was on board with Herod's beautification efforts and wanted to make the temple grounds even more astonishing? Was it because He was a big fan of the high priest and the priesthood? Was it because He wanted everybody to see how religious and patriotic He was? These may have been some of the reasons why others paid the temple tax, but they weren't Jesus' reason.

Jesus paid the tax—and expected His disciples to do the same—so as not to offend those who collected it (17:27). Does this mean that Jesus was suddenly willing to avoid offense and conflict at any cost? Was He willing to capitulate to the unreasonable demands of the powers that be for the sake of peace? Not long before, Jesus didn't hesitate to offend the Pharisees with His teaching (15:12-14). Was He now going soft, weary of controversy? Was His revolutionary teaching losing steam?

No! By conforming to the cultural expectation and simply paying the minimum tax, Jesus was demonstrating to His followers that they needed to pick their battles wisely. On the one hand, there was nothing sinful about paying a temple tax. On the other hand, it wasn't actually obligatory. Because it was neutral, the righteous should prudently weigh the benefits of paying the tax vs. the negative impact of not paying it. Nothing could be gained for the proclamation of the kingdom of God by thumbing noses at the temple-tax collectors. And by simply paying the tax, they would avoid placing a pointless obstacle in the path of outsiders.

In order for Jesus to meet the expectations of the tax collectors, He and the disciples needed the money. Perhaps their own supply of funds had been used up while they were traveling in the region of Caesarea Philippi. So Jesus sent Peter to catch a fish in the Sea of Galilee. That fish would have a shekel in its mouth that would cover the tax for Peter and for Jesus (17:27). Now, I'm not exactly sure why Jesus had Peter acquire the money through such a miraculous means. Perhaps, as Leon Morris suggests, Jesus didn't want to pay the tax with funds that had been donated to the disciples for the purpose of carrying out their preaching ministry.[37]

I find it a little humorous that, in the end, a random fish from the Sea of Galilee paid the temple tax for Jesus! While the two-drachma tax would have equaled about two days of work,[38] catching the fish with one cast of the hook took almost no effort at all. Thus, while Jesus and Peter paid the tax for all practical purposes, neither of them actually expended any energy or spent any of their own (or anybody else's) money in doing so. This shows that although Jesus cared about avoiding offense for the sake of the gospel, He cared little about the tax itself.

APPLICATION: MATTHEW 17:22-27

Living as Dual Citizens

Because none of us will ever face the quandary of whether to pay the temple tax, how does this passage apply to us today? Let me suggest that Jesus' way of dealing with the temple tax is a great illustration of the tensions involved in living as dual citizens. As God's children, we are citizens of heaven (Phil. 3:20). But we are also citizens of earth with rights and responsibilities (e.g., Acts 22:28). We are therefore expected both to honor and obey God and to honor and obey the government over us (Rom. 13:1-5). This includes paying taxes (Rom. 13:6-7)!

Make no mistake: The believer's first obligation is to obey God. Our citizenship in His kingdom is first and foremost. When the laws of the land are directly in conflict with His commands, His truth must prevail, and His will takes immediate precedence. In those cases, we are to obey God rather than men (Acts 4:18-20; 5:27-29). However, in most cases, the laws of the government are in no way contrary to the laws of God. God never dictated how fast we should drive on the highway, but the government does. God never said what percentage of our income we should pay to the government, but our laws do. God never said whether we needed to have our dogs on leashes when walking in public places, but many cities have such laws. In matters like these, we should obey the government.

Yet what about cultural expectations for which there are neither divine commands nor secular laws, but merely societal norms and traditions? In such cases, we must be willing to give up our own preferences for the sake of the gospel. If a countercultural approach to life will bring scorn to the kingdom of God and to His people, we must be willing to surrender our personal rights and conform to the expectations of our society—again, as long as it doesn't run contrary to God's Word. To help us think through some of these issues, let me ask a few questions.

Are you a good citizen of your country? Or do you take secret delight in breaking some of its laws, making excuses like *God doesn't care how fast I drive*? Remember your dual citizenship. In matters about which God has not spoken but your government has, you must submit to the authorities over you.

What is your understanding of freedom regarding neutral or gray issues? Do you think freedom in this case means doing whatever pleases you, regardless of how it may offend outsiders or place obstacles in their path to Christ? Do you push your liberty too far and then rationalize your way around a self-centered lifestyle? Think about what course of action will bring the least scorn on the people of God by casting the gospel in a negative light.

Life Lessons Learned from Children
MATTHEW 18:1-14

NASB

1 At that ªtime the disciples came to Jesus and said, "Who then is greatest in the kingdom of heaven?" 2 And He called a child to Himself and set him ªbefore them, 3 and said, "Truly I say to you, unless you ªare converted and become like children, you will not enter the kingdom of heaven. 4 Whoever then humbles himself as this child, he is the greatest in the kingdom of heaven. 5 And whoever receives one such child in My name receives Me; 6 but whoever causes one of these little ones who believe in Me to stumble, it ªwould be better for him to have a ᵇheavy millstone hung around his neck, and to be drowned in the depth of the sea.

7 "Woe to the world because of *its* stumbling blocks! For it is inevitable that stumbling blocks come; but woe to that man through whom the stumbling block comes!

8 "If your hand or your foot causes you to stumble, cut it off and throw it from you; it is better for you to enter life crippled or lame, than ªto have two hands or two feet and be cast into the eternal fire. 9 If your eye causes you to stumble, pluck it out and throw it from you. It is better for you to enter life with one eye, than ªto have two eyes and be cast into the ᵇfiery hell.

NLT

1 About that time the disciples came to Jesus and asked, "Who is greatest in the Kingdom of Heaven?"

2 Jesus called a little child to him and put the child among them. 3 Then he said, "I tell you the truth, unless you turn from your sins and become like little children, you will never get into the Kingdom of Heaven. 4 So anyone who becomes as humble as this little child is the greatest in the Kingdom of Heaven.

5 "And anyone who welcomes a little child like this on my behalf* is welcoming me. 6 But if you cause one of these little ones who trusts in me to fall into sin, it would be better for you to have a large millstone tied around your neck and be drowned in the depths of the sea.

7 "What sorrow awaits the world, because it tempts people to sin. Temptations are inevitable, but what sorrow awaits the person who does the tempting. 8 So if your hand or foot causes you to sin, cut it off and throw it away. It's better to enter eternal life with only one hand or one foot than to be thrown into eternal fire with both of your hands and feet. 9 And if your eye causes you to sin, gouge it out and throw it away. It's better to enter eternal life with only one eye than to have two eyes and be thrown into the fire of hell.*

10 "See that you do not despise one of these little ones, for I say to you that their angels in heaven continually see the face of My Father who is in heaven. 11 [ᵃFor the Son of Man has come to save that which was lost.]

12 "What do you think? If any man has a hundred sheep, and one of them has gone astray, does he not leave the ninety-nine on the mountains and go and search for the one that is straying? 13 If it turns out that he finds it, truly I say to you, he rejoices over it more than over the ninety-nine which have not gone astray. 14 So it is not *the* will ᵃof your Father who is in heaven that one of these little ones perish.

18:1 ᵃLit *hour* 18:2 ᵃLit *in their midst* 18:3 ᵃLit *are turned* 18:6 ᵃLit *is better* ᵇLit *millstone turned by a donkey* 18:8 ᵃLit *having;* Gr part. 18:9 ᵃLit *having;* Gr part. ᵇLit *Gehenna of fire* 18:11 ᵃEarly mss do not contain this v 18:14 ᵃLit *before*

10 "Beware that you don't look down on any of these little ones. For I tell you that in heaven their angels are always in the presence of my heavenly Father.*

12 "If a man has a hundred sheep and one of them wanders away, what will he do? Won't he leave the ninety-nine others on the hills and go out to search for the one that is lost? 13 And if he finds it, I tell you the truth, he will rejoice over it more than over the ninety-nine that didn't wander away! 14 In the same way, it is not my heavenly Father's will that even one of these little ones should perish.

18:5 Greek *in my name.* 18:9 Greek *the Gehenna of fire.* 18:10 Some manuscripts add verse 11, *And the Son of Man came to save those who are lost.* Compare Luke 19:10.

We have various post–New Testament traditions—enhanced by ancient iconographers, medieval sculptors, Renaissance artists, and misguided churchmen—to thank for concocting inflated (I would say mistaken) identities of the twelve disciples who walked with Jesus. Many have learned from these traditions to call them *Saint* Peter, *Saint* James, *Saint* Andrew, and even *Saint* John *the Divine.* On top of that, the disciples have been portrayed in holy garb with glittering gold frames, or in larger-than-life marble statues, or on canvas with glowing halos and angelic faces, sometimes posed as kneeling with praying hands and bowed heads, demonstrating utter humility.[39]

But when we open up the Gospels, we get a different picture. When the curtain is drawn back on Matthew 18, we catch those "high and holy" disciples arguing over which one of them is the greatest—like a room full of adrenaline-driven pro wrestlers or trash-talking boxers. Can you imagine the saintly disciples of the writers and artists of old duking it out over which of them was number one, with frocks torn and halos bent out of shape? The truth is, the twelve disciples weren't perfectly pious saints who were simply meek models of selfless humility. Rather, they were competitive, hard-charging, slow-learning, self-serving Galileans who, when left to themselves, argued over which one of them was the greatest. In other words, they were typical works in progress . . . like us.

When Jesus walked among His very imperfect disciples, He was concerned about their tendency to call attention to their own achievements instead of putting others before themselves. On one occasion, He chose to expose this tendency in a most unusual way: by using a small child to teach some vital life lessons that are true in every generation.

— 18:1 —

Within an hour of their arrival back in Capernaum, Jesus called some of His disciples together in the house where He was staying and asked them what they had been discussing among themselves during their long walk from Caesarea Philippi (Mark 9:33). As it turns out, they had been debating about which one of them was the greatest. Being omniscient, Jesus already knew this, but as they say, "Confession is good for the soul." The disciples must have known that their self-centered discussion about who was number one would meet with Jesus' disapproval, because they responded to His question with silence (Mark 9:34).

What had precipitated that misguided debate? Perhaps Peter, James, and John had been behaving arrogantly toward the other nine because they had been chosen to accompany Jesus up Mount Hermon to witness the Transfiguration. When asked what happened on the mountain, they would have been tight-lipped according to Jesus' command (Matt. 17:9). This would have increased the tension between disciples already disposed to wrangle over their positions in relationship to Jesus. If that's what was going on, then the three seem to have strangely forgotten the fact that earlier Jesus had been standing in blazing glory while they were reduced to trembling wrecks on the ground. And the Twelve seem to have ignored the fact that Jesus had just told them that He would be betrayed and killed in Jerusalem. Instead of letting those realities sink in and transform their personal priorities, they argued with each other over pride of place.

Ashamed of their jostling, they stayed silent when Jesus asked what they had been talking about. Instead of fessing up, they turned the particular debate about which of them was greatest into a more general theological question: "Who then is greatest in the kingdom of heaven?" (18:1). Of course, that theoretical question was simply a smoke screen intended to get Jesus to settle their actual question indirectly: Who (*among us*) is the greatest?

— 18:2-6 —

Jesus answered their question in an unexpected but compelling and convicting way. He called to Himself a small child and stood the child before the disciples (18:2). If Jesus was staying in Peter's home in Capernaum, perhaps the child was Peter's own son or daughter, or maybe a cousin or family friend. We aren't told if the child was a boy or girl; the Greek term is neuter and simply signifies a small child, likely a toddler.[40] By placing the child front and center, Jesus was definitely making a bold move. If in the old English adage children were meant to be seen and not heard, then in ancient Israel children were not even meant to be seen! R. T. France states, "A *child* was a person of no importance in Jewish society, subject to the authority of his elders, not taken seriously except as a responsibility, one to be looked after, not one to be looked up to."[41] So there the child stood, no doubt a bit bewildered, surrounded by twelve self-important disciples, simply staring. They were wondering what on earth Jesus had in mind.

But then Jesus explained: "Unless you are converted and become like children, you will not enter the kingdom of heaven" (18:3). I can imagine the disciples wincing at that news. Their question was about who was the greatest in the kingdom. Jesus' answer was that there wouldn't even be a place in the kingdom for them if they weren't like little children. Talk about turning the tables! The child stood in their presence by direct invitation from Jesus. He or she didn't belong there and couldn't have earned a place. But unlike the disciples, who were jostling for first place, the child had no agenda, no stuff to strut, no desire for applause, not even an awareness of the reason for being brought into the group. Chances are pretty good that the child was extremely uncomfortable being invited into the very presence of Jesus—in fact, standing at His right hand! The child knew—as did everybody else—that children didn't belong in that room, much less at the center of attention. What a picture of unmerited favor! What a picture of grace!

Jesus further explained that the key to having a place in the kingdom is humility. The child had no pride, no arrogance, no conceit, no expectations, no desire for promotion, no spirit of entitlement, and no phony piety. It was a what-you-see-is-what-you-get moment. Those who humble themselves like that little child—that is, those who understand their utter dependence on the mercy and grace of Jesus for their admission and position in relation to Him—will be regarded as greatest in the kingdom of heaven (18:4).

Though some modern approaches to parenting place children at the center of attention, in the first century that was certainly not the case. It was normal to look past children as small, inexperienced, messy, untaught, and more or less useless until they were old enough to be productive. Until they grew up, children were viewed as being in the way. As Jesus continued to turn the disciples' social world upside down, He pointed again to the small child—among the least-valued members of society—and began speaking in terms that placed children at the pinnacle of the Lord's concern. Jesus noted that showing kindness to a child—who would have been among the lowest-ranking members of society—was equivalent to showing kindness to the top-ranking member of the kingdom, King Jesus Himself (18:5).

And the converse is also true: If somebody treats such a valued member of God's family with contempt, causing them to stumble by failing to value them as God does, that person will suffer severe consequences (18:6). Jesus used a dramatic image to describe the judgment for causing harm to a helpless, innocent child. Such a person would be better off drowning in the sea with a millstone around his or her neck! The allusion to a millstone would have conjured up the image of a large, heavy stone used to grind grain into flour. Clearly, if somebody sank to the bottom of the sea with such a weight, there would be no recovery.

Without detracting from the literal love and concern Jesus had for children (see 19:13-15), we should note that He was arguing from the lesser to the greater. If God so highly valued the least-appreciated and lowest-regarded members of a physical household, then how could members of God's spiritual family regard with contempt *any* of their spiritual brothers and sisters? How could the disciples argue with each other about who was greatest in the kingdom when it is the one with childlike humility who is the greatest of all? In the fast-paced, hurry-up race of life, it's easy to rush past those who are slow and can't keep up. It's easy to push aside the ones society doesn't

© Michael Svigel

Replica of an **ancient millstone** used for crushing olives value. Jesus called His disciples to make room for such people, to accept them, to protect them, and even to exalt them.

— 18:7-11 —

Jesus then picked up the theme of placing "stumbling blocks" in the paths of others. The term translated "stumbling block" in 18:7 is *skandalon* [4625]; the verb form, *skandalizō* [4624], from which we get our word *scandalize*, was used in 18:6 in the sense of "causing to stumble." Jesus condemned the world for its plethora of temptations that coax the weak, the innocent, the unlearned, and the naïve down a path of sinfulness. The word "woe," which Jesus expresses toward the world, suggests a strong exclamation of deep emotion—either sorrow or anger. Though these snares are inevitable in a fallen world, those who perpetrate the wickedness are called out and will suffer dire consequences.

In 18:8-9, Jesus leveled the same severe warning against those things in our lives that lead to personal sin and transgression. After all, those who cause others to stumble began by stumbling themselves, and those personal patterns of sin develop for us when we allow stumbling blocks in our own lives. This brings up an often-neglected dimension to sin: Succumbing to temptation is never personal and private. The consequences always affect others in ways we can't necessarily predict. If we let stumbling blocks into our own lives, eventually a chain reaction will ensue that causes others to stumble as well. As He did in Matthew 5:29-30 regarding lust, Jesus employed hyperbole to drive home the seriousness of keeping oneself from sin. Hyperbole is a figure of speech involving obvious exaggeration intended to make an emotional impact on the hearers. Jesus wasn't advocating literal self-mutilation as a solution for removing stumbling blocks in our lives. Rather, He wanted His followers to have uncompromising standards when it came to temptation and sin.[42]

It may seem that Jesus' teaching had gotten off track. Didn't He start by scolding His disciples for arguing over who was the greatest . . . then veer off into valuing children . . . and now wander into a discussion about the seriousness of sin? Actually, Jesus was setting up a contrast between the self-centered life and the other-centered life. Craig Blomberg notes, "A stark contrast thus remains between those who recognize their complete dependence on God, and who therefore welcome other believers in humility and service, and those, including professing believers, who lead themselves and others to sin."[43] Two paths stood before the disciples—one of selfishness, pride, and a spiraling into sin that would destroy self and others; the other of selflessness, humility, and leading even the weakest believers into righteousness.

Returning to the spiritual lesson related to those who appear to be least in the kingdom but who are actually greatest, Jesus urged the disciples not to devalue and discount such people. How easy to undervalue or discount little children, or, for that matter, other believers who are weak and fragile in their faith. By showing preferential treatment to those who are gifted or wealthy or famous or powerful, we turn our backs on those less noticeable members of the church who often exhibit the character of Christ better than others. Like children who live under a special watchful eye of heaven, those with simple, childlike faith are watched over by the angels themselves (18:10). The God-man Himself gave up His life for such seemingly insignificant ones, who would be utterly lost without Him (18:11).[44] If heaven places such a value on lost and weak souls, shouldn't we?

— 18:12-14 —

The whole purpose of Jesus' living object lesson with the little child was to set forth the gracious and unwavering concern His followers are to have for those who are normally least valued or least desired. Among this category are those who are lost or have wandered from the straight path. I can think of numerous children of believing parents who have forsaken the faith in which they were raised. And entire post-Christian nations have a "been there, done that" attitude toward Christianity. They are lost. How easy it would be for us to neglect them, to write them off, and to worry only about our own membership in the "Jesus club."

Jesus challenged this self-centered attitude. Shepherds are known for their dedication to all their sheep and for their diligence in seeking out even one that has wandered away, gotten sick, or been injured (18:12). All of us are called to the compassion and commitment of a good shepherd who would not make the retrieval of the wandering sheep a distraction and annoyance but would make it a priority and a passion. How easy it would be for us to do a cost-benefit analysis and determine that one soul just isn't worth endangering the comfort of the rest of the flock. But Jesus encourages just the opposite. When that one sheep is found, the shepherd rejoices, just as our heavenly Father rejoices over the conversion of one little child, or one believer with childlike faith (18:13-14).

APPLICATION: MATTHEW 18:1-14

Becoming like a Child

Most of us, like the disciples, are soaked to our ears in pride. We compare ourselves with others, usually to highlight our own virtues and strengths. We criticize others to emphasize their weaknesses and underscore our own importance. We constantly seek to find the greatest, smartest, fastest, richest, and prettiest among us. Admit it: When you're shown a group photo from a gathering where you were present, the first person you look for is yourself. When a project we were involved in is completed and the participants are announced, we long to hear our names mentioned. And unfortunately, getting older doesn't automatically mean we become less self-interested and self-centered. In fact, sometimes it's just the opposite.

We need to remember the little child standing in Christ's presence. That child represented two vital qualities we all need to cultivate: *childlike innocence*, in which our focus is simply on being who we are rather than putting on appearances; and *childlike humility*, in which we see other people as more important than ourselves. When we truly learn these qualities, we'll begin to live like Christ, seeing ourselves and others in the right light. Think about Paul's words concerning Christlike character: "Do nothing from selfishness or empty conceit, but with humility of mind regard one another as more important than yourselves; do not merely look out for your own personal interests, but also for the interests of others" (Phil. 2:3-4). This, Paul says, is the same attitude as Christ's (Phil. 2:5).

Jesus' illustration of becoming like a child also reminds us that we're all equally valued in God's eyes. That helps explain why, when the Lord Jesus Christ died, He died for *all*—including you and me. No one is too young, too old, too lost, too sinful, too insignificant, too unsophisticated, or too poor. But unless the Spirit converts our hearts and we come to Jesus like little children, we *will* be too prideful, too stubborn, too selfish, or too arrogant. In your initial conversion to Christ, as well as in your walk with Him as a child of the King, continually remember this admonition to become like a child in His presence.

Caring Enough to Confront
MATTHEW 18:15-20

NASB

15 "If your brother sins[a], go and [b]show him his fault [c]in private; if he listens to you, you have won your brother. 16 But if he does not listen *to you*, take one or two more with you, so that BY THE MOUTH OF TWO OR THREE WITNESSES EVERY [a]FACT MAY BE CONFIRMED. 17 If he refuses to listen to them, tell it to the church; and if he refuses to listen even to the church, let him be to you as [a]a Gentile and [a]a tax collector. 18 Truly I say to you, whatever you [a]bind on earth [b]shall have been bound in heaven; and whatever you [c]loose on earth [b]shall have been loosed in heaven.

19 "Again I say to you, that if two of you agree on earth about anything that they may ask, it shall be done for them [a]by My Father who is in heaven. 20 For where two or three have gathered together in My name, I am there in their midst."

18:15 [a]Late mss add *against you* [b]Or *reprove* [c]Lit *between you and him alone* 18:16 [a]Lit *word* 18:17 [a]Lit *the* 18:18 [a]Or *forbid* [b]Gr fut. pft. pass. [c]Or *permit* 18:19 [a]Lit *from*

NLT

15 "If another believer* sins against you,* go privately and point out the offense. If the other person listens and confesses it, you have won that person back. 16 But if you are unsuccessful, take one or two others with you and go back again, so that everything you say may be confirmed by two or three witnesses. 17 If the person still refuses to listen, take your case to the church. Then if he or she won't accept the church's decision, treat that person as a pagan or a corrupt tax collector.

18 "I tell you the truth, whatever you forbid* on earth will be forbidden in heaven, and whatever you permit* on earth will be permitted in heaven.

19 "I also tell you this: If two of you agree here on earth concerning anything you ask, my Father in heaven will do it for you. 20 For where two or three gather together as my followers,* I am there among them."

18:15a Greek *If your brother.* 18:15b Some manuscripts do not include *against you.* 18:18a Or *bind,* or *lock.* 18:18b Or *loose,* or *open.* 18:20 Greek *gather together in my name.*

Strange as it may sound, one of the most obvious proofs of parents' love for their children is their commitment to discipline them when they go astray. Children, of course, don't like to accept it—especially when they see "anything goes" parents allowing their children to do what they want when they want with few repercussions for wrongdoing. But the fact remains: It's the mother or father who fails to confront—who doesn't deal with wrong in their children's lives—who is uncaring and irresponsible.

Our heavenly Father faithfully disciplines those He loves. The author of Hebrews quotes the wise words of Proverbs 3:11-12 to explain the Lord's discipline of His spiritual children:

"MY SON, DO NOT REGARD LIGHTLY THE DISCIPLINE
    OF THE LORD,
NOR FAINT WHEN YOU ARE REPROVED BY HIM;
FOR THOSE WHOM THE LORD LOVES HE DISCIPLINES,
AND HE SCOURGES EVERY SON WHOM HE RECEIVES."
    (Heb. 12:5-6)

Discipline, accountability, confrontation—these are not signs of the Lord's hatred toward people, but proof of the Lord's love for His children.

What's true of our earthly parents and of our heavenly Father is also true of those in the body of Christ. And there are benefits to being accountable to one another. Through proper accountability in the community of believers, we truly exercise love for our brothers and sisters in Christ. Accountability includes loving and learning from one another, observing and affirming one another, encouraging and counseling one another, and *also* confronting and disciplining one another. It's not that we confront because we like to intrude in people's lives. We confront because we care.

Though it's a brief passage, Jesus' instructions concerning accountability and discipline in Matthew 18:15-20 are essential for understanding our responsibilities in this important matter. We'll learn when discipline is necessary, as well as how and why it's carried out. Discipline and accountability may not be popular among Christians today, but they are necessary for balanced spiritual growth.

— 18:15 —

I wish it were true that the Lord keeps all believers on the straight and narrow path from the moment they're indwelled by the Spirit to the day they enter His presence. It would make ministry, marriage, parenting, and life in general so much easier if believers always responded instantly to the inner promptings of the Spirit to discern right from wrong and do what's right without external motivation or correction. But that description of the spiritual life is what we're looking forward to in eternity; it's not the reality we face in this "in-between time" as we await our ultimate redemption.

Thus, Jesus began his next instruction with the very realistic scenario all of us are bound to face over and over again in life: "If your brother sins . . ." (18:15). Though Jesus used "brother" in the illustrative example of a wayward fellow believer, He could just as well have used "sister" or "brother or sister." Addressing male disciples, it made the most sense to project a scene in which one of their own compatriots committed a sin against them that called for accountability. However, the principles apply more widely.

Before we walk through Jesus' step-by-step process of accountability, confrontation, and church discipline, it would help to take a step back and consider five general principles that help bring clarity and balance to our understanding of this important topic.

First, *confronting serious sin is loving.* This is the greatest problem with so-called inclusive churches. People often say, "We don't care how the people in our fellowship live. That's between them and God. The main thing is that we all love Jesus and love each other." But that's not love. If your child wants to drink poison, you don't say, "Well, I personally wouldn't do that, but I don't want to hurt their feelings. I'll let my child make their own decision, and I'll respect their choice." Why would we have the same attitude toward those who are engaging in sinful, destructive lifestyles?

Second, *confronting serious sin requires us to have the fortitude to do what's right.* If you or your church obey Christ's words in Matthew 18:15-20 (and the similar principles in 1 Corinthians 5), you will be called all sorts of names: intolerant, unloving, vengeful, legalistic, judgmental, cultish. You could be slandered, sued, and persecuted, not only by the sinners involved and those already antagonistic toward the church, but also by those within the church who are confused or who don't have the stomach for doing the right thing. Waiting in the wings of many grace-preaching churches are people ready to tag a person as a legalist whenever he or she takes a stand against serious, unrepentant sin. But we must commit ourselves to doing what is right, even when it's unpopular.

Third, *confronting serious sin is not optional.* We'll soon walk through Jesus' clear guidelines in Matthew 18:15-20, which will ensure that our understanding of the process conforms to God's standards. We need to read those words, study them, meditate on them, and then carefully and prayerfully apply them. We'll see that the text leaves no room for backing down from confrontation or backing out of the process. For the sake of the church's health and holiness, and for the sinner's rescue and restoration, we must all engage in this process when wisdom dictates.

Fourth, *confronting serious sin is not penal but remedial.* James wrote, "He who turns a sinner from the error of his way will save his soul from death and will cover a multitude of sins" (Jas. 5:20). Invariably, there are self-proclaimed Christian "bouncers" who feel like it's their mission to snatch sinners from churches, escort them to the door, and rough them up enough to guarantee they never show their faces in the sanctuary again. Such an approach is completely wrongheaded. The purpose of church discipline is not to humiliate, infuriate, or irritate wandering saints. The purpose is to urge them to see the error of their ways and to shepherd them back to repentance and fellowship. Is your attitude that of a bouncer or a shepherd?

Finally, *confronting serious sin is not for outsiders but for insiders.* Church discipline is to be carried out *by* believers and *for* believers. The process outlined in Matthew 18 doesn't describe how we are to engage those outside the fellowship of our brothers and sisters in Christ. Paul wrote in 1 Corinthians 5:12-13, "For what have I to do with judging outsiders? Do you not judge those who are within the church? But those who are outside, God judges. Remove the wicked man from among yourselves."

In light of these basic biblical principles, we return to Jesus' case study: a brother (or sister) in the faith commits a sin. Some ancient manuscripts add the words "against you," making the matter personal. In any case, the fact that we are to address the issue with our brother "in private" (Matt. 18:15) at least suggests that the matter is not one of open scandal or an offense against a larger group or the whole church, such as heresy, apostasy, or blasphemy. However, the one who has done wrong has not been forthcoming, has not acknowledged the sin, and has made no confession or attempt to reconcile or make it right.

When we become aware of this kind of harbored sin and unrepentant heart, we are to respond in love—especially if the sin is against us personally. Proverbs 27:6 says, "Faithful are the wounds of a friend, but deceitful are the kisses of an enemy." Yes, confrontation may hurt the other person's feelings and put him or her on the defensive. But ignoring the offense is not loving. Simply praying is an incomplete response. Telling others erodes into gossip. Those who are open to sharing accountability in the community must always be ready to confront others and to receive another's confrontation. Such confrontation is *not* the same thing as legalism. When handled carefully and correctly, with humility and compassion, it is concrete evidence of true love for others.

I love the way Paul puts it in Galatians: "Brethren, even if anyone is caught in any trespass, you who are spiritual, restore such a one in a spirit of gentleness" (Gal. 6:1). Much of the time, if we exhibit such a caring, compassionate, gentle attitude, the straying believer will listen, and when that happens, "you have won your brother" (Matt. 18:15). At that point, the process is over. Forgiveness is extended, repentance and confession are achieved, that person's relationship with the Lord is mended, and reconciliation between two believers is restored.

Let me make one more point. I know that in our age of emails, texting, and messaging, it's really tempting to try to resolve interpersonal conflicts and to engage in accountability by dropping a few hastily typed words and clicking "send." But in almost all cases, these are the wrong media. Even a handwritten or typed letter printed and mailed is less than ideal. As one commentator notes, "More trouble has been caused by the writing of letters than by almost anything else. A letter may be misread or misunderstood; it may quite unconsciously convey a tone it was never meant to convey. If we have a difference with someone, there is only one way to settle it—and that is face to face. The spoken word can often settle a difference which the written word would only have exacerbated."[45]

If an in-person, face-to-face connection isn't possible, then the next best thing would be a video conference or chat. If that won't work, then a phone call would be better than a written note. Yes, such personal confrontation is inconvenient. It will take planning, time, energy, and possibly money. And it will be less comfortable than a quickly drafted message through social media. But trust me—it will be worth it, especially if your brother or sister in Christ is convicted and takes steps toward restoration.

— 18:16 —

Of course, the Bible tells it like it is, not like we wish it to be. The truth is, an initial private conversation isn't always successful. If a believer's discreet confrontation of an erring brother or sister fails to result in repentance, a second step is necessary. Jesus drew on a general Old Testament principle of establishing a case on the basis of more than just one person's testimony. Deuteronomy 19:15 says, "A single witness shall not rise up against a man on account of any iniquity or any sin which he has committed; on the evidence of two or three witnesses a matter shall be confirmed."

Jesus applied this principle to the need for involving a widening circle of believers in holding a sinning brother or sister accountable. If the caring voice of one believer fails to result in repentance, that believer should next bring "one or two" others along, thus meeting the biblical requirement of "two or three witnesses" (Matt. 18:16). Does this mean that the one or two others had to have been eyewitnesses of the stubborn believer's sin? No. Although the original principle from Deuteronomy of having two or three witnesses referred to a formal legal proceeding in which a person was accused of a crime on the basis of two or three actual eyewitnesses, Jesus was simply quoting the verse to glean a general principle that involving a couple more people in the intervention would make it more convincing or persuasive. It would also communicate that the confrontation was taking on a more official and serious tone. And if the sinning believer still refused to change course, those two or three witnesses could serve to testify that the person did not, in fact, respond positively to sincere exhortation.

If you're in a situation in which you must take this second step, choose the other one or two people carefully. Prudence, impartiality, experience, integrity, maturity, and biblical and theological knowledge are key. So are compassion, patience, kindness, and genuine love for the sinning individual. Remember, the goal is not to corner the person or to gang up on him or her. The goal is to draw on the combined wisdom provided by a plurality of godly men or women. As Proverbs 11:14 says, "In abundance of counselors there is victory."

However, even at this point, victory is never guaranteed. Just as the person rejected the accountability of the initial private confrontation, he or she could very well react defensively and stubbornly in response to the two or three.

— 18:17 —

Jesus accounted for the worst-case scenario. Unfortunately, I've been in several situations throughout my decades of ministry that have reached this unhappy place. Nobody ever wants it to go this far, but when it does, it's important to keep at the forefront the guidelines established by Jesus.

After the offender has rejected the counsel of two or three fellow believers, the process takes on a more formal and serious character. Jesus said that if it reaches this point, then "tell it to the church" (18:17). This is the second of two uses of the term *ekklēsia* [1577]—translated "church"—in Matthew. The first was in 16:18, where Jesus said, "Upon this rock I will build My church." The word "church" is never used in the Gospels of Mark, Luke, or John. It appears in Acts 5:11 and then frequently thereafter in the remainder of the New Testament as a technical term for the new community of disciples of Jesus Christ, established by the baptism of the Holy Spirit (1 Cor. 12:13).

Even here, in appealing to the congregation, the immediate purpose is not to remove the person from membership, to shun them, or to subject them to the most public form of humiliation and shame. Rather, Jesus said, "*If* he refuses to listen even to the church," then severe consequences would follow (Matt. 18:17, emphasis mine). The purpose, then, of bringing the matter to the attention of the church is to provide a final opportunity for persuasion of wrongdoing and appeal for repentance.

Keeping this goal in mind, we should understand the word "church" as not necessarily referring to the entire gathered congregation at a Sunday-morning service. It could refer to the representatives of the church, like the elders, or to a small, carefully selected group of qualified, mature individuals. If we remember that the goal is the fellow believer's repentance and restoration, the "two or three witnesses" should consider carefully and wisely what group of people would most likely be effective in putting the right kind of loving but firm pressure on the person. Rarely would that be the entire gathered church—and almost never in the normal worship service!

Here, in a face-to-face context, in which a small group of caring brothers and sisters is present, the offender is again made aware of the wrongdoing in hopes of bringing about repentance, confession, and full reconciliation. However, if that still doesn't occur, then—and only then—is that individual removed from being a fully functioning member of the church community. Jesus used strong language for that final, sad step. That person is to be treated like "a Gentile and a tax collector" (18:17)—that is, like an outsider who does damage to those who should be brothers and sisters. This formal removal from the church's fellowship is treated more directly by Paul in 1 Corinthians 5:1-5. It is a sobering action, but it is necessary for the discipline of the individual offender and for the good of the church.[46]

Lest any walk away from this issue of accountability, confrontation, and church discipline with misunderstanding or with an unbalanced perspective, listen to the way one expositor and seasoned pastor characterizes the situation: "The work of discipline should be undertaken with the greatest care. Done in the wrong way or in the wrong spirit it can do great damage by fostering self-righteousness and legalism, just as discipline not done at all causes great damage by allowing sin's influence to spread like leaven."[47] Maintaining that kind of balance between being too hard and being too soft, between legalism and license, is vital throughout the process.

— 18:18-20 —

Jesus' words in Matthew 18:18 should sound familiar to you. He spoke them before, at 16:19, when He said that Peter—as a representative of the apostles—had been given "the keys of the kingdom of heaven." In that context, He instructed Peter, "Whatever you bind on earth shall have been bound in heaven, and whatever you loose on earth shall have been loosed in heaven." The statement in 18:18 is almost identical to that in 16:19, with one very important difference: Whereas Jesus' words to Peter in Matthew 16 were stated in the singular ("whatever you [singular] bind on earth . . ."), His words in Matthew 18 are stated in the plural ("whatever you [plural] bind on earth . . ."). In the present context, the plural "you" applies generally to those members of the church involved in the final step of church discipline.

What's the significance of this parallel? Remember that the authority to "bind and loose" given to Peter as a representative of the first-generation apostles was related to Peter's unique role in initially opening up the way (having the "keys of the kingdom") for the admission of people into the visible membership of the church, based on the confirmation that those people had been accepted by the Holy Spirit for salvation.[48] As the use here of the same expression shows, the authority and responsibility for admission to membership—and dismissal from membership—in the church is not relegated to Peter only,[49] but also falls generally on the local churches themselves. However, it should be noted that the church has authority only to reflect the mind of Christ and God's own acceptance or rejection of a person based on a profession of faith and a lifestyle of sanctification.

Only after due process can a church remove an unrepentant sinner from membership. And this process is intended to reveal and prove God's will in the matter. The idea behind Matthew 18:18 (and 16:19) is not that God is compelled to conform to the church's decisions. Rather, when the church follows Christ's pattern for discipline, it conforms its decisions to what God has already done and thereby receives heaven's approval and authority. This is what makes the difficult task of church discipline effective.

Jesus concluded this discussion on discipline with an intriguing promise that God would honor the requests of "two" who agree on earth about a matter (18:19). In fact, Jesus promised, "Where two or three have gathered together in My name, I am there in their midst" (18:20). These verses—especially 18:20—have been ripped out of context and used by misguided Christians to claim that whatever they ask for, God will grant. But the context here is still the issue of church discipline. The connection of these two verses with what precedes is made clear in how Jesus begins these statements: "*Again* I say to you . . ." (18:19, emphasis mine).

The point is that as soon as the proper process of accountability, confrontation, and discipline begins, Jesus is present, and God the Father is working through the interactions that take place. Even in the private, one-on-one confrontation, two believers are present in Jesus' name, and the result will be that God will confirm and empower the actions that are taken in conformity with His Word.

APPLICATION: MATTHEW 18:15-20

Essential Balance in Accountability

It seems to me that in churches today the tendency is to steer a wide path around Matthew 18:15-20. When confrontation and church discipline appear on the horizon, Christians often opt to head in the other direction. Whether it's because of the discomfort of having to confront somebody or the fear of an angry encounter or worries about "invasion of privacy" and legal repercussions, church discipline hasn't fared well.

Admittedly, confrontation isn't easy. Nor is it popular. And rarely does it work out nicely and neatly with a smooth transition from step one to step two to step three. Life is messy. Sin is messy. And church discipline is messy. But the church of Jesus Christ is supposed to act not like a business or a club but like a family. Families care enough to confront and to maintain the health of relationships by holding members accountable.

This is why we need to guard against extremes in the application of accountability and the exercise of church discipline. On the one hand, a church can become too severe. It can resemble a strict, harsh, military-like institution that's demanding, legalistic, and lacking in grace and mercy. On the other hand, a church can become a sort of spiritual country club that has no requirements for membership, no standards of holiness, no biblical boundaries, and a generally soft approach to morality. Neither of these extremes is healthy. A proper balance is key.

To help maintain this essential balance in accountability, let me suggest reading, memorizing, meditating on, and living out the principles of Galatians 6:1-2:

> Brethren, even if anyone is caught in any trespass, you who are spiritual, restore such a one in a spirit of gentleness; each one looking to yourself, so that you too will not be tempted. Bear one another's burdens, and thereby fulfill the law of Christ.

Don't rush through those words. Absorb them, ponder them, and take them to heart. Remember, the ultimate objective is restoration, assisting wayward saints through the process of finding healing, hope, personal dignity, and purposeful living. We want a full recovery, which is much more likely when we confront with humility, grace, and understanding. And as believers recommit to walking in righteousness and truth, we want to build up their lives with a positive attentiveness to holiness and godly living and keep from dwelling negatively on past guilt and shame.

How Often Should We Forgive?
MATTHEW 18:21-35

NASB

21 Then Peter came and said to Him, "Lord, how often shall my brother sin against me and I forgive him? Up to seven times?" 22 Jesus said to him, "I do not say to you, up to seven times, but up to seventy times seven.

23 "For this reason the kingdom of heaven ªmay be compared to a king who wished to settle accounts with his slaves. 24 When he had begun to settle *them,* one who owed him ªten thousand talents was brought to him. 25 But since he ªdid not have *the means* to repay, his lord commanded him to be sold, along with his wife and children and all that he had, and repayment to be made. 26 So the slave fell *to the ground* and prostrated himself before him, saying, 'Have patience with me and I will repay you everything.' 27 And

NLT

21 Then Peter came to him and asked, "Lord, how often should I forgive someone* who sins against me? Seven times?"

22 "No, not seven times," Jesus replied, "but seventy times seven!*

23 "Therefore, the Kingdom of Heaven can be compared to a king who decided to bring his accounts up to date with servants who had borrowed money from him. 24 In the process, one of his debtors was brought in who owed him millions of dollars.* 25 He couldn't pay, so his master ordered that he be sold— along with his wife, his children, and everything he owned—to pay the debt.

26 "But the man fell down before his master and begged him, 'Please, be patient with me, and I will pay it all.' 27 Then his master was filled

NASB

the lord of that slave felt compassion and released him and forgave him the ᵃdebt. ²⁸But that slave went out and found one of his fellow slaves who owed him a hundred ᵃdenarii; and he seized him and *began* to choke *him,* saying, 'Pay back what you owe.' ²⁹So his fellow slave fell *to the ground* and *began* to plead with him, saying, 'Have patience with me and I will repay you.' ³⁰But he was unwilling ᵃand went and threw him in prison until he should pay back what was owed. ³¹So when his fellow slaves saw what had happened, they were deeply grieved and came and reported to their lord all that had happened. ³²Then summoning him, his lord said to him, 'You wicked slave, I forgave you all that debt because you pleaded with me. ³³Should you not also have had mercy on your fellow slave, in the same way that I had mercy on you?' ³⁴And his lord, moved with anger, handed him over to the torturers until he should repay all that was owed him. ³⁵My heavenly Father will also do the same to you, if each of you does not forgive his brother from ᵃyour heart."

18:23 ᵃLit *was compared to*   18:24 ᵃA talent was worth more than fifteen years' wages of a laborer   18:25 ᵃOr *was unable to*   18:27 ᵃOr *loan*   18:28 ᵃThe denarius was a day's wages   18:30 ᵃLit *but*   18:35 ᵃLit *your hearts*

NLT

with pity for him, and he released him and forgave his debt.

²⁸"But when the man left the king, he went to a fellow servant who owed him a few thousand dollars.* He grabbed him by the throat and demanded instant payment.

²⁹"His fellow servant fell down before him and begged for a little more time. 'Be patient with me, and I will pay it,' he pleaded. ³⁰But his creditor wouldn't wait. He had the man arrested and put in prison until the debt could be paid in full.

³¹"When some of the other servants saw this, they were very upset. They went to the king and told him everything that had happened. ³²Then the king called in the man he had forgiven and said, 'You evil servant! I forgave you that tremendous debt because you pleaded with me. ³³Shouldn't you have mercy on your fellow servant, just as I had mercy on you?' ³⁴Then the angry king sent the man to prison to be tortured until he had paid his entire debt.

³⁵"That's what my heavenly Father will do to you if you refuse to forgive your brothers and sisters* from your heart."

18:21 Greek *my brother.*   18:22 Or *seventy-seven times.*   18:24 Greek *10,000 talents* [375 tons or 340 metric tons of silver].   18:28 Greek *100 denarii.* A denarius was equivalent to a laborer's full day's wage.   18:35 Greek *your brother.*

Forgiveness is not an elective in the curriculum of the Christian life. It's a required course. In fact, it's part of Christianity 101. Every believer must learn it. Though the concepts are simple, the exams are hard to pass. But what a relief when we pass them!

Now, it's not *vertical* forgiveness we have in mind here—that is, the forgiveness we have from God through Jesus Christ. That forgiveness happened once for all at the Cross, and we personally received it when we believed in Jesus. Rather, we're addressing *horizontal* forgiveness— forgiving one another—which needs to happen repeatedly throughout our lives. Without that forgiveness, we drag along with us long-standing feelings of resentment that will ultimately erode into anger, bitterness, hatred, and mental torment. Unforgiveness imprisons us in the past, locking out all potential for inner peace and freedom.

While Jesus was training His disciples, He dealt with the subject of forgiveness head-on. In light of their future, which would include mistreatment and persecution, forgiveness was something Jesus' disciples needed to come to terms with. As Jesus was talking about forgiveness, Peter came up with a practical question that is still being asked to this day: How often should we forgive?

— 18:21-22 —

Jesus had begun His earlier teaching concerning accountability and confrontation by saying, "If your brother sins, go and show him his fault in private; if he listens to you, you have won your brother" (18:15). After Jesus affirmed the church's responsibility to "bind and loose" (see 18:18)—that is, to grant and withhold "community forgiveness" affecting a sinning believer's active membership in the church—Peter approached Jesus with a reasonable follow-up question: "How often shall my brother sin against me and I forgive him?" (18:21). This question reaches back to 18:15—the private confrontation that results in a believer's acknowledgment of wrongdoing and immediate reconciliation. Peter's inquiry related to the limits on forgiveness and mercy. To put his question another way, "At what point do we start looking foolish? Yes, we want to be people of peace, but eventually we'll be treated like doormats if we keep on forgiving over and over again, right?"

According to the rabbis at that time, the going rate for forgiving somebody who sinned against you repeatedly was three times.[50] Having sat under Jesus' teaching, which emphasized grace and mercy (often in contrast to the Pharisees' legalism), Peter doubled the number of the rabbis' limit and even added one more to make it a perfect seven. I'll bet Peter expected to be commended for being so bighearted. Maybe Jesus would even lay on another "Blessed are you, Simon Barjona, because flesh and blood did not reveal this to you, but My Father who is in heaven" (see 16:17). Wrong!

In fact, Jesus made Peter's "seven times" look stingy. Forgiveness was to be extended not seven times, but "seventy times seven" (18:22). If Peter had begun counting on his fingers or calculating in the sand to multiply the numbers, he would have completely missed the point. Jesus wasn't giving a literal limit so that people could keep track; He was employing a figure of speech. He took Peter's number and multiplied it to a surprisingly high number. Think about it. How likely is it that any of us would face a scenario in which a fellow believer in Christ sinned against us 490 times? Not likely at all. But even if we did, Jesus' point was not to keep count, but not to count at all.

<h2 style="text-align:center">— 18:23-27 —</h2>

Using a detailed parable, Jesus undergirded His principle of limitless forgiveness with a solid theological truth that could essentially be stated in one sentence: "Be kind to one another, tender-hearted, forgiving each other, just as God in Christ also has forgiven you" (Eph. 4:32). So why didn't Jesus just say that, or perhaps, "Show forgiveness to others with the same limitless mercy God has shown you"? Why tell a story? Because stories illustrate truth in a dramatic, memorable way that captures our attention, involves our emotions, and gives us ideas and images on which to ponder and meditate.

The story in Matthew 18:23-34 illustrates a vital principle of the kingdom of heaven. When Jesus mentions "the kingdom," He's often not talking about the *place* we call heaven—that spiritual realm where God dwells. Frequently, Jesus is seeking to bring out aspects of kingdom living, a lifestyle with distinct principles, priorities, and allegiances. In such cases, the "kingdom of heaven" or "kingdom of God" is discussed to encourage followers to imitate the model of Jesus, the King. As believers and members of the church—the mysterious spiritual form of the kingdom on earth—we emulate the character of the King and are transformed into His likeness. And in this realm of kingdom living, the grace and mercy expressed in limitless forgiveness are paramount.

In this story, Jesus tells about a king who decides to settle accounts, a servant who owes that king an overwhelming amount of money that's impossible to repay, and another servant who owes the first servant a paltry amount. Besides these three characters, there is a prison filled with torturers. These are the elements of the drama that unfolds in Jesus' parable. Let me briefly summarize the major events and plot twists in the story.

First we see vertical forgiveness, illustrated when the king seeks to settle accounts with His subjects who owe him money (18:23). One of them owes the king "ten thousand talents" (18:24). Though this amount is not easy to reckon in modern currency, estimates range from millions to trillions of dollars![51] Regardless of the exact amount—Jesus was probably just alluding to the highest imaginable amount of debt—the point is that in no case would that man have been able to pay off his debt. He

SATISFYING AN IMPOSSIBLE DEBT

MATTHEW 18:23-27

Our inability to pay our obligation to honor and obey God, as well as our ever-increasing debt of sin and guilt before Him, leaves us in a dreadful plight. The only One who could afford to pay our debt is God Himself—but He doesn't owe it. And as Matthew 18:24-25 illustrates, fallen humanity owes God an infinite debt, but humans are unable to pay it. What a seemingly unsolvable dilemma: The one who owes it can't pay it, and the One who can pay it doesn't owe it!

This catch-22 has led many Christians to use the expression "substitutionary atonement" to describe the nature of Christ's perfect, sinless life lived in our stead and His sacrificial death in our place. In his classic work *Why God Became Man*, the medieval theologian Anselm of Canterbury (c. 1033–1109) famously explained how the Incarnation of God the Son resolved the problem of our guilt and our inability to absolve ourselves of it:

> For God will not do it, because he has no debt to pay; and man will not do it, because he cannot. Therefore, in order that the God-man may perform this, it is necessary that the same being should be perfect God and perfect man, in order to make this atonement. For he cannot and ought not to do it, unless he be very God and very man. Since, then, it is necessary that the God-man preserve the completeness of each nature, it is no less necessary that these two natures be united entire in one person, just as a body and a reasonable soul exist together in every human being; for otherwise it is impossible that the same being should be very God and very man.[52]

Because Adam and Eve plunged humanity into a fallen state, not only do people fail to render the obedience God is due, but they also continue to dig themselves deeper and deeper into a pit of sin and guilt. But because of the great mercy of God, the eternal Son of God took on humanity and lived a perfect, sinless life as our representative, winning infinite merit on our behalf. Not only that, but He willingly gave up His life, dying on the cross as our substitute, the righteous in place of the wicked, thus canceling the debt owed for all our sin. What good news!

would be utterly doomed to whatever fate the king determined. Justice would have dictated that the man, his wife, his children, and all his possessions be sold (18:25), and even then, the amount gained would be but a drop in the bucket of the debt. In a dramatic, emotional scene, the doomed man begs for mercy from the king, who is so moved by compassion that he forgives him the debt (18:26-27).

By the close of this first scene, it is obvious that the king represents

God the Father, to whom each of His subjects owes an infinite debt of love, honor, and obedience. However, we have all failed to pay Him what we owe, "for all have sinned and fall short of the glory of God" (Rom. 3:23). Each of us subjects of the King have dug ourselves into a bottomless pit of sin and guilt, the just wages of which is death (Rom. 6:23).

— 18:28-30 —

The next scene in this parable shifts the focus from *vertical forgiveness*, between the desperately indebted subject and the king, to *horizontal forgiveness*, between the forgiven subject and a fellow servant. Having been completely forgiven of an impossible debt, the first subject finds a man who owes him a paltry sum. Instead of passing forward the forgiveness he received from the king, the servant demands payment in full (18:28). In an almost exact replay of the earlier plea for mercy, the second servant, who owes almost nothing, asks for a brief reprieve so he can find the money to pay the first servant back (18:29). But that's where the replay ends, as the forgiven man refuses to show similar mercy to his fellow servant (18:30).

A proper response to this scene would be disgust. Had the first man—forgiven of an immeasurable debt—no decency? Did his (vertical) forgiveness from the king mean nothing to him? How hypocritical! Of all people, that man should be willing—in fact, eager—to extend to others the same kind of mercy he himself had been shown, especially to somebody who, given just a little time, could easily pay back the few measly bucks!

— 18:31-34 —

The story doesn't end there. The first servant gets what's coming to him, though not in the sense of the impersonal Eastern notion of karma. Other subjects of the king become clearly appalled at the first man's behavior. They presumably know about the great mercy that was shown him and can't believe the way he is treating the second servant. They promptly report the gross hypocrisy to the king (18:31).

Needless to say, the king is not at all pleased. He calls the forgiven servant back and openly rebukes him: "Should you not also have had mercy on your fellow slave, in the same way that I had mercy on you?" (18:33). Clearly, the answer is yes. But it's too late. Because the debtor failed to extend forgiveness to his equal, the king withdraws his forgiveness and restores the full debt on the man. He essentially hands

A Story of Forgiveness

MATTHEW 18:21-35

Years ago, I preached a sermon called "Finding Healing through Forgiveness." It became one of the most popular and most requested messages at Insight for Living—not because of my exposition and application but because in it my wife, Cynthia, shared her powerful testimony of being set free through forgiveness.

Cynthia grew up in a home with an always-angry father who was verbally and physically abusive. That family upbringing had long-lasting effects in our own family, and it didn't help at all that my own parents didn't really agree with our getting married. As we began to have children and our family grew, all kinds of complications arose between Cynthia and my mother. These went beyond the typical "wife vs. mother-in-law" rivalry. My mother wasn't an easy person to like much of the time, and Cynthia really struggled with that strained relationship. As so often happens to people in situations where relationships are broken and transgressions are compounded, Cynthia suffered from depression, and this affected her other relationships as well.

But then Cynthia took a course that changed her life. During that time, she discovered that the prison doors of emotional torment can be opened and that freedom can come through forgiveness and reconciliation. You don't even have to wait for somebody to ask for forgiveness. You can release the past and let go of the power it has over you, and as you do, it will be as though the torments of prison are relieved. Convicted of her own role in the broken relationship and convinced of her need for forgiveness, Cynthia said to me, "When your mother comes over today, I'm going to make things right. I'm going to sit down with her and tell her how much I love her for giving me the husband I have and for providing the home that she did for you. And that I've not handled things well as a young mother. And would she please forgive me?"

(continued on next page)

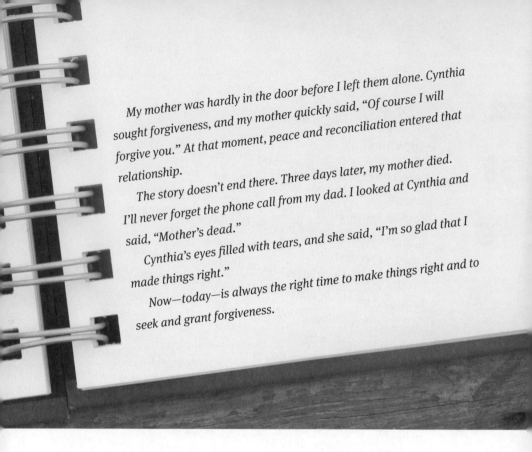

My mother was hardly in the door before I left them alone. Cynthia sought forgiveness, and my mother quickly said, "Of course I will forgive you." At that moment, peace and reconciliation entered that relationship.

The story doesn't end there. Three days later, my mother died. I'll never forget the phone call from my dad. I looked at Cynthia and said, "Mother's dead."

Cynthia's eyes filled with tears, and she said, "I'm so glad that I made things right."

Now—today—is always the right time to make things right and to seek and grant forgiveness.

the ungrateful, wicked, hypocritical servant a bill he will never be able to pay (18:34).

From this scene we learn two important truths we should never forget. First, for a believer forgiven by God, the refusal of forgiveness toward another is the peak of hypocrisy. Since each one of us has been the recipient of maximum mercy and endless grace, which we could never hope to repay, the least we can do is forgive others. Second, believers who refuse to forgive find themselves in a prison of unforgiveness, constantly tormented.

— 18:35 —

Finished with His parable, Jesus brought the message home. If a person refuses to show horizontal forgiveness toward someone who has wronged them and who has asked for mercy, God will also withhold forgiveness, casting the stubbornly unforgiving believer into a self-made prison of mental, emotional, and spiritual anguish. Refusal to forgive has its own built-in consequences. Those who harbor grudges and maintain bitter feelings toward others will be trapped in unrest and agony that will eat them up from the inside.

I love the way one of my mentors, Ray Stedman, explained the "torment" experienced by those who fail to forgive:

> This is a marvelously expressive phrase to describe what happens to us when we do not forgive another. It is an accurate description of gnawing resentment and bitterness, the awful gall of hate or envy. It is a terrible feeling. We cannot get away from it, we cannot escape it. We find ourselves powerless to avoid it. We feel strongly this separation from another, and, every time we think of them, we feel within the acid of resentment and hate eating away at our peace and calmness. This is the torturing that our Lord says will take place.[53]

It should be inconceivable to us that believers would withhold forgiveness from those who seek it. Those who have experienced God's no-strings-attached forgiveness in Christ must always be eager to extend mercy to others, especially since they have the Holy Spirit dwelling in them, enabling them to do what would seem naturally impossible. It's no wonder, then, that our vertical fellowship with God is so negatively affected when we fail to maintain horizontal fellowship with others. When it comes to forgiving others unconditionally, believers are, quite literally, without excuse.

APPLICATION: MATTHEW 18:21-35

Doing for Others What God Has Done for You

It may be that a person fails to pass forgiveness on to others because he or she has never actually experienced true forgiveness from God. As the old adage goes, "You cannot impart to others what you do not possess yourself." People who do not personally understand God's grace and who have never genuinely received forgiveness won't know what it means to forgive others.

However, Matthew 18:21-35 isn't just applicable to unbelievers. Believers in Christ can be just as stubborn and hard-hearted when it comes to forgiving others. And when they withhold forgiveness, they find themselves locked in a prison of their own, being tormented by anger, bitterness, disappointment, depression, broken relationships, and countless other mental and emotional maladies. Besides that, they will find their vertical relationship with the Lord God affected. Prayers aren't answered. The comfort of the Spirit and assurance of His presence wane. Without doubt, the discipline of a loving Father will fall on those who refuse to extend mercy and grace to others.

The saddest thing about those who suffer in the prison of unforgiveness is that they hold the key to their own cell! With the help of the Holy Spirit, they can extend forgiveness and free themselves from the past memories and present agonies.

Take some time to evaluate your own relationships in your family, your church, and your workplace—both in your past and in your present. Who needs your forgiveness? From whom are you withholding mercy? Is it your mother or father? One of your siblings? A child? An ex-husband or ex-wife? Maybe a mother- or father-in-law? Family members can wrong us and hurt us in so many ways. And that kind of pain can be especially hurtful because it comes from people who are supposed to fulfill loving, supportive roles in our lives. Do you need to reach out a hand of forgiveness to a family member?

Or perhaps you need to forgive a former or current boss, co-worker, or employee who has done you wrong. Maybe you're even still reeling from the consequences of whatever that person did. Or perhaps a former pastor, coach, mentor, or teacher needs to be shown mercy that only you can extend.

What if the person who harmed you has died? No matter. Bring the issue to the Lord and release that person's power over you. Extend forgiveness, even toward those who don't—or can't—ask for it. Remember that "God demonstrates His own love toward us, in that while we were yet sinners, Christ died for us" (Rom. 5:8). Follow the example of Jesus, who, from the cross, extended unconditional forgiveness to His executioners, even when they didn't ask (Luke 23:34).

Debate over Divorce
MATTHEW 19:1-12

NASB

[1] When Jesus had finished these words, He departed from Galilee and came into the region of Judea beyond the Jordan; [2] and [a] large crowds followed Him, and He healed them there.

NLT

[1] When Jesus had finished saying these things, he left Galilee and went down to the region of Judea east of the Jordan River. [2] Large crowds followed him there, and he healed their sick.

³*Some* Pharisees came to ᵃJesus, testing Him and asking, "Is it lawful *for a man* to ᵇdivorce his wife for any reason at all?" ⁴And He answered and said, "Have you not read that He who created *them* from the beginning MADE THEM MALE AND FEMALE, ⁵and said, 'FOR THIS REASON A MAN SHALL LEAVE HIS FATHER AND MOTHER AND BE JOINED TO HIS WIFE, AND THE TWO SHALL BECOME ONE FLESH'? ⁶So they are no longer two, but one flesh. What therefore God has joined together, let no man separate." ⁷They said to Him, "Why then did Moses command to GIVE HER A CERTIFICATE OF DIVORCE AND SEND *her* AWAY?" ⁸He said to them, "Because of your hardness of heart Moses permitted you to ᵃdivorce your wives; but from the beginning it has not been this way. ⁹And I say to you, whoever ᵃdivorces his wife, except for ᵇimmorality, and marries another woman ᶜcommits adulteryᵈ."

¹⁰The disciples said to Him, "If the relationship of the man with his wife is like this, it is better not to marry." ¹¹But He said to them, "Not all men *can* accept this statement, but *only* those to whom it has been given. ¹²For there are eunuchs who were born that way from their mother's womb; and there are eunuchs who were made eunuchs by men; and there are *also* eunuchs who made themselves eunuchs for the sake of the kingdom of heaven. He who is able to accept *this,* let him accept *it.*"

19:2 ᵃLit *many*   19:3 ᵃLit *Him* ᵇOr *send away*
19:8 ᵃOr *send away*   19:9 ᵃOr *sends away* ᵇLit *fornication* ᶜSome early mss read *makes her commit adultery* ᵈSome early mss add *and he who marries a divorced woman commits adultery*

³Some Pharisees came and tried to trap him with this question: "Should a man be allowed to divorce his wife for just any reason?"

⁴"Haven't you read the Scriptures?" Jesus replied. "They record that from the beginning 'God made them male and female.'*" ⁵And he said, "'This explains why a man leaves his father and mother and is joined to his wife, and the two are united into one.'* ⁶Since they are no longer two but one, let no one split apart what God has joined together."

⁷"Then why did Moses say in the law that a man could give his wife a written notice of divorce and send her away?"* they asked.

⁸Jesus replied, "Moses permitted divorce only as a concession to your hard hearts, but it was not what God had originally intended. ⁹And I tell you this, whoever divorces his wife and marries someone else commits adultery—unless his wife has been unfaithful.*"

¹⁰Jesus' disciples then said to him, "If this is the case, it is better not to marry!"

¹¹"Not everyone can accept this statement," Jesus said. "Only those whom God helps. ¹²Some are born as eunuchs, some have been made eunuchs by others, and some choose not to marry* for the sake of the Kingdom of Heaven. Let anyone accept this who can."

19:4 Gen 1:27; 5:2.   19:5 Gen 2:24.   19:7 See Deut 24:1.   19:9 Some manuscripts add *And anyone who marries a divorced woman commits adultery.* Compare Matt 5:32.   19:12 Greek *and some make themselves eunuchs.*

Marriage . . . divorce . . . remarriage—talk about hot issues! I can't think of many more active battlegrounds of disagreement among Christians than these. I'm not talking about disagreements between liberals and conservatives or between those who take the Bible literally and those who tend to stretch its meaning. I'm talking about disagreements among Christians who wholeheartedly believe in the inspiration and inerrancy of Scripture, who hold it as the final authority in all matters of faith and practice, and who interpret its words in their most natural sense as understood with respect to the original historical context. I personally know excellent pastors and exceptional Bible scholars on all sides of the issue of divorce and remarriage.

Although there's room for different positions on this issue among godly believers, some very twisted interpretations abound. These are driven by self-serving applications and rationalizations. Some married couples have convinced themselves that, in the name of "love," it's better for them to be divorced friends than married enemies. Others feel that if they meet the low criteria for divorce set by the state, such as "irreconcilable differences," then they're okay in God's eyes.

On the one hand, to excuse their own practices or to avoid controversy in a culture where divorce is rampant, some teachers twist the Scriptures and lower their moral standards below those the Bible sets. On the other hand, in hopes of stemming the tide of divorce and promoting family unity at all costs, some teachers have bent Scripture in the other direction, raising the standard even higher than what the Bible teaches. These two approaches aren't new. In fact, teachers of Scripture throughout time have often gone off the road to the right or to the left, failing to maintain a proper, balanced approach to marriage, divorce, and remarriage.

In Matthew 19:1-12, we find Jesus caught in the midst of competing schools of thought regarding divorce. At least, this is what appears to be happening on the surface. As we dig a little deeper, we see that what was actually going on was that the Pharisees were using an ongoing debate over divorce to try to catch Jesus in some contradiction, either with the Law itself or with one or more of the prevailing interpretations of the Law. As we can expect, their attempts would be foiled as Jesus—the great Teacher and divine Interpreter—set the record straight.

— 19:1-2 —

In the transition from chapter 18 to chapter 19, Matthew notes the geographical shift from Capernaum in Galilee to the area of Judea (19:1)—the center of political and religious life in Israel. Already Jesus had told His disciples that He would "go to Jerusalem, and suffer many things from the elders and chief priests and scribes, and be killed, and be raised up on the third day" (16:21). However, the disciples seem to have

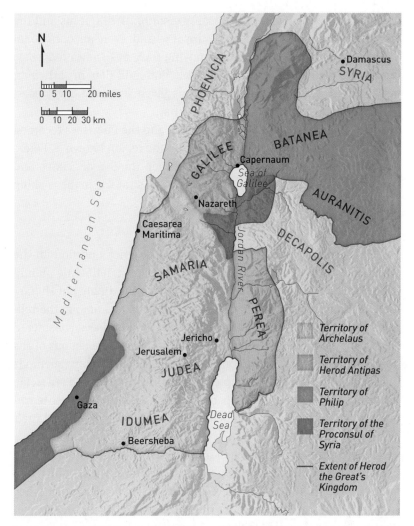

The regions ruled by Herod the Great were divided between his sons when he died in 4 BC. The region of Perea, east of the Jordan River, was, like Galilee, under the jurisdiction of Herod Antipas.

pushed that idea out of their minds, preferring to imagine a mighty and glorious entry and reception.

A large crowd followed Jesus (19:2). He healed the sick, still as engaged as ever in His mission to manifest the divine power of the coming kingdom. Through these miracles, He continued to reveal to those who had eyes to see and ears to hear that He was, in fact, the King, Israel's long-awaited Messiah. But, of course, not everybody was willing to see the truth right in front of their noses.

Among the spiritually blind were the very leaders of the Jews who would soon be responsible for Jesus' execution. While Jesus and the disciples were in Galilee, the Pharisees—and even an occasional Sadducee—would show up like annoying flies, easily swatted away. But as they neared the province of Judea, and Jerusalem in particular, the Pharisees would begin circling Jesus like a swarm of angry bees, desperate to protect their hives of hypocrisy.

When the confrontation between Jesus and the Pharisees recorded in Matthew 19:3-9 took place, Jesus was in the region known as Perea, on the east side of the Jordan River between the Sea of Galilee and the Dead Sea. This location would prove to be strategic in the ensuing debate.

— 19:3-6 —

The Pharisees approached Jesus with a sneaky trick question for the purpose of putting Him to the test (19:3). It was a deliberate plan to lasso Him into a controversy they knew would inevitably put Him on the blacklist of key political figures and influencers among the religious leadership in Jerusalem. Remember, the Pharisees considered Jesus their archnemesis. They despised Him. They were jealous of His popularity and looked down on His simple, folksy teaching methods that cut through their own complex, legalistic contrivances like a sickle through grass. They hated Him because He confronted their false teachings, undermined their self-proclaimed authority, and exposed their hypocritical lifestyles.

The Pharisees had often been on the lookout for ways to discredit Jesus in the eyes of the general public, tearing Him down to build themselves up. But now, as Jesus got nearer and nearer to Jerusalem, they were especially on the prowl for some scrap of juicy, incriminating evidence to make it easier for them to arrest Him, try Him, and execute Him. Their approach here was to trick Him into committing to one of the two prevalent schools of thought regarding the issue of marriage, divorce, and remarriage, and then catch Him in some kind of contradiction to the Law. Early on in Jesus' ministry, the Pharisees likely believed that He was just an uneducated hillbilly who should be easy to take down. At every turn, though, Jesus proved to be a genius who instead shed light on his adversaries' own ignorance.

As far as theological controversies go, the Pharisees went straight for the jugular. The question they posed was eminently practical, as it related to responsibilities in marriage, the bases for divorce, and the related issue of remarriage after divorce. The question also concerned biblical interpretation, specifically how to understand the conditions of Deuteronomy 24:1: "When a man takes a wife and marries her, and it happens that she finds no favor in his eyes because he has found some indecency in her, and he writes her a certificate of divorce and puts it in her hand and sends her out from his house . . ." And the question was theological, as it pertained to God's original intention for marriage and the relationship of the Mosaic Law to that intention.

But the question was also political. Not only had two opposing "denominations" of the Pharisees been arguing for some time over the right understanding of divorce, but the question was also posed while they were in the region of Perea. This area was under the rule of Herod Antipas. He was the one who had had John the Baptizer imprisoned for condemning his illegitimate divorce from his wife and his marriage to Herodias (Matt. 14:3-4). From Jesus' previous public teaching on the matter (5:31-32), the Pharisees knew that He would likely come down on the same side of the issue as John the Baptizer. Perhaps, they hoped, this would get Him into similar political trouble with Herod. Any answer Jesus gave was sure to spring a trap and catch Him in some deeper controversy.

The debate among the Pharisees themselves centered on the meaning of the words "he has found some indecency in her" (Deut. 24:1). The interpretations of this expression tended to go in one of two directions in Jesus' day. The more conservative school of thought restricted this language to be referring to only sexual immorality, while the more liberal school of thought understood "indecency" to include anything that displeased a husband. The first-century Jewish historian Josephus summed up this common, liberal view: "He that desires to be divorced from his wife for any cause whatsoever (and many such causes happen among men), let him in writing give assurance that he will never use her as his wife any more."[54] (For more information, see the feature "Irreconcilable Differences: Two Schools of Thought on Divorce" on page 100.)

With this background to the debate, we can understand the Pharisees' question: "Is it lawful for a man to divorce his wife for any reason at all?" (Matt. 19:3). I suppose this question was posed by the more conservative teachers. But they weren't trying to win Jesus' support so as to gain points against their liberal opponents. Rather, they were attempting to set up a trip wire that Jesus would spring, entangling Himself in a net of complex biblical, theological, practical, and political controversy from which He wouldn't be able to extricate Himself. Little

IRRECONCILABLE DIFFERENCES: TWO SCHOOLS OF THOUGHT ON DIVORCE

MATTHEW 19:3

The issue of divorce and remarriage has for centuries generated great debate among biblical scholars, pastors, and teachers. Along with Jesus' brief statement in the Sermon on the Mount recorded in Matthew 5:31-32, His interaction with the Pharisees regarding divorce in Matthew 19:1-9 has produced several different opinions on how to interpret and apply His teaching—from the very strict to the very liberal. In Jesus' day, the situation was similar. Two schools of thought had developed among the Pharisees regarding the interpretation of Deuteronomy 24:1-4, which states,

> "When a man takes a wife and marries her, and it happens that she finds no favor in his eyes because he has found some indecency in her, and he writes her a certificate of divorce and puts it in her hand and sends her out from his house, and she leaves his house and goes and becomes another man's wife, and if the latter husband turns against her and writes her a certificate of divorce and puts it in her hand and sends her out of his house, or if the latter husband dies who took her to be his wife, then her former husband who sent her away is not allowed to take her again to be his wife, since she has been defiled; for that is an abomination before the LORD, and you shall not bring sin on the land which the LORD your God gives you as an inheritance."

The Mishnah preserves the oral traditions of two rabbinical scholars and their followers concerning the reasons for divorce—the more conservative Shammai and the more liberal Hillel:

> The School of Shammai say: A man may not divorce his wife unless he has found unchastity in her, for it is written, *Because he hath found in her* indecency *in anything.* And the School of Hillel say: [He may divorce her] even if she spoiled a dish for him, for it is written, *Because he hath found in her indecency in* anything. R. Akiba says: Even if he found another fairer than she, for it is written, *And it shall be if she find no favor in his eyes.*[55]

Obviously, different teachers of the Law didn't see eye to eye on the matter of permissible divorce. However, with regard to remarriage, the rabbis at the time were in general agreement that if a divorce was conducted for allowable reasons, a divorced woman who received a bill of divorce from her husband was entirely free to remarry, as was the man who had separated from his wife by a legitimate divorce. In fact, with respect to the variations in bills of divorce at the time, the Mishnah states, "The essential formula in the bill of divorce is, 'Lo, thou art free to marry any man.'"[56] The point of the divorce was not merely the dissolution of marriage, but also the freedom to remarry.

did they know that they weren't dealing with some amateur interpreter of the Law of Moses . . . they were dealing with the Author Himself!

In His response, Jesus quite clearly steered far from the liberal interpretation of the Law. But He did so in an entirely unexpected way. Unlike the Pharisees, Jesus didn't appeal to some famous rabbi or apply the Scripture text to some far-fetched hypothetical scenario. Nor did He give a simple yes or no answer. Rather, He went far back in time, before any school of thought and even before Moses himself. He went back to Genesis itself and the original purpose and design of marriage, quoting Genesis 1:27 ("Male and female He created them") and Genesis 2:24 ("For this reason a man shall leave his father and his mother, and be joined to his wife; and they shall become one flesh").

Jesus' point was this: When we go back to the beginning, before the Fall, when God established marriage between a man and a woman, we see that divorce was not part of His original intention. In the beginning, God appointed marriage to be between one man and one woman—not a group of men and group of women, either simultaneously or in succession. Also, there was to be a special joining or bonding within that relationship between the one man and one woman. The word Matthew used for "joined" in Matthew 19:5 is a form of *kollaō* [2853], which means "to join closely together, bind closely, unite," originally conveying the sense of gluing or cementing things together for the purpose of permanently uniting.[57] God's original intention for marriage, then, was *permanence*. The special unity of marriage is reinforced by the fact that the two become "one flesh," which is both metaphorical and literal. Metaphorically, they are "joined at the hip," complementing each other emotionally, mentally, spiritually, socially, and physically. Literally, the sexual union within marriage can result in procreation—one new person born from the joining of the two. Based on these biblical and theological statements from Genesis, Jesus drew the following practical conclusion: "What therefore God has joined together, let no man separate" (19:6).

— 19:7-9 —

The Pharisees anticipated that Jesus would come down against divorce, and they had a response ready at hand (19:7). Note that they weren't really interested in the right answer to the question, nor its biblical or theological foundation in creation. They didn't really want an answer or a lesson; they wanted Jesus' body on a cross! But He didn't snap at their bait with a yes-or-no answer. Rather, He pointed them to the primary passage they had neglected in their own biblical bickering and pitted the liberal approach to divorce against God Himself!

In their response, they essentially argued, "If what You say is true, that divorce was not part of God's intention for marriage, then why would Moses—the great revealer of the Law—command that a man give his wife a certificate of divorce and send her away?" Here, they tried to pit Jesus against Moses—His words against the Law. Ignoring Jesus' argument from Genesis 1 and 2, they went back to Deuteronomy 24:1-4. The argument, in their minds, was compelling: If it were unlawful to divorce a wife, based on the words of Genesis, then Moses was breaking God's law by providing for divorce in Deuteronomy.

Jesus no doubt knew that they would rush to that place in Scripture. He saw it coming and wasn't at all fazed by their strategy. In His immediate response, He pointed out what was a blatant misreading of the Law and corrected them: Moses had never *commanded* husbands to give a certificate of divorce. Moses had issued no such *requirement* that men divorce their wives. Rather, the Law acknowledged that men and women, in their fallen, weak condition, had already been divorcing and would continue to do so. Jesus rightly noted that the wording in Deuteronomy was not expressing a command but a *concession*—if certain conditions were met. Because of the hardness of the human heart, divorce had been permitted by God under a specific circumstance, but this was only a concession in view of a lost ideal. Jesus didn't budge one inch from the ideal established in Genesis 2. Don't miss this important line "But from the beginning it has not been this way" (Matt. 19:8). In short, the Pharisees argued that Moses had *commanded* divorce, while Jesus countered that Moses had merely *permitted* divorce.

One biblical scholar offers this great illustration:

> Just as a car is made to drive safely on the road, not to skid around colliding with other cars, so marriage was made to be a partnership of one woman and one man for life, not something that could be split up and reassembled whenever one person wanted it. . . . Moses didn't say, as it were, "when you drive your car, this is how to have an accident"; rather, "when you drive a car, take care not to have an accident; but if, tragically, an accident occurs, this is how to deal with it."[58]

When it comes to handling difficulties, there's a major difference between commanding and permitting, whether it's driving your car on a road where wrecks occur or dealing with your marriage when troubles

EXCURSUS: THE BIGGER PICTURE—PAUL ON DIVORCE IN 1 CORINTHIANS 7

MATTHEW 19:9

Because of the narrow scope of the Pharisees' questioning in Matthew 19:3-9 regarding the language of Deuteronomy 24:1, Jesus didn't cover every contingency related to permissible divorce. He didn't get into all of the various scenarios and exceptions. However, years later, the apostle Paul took time to fill in some of the gaps and give us a bigger picture regarding this important issue.

Paul stated up front that "the wife should not leave her husband . . . and that the husband should not divorce his wife" (1 Cor. 7:10-11). This general statement is similar to Jesus' reference to the ideal for marriage as being between one man and one woman for life (Matt. 19:4-6). In fact, with the words "not I, but the Lord," Paul pointed out to his readers that this teaching was a reiteration of Jesus' own words on the subject of divorce (see Matt. 5:32; 19:4-6). By referring to Jesus' teaching on this matter, now recorded in the Gospels, Paul reaffirmed the basic biblical principle of marriage: permanence. This being the case, Christians should do everything in their power to nurture and build their marriages with the intent of permanence.

Without denying the seriousness of the ideal that marriage should be a lifelong commitment, Paul, like Jesus, acknowledged the reality of our fallen world, which challenges the ideal of permanence. Some marriages become so twisted by the Fall that the ideal is not always upheld. Paul faced this reality head-on, giving practical guidelines for handling painful and dysfunctional marriages. For Christians whose marital bonds have been severed by the sharp edges of sin or selfishness,

Paul counseled that such divorced couples should either remain unmarried or be reconciled to one another (1 Cor. 7:11). Paul didn't indicate the cause of separation in cases like this. Perhaps it's abandonment or some other crisis leading to separation. Perhaps it's simply a case of "irreconcilable differences." The language seems to suggest mild reasons for leaving, like common marital conflicts, rather than serious matters, such as unrepentant adultery or overt abuse. Jesus Himself allowed for Christians to remarry if their divorces have been precipitated by sexual immorality (Matt. 19:9).

But what about a marriage in which only one person is a believer? Should these unions continue, or should spiritual incompatibility allow for dissolution? Jesus never addressed this issue. Paul, however, provided spiritually sound advice based on his God-given apostolic authority. Paul's phrase "I say, not the Lord" (1 Cor. 7:12) doesn't mean that he was merely giving his own private opinion on the matter. Rather, it simply means that Paul's instructions were not based on any direct command from Christ. Here the Holy Spirit was speaking to new situations through the pen of the inspired, prophetic apostle. Regarding marriages in which one person is an unbeliever, Paul said that if the unbelieving spouse is willing to remain with the believing partner, the believer should not seek separation (1 Cor. 7:12-16).

Clearly, Paul valued the believer's faithfulness to the marriage vow as the ideal, but he also knew that in our fallen world, unbelieving spouses don't always endure in such a union. What happens when a non-Christian spouse divorces a Christian

(continued on next page)

intensify. Moses didn't command the Jews to wreck their cars and get new ones. And he certainly didn't allow for men to simply trade in their car when they wanted a newer model! Rather, the Law given to Moses gave a few rules for minimizing the damage caused by a wrecked marriage.

Similar to the more conservative view of the time, Jesus' interpretation of the basis for divorce outlined in Deuteronomy 24:1—"indecency"—was "immorality" (Matt. 19:9). The term Matthew used for "immorality" here is *porneia* [4202]. This Greek word describes a broad range of sexual indecencies, not just adultery (which was often indicated by the specific term *moicheia* [3430]). In fact, the verb form of this second term appears later in the same verse to describe the action of those men who divorce their wives for any reason other than sexual indecency. And although Jesus clearly stated that sexual immorality was an acceptable reason for divorce to be *permitted*, He never said that divorce was *required* in such a case.

We also need to remember that Jesus was specifically addressing the Pharisees' interpretation of Deuteronomy 24:1 and what was meant by the Hebrew word *ervah* [H6172]—"indecency." The term literally meant "nakedness," but it was used euphemistically for "shameful exposure" in the sense of "improper behavior."[59] Jesus corrected the more liberal Pharisees' overly broad interpretation of the term in favor of the narrower sense of "sexual immorality."

A study of all the passages in the Bible on the issue of divorce leads to the conclusion that divorce is allowable under a few circumstances—*allowable, but not encouraged*. Other serious violations of the marriage covenant that potentially allow for divorce, when reconciliation isn't possible, might include mental or emotional cruelty, physical danger to a spouse or children, cases of ongoing brutality and abuse, and abandonment. (See the excursus "The Bigger Picture—Paul on Divorce in 1 Corinthians 7" starting on page 103.)

— 19:10-12 —

I imagine that just as quickly and quietly as the Pharisees arrived to challenge Jesus, they scooted! Enraged that they couldn't catch Him in a contradiction with Scripture and embarrassed that they couldn't out-argue Him in public, they left. Jesus had clearly passed their insidious test, doing so by utterly deconstructing their questions and dismantling their trap. Jesus may have defeated the Pharisees here, but He didn't destroy their plot. They would simply regroup and come at Him again from another angle.

After this debate, the disciples were blown away. They had grown up in a world not unlike our own, in which divorce for almost any reason was often acceptable and made possible by loose legislation. They had been raised to think, *I can marry, and if it doesn't work out, I can just find another partner later.* But in this exchange between Jesus and the Pharisees, they heard their Master not only take the more conservative path regarding allowances for divorce but also greatly increase the sanctity of marriage between one man and one woman for life. Maybe, they reasoned, it would be better not to be married than to live in such a permanent relationship for the rest of one's life (19:10).

Jesus recognized that marriage is no lifelong honeymoon. It is hard work—in fact, impossible for those operating strictly in the flesh. Marriage is a calling that requires a God-given ability to fulfill (19:11).[60] However, it isn't the only calling. Jesus noted, as Paul did in 1 Corinthians 7:25-35, that the life of singleness is also an option for those committed to the kingdom of God (Matt. 19:12). The term "eunuch" (from the Greek *eunouchos* [2135]) typically referred to a male servant who was castrated as part of his dedication to his master's service.[61] Here Jesus referred to three categories of men who were functionally in the same situation—lifelong singleness. These included (1) those who were born with some kind of physical defect that rendered them unable to have children (with the likely result of remaining unmarried), (2) those who had been castrated for special service, and (3) those who voluntarily chose to live as if they were eunuchs for the sake of the kingdom. Jesus and the apostle Paul both fell into this final category. However, such a lifestyle also has its challenges and requires the grace of God to accomplish. Singleness, like marriage, is not for everyone.

From these teachings, we can glean a few important principles. First, some people are meant for marriage, including its responsibilities, privileges, complications, and delights. It is a high and holy calling. Second, some people are not meant for marriage. For whatever reason, some men and women are called to remain single and serve the Lord in that state. It's not acceptable for others to judge these people or to become suspicious of their motives, nor is it anyone's responsibility to "intervene" in their lives. Third, some people could be married, but they make decisions about priorities that lead them to give full attention to the things of Christ and His kingdom. Perhaps this is a permanent, lifelong decision, or perhaps it is temporary. In any case, sometimes ministry requires a commitment to singleness—though God doesn't call anyone already married to divorce a spouse for ministry. Finally, all of us must give ourselves and others room to live our lives before the Lord as He guides and provides. We must operate our lives in the liberty we have in Christ and guard against unbiblical expectations.

APPLICATION: MATTHEW 19:1-12

Personal and Practical Perspectives on Divorce

By way of application, I'd like to share my own perspective on some of the sticky issues of divorce in a similar spirit to Jesus, who said, "Let anyone accept this who can" (19:12, NLT). Consider both the words Jesus used and His tone. Rather than laying down a hard-and-fast set of rules, Jesus and the New Testament writers offer principles we need to prayerfully and intelligently think through and wisely apply to every situation we face. I know many would prefer clear, precise, all-encompassing rules with stringent boundaries—rules that are permanent and binding. But not every issue related to divorce and remarriage can be settled by quoting a specific statement of Jesus or citing a particular passage of Scripture. The issues connected with divorce are too varied and too complicated to be resolved in that simple manner. Though the Bible provides the foundation and structure of our thinking about these issues, we still need to *think*. So, in this spirit, let me offer four principles.

First, *the ideal is that marriage should be an indissoluble union between one man and one woman*. Such a union is based on mutual commitment, love, and faithfulness, and it results ideally in a harmonious and fulfilling relationship only death can end. But make no mistake—even a marriage like that lasts only because of the determined effort of both husband and wife, who work at their marriage because they're unselfish, cooperative, and willing to compromise. They're mutually agreeable to change and to adapt for each other. They're willing to release their rights and forgive the other for wrongdoing—and to do so throughout the years of marriage. This requires the enabling grace of God, much prayer, and a shared commitment to Christ. That's the ideal.

Second, *life is not, and never can be, tidy, orderly, or perfect.* Because of everyone's sinfulness, the unexpected and unpredictable intrude into every marriage. What wasn't known during premarital counseling, at the wedding, or even during the honeymoon becomes crystal clear during the years of marriage. Secrets that had never been told are now revealed, and they often take a toll. Hidden traits that had not been known are now exposed. And painful realities that were not resolved prior to marriage emerge, causing a breakdown in the once harmonious union. A relationship that was meant to be fulfilling, unified, and rewarding can feel empty, chaotic, and miserable. Serious attempts to find solutions often prove futile, and in spite of those attempts to heal the wounds, things only get worse. What was once difficult can even become dangerous to health and life. And what a couple had hoped would lead to reconciliation and restoration of the relationship results in an unworkable impasse that can't be overcome and a chasm that can't be bridged. That's a sad reality of many relationships in this fallen world.

Third, *we who are not a part of the breakdown of a marriage cannot fully (or even correctly) evaluate the depth of the misery.* We can have a tendency to watch a marriage break down and form negative opinions of the couple, based on verses of Scripture we can cite—like the Pharisees did with Deuteronomy 24:1—or based on a quote of Jesus that we can recall. We do this without considering the full context of those words or everything else the Spirit has revealed on the matter. And we don't know enough to judge those involved in the breakdown. In fact, it's often something we don't know that is a major cause of the conflict, because it can only be known within that intimate situation. I've seen enough of these miserable relationships close-up to know that, often, the person who is guilty of day-to-day, sadistic cruelty, selfishness, or constant criticism, or of afflicting mental anguish, appears to the public to be a model of piety and godliness. And we're deceived into thinking that that person is the one in the right when, in fact, he or she may be the very reason for the breakdown. The circumstances of most relationship breakdowns are complicated and are rarely black and white.

Finally, *to expect two people who find themselves in such incurable misery to remain bound to a lifetime of unhealthy disharmony—and possibly danger—seems unrealistic.* Surely this is not what God requires of them. A separation is often needed, and a divorce is sometimes necessary, for the health and safety of one or both partners—and for their children. This is especially the case if a couple has tried every possible means to resolve and rectify the situation. Yes, we strive for the ideal of lifelong marriage, but we must also deal with the reality of marriage breakdown and divorce.

This hasn't always been my position. I used to take a much more strict, idealistic, and, frankly, *unrealistic* view of marriage, divorce, and remarriage. But as I've studied and meditated on Scripture over the decades and applied it to real life throughout my years of ministry, I've come to the place now where I can't go anywhere else but here. I believe in marriage and embrace the ideal of permanence with all my heart. I've been a happy, fulfilled participant in marriage to the same woman for virtually all my adult years. But I also know that there are some who can't pull it off, though they want it as much as I did when I got married. For whatever reasons—and the reasons are complicated—they realize it's impossible for them to stay with their spouses. Individual recovery from such a breakdown is possible. If you've found yourself in this situation, the loving God of great mercy and grace has room in His plan for you to move to a healthy and safe place, away from a disastrous—and possibly dangerous—situation.

Who Is Closest to the Kingdom of Heaven?
MATTHEW 19:13-30

NASB

¹³Then *some* children were brought to Him so that He might lay His hands on them and pray; and the disciples rebuked them. ¹⁴But Jesus said, "ᵃLet the children alone, and do not hinder them from coming to Me; for the kingdom of heaven belongs to such as these." ¹⁵After laying His hands on them, He departed from there.

¹⁶And someone came to Him and

NLT

¹³One day some parents brought their children to Jesus so he could lay his hands on them and pray for them. But the disciples scolded the parents for bothering him.

¹⁴But Jesus said, "Let the children come to me. Don't stop them! For the Kingdom of Heaven belongs to those who are like these children." ¹⁵And he placed his hands on their heads and blessed them before he left.

¹⁶Someone came to Jesus with

said, "Teacher, what good thing shall I do that I may obtain eternal life?" [17] And He said to him, "Why are you asking Me about what is good? There is *only* One who is good; but if you wish to enter into life, keep the commandments." [18] *Then* he said to Him, "Which ones?" And Jesus said, "YOU SHALL NOT COMMIT MURDER; YOU SHALL NOT COMMIT ADULTERY; YOU SHALL NOT STEAL; YOU SHALL NOT BEAR FALSE WITNESS; [19] HONOR YOUR FATHER AND MOTHER; and YOU SHALL LOVE YOUR NEIGHBOR AS YOURSELF." [20] The young man said to Him, "All these things I have kept; what am I still lacking?" [21] Jesus said to him, "If you wish to be ᵃcomplete, go *and* sell your possessions and give to *the* poor, and you will have treasure in heaven; and come, follow Me." [22] But when the young man heard this statement, he went away grieving; for he was one who owned much property.

[23] And Jesus said to His disciples, "Truly I say to you, it is hard for a rich man to enter the kingdom of heaven. [24] Again I say to you, it is easier for a camel to go through the eye of a needle, than for a rich man to enter the kingdom of God." [25] When the disciples heard *this*, they were very astonished and said, "Then who can be saved?" [26] And looking at *them* Jesus said to them, "With people this is impossible, but with God all things are possible."

[27] Then Peter said to Him, "Behold, we have left everything and followed You; what then will there be for us?" [28] And Jesus said to them, "Truly I say to you, that you who have followed Me, in the regeneration when the Son of Man will sit on ᵃHis glorious throne, you also shall sit upon twelve thrones, judging the twelve tribes of Israel. [29] And everyone who has left houses or brothers or sisters

this question: "Teacher,* what good deed must I do to have eternal life?"

[17] "Why ask me about what is good?" Jesus replied. "There is only One who is good. But to answer your question—if you want to receive eternal life, keep* the commandments."

[18] "Which ones?" the man asked.

And Jesus replied: "'You must not murder. You must not commit adultery. You must not steal. You must not testify falsely. [19] Honor your father and mother. Love your neighbor as yourself.'*"

[20] "I've obeyed all these commandments," the young man replied. "What else must I do?"

[21] Jesus told him, "If you want to be perfect, go and sell all your possessions and give the money to the poor, and you will have treasure in heaven. Then come, follow me."

[22] But when the young man heard this, he went away sad, for he had many possessions.

[23] Then Jesus said to his disciples, "I tell you the truth, it is very hard for a rich person to enter the Kingdom of Heaven. [24] I'll say it again—it is easier for a camel to go through the eye of a needle than for a rich person to enter the Kingdom of God!"

[25] The disciples were astounded. "Then who in the world can be saved?" they asked.

[26] Jesus looked at them intently and said, "Humanly speaking, it is impossible. But with God everything is possible."

[27] Then Peter said to him, "We've given up everything to follow you. What will we get?"

[28] Jesus replied, "I assure you that when the world is made new* and the Son of Man* sits upon his glorious throne, you who have been my followers will also sit on twelve thrones, judging the twelve tribes of Israel. [29] And everyone who has given up houses or brothers or sisters or father

NASB

or father or mother [a]or children or farms for My name's sake, will receive [b]many times as much, and will inherit eternal life. 30But many *who are* first will be last; and *the* last, first.

19:14 [a]Or *Permit the children*   19:21 [a]Or *perfect*
19:28 [a]Lit *the throne of His glory*   19:29 [a]One early ms adds *or wife*   [b]One early ms reads *a hundred times*

NLT

or mother or children or property, for my sake, will receive a hundred times as much in return and will inherit eternal life. 30But many who are the greatest now will be least important then, and those who seem least important now will be the greatest then.*

19:16 Some manuscripts read *Good Teacher.*
19:17 Some manuscripts read *continue to keep.*
19:18-19 Exod 20:12-16; Deut 5:16-20; Lev 19:18.
19:28a Or *in the regeneration.*   19:28b "Son of Man" is a title Jesus used for himself.
19:30 Greek *But many who are first will be last; and the last, first.*

By the rules of this world, the more wealthy, famous, important, and powerful you are, the less approachable, accessible, and available. None of us can stroll into the White House, knock on the door of the president of the United States, and ask for a few minutes of time to talk. If we were to see an Academy Award–winning actress dining at a pricey Hollywood restaurant, who of us would be able to slip into an empty seat at the table and ask about her next project? In our world, inaccessibility is a measure of importance.

Not so with Jesus. As usual, He defied cultural expectations and turned the rules of the world upside down. He didn't favor the powerful, give special access to the elite, or make extra space for the influential. He was eminently approachable, accessible, and available . . . to *everyone.* Jesus was in touch with every kind of person—young and old, poor and rich, sick and healthy, corrupt and honest, harsh and courteous, hateful and loving, humble and proud, the devoted follower and the cruel critic. His refusal to construct social barriers and to limit access is nothing short of astonishing.

Seldom do we come across an example of His widespread accessibility as striking as what we see in Matthew 19:13-30. First, we meet a group of innocent little children who were brought to Jesus by their parents for a blessing. Then we listen in on a conversation Jesus had with a very rich man who was anything but innocent. As we walk through these two episodes, let's pay careful attention to the reaction of the disciples, who were learning some important lessons about who was closest to the kingdom of heaven.

— 19:13-15 —

Think about this: Jesus exuded such a gracious, welcoming spirit that even parents of small children felt completely free to bring their young to Him without an invitation or special permission. When the scene opens in Matthew 19:13, we see parents bringing their kids into Jesus' presence, asking for His touch and a prayer or blessing. They had no fear or hesitation as they bundled up their babies or toddlers and ushered them into the presence of the most important man who ever walked the face of the earth.

Jesus did have His own self-appointed "security team"—the disciples. They stepped in and rebuked the parents for what they perceived as an appalling affront to social decorum. They had learned, especially in the last few days, just how powerful and glorious Jesus really was, and it appears that they took it upon themselves to serve as Jesus' bouncers or bodyguards by limiting access to the Master only to those who met muster according to their standards. Clearly, small children didn't measure up.

Yet Jesus immediately rebuked their tight, grim-faced resistance to the noisy crowd of children and parents gathering in for a blessing: "Let the children alone, and do not hinder them from coming to Me" (19:14). What an unexpected, delightful scene! Jesus invited those kids in with open arms, placing His hands on their heads and shoulders, while the disciples no doubt stood disoriented by the scene. Was He not the King, Israel's long-awaited Messiah? Why waste His precious time with such insignificant people—with their unpleasant odors, runny noses, toothless smiles, and silly questions?

I love William Barclay's observations about this passage: "There is a strange difference between Jesus and many famous preachers or evangelists. It is often next to impossible to get into the presence of one of these famous ones. They have a kind of retinue and bodyguard which keep the public away lest the great figure be wearied and bothered."[62] Jesus was nothing of the sort, and He wouldn't allow His disciples to wear the badges of His personal security escort. As soon as they tried to limit access to Him, the Lord put them in their place. Children, as much as anybody, were worthy of Jesus' time and His gentle touch.

Earlier, when the disciples had asked who was the "greatest in the kingdom of heaven" (18:1), Jesus had answered, "Unless you are converted and become like children, you will not enter the kingdom of heaven" (18:3). Something about a child's simplicity, openness, honesty, and wonder perfectly illustrates the kind of person who is closest to the kingdom of heaven in attitude and actions. No pretenses, no agenda, no inhibitions, no reluctance, no self-consciousness—children displayed none of those things that hold back heavy-laden adults from approaching Jesus with nothing but their own desperate neediness.

And these children stood in direct contrast to the next person to show up looking for an audience with the Master.

— 19:16-22 —

After Jesus finished blessing the little children, he departed from there. Soon after, a voice called out to Him from the crowd: "Teacher, what good thing shall I do that I may obtain eternal life?" (19:16). We don't know the man's name. Matthew tells us that he was "young" (19:20) and "owned much property" (19:22). Luke's account adds that the man was a "ruler" among the people (Luke 18:18) and was "extremely rich" (Luke 18:23). Maybe he was the young heir of a vast estate, or a self-made entrepreneur. We don't know. In any case, the man obviously had a well of self-confidence—driven, abrupt, to the point—and more than a little of the pride that comes from being a man of means. However, as Mark's Gospel tells us, the man knelt before Jesus when he asked his question (Mark 10:17). Though instilled with self-assurance, at least the man acknowledged the superior wisdom of Jesus in spiritual matters.

I like how Jesus didn't let the man have control of the conversation for an instant. If we read Matthew, Mark, and Luke together, it seems that the man was engaging in a bit of flattery as well as self-justification. In response to being called "good" (Mark 10:17; Luke 18:18), Jesus suggested that the man didn't know what he was saying: "Why do you call Me good? No one is good except God alone" (Luke 18:19). Matthew's account notes how Jesus turned this flattery into an exposé of the man's insufficient notion of "good" (Matt. 19:17). In the rich man's eyes, moral or ethical goodness was measured on a horizontal scale—comparing righteousness among people. In the man's worldly eyes, Jesus was pretty high on the "goodness scale." Jesus blasted that whole concept of horizontal righteousness and replaced it with a divine standard: "There is only One who is good" (19:17). The standard for goodness and righteousness is not how much better we are than the people around us but how we measure up to God's perfect holiness.

Because God is the valid benchmark for perfect righteousness, the Law that He provided is a helpful revelation of His expectations. If the man was serious about doing good things to "obtain eternal life" (19:16), then Jesus' response makes perfect sense: "If you wish to enter into life, keep the commandments" (19:17). On the one hand, this is a valid offer. Theoretically, if a person had innate righteousness and goodness, he or she would keep all the commands perfectly, with a willing heart and humble spirit, as an act of loving worship toward God. Such a person—if they ever existed—would please God in every respect and would merit eternal life. *Theoretically.* In reality, the only person with such innate righteousness and goodness is the God-man, Jesus Christ. He alone was born without the total depravity and fallen sinful nature that characterizes humanity. He alone is "good" in the absolute sense. And He alone could live a perfect life in obedience to God's commands and please Him in every respect. So, while Jesus stated the truth that keeping the commands could open the door to eternal life, He didn't bother to tell the rich young ruler that it was impossible for anybody to do it but Himself!

Why was Jesus doing this? Was He toying with the man? No, He was teaching him an important lesson about the vast difference between self-righteousness and God's gift of righteousness. Remember the original question: "What good thing shall *I do* that *I may obtain* eternal life?" (19:16, emphasis mine). This notion of working one's way into favor with God, doing enough of the right good deeds, avoiding certain sins, and building equity in God's kingdom was a very popular idea in first-century Judaism. And it still is today. But the man's presuppositions about the nature of eternal life—and how a fallen, depraved sinner could achieve it—were completely wrong. To teach him (and us) the folly of that works-righteousness thinking, Jesus gave the man a good answer to a bad question: "You want to know what to *do* to obtain eternal life? Okay, I'll tell you: Keep the commands."

The man didn't miss a beat: "Which ones?" (19:18). Surely, like a lot of boys and girls today who have grown up in Christian homes and gone to church regularly, the rich young ruler knew the Ten Commandments. In fact, they probably occupied much of his attention, serving like a checklist of righteousness. As long as he was in the clear on the "Big Ten," he would be well on the road to life. Knowing the man's heart and his desire to justify himself, Jesus listed a few of the commandments from the Law—all having to do with our relationships with others (19:18-19). As He did, the man checked each one off as "mission accomplished":

- Don't murder . . . *check!*
- Don't commit adultery . . . *check!*
- Don't steal . . . *check!*
- Don't bear false witness . . . *check!*
- Honor your father and mother . . . *check!*
- Love your neighbor as yourself . . . *check!*

I have serious doubts that the man would have actually been able to live up to the deeper, internal righteousness that Jesus had preached about in His Sermon on the Mount (5:21-48). Clearly, he had no idea that Jesus had already addressed the issue of external, visible righteous acts and internal, invisible righteousness of the heart. When the young man claimed that he had kept all those commandments, Jesus let it go. I'm sure He could have poked and probed, revealing some area of neglect, a secret lust or hatred, a disrespect of parents, or some other blind spot. But instead, Jesus once again went straight for the jugular: in this case, the source of the man's pride, power, and self-confidence—his riches.

Jesus knew all the stuff the man was clinging to. All those toys he loved so much. Perhaps the man regarded his boundless wealth as a sign of God's blessing and favor, a reward here on earth for being so diligent to keep the commandments. So Jesus cut to the quick. To be truly perfect and complete in obedience to God's commands, the man would have to get rid of all his riches—sell everything he had and give the proceeds to the poor (19:21). In that way, he would truly fulfill the command he so hastily claimed to have accomplished: "Love your neighbor as yourself" (19:19-20). Having disposed of his entire estate, the man would be free to pledge allegiance to the true source of eternal life and the only one who could offer it. He could join the band of followers who lived from day to day depending only on God for provisions.

Knowing that the man wanted to justify himself in the eyes of God, the disciples, and the crowd of onlookers, Jesus raised the bar of works righteousness so high that He knew the man wouldn't be able to accomplish it. The man had asked the wrong question: "What good thing shall I do?" (19:16). Jesus told him. But even if the man had actually given everything to the poor and followed Jesus, the list of "good things" would have continued forever. Why? *Because there is no good thing a person can do to obtain eternal life.* The man should have said, "Lord, I'm a sinner in need of salvation. Have mercy on me!"

When the man saw that the bar was set this high, he gave up. Overcome with grief, he walked away (19:22). What a tragic addiction! Though young, the man was already so proud of his possessions and so unwilling to part with the social position they brought him that he would rather cling to those possessions than have a chance at eternal life. And this can happen to anybody. If left to ourselves and to our own works righteousness, nothing we do can ever be enough.

Eventually God will demand something from us we won't be able to surrender. That's the nature of the Law. Our good deeds are never enough. Only God, in His mercy and grace, can save such desperate, stubborn sinners.

— 19:23-26 —

The rich young ruler had slinked away in despair. The kingdom of heaven, which he had thought was just one good deed away, was now out of reach. He couldn't meet the high demands of total sacrifice and complete surrender.

Perhaps shaking His head in pity, Jesus instructed His disciples about just how far away the rich man had been from earning eternal life by good works: "It is easier for a camel to go through the eye of a needle, than for a rich man to enter the kingdom of God" (19:24). The idea that it was difficult for a rich man to enter the kingdom of heaven would have shocked first-century Jews. In a religious and social culture in which obedience to the Law was seen as directly correlated to material blessings in the Promised Land (see Deut. 28:1-14), it didn't take a stretch of the imagination to assume that those Jews who were blessed with great wealth and property were receiving the just rewards for their righteousness. And if they were thus blessed in this life for their righteousness, surely they were well on the path to the kingdom of God and eternal life! R. V. G. Tasker explains: "As the Jews were apt to regard material prosperity as a mark of divine favour, and the possession of riches as a kind of virtue, it is not as surprising as it might otherwise appear that the disciples' reaction to this statement of Jesus was stark amazement."[63]

It's so easy to think, *If I were rich, I'd have it made! Life would be easier. I wouldn't worry about the future. I could take care of my family. And I could help others, too!* But Jesus' interaction with the rich young ruler reveals the dark side of riches—how it can damage a person's ego and drive him or her further from genuine, humble dependence on God. Wealth encourages false independence and blind arrogance. This is illustrated well in Jesus' message to the church in Laodicea recorded in the book of Revelation. In His words of rebuke to that lukewarm church, He said, "You say, 'I am rich, and have become wealthy, and have need of nothing,' and you do not know that you are wretched and miserable and poor and blind and naked" (Rev. 3:17).

Again, Jesus turned the Jews' socioeconomic world on its head. Rather than being a blessing, wealth is seen as a heady intoxicant. It leads people into thinking they don't actually need God. Unlike children, who have no power, no defense, no resources, and no ability to accomplish what they want in life, the rich are blindly self-sufficient, independent, and proud. Truth be told, being rich has a way of luring our eyes away from the Lord and onto the things of this world. It creates a stubborn resistance against humble and helpless dependence.

Left to himself in his state of self-centered pride and self-justifying piety, the rich young ruler was hopelessly lost. In such a condition, the man's salvation wasn't merely difficult—*it was impossible.* Jesus' image of squeezing a large camel through the tiny eye of a needle was meant to communicate the utter impossibility of stripping oneself of pride and working oneself to heaven. The disciples understood this well when they asked, "Then who can be saved?" (Matt. 19:25).

Jesus' answer cleared up the matter and taught an essential lesson on the biblical doctrine of salvation (19:26). Self-effort of any kind does not result in salvation. That is, salvation is impossible by human effort. But when God does a work in a person's heart by the power of the Holy Spirit, He brings that person to humble faith in Christ, repentance from self-reliance, and submission to His authority. With God, *any heart can be changed.* What's impossible for people to accomplish is entirely possible for God. The rich young ruler's problem wasn't his riches per se, but the deceptive self-importance that accompanied his wealth. Just as the man may have earned extreme prosperity by human effort, he wanted to earn eternal life by doing good things. Impossible! Eternal life can't be earned and can't be bought. It can only be received by grace alone through faith alone in Christ alone (Eph. 2:8-9).

— 19:27-30 —

It would take the coming of the Holy Spirit for the disciples to come to terms with the notion of salvation by grace through faith in its fullest sense. Eventually, the teaching ministry of the Spirit would reveal to them that salvation is a gift that can't be earned, a gift entirely dependent on the righteousness of Christ and His finished work on the cross. And they would learn that the good works of a life of obedience and sacrifice are not the *cause* of salvation, but the *effect* of having a saving relationship with Christ (Eph. 2:8-10; Phil. 2:12-13).

But in the aftermath of learning about the uselessness of the rich young ruler's wealth, the disciples did a little self-reflection. They sized up their own situation and saw that they had, in fact, left everything and followed Jesus. From fishing boats to tax booths, livelihoods and secure futures had been abandoned for the sake of trailing Jesus wherever He went. Speaking for the disciples, Peter asked, essentially, "Well, Jesus, we disciples may have a lot of struggles, but being rich isn't one of them. We've walked away from prosperous businesses and other opportunities to make a lot of money. So, if you don't mind my asking . . . what will there be for us in the coming kingdom?" (see Matt. 19:27).

EXCURSUS: A FUTURE FOR ISRAEL?

MATTHEW 19:28

Many Christians today are convinced that God's plan for ethnic Israel has come to an end. Some believe that the promises about Israel being a glorious nation and receiving future blessing in the Holy Land have been abolished because of Israel's past unfaithfulness. Others have determined that these promises have been fulfilled in a spiritual sense through Christ and the church. Some theologians propose that Israel has been replaced by the church and that ethnic Jews have been divorced by God, having no future in God's plan.

But the New Testament assures us that God plans to bring about the fulfillment of those promises through Jesus Christ. Although most ethnic Jews have been in a state of unbelief since the time of Jesus, God will one day bring a remnant to faith in Christ and restore them in the land promised to their forefathers (e.g., Gen. 13:14-15). Jesus Himself promised the apostles, "In the regeneration when the Son of Man will sit on His glorious throne, you also shall sit upon twelve thrones, judging the twelve tribes of Israel" (Matt. 19:28). Before Christ's ascension, the disciples eagerly inquired about the timing of that earthly kingdom when they asked, "Lord, is it at this time You are restoring the kingdom to Israel?" (Acts 1:6). It is significant that Jesus didn't reject their literal interpretation and expectation of a future fulfillment of these earthly promises. Instead, He simply told them that they would not be able to know the timing of this restoration (Acts 1:7-8).

Years later, the apostle Paul addressed the issue of Israel's unbelief by declaring that their rebellion would one day be reversed: "A partial hardening has happened to Israel until the fullness of the Gentiles has come in; and so all Israel will be saved" (Rom. 11:25-26). In other words, when God has accomplished His purposes through the church in bringing droves of Gentiles to Christ, He will again turn His attention to the nation of Israel and bring them to faith in Christ. We can see the beginnings of this future for Israel in the prophecy of the sealing of the 144,000 in Revelation 7:1-8. This will occur during the end-times events leading up to the return of Christ.

Why is the restoration of Israel important? Because God's very reputation as a promise keeper is at stake! With explicit reference to the calling of Israel, Paul said, "For the gifts and the calling of God are irrevocable" (Rom. 11:29). It's as simple as that. If we can't trust God to keep His promises to Israel (see Jer. 31:35-37), how can we trust Him to keep His promises to us (Rom. 8:35-39)? Never doubt it: God will do what He said He will do!

At first glance, this question may appear presumptuous of Peter, but it was asked in sincerity. The fact that he asked it suggests that they hadn't given it much thought. They knew the kingdom was coming. They knew they had embraced Jesus as the King, the long-awaited Messiah. When Jesus promised the rich young ruler that giving up everything would result in "treasure in heaven" (19:21), that got the disciples thinking about whether something glorious was in store for them. Did the same promise go for them even though they hadn't given up such sizeable estates?

Jesus turned the attention of the disciples away from the present age and its temporary treasures toward "the regeneration"—that time when the kingdom will fully come on earth and Jesus will sit on His glorious throne. At that time, the twelve disciples will be exalted to sit on twelve thrones as co-regents with Christ to reign over the twelve tribes of Israel (19:28; see Rev. 20:4-11).

How encouraging Jesus' words must have been to those men who had literally walked away from their livelihoods to be close followers of Him! Jesus reassured them that they had not made a foolish decision in giving up everything for a life of discipleship. They may have given up fishing nets, but they would be rewarded with thrones. They may have abandoned houses, farms, family, and friends for the sake of total allegiance to the King, but they would receive "many times as much" when they entered eternal life (Matt. 19:29).

But not in this world.

In this world, people like the rich young ruler are on top. They're "first," having everything money can buy. Others, like the disciples, are "last," on the bottom of the social and economic ladder. But in the next world, in God's kingdom, those who have been on top will be on the bottom, and those who have been scrounging in the dirt will be crowned with glory (19:30).

APPLICATION: MATTHEW 19:13-30

Two Contrasting Perspectives

Each of us stands between two very different social, economic, and spiritual perspectives. On the one side are small children brought to Jesus for a blessing. On the other is the rich young ruler who believed he was already blessed! In this episode from Matthew's Gospel, we see the children brought to Jesus—helpless, without an agenda, with no sense of self-worth or merit. In contrast, we see the wealthy man offering his own self-righteousness as payment for a heavenly reward. Let's consider these two contrasting perspectives and consider carefully where our own hearts lie.

Think about the perspective of the small children. For a lot of us, when we were little children, life was simple and uncomplicated. We had very little self-consciousness, and the competitive spirit we had and the desire to get more stuff that we experienced tended to be short-lived and easily forgotten. There was also a general trust toward those to whom we were entrusted. We loved those who loved us, and we largely obeyed those placed over us for our care and protection. Regarding "stuff," yes, we had toys, but they were to play with, to enjoy, to share, and to carry around with us. They weren't that expensive. They didn't own us. We operated our lives with no agenda, and it was as life was meant to be—fun and relaxing. Life was mostly about relationships, not about stuff.

Now think about how things changed as we grew up. We grew to love things and to use people to get what we wanted. Now, what we acquire easily becomes too important. We get selfish, myopic, and greedy, being driven by our own agendas, which keep us from being aware of others. Though getting more stuff, we don't become content. Instead, we get greedier, more competitive, more ambitious, and more self-centered. We may make acceptable salaries, but we want them to be higher. We may have comfortable lifestyles, but we want luxury. All our needs may be met, but what about all our wants?

Amid these two very different perspectives on life—the simplicity of childhood and the complexity of adulthood—we stand and hear Jesus' voice. He tells us to be like little children, "for the kingdom of heaven belongs to such as these" (19:14). He exposes the truth about eternal life and true blessedness: It's not in the stuff we have. It's not about the toys. It's not about getting more. It's about coming to Him with nothing and letting Him change our hearts and fill our lives with real meaning. It's about giving and releasing. About believing in Him and following Him.

We don't need any toys when death comes. We need only Jesus. If today you find yourself closer to the perspective of the rich young ruler, clinging to your toys and feigning righteousness, let go. Let the Spirit of God bring you to Jesus—helpless, desperate, and hopeful. He alone can bless you. He alone can usher you into the kingdom and bless you with every spiritual blessing, which will make the vast treasures of this world seem like worthless trash.

Letting God Be God
MATTHEW 20:1-16

NASB

¹ "For the kingdom of heaven is like ᵃa landowner who went out early in the morning to hire laborers for his vineyard. ² When he had agreed with the laborers for a ᵃdenarius for the day, he sent them into his vineyard. ³ And he went out about the ᵃthird hour and saw others standing idle in the market place; ⁴and to those he said, 'You also go into the vineyard, and whatever is right I will give you.' And *so* they went. ⁵ Again he went out about the ᵃsixth and the ninth hour, and did ᵇthe same thing. ⁶ And about the ᵃeleventh *hour* he went out and found others standing *around;* and he said to them, 'Why have you been standing here idle all day long?' ⁷ They said to him, 'Because no one hired us.' He said to them, 'You go into the vineyard too.'

⁸ "When evening came, the ᵃowner of the vineyard said to his foreman, 'Call the laborers and pay them their wages, beginning with the last *group* to the first.' ⁹ When those *hired* about the eleventh hour came, each one received a ᵃdenarius. ¹⁰ When those *hired* first came, they thought that they would receive more; ᵃbut each of them also received a denarius. ¹¹ When they received it, they grumbled at the landowner, ¹²saying, 'These last men have worked *only* one hour, and you have made them equal to us who have borne the

NLT

¹ "For the Kingdom of Heaven is like the landowner who went out early one morning to hire workers for his vineyard. ² He agreed to pay the normal daily wage* and sent them out to work.

³ "At nine o'clock in the morning he was passing through the marketplace and saw some people standing around doing nothing. ⁴So he hired them, telling them he would pay them whatever was right at the end of the day. ⁵So they went to work in the vineyard. At noon and again at three o'clock he did the same thing.

⁶ "At five o'clock that afternoon he was in town again and saw some more people standing around. He asked them, 'Why haven't you been working today?'

⁷ "They replied, 'Because no one hired us.'

"The landowner told them, 'Then go out and join the others in my vineyard.'

⁸ "That evening he told the foreman to call the workers in and pay them, beginning with the last workers first. ⁹ When those hired at five o'clock were paid, each received a full day's wage. ¹⁰ When those hired first came to get their pay, they assumed they would receive more. But they, too, were paid a day's wage. ¹¹ When they received their pay, they protested to the owner, ¹² 'Those people worked only one hour, and yet you've paid them just as much as

burden and the scorching heat of the day.' ¹³But he answered and said to one of them, 'Friend, I am doing you no wrong; did you not agree with me for a denarius? ¹⁴Take what is yours and go, but I wish to give to this last man the same as to you. ¹⁵Is it not lawful for me to do what I wish with what is my own? Or is your eye ᵃenvious because I am ᵇgenerous?' ¹⁶So the last shall be first, and the first last."

20:1 ᵃLit *a man, a landowner* 20:2 ᵃThe denarius was a day's wages 20:3 ᵃI.e. 9 a.m. 20:5 ᵃI.e. noon and 3 p.m. ᵇLit *similarly* 20:6 ᵃI.e. 5 p.m. 20:8 ᵃOr *lord* 20:9 ᵃThe denarius was a day's wages 20:10 ᵃLit *each one a denarius* 20:15 ᵃLit *evil* ᵇLit *good*

you paid us who worked all day in the scorching heat.'

¹³"He answered one of them, 'Friend, I haven't been unfair! Didn't you agree to work all day for the usual wage? ¹⁴Take your money and go. I wanted to pay this last worker the same as you. ¹⁵Is it against the law for me to do what I want with my money? Should you be jealous because I am kind to others?'

¹⁶"So those who are last now will be first then, and those who are first will be last."

20:2 Greek *a denarius*, the payment for a full day's labor; similarly in 20:9, 10, 13.

I've noticed over the years that people waste a lot of time and effort minding God's business when they should be minding their own. Most of us have probably had the feeling at times that God wasn't managing things fairly, equitably, or justly. Maybe we didn't put those thoughts into words, but they've likely crossed our minds when things just don't seem right:

- A friend shows up at work in a new car, and you're still driving the fifteen-year-old clunker.
- A colleague is promoted ahead of you even though you have seniority.
- Your health is failing in middle age, while a much older friend is a paragon of strength.
- Your son has a disability, while another family has several kids with no health issues.
- A tornado destroyed your home without tearing a shingle off your neighbor's roof.

These examples could be multiplied by the dozens because every time we turn around we seem to be dealing with another one of life's "unfair" situations. The temptation, of course, is to grumble, *How unjust of God to allow that!*

Such a response reveals how shortsighted we humans really are. As we evaluate things, we react negatively against what appear to be special favors being granted to others, especially when we are concurrently enduring a series of painful trials. *Why do others seem to sail through life with hardly a blip on their screens?* In spite of living faithfully before God, sickness or accidents befall us, bringing us to our knees. Why? Is God unfair? Is He unjust? Doesn't He care?

In the Parable of the Day Laborers in the Vineyard (20:1-16), Jesus teases out for His disciples what it really looks like that "the last shall be first, and the first last" (20:16; cf. 19:30). In the process, He helps us with the issue of the fairness of God by telling us, in effect, "Stop grumbling about your lot in life. Let God be God."

— 20:1-7 —

Jesus told the parable recorded in Matthew 20:1-16 in the immediate context of the rich young ruler who had been possessed by his possessions (19:16-22). After Jesus told him how he could tap into the one thing he didn't have and couldn't buy—an authentic relationship with God through a personal relationship with Christ—the man wanted nothing to do with it. Why? Because to surrender himself to the free grace and loving embrace of God would inevitably lead to also surrendering himself to His priorities, His provisions, and His place for him in this world. Unconditional allegiance to Christ means that we let God be God. How difficult it is for those who are at the top of the social ladder to hand that position over to somebody else—even if it's the benevolent Creator and Sustainer of all things!

The rich young man exited the scene full of himself and full of his wealth, but empty of God and empty of anything that really mattered. Seeing the man's refusal to surrender even a coin of his self-reliance, Peter asked what kind of reward the disciples would have for surrendering their lives and livelihoods for the sake of following Jesus (19:27). Jesus' parable in Matthew 20 provides a vivid illustration of a profound truth, unpacking the frequently quoted but often misunderstood principle that "[the] first will be last; and the last, first" (19:30; cf. 20:16).

Like all good stories, this parable about the laborers in the vineyard has an interesting cast. The main character is the landowner. He's in charge of the land, the hiring of workers, and the fair payment of those workers. The story starts out with what would have been a very familiar scene in the first century, as it has been in many urban areas throughout history, even up to this day. James Morier, in his travelogue of journeys through Persia, Armenia, and Asia Minor, recorded a scene in a marketplace of Hamadan, one of the oldest cities in Iran. Though his observations were made in the nineteenth century, this could have fallen right out of the scene Jesus paints in Matthew 20:

Here we observed every morning before the sun rose, that a numerous body of peasants were collected with spades in their
hands, waiting as they informed us, to be hired for the day to work
in the surrounding fields. This custom, which I have never seen
in any other part of Asia, forcibly struck us as a most happy illustration of our Saviour's parable of the labourers in the vineyard,
in the 20th chapter of Matthew; particularly when passing by the
same place late in the day, we still found *others standing idle,* and
remembered His words, *Why stand ye here all the day idle?* as most
applicable to their situation; for in putting the very same question
to them, they answered us, *Because no man hath hired us.*[64]

Typically, workers would have arrived at a marketplace before dawn,
eager to earn a day's wage, which was a denarius (20:2). A landowner
would hire just the number he needed and could afford; he would do
this early in the day so as to get maximum benefit for the cost of labor.
So, at this point in the parable, nothing would sound strange to the ears
of the disciples. The principles of "you get what you pay for" and "you
earn what you work for" would have applied.

However, the story begins to take a turn toward the unfamiliar
in 20:3-7. While a real-life landowner would have known how many
workers his vineyard required and the amount of labor that needed to
be done, the man in the story returns to the marketplace about every
three hours during the day to find more workers. The first hour of the
day would have been around sunrise (usually about 6:00 a.m.). Three
hours later, around 9:00, the owner of the vineyard found other workers standing idle and instructed them to join the original workers in
the vineyard. Notice that the story doesn't suggest that the landowner
sized up the amount of work in his vineyard, determined that the original slate of laborers wasn't enough, and then went out to recruit a few
more. The motivation behind calling the second wave of workers seems
to have been because they were "standing idle" and would therefore
not have money to support their families (20:3).

The 9:00 a.m. workers agreed to join the labor for a wage that would
be "right" (20:4). The Greek term *dikaios* [1342], when appearing in the
neuter gender, as it does in 20:4, connotes "obligatory in view of certain
requirements of justice."[65] Since the twelve-hour day was typically broken into four quarters (6:00 a.m.–9:00 a.m.; 9:00 a.m.–noon; noon–3:00
p.m.; 3:00 p.m.–6:00 p.m.), those hired at 9:00 would have rightly expected to receive three-fourths of a denarius for their labor. That would
have been fair according to any reasonable economic principles.

Jesus' parable would have sounded stranger and stranger as the owner of the vineyard kept going out throughout the day to hire other unemployed workers from the marketplace—a third wave at noon, a fourth at 3:00 in the afternoon (20:5). Of course, these stragglers who showed up late in the day would have fully expected to receive a half- and quarter-day's wage, respectively. That would have been just.

Finally, pushing the story to the brink of the ridiculous, Jesus mentions one last sweep of the landowner through the marketplace at the "eleventh hour," about 5:00 p.m. (20:6). This would have been the time that the other laborers in the vineyard were looking toward the setting sun and looking forward to going home. Perhaps some had already begun tidying up their workplaces and packing up their tools. Why would an owner add even more laborers to an already overstaffed workforce so late in the day? Because they had been standing idle all day long, nobody else had hired them, and they would therefore have no money with which to provide for their families.

I can imagine the confusion of the all-day, or even half-day, laborers when that last group of workers joined the force. Think about the muffled comments that would have passed among the earlier workers who had already put in many hours:

- "Where were you hours ago when we really needed you?"
- "What's the point of working now when you'll only make a twelfth of a day's wage?"
- "Why didn't you accept the owner's invitation at noon or 3:00 like the others?"
- "What have you been doing all day?"

Then again, maybe they didn't say anything at all. Knowing the landowner would be just and fair, I'm sure they expected that the late-coming cleanup crew would get only a few pennies for their meager contributions.

— 20:8-16 —

In accordance with Jewish Law, the owner saw that the laborers were paid at the end of the workday (20:8; see Lev. 19:13). He had the foreman of the vineyard assemble the laborers by groups in the opposite order in which they were hired. Those who had arrived at the eleventh hour, who probably had barely broken a sweat, came first to receive their "just" wages.

Put yourself for a moment in the shoes of the original group of workers who had been toiling in the tangled vines since the break of dawn.

You were promised a full denarius—the typical amount for a day's labor. You watch as the last group of workers ambles forward to receive their pittance for an hour's work. But the foreman hands the Johnny-come-latelies a full denarius—as if they had worked the whole day! You begin to wonder whether the owner has forgotten that he called forward those whom he had hired last. Maybe those denarii were meant for your group. But then you remember that the owner clearly said to pay the workers from last to first (Matt. 20:8). So, you do the math: If those who worked about a twelfth of a day are receiving a whole denarius, then you, who have worked twelve times longer, will get about twelve denarii!

This line of thinking would have been natural. It would have been fair. In fact, it would have been entirely reasonable for each group to expect their pay to be prorated according to the number of hours they worked. But the point of Jesus' surprising parable isn't that people get what they deserve or that people should work hard for their wages. It is about God's *grace*, illustrated in the overwhelming mercy, generosity, and goodness of the landowner. To underscore the great benevolence of this employer, Jesus noted that regardless of when they showed up on the jobsite and how long they worked—even if it was just one hour—each laborer received a denarius.

Any good story includes an element of conflict—a challenge to overcome, a problem to solve, or a question to answer. In Jesus' parable, the conflict erupts when those workers who had put in a full day of arduous labor saw that the owner of the vineyard was paying each worker the same amount. Quite reasonably, that first wave of workers, who had agonized in the hot sun all day, thought they would get considerably more than those who worked for only one hour. In response to what they saw as injustice, they "grumbled at the landowner" (20:11). Their words suggest resentment, anger, and the feeling that they had been treated unfairly.

The landowner reminds the grumbling workers who had labored all day that they had agreed to work for a denarius, and this was exactly what they had received (20:13). The truth is, the employer was being entirely just in giving them the agreed-upon amount. It was a normal day's wage, with which they could sufficiently feed their families. Those men had no grounds for accusing the owner of the vineyard of any wrongdoing. Had he promised them ten denarii and paid them only one, then they would have had reason to complain. But the owner was being completely just, giving them what they deserved.

Yet the owner was not only just, he was also generous. Knowing that those who had only worked an hour . . . or three . . . or six . . . wouldn't have enough money to support their families if he prorated their pay, he decided to treat them with grace and generosity by giving them not what they deserved but what they needed—a full day's wage (20:14). Because the money belonged to him to do with as he chose, the landowner had the freedom to give it to anybody at any time under any conditions (20:15). How natural it is for worldly-minded people to become envious when a generous person demonstrates such grace! This is exactly the reaction of the grumblers.

The response of the landowner in the parable is meant to mirror the grace, mercy, and goodness of God the Father in His benevolent dealings with people. God's economy isn't based on merit and wages, hard labor and good works. Though we serve Him knowing that He will reward us, we're not motivated by rewards. And though we know that He will provide us with everything we need to carry out the work in the vineyard of His kingdom, we're to be satisfied with how and what He provides, even if it's different from His provision for the needs of others. Our response to God's goodness and generosity—even if it's directed toward others—should be thankfulness and appreciation, knowing that God owes us nothing, and we owe Him everything.

If we're ever tempted to think that God isn't forking over what He owes us, or that He's unfairly giving to those who don't deserve it while overlooking our own stellar performances, or that he's unjustly placing upon us burdens that other believers don't have to bear, we must remember the story of the laborers in the vineyard. Remember that in God's economy—fueled by grace, not merit—"the last shall be first, and the first last" (20:16). We must let God be God, acknowledging His wisdom and sovereignty in giving to His children how, what, and when He sees fit.

APPLICATION: MATTHEW 20:1-16

Grace Abounds

For most people in this world who have never learned the reality of God's grace, everything is based on human merit. And when somebody senses that another person is getting something they didn't earn or don't deserve, the grumbling begins. "That's not fair" becomes a muttered mantra that can easily grow into a battle cry.

Where are you in Jesus' parable? As believers, we're all among the laborers, but in which camp do you find yourself? Are you among the grumblers, with your eyes fixed on what others have? Do you begrudge them God's abounding grace? Do you live your life on the ragged edge of comparison? It's time to realize where your battle really lies and who you're really struggling against. It's not the person who was given something you think was undeserved. You're having trouble letting God be God. You're being critical of His mercy, grace, generosity, and goodness.

Let me be blunt. If you're one of the grumblers, you need to get your nose out of God's business. You need to let God be God. You need to forget about the haves and have-nots of this world, put your hand to the plow, and continue laboring in God's kingdom. So what if you've been a faithful believer since childhood and some recent convert gets all the glory? That's God's business, not yours. What does it matter if you seem to be burdened by struggles while less mature believers seem to be coasting through life? God will do what's right. Check out the words of Hebrews: "For God is not unjust so as to forget your work and the love which you have shown toward His name" (Heb. 6:10).

In short, let God be God! Leave your life—and the lives of others—to Him. I love the short poem by John Oxenham entitled "God's Handwriting." It sums up well a vital perspective we can strive for whenever we're tempted to grumble about how God exercises His sovereign, abounding grace:

> He writes in characters too grand
> For our short sight to understand;
> We catch but broken strokes, and try
> To fathom all the mystery
> Of withered hopes, of death, of life,
> The endless war, the useless strife,—
> But there, with larger, clearer sight,
> We shall see this—
> HIS WAY WAS RIGHT.[66]

Roadside Reminders and Reproofs
MATTHEW 20:17-34

NASB

¹⁷As Jesus was about to go up to Jerusalem, He took the twelve *disciples* aside by themselves, and on the way He said to them, ¹⁸"Behold, we are going up to Jerusalem; and the Son of Man will be ᵃdelivered to the chief priests and scribes, and they will condemn Him to death, ¹⁹and will hand Him over to the Gentiles to mock and scourge and crucify *Him*, and on the third day He will be raised up."

²⁰Then the mother of the sons of Zebedee came to ᵃJesus with her sons, bowing down and making a request of Him. ²¹And He said to her, "What do you wish?" She said to Him, "Command that in Your kingdom these two sons of mine may sit one on Your right and one on Your left." ²²But Jesus answered, "You do not know what you are asking. Are you able to drink the cup that I am about to drink?" They said to Him, "We are able." ²³He said to them, "My cup you shall drink; but to sit on My right and on *My* left, this is not Mine to give, but it is for those for whom it has been prepared by My Father."

²⁴And hearing *this*, the ten became indignant with the two brothers. ²⁵But Jesus called them to Himself and said, "You know that the rulers of the Gentiles lord it over them, and *their* great men exercise authority over them. ²⁶It is not this way among you, but whoever wishes to become great among you shall be your servant, ²⁷and whoever wishes to be

NLT

¹⁷As Jesus was going up to Jerusalem, he took the twelve disciples aside privately and told them what was going to happen to him. ¹⁸"Listen," he said, "we're going up to Jerusalem, where the Son of Man* will be betrayed to the leading priests and the teachers of religious law. They will sentence him to die. ¹⁹Then they will hand him over to the Romans* to be mocked, flogged with a whip, and crucified. But on the third day he will be raised from the dead."

²⁰Then the mother of James and John, the sons of Zebedee, came to Jesus with her sons. She knelt respectfully to ask a favor. ²¹"What is your request?" he asked.

She replied, "In your Kingdom, please let my two sons sit in places of honor next to you, one on your right and the other on your left."

²²But Jesus answered by saying to them, "You don't know what you are asking! Are you able to drink from the bitter cup of suffering I am about to drink?"

"Oh yes," they replied, "we are able!"

²³Jesus told them, "You will indeed drink from my bitter cup. But I have no right to say who will sit on my right or my left. My Father has prepared those places for the ones he has chosen."

²⁴When the ten other disciples heard what James and John had asked, they were indignant. ²⁵But Jesus called them together and said, "You know that the rulers in this world lord it over their people, and officials flaunt their authority over those under them. ²⁶But among you it will be different. Whoever wants to be a leader among you must be your servant, ²⁷and whoever wants

first among you shall be your slave; [28]just as the Son of Man did not come to be served, but to serve, and to give His [a]life a ransom for many."

[29]As they were leaving Jericho, a large crowd followed Him. [30]And two blind men sitting by the road, hearing that Jesus was passing by, cried out, "Lord, have mercy on us, Son of David!" [31]The crowd sternly told them to be quiet, but they cried out all the more, "Lord, Son of David, have mercy on us!" [32]And Jesus stopped and called them, and said, "What do you want Me to do for you?" [33]They said to Him, "Lord, *we want* our eyes to be opened." [34]Moved with compassion, Jesus touched their eyes; and immediately they regained their sight and followed Him.

20:18 [a]Or *betrayed*   20:20 [a]Lit *Him*   20:28 [a]Or *soul*

to be first among you must become your slave. [28]For even the Son of Man came not to be served but to serve others and to give his life as a ransom for many."

[29]As Jesus and the disciples left the town of Jericho, a large crowd followed behind. [30]Two blind men were sitting beside the road. When they heard that Jesus was coming that way, they began shouting, "Lord, Son of David, have mercy on us!"

[31]"Be quiet!" the crowd yelled at them.

But they only shouted louder, "Lord, Son of David, have mercy on us!"

[32]When Jesus heard them, he stopped and called, "What do you want me to do for you?"

[33]"Lord," they said, "we want to see!" [34]Jesus felt sorry for them and touched their eyes. Instantly they could see! Then they followed him.

20:18 "Son of Man" is a title Jesus used for himself.   20:19 Greek *the Gentiles.*

When somebody just doesn't "get it," even though something has been explained several times, we might say that person just "isn't on the same page." That saying comes from the very real experience of trying to follow along on one page while a teacher or reader is actually reading from another page. Confusion, frustration, and even embarrassment ensue. Being literally on the wrong page is usually easy to fix—just flip until you find the right one, or ask somebody nearby for the page number. Sometimes, however, we find ourselves so lost and out of sync with the person trying to teach us that we're just as likely to give up as we are to get help.

I had an experience like that the summer before my second year in seminary. I decided to take a crash course in Hebrew with a brilliant young professor, Dr. Bruce Waltke. Very quickly, though, I realized I was in over my head. Hebrew reads from right to left. It has no letters that look like real vowels, just little dots and dashes often called "pointings." And the vocabulary, grammar, and syntax is so foreign to English speakers that those words on the page might as well have been ants foraging for food. If I may state the obvious, this was a case of a confused Chuck Swindoll and a brilliant Bruce Waltke not being on the same page! Yes, I eventually made sense of that bizarre but beautiful language and have used it for decades in ministry, but that summer crash course was as brutal as you can imagine.

"Not being on the same page" happens when someone in charge is communicating something, often of great importance, but those listening, for whatever reason, have simply tuned out. Perhaps, as in my experience with summer Hebrew, the teacher's material is just so foreign and so outside our experiences and expectations that the learning curve is more like a cliff than a slope. That is exactly what we find in the scene recorded in Matthew 20:17-19 and its follow-up in 20:20-28. Though the twelve disciples had been with Jesus for almost three years, those men were not on the same page as their Master.

— 20:17-19 —

For the third time, Jesus informed His disciples that He was on His way to the Cross. The first time He had shared this privileged information, Peter had rebuked Him (16:21-23). The second time, the disciples were "deeply grieved" (17:22-23). This time, the announcement seems to have gone in one ear and out the other, despite the fact that Jesus had already indicated that every step they took toward Jerusalem was a step toward the inevitable mocking, scourging, and crucifixion (16:21; 20:18-19).

Nothing about Jesus' itinerary of torture and execution in Jerusalem was, on the surface, difficult to understand. He even took the disciples aside by themselves so they wouldn't be distracted by the crowds of people as He told them about it (20:17). He could look them in the eye, answer any questions they might have, and make it crystal clear what was ahead. Although Matthew doesn't record the disciples' immediate response at this point, the Gospel of Luke fills in this detail: "But the disciples understood none of these things, and the meaning of this statement was hidden from them, and they did not comprehend the things that were said" (Luke 18:34).

The disciples clearly weren't on the same page as Jesus! They were neither ready nor willing to hear anything about His upcoming betrayal, arrest, suffering, and crucifixion, nor, for that matter, were they able to grasp the significance of His resurrection. What in the world were they thinking?

The answer to that question becomes clear in the next scene. They were thinking about themselves!

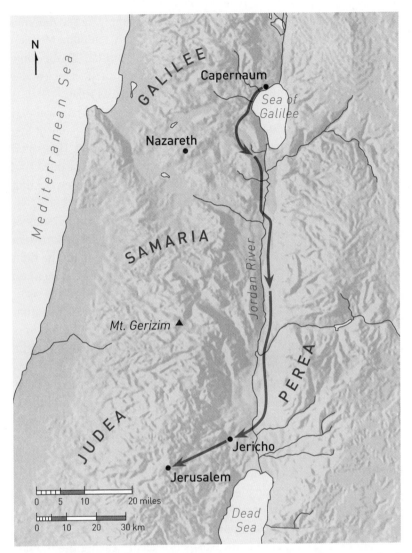

This is the likely route taken by Jesus and the disciples from Galilee "up to Jerusalem" (20:17), through Jericho (20:29).

— 20:20-28 —

The disciples had been following Jesus for about three years. They had given up their careers, walked away from financial security, and spent most of their time away from their wives and children. During this time, they heard the word "kingdom" over and over again. But whenever Jesus said "kingdom," they immediately pictured something like the kingdoms of this world, except with Jesus and themselves in charge. Yes, Jesus talked about the spiritual dimensions of the kingdom, but with their worldly political framework firmly in place, they simply tucked that into their unflinching conception of a world empire with a militant Messiah who would overthrow the Romans. It would be "spiritual" in the same way Israel was always meant to be spiritual—by being a theocracy under God. The disciples were clearly not on the same page as Jesus.

Now they were on their way to Jerusalem, the seat of political and religious power in Judea. As they neared the city, their dreams of taking part in the glorious messianic kingdom began to grow. The payoff for their lives of discipleship was coming! In fact, some of them had already been talking with their family members about the reward that was coming. This explains what happened next.

As if out of nowhere, the mother of James and John, the "sons of Zebedee," approached Jesus with a bold request: that in Jesus' kingdom her two sons would have the most exalted positions—one on the right and one on the left of Jesus (20:20-21). Though Matthew doesn't mention her name, commentators believe she was most likely Salome, the sister of Jesus' mother and therefore Jesus' aunt (cf. John 19:25).[67] If so, that would make James and John cousins of Jesus.[68] Because the brothers of Jesus were not yet disciples, those two cousins would have been the closest kin among His followers. Perhaps, then, this gave them the idea that by royal rights they ought to have the highest positions in the kingdom with Jesus—in fact, occupying the positions of second- and third-in-command. I almost hesitate to mention the other possibility that all of Jesus' talk of His betrayal and execution would have led worldly-minded men to consider the prospect of immediate succession to the throne. If this was involved, then how deeply steeped they were in their carnal expectation of a kingdom that followed the rules of this world!

Another point I need to make is that although their mother was the mouthpiece of the request, James and John were the originators and instigators. The Gospel of Mark makes this clear, leaving the mother out of the account completely and noting that the request came from the two brothers (Mark 10:35-37). R. V. G. Tasker notes, "It is clear that, in fact, the request emanated from the brothers themselves, for the remaining ten apostles, when they hear about it, do not in Matthew's narrative any more than in Mark's turn in indignation upon the mother but upon her sons."[69]

Jesus' answer confirms that the Zebedee boys were behind the whole request, and He knew it. In His response, Jesus didn't speak directly to His aunt Salome, who was bowing down before Him. Rather, He used the second person plural, addressing the two boys who had put her up to it. What a surprise that must have been for them to have their cover blown. His response: "You [two] do not know what you [two] are asking" (Matt. 20:22).

I sense a mixture of exasperation and disappointment in Jesus' words, as if He were saying to James and John, "You just don't get it, do you?" When He asked if they were able to "drink the cup" He was about to drink, they answered without hesitation: "We are able." But they still didn't have a clue what He was talking about. My guess is that they thought Jesus was talking about some kind of festive banquet, or the spoils of victory associated with the crown and the kingdom. But He was actually talking about the suffering He was facing with the agony of the Cross ahead (see 26:39). Had they fully grasped the point of Jesus' repeated warnings of His coming death and resurrection, they would have known that to follow Him as a disciple meant that suffering comes before significance, brokenness before usefulness, humility before authority, the bitter cup of pain before the sweet glories of promotion!

While they still weren't on the same page, Jesus confirmed that they would, in fact, drink His cup (20:23). James would be the first of the twelve disciples to lose his life in martyrdom when King Herod "had James the brother of John put to death with a sword" (Acts 12:2). Then, about sixty years later, the apostle John would, according to tradition, be the last of the Twelve to die, having lived through persecution, imprisonment, torture, exile, and even an attempt to boil him alive in oil.[70] By the end of his life, John would understand Jesus' words that he would "drink the cup" as Jesus had. In the opening chapter of the book of Revelation, John described himself as a "partaker in the tribulation and kingdom and perseverance which are in Jesus" while he was "on the island called Patmos because of the word of God and the testimony of Jesus" (Rev. 1:9). At the time of the disciples' ascent toward Jerusalem, however, James and John seemed to have no idea that Jesus was talking about suffering for the sake of the kingdom.

Jesus then attempted to set the record straight regarding those coveted high positions in the future kingdom. Those places of honor would be given to those whom God the Father chose. A high position in the kingdom isn't something that can be earned. And it certainly isn't something that can be inherited through close family connections. Those are the ways of the world. Jesus' words suggest that those places "have already been assigned" in the plan and purpose of God.[71] Therefore, the way the disciples were wrangling and jostling among themselves over such positions was utterly futile.

Yet wrangle and jostle they did! Matthew recalls that the other ten disciples who had been standing by watching the whole awkward scene unfold had become "indignant" with James and John (Matt. 20:24). Why? Because each of them wanted to have access to one of those places of privilege at Jesus' right or left hand. Not one of them was on the same page as Jesus. No matter how plainly Jesus spelled out His coming suffering and death, no matter how clearly He taught them that they would follow in His footsteps, and no matter how hard He tried to show them that His kingdom was not like the kingdoms of this world, not one of them got it.

Being the patient teacher that He was, Jesus called another huddle of the Twelve to set things straight again. I can imagine Him forming a circle, staring into each man's eyes, and speaking very slowly. First, He set up a negative example as a clear point of contrast: the way of the nations. Their rulers "lord it over" those who are under them in their worldly kingdoms, and such rulers "flaunt their authority over those under them" (20:25, NLT). Note the "over"/"under" emphasis. According to the ways of the world, the king on the throne and those who have high positions on his right and left function like domineering superiors ordering commands to their lowly underlings. But such a picture of authority in God's order is completely wrong!

Thus, Jesus said, loudly and clearly, "It is not this way among you" (20:26). God's kingdom stands in utter contrast to the ways of the kingdoms of the nations. On Jesus' leadership team, there is no place for self-serving ambition, personal promotion, shameless nepotism, presumptuous arrogance, or unbridled narcissism. Rather, "Whoever wishes to become great among you shall be your servant, and whoever wishes to be first among you shall be your slave" (20:26-27).

You could have probably heard their jaws drop when Jesus uttered those words. The words were revolutionary. They turned the world's ways on their head. Once again, Jesus was unpacking the meaning of His statement that "the last shall be first, and the first last" (20:16). And with each pass at this confusing teaching, He hoped the disciples would get closer and closer to understanding His mission, which would become their own mission when He departed this world. Only when they fully grasped this mission would they understand what true greatness in the kingdom of heaven really is. He concluded the lesson by pointing to Himself as the ultimate example of what He had just been trying to teach them: "The Son of Man did not come to be served, but to serve, and to give His life a ransom for many" (20:28).

— 20:29-34 —

In the very next scene, Jesus lived out the words he had just shared: "The Son of Man did not come to be served, but to serve" (20:28). As Jesus and the disciples were traveling through Jericho, a great crowd had been gathering around Him (20:29). At this point, two blind men, who were sitting along the road, inquired about all the noise and excitement. Upon learning that Jesus was passing by, they began crying out, "Lord, have mercy on us, Son of David!" (20:30). When they were hushed by the crowd, they lifted their voices even more (20:31).

Think about this. Simply from small bits of overheard murmuring coming from the passing crowd, those blind men pieced together a simple but true confession of faith. This man was the Son of David—that is, Israel's King, the long-awaited Messiah! They knew enough of the messianic prophecies to know that with the coming of the Messiah came healing, liberation, and times of refreshing for the people of Israel. By addressing Jesus as "Lord," they acknowledged His sovereignty. And by asking for mercy, they acknowledged their unworthiness, their miserable condition in this fallen world, and—most importantly—Jesus' ability to relieve them of their suffering.

In His mission as a servant, Jesus stopped, welcomed them into His presence, and asked how He could help them: "What do you want Me to do for you?" (20:32). Isn't that wonderful? Don't rush past those two important words: *for you.* Jesus lived every moment of His life for others. While the exuberant crowd seemed to care only about themselves (20:31), and while the disciples wrangled over who was greatest among them (20:20-24), Jesus turned His attention to the lowliest members of society, stooped down, and condescended to *serve!*

The request of the blind men was as simple as their confession: They wanted to see (20:33). At this moment Matthew gives us insight into Jesus' inner motive for His service. Some people serve others because they get paid to do it. Others serve to score points with people around them. Others serve to fulfill some vow, social obligation, or religious requirement. Jesus, however, served because He was "moved with compassion" (20:34). His deep love fueled His desire for service. Without hesitation, Jesus touched their eyes. One moment, they saw darkness; the next moment, they were looking into the light of Jesus' eyes.

APPLICATION: MATTHEW 20:17-34

Getting on the Same Page as Jesus

For the disciples, getting on the same page as Jesus was a slow, agonizing, baby-step-by-baby-step process—more like an ordeal. They didn't get it, even after repeated instructions and numerous examples. These lessons have been recorded in the Gospel of Matthew to serve as instructions and examples for all followers of Jesus, including us. The question is: Are we on the same page as Jesus, or are we adrift in the fog of worldly priorities like the disciples?

Allow me to ask a question to help you do an honest audit of your servanthood: *Are you leading by serving?* Let me make this specific. Husband, are you serving your wife? Pastor, are you serving your church? Employer, are you serving your employees? Parent, are you serving your children? Now, Jesus' kingdom of servanthood isn't merely a reversal of the world's "lord it over" leadership. It works in both directions. We're to serve one another (Gal. 5:13). Husband, serve your wife. Wife, serve your husband. Children, serve your parents. Parents, serve your children. I think you get the picture. If you do, you're one step closer to being on the same page as Jesus in His kingdom mission.

But what does it mean to be a servant? To start, it means helping someone who may not say thank you. It means doing something kind for someone who won't even know you did it. It means applauding the accomplishments of others even if they would never return the compliment. It means going out of your way to come to another's aid, to accept and honor them—even if that person is a "nobody" in the eyes of the world. And it means treating with equal respect and value the CEO and the file clerk, the senior pastor and the volunteer parking attendant, the computer genius and the trash collector.

Ultimately, the disciples—or at least eleven of them—got on the same page with Jesus. They finally realized that it wasn't about them. They discovered that their mission was to love one another, just as Christ loved them. If they could learn this countercultural, otherworldly lesson, so can we.

Who's Riding What and Why?
MATTHEW 21:1-11

NASB

[1] When they had approached Jerusalem and had come to Bethphage, at the Mount of Olives, then Jesus sent two disciples, [2] saying to them, "Go into the village opposite you, and immediately you will find a donkey tied *there* and a colt with her; untie them and bring them to Me. [3] If anyone says anything to you, you shall say, 'The Lord has need of them,' and immediately he will send them." [4] This [a] took place to fulfill what was spoken through the prophet:

[5] "SAY TO THE DAUGHTER OF ZION,
　'BEHOLD YOUR KING IS COMING
　　TO YOU,
　GENTLE, AND MOUNTED ON A
　　DONKEY,
　EVEN ON A COLT, THE FOAL OF A
　　BEAST OF BURDEN.'"

[6] The disciples went and did just as Jesus had instructed them, [7] and brought the donkey and the colt, and laid their coats on them; and He sat on [a] the coats. [8] Most of the crowd spread their coats in the road, and others were cutting branches from the trees and spreading them in the road. [9] The crowds going ahead of Him, and those who followed, were shouting,

"Hosanna to the Son of David;
BLESSED IS HE WHO COMES IN THE
　NAME OF THE LORD;
Hosanna in the highest!"

[10] When He had entered Jerusalem, all the city was stirred, saying, "Who is this?" [11] And the crowds were saying, "This is the prophet Jesus, from Nazareth in Galilee."

21:4 [a] Lit *has happened* **21:7** [a] Lit *them*

NLT

[1] As Jesus and the disciples approached Jerusalem, they came to the town of Bethphage on the Mount of Olives. Jesus sent two of them on ahead. [2] "Go into the village over there," he said. "As soon as you enter it, you will see a donkey tied there, with its colt beside it. Untie them and bring them to me. [3] If anyone asks what you are doing, just say, 'The Lord needs them,' and he will immediately let you take them."

[4] This took place to fulfill the prophecy that said,

[5] "Tell the people of Jerusalem,*
　'Look, your King is coming to
　　you.
He is humble, riding on a donkey—
　riding on a donkey's colt.'"*

[6] The two disciples did as Jesus commanded. [7] They brought the donkey and the colt to him and threw their garments over the colt, and he sat on it.*

[8] Most of the crowd spread their garments on the road ahead of him, and others cut branches from the trees and spread them on the road. [9] Jesus was in the center of the procession, and the people all around him were shouting,

"Praise God* for the Son of David!
Blessings on the one who comes
　in the name of the LORD!
Praise God in highest heaven!"*

[10] The entire city of Jerusalem was in an uproar as he entered. "Who is this?" they asked.

[11] And the crowds replied, "It's Jesus, the prophet from Nazareth in Galilee."

21:5a Greek *Tell the daughter of Zion.* Isa 62:11. **21:5b** Zech 9:9. **21:7** Greek *over them, and he sat on them.* **21:9a** Greek *Hosanna,* an exclamation of praise that literally means "save now"; also in 21:9b, 15. **21:9b** Pss 118:25-26; 148:1.

We know it today as Palm Sunday—the day of the Triumphal Entry, four days before the Last Supper, five days before the Crucifixion, one week before the Resurrection. This was the day that kicked off the series of events Christians have traditionally called Holy Week.

The four Gospels devote nearly one-third of their length to the final few days of Jesus' life and ministry. Only two of the four Gospels (Matthew and Luke) mention the events surrounding His birth. All four offer only a page or two on His resurrection. But when it comes to the dramatic events leading up to His passion and crucifixion, and the account of His death itself, each writer lingers over the details.

As the day drew near for the Son of God to suffer and die, it was as if time stood still and the universe sucked in its breath. God's Spirit moved each Gospel writer to take his time with Holy Week—to write carefully, to proceed slowly, to reflect deeply. Because eternal life depended on it.

As our walk through Matthew's narrative brings us to these final days of Jesus' earthly life, we need to take our time and let the wonder in.

— 21:1-5 —

Jesus and His disciples had been walking for days from Galilee toward Jerusalem to take part in the annual Passover celebration. Accompanying them during the last leg of the journey would have been any additional men and women counted among Jesus' broader circle of disciples, the typical crowd of hangers-on who had continued from Jericho, and probably the two blind men Jesus had healed along the road through Jericho, who had followed Him after their sight was restored (20:34).

Coming from Jericho, Jesus and a crowd of followers approached Jerusalem from the east, through Bethphage and across the ridge of the Mount of Olives.

The last 18 miles, from Jericho to Jerusalem, is a fairly steep uphill climb, which under normal circumstances would have dissuaded the half-hearted from accompanying Jesus. Yet with the Passover feast looming, Jesus and His followers would have blended into a growing crowd of pilgrims making their way toward Jerusalem. The Gospel of John reports that as Jesus and

EXCURSUS: THE "TALE" WAGGING THE DONKEY?

MATTHEW 21:1-7

The accounts of the Triumphal Entry in the other three Gospels mention only the colt, the young donkey that Jesus actually rode (Mark 11:2, 7; Luke 19:30, 35; John 12:14). Matthew alone reports that the disciples retrieved both the colt and its mother, referring to the two animals throughout the account (Matt. 21:2-3, 7). This discrepancy between Matthew and the other Gospels has led some skeptics and critics of the Bible to suggest that Matthew added the colt's mother to the story in order to better fit the prophecy of Zechariah 9:9, which says, "Behold, your king is coming to you . . . humble, and mounted on a donkey, even on a colt, the foal of a donkey."

The Hebrew text literally reads, "riding upon a donkey, and upon a young male donkey, the son of a donkey." Meanwhile, the Greek translation of the Hebrew Bible well known at the time (the Septuagint) reads, "sitting upon a donkey and a young colt." In either case, the conjunction "and" could have led to the understanding that both a young colt and its mother would be involved in the Triumphal Entry. However, it was typical of Hebrew poetry in its use of parallelism to reiterate one idea with different words. Thus, Jewish readers of Zechariah 9:9 would have understood that the coming king would not be riding on two animals but, as the NASB translation rightly renders it, would be "mounted on a donkey, *even* on a colt, the foal of a donkey" (emphasis mine).

So, did Matthew misunderstand Hebrew parallelism? Furthermore, did he then make up an account that included two animals in order to match his misreading of the prophecy of Zechariah? Is this a case of the tail—or *tale*—wagging the donkey?

Regarding the first question, it is extremely unlikely that Matthew, of all people, would have failed to grasp the simple concept of parallelism in Hebrew poetry—something even a first-year student of Hebrew is able to identify. Regarding the second question, I agree with R. V. G. Tasker, who argues, "When Matthew states that the foal was brought with her dame he is recording a fact, and not rather unintelligently adapting his material in the interest of a literal fulfillment of prophecy."[72]

The fact is, though two beasts of burden were present at the Triumphal Entry, Jesus didn't ride on both animals at once. In no case would that be a believable scenario. Jesus rode on the younger donkey, upon which no one had ever ridden. Mark, Luke, and John focus full attention on the single animal, the colt, upon which Jesus rode. They saw no need to mention the other beast of burden that would have been carrying only excess baggage and clothing.

While the colt's mother is not explicitly mentioned in Mark, Luke, and John, Matthew's account answers a very important question that would have struck a first-century reader of the other Gospel accounts: If the colt had never been ridden or even sat upon, how was it able to remain calm in the midst of a noisy crowd? This may not seem like a big deal to most of us who have only seen mature, trained donkeys ridden at a carnival or petting zoo. But it likely would have been baffling to a first-century reader. John Peter Lange highlights the significance of having the young donkey's mother present during the short ride from Bethphage to Jerusalem: "If this foal had never borne a rider, it was necessary that the mother should be led by its side, in order to quiet it for such a service."[73]

His disciples neared Jerusalem, they came to the town of Bethany, where they stayed at the home of Martha, Mary, and Lazarus (John 12:1-2).

Bethany lay on the eastern slope of the Mount of Olives, about 2 miles from the walls of Jerusalem. Bethphage was a little farther up, about halfway between Bethany and Jerusalem, technically a part of Jerusalem itself.[74] It was to the small village of Bethphage that Jesus was pointing when He told His disciples to retrieve a donkey and colt from "the village opposite you" (Matt. 21:2; see Mark 11:1-2; Luke 19:30).

It may be tempting to read Jesus' instructions as if He were commandeering the property of complete strangers to exercise His divine right and exhibit His divine power of omniscience. Some have even seen this as an instance of *angareia*, the right of official requisitioning that "belonged to royalty and was claimed also by Rabbis."[75] If so, then Jesus was making both a political and a religious statement in the procurement of the animals, exercising His right as a sovereign dignitary. However, it's more likely that Jesus knew the owners of the animals and was instructing the disciples to follow a prearranged plan.

In any case, Matthew records that Jesus had His disciples fetch two animals—a donkey and her colt—upon which no one had ever ridden. Matthew explains the prophetic significance of this act by paraphrasing Zechariah 9:9, which says,

> Rejoice greatly, O daughter of Zion!
> Shout in triumph, O daughter of Jerusalem!
> Behold, your king is coming to you;
> He is just and endowed with salvation,
> Humble, and mounted on a donkey,
> Even on a colt, the foal of a donkey.

When Jesus took His seat on a young donkey and rode into Jerusalem, a loud and clear message would be proclaimed without words—"Your King is coming to you" (Matt. 21:5). Matthew shines a light on this fulfillment of prophecy to underscore the overarching purpose of his Gospel: to demonstrate to his Jewish readers that Jesus is indeed the King, Israel's long-awaited Messiah.

— 21:6-11 —

As instructed, the disciples fetched the colt and its mother from Bethphage, and they loaded them with coats. Jesus mounted the smaller of the two, using the coats as a sort of makeshift saddle (21:6-7). From there, Jesus, surrounded by a retinue of close disciples as well as a wider circle of followers, began the slow but short journey over the Mount of Olives, up its eastern slope from Bethany, through Bethphage, then down the western slope into the Kidron Valley and on to the gates of Jerusalem.

The geography of this event is important. Because of the journey through peaks and valleys from Bethany to Jerusalem, thousands of pilgrims on the road would have been able to see from a distance the man riding on a young donkey. The presence of the colt's mother beside him would have been a clue that the rider was making some kind of statement. I'm sure that with that many devoted Jews seeing the scene from either above or below, several in the crowd would have made the connection with the messianic prophecy of Zechariah 9:9.

On the profound significance of Jesus' ride, William Barclay notes,

> He proposed to ride into Jerusalem in a way that would be an unmistakable claim to be the Messiah, God's anointed king. . . . He entered in such a way as to focus the whole limelight upon himself and to occupy the centre of the stage. . . . It was a deliberate claim to be king, a deliberate fulfilling of the picture in Zechariah 9:9. But even in this Jesus underlined the kind of kingship which he claimed. . . . Only in war did kings ride upon a horse; when they came in peace they came upon a donkey.[76]

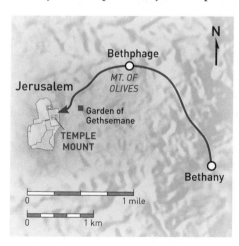

Jesus' route on the colt from Bethany, over the Mount of Olives through Bethphage, and through the Kidron Valley into Jerusalem provided numerous vantage points for the pilgrims to see him even from a distance.

The behavior of many members of the growing crowd making their way to Jerusalem that day demonstrates that numerous pilgrims understood the significance of Jesus' actions. In acclamation and honor, they spread their garments on the road or spread large palm branches out before the path of the donkey. Stanley Toussaint explains the significance of this: "To make a carpet out of garments for the way of a king is said to be a common form of homage to this day. The waving of palm branches was done to welcome kings. Every outward indication pointed to the entrance of a king into Jerusalem."[77]

Besides their actions, their words confirmed an exuberant acceptance that Jesus was, in fact, their King, the long-awaited Messiah. Both those ahead of Jesus and those behind were shouting and praising Him with the words "Hosanna to the Son of David; blessed is He who comes in the name of the LORD; Hosanna in the highest!" (Matt. 21:9). Besides clearly identifying Jesus as the Son of David, that is, the Messiah, the crowd was repeating the word "Hosanna," a one-word prayer that means "O Lord, save now!" It was a petition for deliverance from oppression. The crowd drew inspiration for these words from Psalm 118:25-26:

> O LORD, do save, we beseech You;
> O LORD, we beseech You, do send prosperity!
> Blessed is the one who comes in the name of the LORD;
> We have blessed you from the house of the LORD.

What a moment! Those men, women, and children knew they were living out the prophecies of Scripture. It was as if the ancient words of God suddenly came to life before their eyes. They were personally witnessing the fulfillment of prophecy and the realization of deep anticipation.

As Jesus and the crowd passed through the Kidron Valley and neared the eastern gate of Jerusalem, the shouts and cheers of high praise would have carried across the city, possibly reverberating throughout the valley. The entire city—including scowling Pharisees, irritated priests, and stern-faced Roman soldiers—likely would have heard the joyous noise, each interpreting it differently. Perhaps the Pharisees heard it as another threat to their own control over the people. Maybe the priests would have seen it as a terrible intrusion on the solemnity of the Passover week. And the Romans would have begun to worry about insurrection or revolt if they had understood the significance of the One riding the colt. What was obvious in the eyes of the Jews would have been unclear to the Romans, who would have expected a king to ride in on a stallion.

As word got around about the arrival of the man on a colt, everybody soon learned His identity: "the prophet Jesus, from Nazareth in Galilee" (Matt. 21:11). The Gospel of Luke records attempts by the ill-tempered Pharisees to calm the crowd, demanding that Jesus Himself rebuke the people because they dared to insinuate that He was the long-awaited Messiah. The Lord's response would have caused them to burn with

Living Out a Long-Awaited "Prophecy"

MATTHEW 21:9

I was raised in a very modest home. Our little place on Quince Street in East Houston cost my folks about $6,000. We had three little bedrooms and one tiny bath. My older brother, Orville, my older sister, Luci, and I grew up there through our teenage years.

My father was a diligent laborer. During World War II he was a little too old for the military draft, so he was part of the workforce that helped push our country through the war. My mother didn't work outside the home. We three kids were enough to handle. She loved the Lord and wanted us kids to love the Lord. The first part—her loving the Lord—was working for her, but the last part was a little later in coming, at least for me.

One day when I was about twelve years old, I was getting ready to go out and play sandlot football. As I was running through the kitchen my mother said, "Charles, come here. I want to show you something."

I could sense by the tone of her voice that a mother's sermon was coming. I didn't have time for it, so I said, "Mom, can I do it later when I come back?"

"No," she said, "you're going to come here right now. I want to show you what the Lord gave me. And it has you in mind."

I thought, "Oh brother! What's this going to be?" So I stood there, tossing my football up in the air.

"Stand still and listen to me," she said. I froze. Then came the sermon: "I've been reading in Proverbs, and I found the verse for you. It's Proverbs 18:16." She had written it out on a little 4 x 6 card and taped it on the wall above the sink:

> A man's gift makes room for him
> And brings him before great men.

(continued on next page)

"That's great, Mom," I said. "Can I go now?"

Then she said, "No. I'm going to tell you what the Lord has taught me about this."

"Mom, all the guys are waiting out there for—"

"Listen to me," she said. "I believe the Lord is going to use you in ways that we would never guess."

"Great, Mom. I hope He does. Are we through?"

"Listen to me. When you're older, you'll realize that God is fulfilling the truth of this verse in your life."

I tilted my head and read it again: "A man's gift makes room for him and brings him before great men."

In light of our little home and our modest growing-up years, "great people" didn't register with me. But it meant a lot to her; in fact, she had tears in her eyes. She put her arms around me and said, "I want you to know I'm claiming this for you."

I said, "Well, that's great, Mom. Keep claiming. Are we through?"

She didn't like that response, but I slipped out of her grip and raced out of the house.

I would have never guessed as a twelve-year-old how the grace of God would work, how my mother's earnest and insightful prayers would be answered. Time passed. I got out of school, got married, and wound up in Okinawa, serving in the Marine Corps. There I was, 8,000 miles from home, not even thinking about Proverbs 18:16. But through a series of events, I wound up being mentored by a representative from The Navigators. That mentor really helped me grow up as a Christian. It was during those many months on that island I received from the Lord my call into the ministry.

By God's grace, I ended up at Dallas Theological Seminary. Though I was accepted on probation because I didn't have the requisite academic background, God gave me the ability to work hard and excel. During the course of my four years at seminary, I was mentored by some great men of God. Ray Stedman, Howie Hendricks, *and Dwight Pentecost especially shaped my transition into pastoral ministry. I pastored in New England for a while and eventually ended up in Southern California. There I did something I never dreamed of doing: I wrote a book that people actually wanted to read. Before long, the Lord opened the door for me to write more books. Then, by His grace, my preaching wound up on the radio.*

Honestly, all of this came as a surprise to me. I couldn't have choreographed those moves or plotted out this path. My life has been a composite of one surprise after another, blessed by the grace of God—as it is to this day.

In the middle of this journey, back in the 1980s, I was invited to a very special gathering by the Christian Embassy in Washington, DC. In that group, there would be a large number of high-ranking officers from the Pentagon—generals and colonels. There would be a group of ambassadors with their families. Even a member of President Reagan's cabinet. And they had invited me—of all people!—to speak. I realized there were going to be about eight hundred people at that gathering of great men and women. Earlier that afternoon, as I was going through my Bible, thinking through what I wanted to say that evening, I came across Proverbs 18:16, circled.

By that time, my mother had died. But her words returned. I suddenly realized that I was now living the fulfillment of what she had claimed—a statement that had been given to me when I wasn't even interested. At the time, I had shrugged it off. And here I was living out the truth she had claimed for me.

How great it is when we realize that God is bringing about the fulfillment of things He's had planned for us. These are good times to pause and give Him thanks and praise for what He has done. I remember standing up that evening and having to choke back tears as I got started, thinking, Who am I to talk to these great men and women? *I realized that I was who I had always been—what we all are—nothing but a recipient of God's amazing grace.*

rage: "I tell you, if these become silent, the stones will cry out!" (Luke 19:39-40). In a telling case of irony, even the stones "knew" what the stonehearted Pharisees refused to believe: Jesus was the King, Israel's long-awaited Messiah.

APPLICATION: MATTHEW 21:1-11

Our Short Journey

It was a rather short journey between Bethany and the gates of Jerusalem. Jesus probably made it in less than an hour, even on that stubby-legged colt, up and down the Mount of Olives. But for those along that road that Sunday morning, it was a profoundly important journey that had the potential to seal their eternal destinies. That crowded road, with Jesus in view, provides a picture of our own short journey through life, with its twists and turns, peaks and valleys. Eventually the road comes to an end at the golden gate leading into the eternal city, and we either follow Jesus through or find ourselves outside the wall.

Where are you in that crowd? Are you getting as close as you can to Jesus, placing your own garment on the ground as an act of worship and honor, acknowledging Him as your Savior and Lord? Can the people closest to you in life see your devotion to the Messiah, or do you follow Jesus from afar, only with your eyes, keeping your "Hosannas" to yourself?

Are you like those who were swept up in the excitement of the moment, who went along with the crowd, hoping to gain some short-term joy or worldly benefit from getting close to that celebrity from Nazareth . . . only to shout "Crucify Him! Crucify Him!" a few days later? Is your devotion to Christ firm or fickle?

Or are you keeping your distance and avoiding the crowd, perhaps even sneering, scoffing, or turning your nose up at the notion of surrendering everything to the Son of God? Are you a cynic, rejecting everything Jesus claimed to be? Like a Pharisee who wants to silence the crowd? Or a Roman soldier who just wants to keep the peace?

There's only one right response to the One who has come to reign in our lives—total surrender. It's the one response that doesn't come naturally to any of us. We were all taught to fight our way through life, to defend ourselves, to take charge—certainly not to follow some guy on a young donkey, no matter who He claims to be. And yet, with all our hearts, souls, and strength, we are called to join the throng of eternal "Hosannas."

When Jesus Lowered the Boom
MATTHEW 21:12-22

NASB

[12]And Jesus entered the temple and drove out all those who were buying and selling in the temple, and overturned the tables of the money changers and the seats of those who were selling doves. [13]And He said to them, "It is written, 'MY HOUSE SHALL BE CALLED A HOUSE OF PRAYER'; but you are making it a ROBBERS' ªDEN."

[14]And *the* blind and *the* lame came to Him in the temple, and He healed them. [15]But when the chief priests and the scribes saw the wonderful things that He had done, and the children who were shouting in the temple, "Hosanna to the Son of David," they became indignant [16]and said to Him, "Do You hear what these *children* are saying?" And Jesus said to them, "Yes; have you never read, 'OUT OF THE MOUTH OF INFANTS AND NURSING BABIES YOU HAVE PREPARED PRAISE FOR YOURSELF'?" [17]And He left them and went out of the city to Bethany, and spent the night there.

[18]Now in the morning, when He was returning to the city, He became hungry. [19]Seeing a lone fig tree by the road, He came to it and found nothing on it except leaves only; and He said to it, "No longer shall there ever be *any* fruit from you." And at once the fig tree withered.

[20]Seeing *this*, the disciples were amazed and asked, "How did the fig tree wither *all* at once?" [21]And Jesus answered and said to them, "Truly I

NLT

[12]Jesus entered the Temple and began to drive out all the people buying and selling animals for sacrifice. He knocked over the tables of the money changers and the chairs of those selling doves. [13]He said to them, "The Scriptures declare, 'My Temple will be called a house of prayer,' but you have turned it into a den of thieves!"*

[14]The blind and the lame came to him in the Temple, and he healed them. [15]The leading priests and the teachers of religious law saw these wonderful miracles and heard even the children in the Temple shouting, "Praise God for the Son of David."

But the leaders were indignant. [16]They asked Jesus, "Do you hear what these children are saying?"

"Yes," Jesus replied. "Haven't you ever read the Scriptures? For they say, 'You have taught children and infants to give you praise.'*" [17]Then he returned to Bethany, where he stayed overnight.

[18]In the morning, as Jesus was returning to Jerusalem, he was hungry, [19]and he noticed a fig tree beside the road. He went over to see if there were any figs, but there were only leaves. Then he said to it, "May you never bear fruit again!" And immediately the fig tree withered up.

[20]The disciples were amazed when they saw this and asked, "How did the fig tree wither so quickly?" [21]Then Jesus told them, "I tell you

NASB

say to you, if you have faith and do not doubt, you will not only do what was done to the fig tree, but even if you say to this mountain, 'Be taken up and cast into the sea,' it will happen. ²²And all things you ask in prayer, believing, you will receive."

21:13 ªLit *cave*

NLT

the truth, if you have faith and don't doubt, you can do things like this and much more. You can even say to this mountain, 'May you be lifted up and thrown into the sea,' and it will happen. ²²You can pray for anything, and if you have faith, you will receive it."

21:13 Isa 56:7; Jer 7:11.   21:16 Ps 8:2 (Greek version).

Can you remember the last time you got mad . . . about the right thing?

I'm not talking about an out-of-control temper tantrum that turns into steaming rage. I mean being upset for the right reason—what people might call righteous indignation. Righteous anger results when somebody does something that bothers reasonable, moral people. In fact, if you don't experience righteous indignation in such circumstances, it would reveal a careless lack of compassion and justice.

Taking offense to moral wrongs is the kind of anger Paul wrote about in Ephesians 4:26: "Be angry, and yet do not sin." This tells us that there are times when it's right to show anger. What kinds of situations should rightly kindle our ire? It's right to feel anger toward an abuser—whether that's physical, mental, emotional, spiritual, or sexual abuse. It's appropriate to have anger toward a bully who takes advantage of someone smaller, who ridicules a person for being different, or who picks on those who are defenseless or have disabilities. And as believers, we should feel indignation when we witness individuals shamelessly desecrating things that are sacred, selfishly exploiting the poor, or oppressing the innocent—treating with cruelty people created in God's image.

Such wrong acts get to us. *And they should.* It's only human to react this way. However, we fallen humans must be careful that our righteous indignation doesn't get out of control and morph into wicked rage. This is why Paul adds "and yet do not sin" to his "be angry."

Sometimes we forget that Jesus, too, was fully human—with the same physical, mental, and emotional makeup as you and me, but without sin (Heb. 4:15). As the God-man, Jesus had both a fully divine nature and a fully human nature—in one unique person. Theologians coined the expression *theanthropic person*, which combines *theos* [2316], meaning "God," pointing to His divinity, and *anthrōpos* [444], meaning "man," referring to His humanity. Because of His fully divine nature, the God-man could command the weather, heal the sick, walk on water, forgive sins, and raise the dead. Because of His fully human nature, the God-man soiled His diapers as an infant, learned to walk as a child, became weary and slept when He took a long journey, ate when He was hungry, wept when He was grieved, and died when He was crucified.

And yes, because Jesus was fully human, He got angry. But because He was fully divine, His anger was always just, His response always measured, His actions always appropriate.

People are often shocked when they read accounts like the two in Matthew 21:12-22. Many Christians are taught only a one-sided view of Jesus, namely that He is "gentle Jesus, meek and mild." Without question, the Messiah modeled humility and gentleness; He was the personification of grace and mercy. But He was more—far more—than that. Because He was jealous for the holiness and glory of God and had the highest regard for proper prayer and authentic worship, He couldn't tolerate anything that compromised those important marks of true spirituality, especially if hypocrisy played a part in the process.

As Jesus encountered the gross sacrilege taking place in the temple— all the buying and selling and acts of extortion in a bazaar-like setting— He reached His limit. And as we'll see, even the next morning He was still fired up when He condemned an unfruitful fig tree as a symbol for the condemnation of the wicked rebels of Israel.

— 21:12-13 —

I suppose onlookers could overlook the first overturned table as a clumsy mistake. But then the commotion increased. They saw Jesus moving through the crowded, outer Court of the Gentiles flipping tables of money changers and kicking over the padded seats of those who had been bilking common people out of their money. They quickly realized that something big was going down. What was it that drew out such holy ire from the Son of God?

When Jesus and His disciples neared the temple, they saw what amounted to a religious circus. While many places of interest today make a visitor exit through a gift store, the religious elite who ran the big business that was the temple in the first century made all worshipers enter through what amounted to a religious carnival. Kent Hughes describes it this way: "Merchants shouted from their stalls to the customers, and noisy, haggling, pushy pilgrims jostled one another for position. . . . The aroma of the livestock, accentuated by the enclosure, made it like a county fair and the Stock Exchange all rolled into one!"[78]

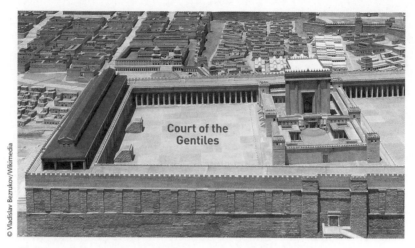

© Vladislav Bezrukov/Wikimedia

The first-century temple, renovated by Herod the Great, included the large **Court of the Gentiles**, where non-Jews could come for worship.

To understand Jesus' seemingly harsh actions, we need to consider a little historical background. The bustling marketplace on the temple mount had been called "Annas's Bazaar," named after the retired high priest, Annas, who was also the father-in-law of the current high priest, Caiaphas. Annas had ruled as Israel's high priest for almost a decade, during which he had established an extensive financial network in the temple that systematically extorted money from worshipers. Here's how the operation worked: As worshipers made their pilgrimage to Jerusalem from all over the world to take part in feasts and offer the required sacrifices at the temple, the chief priests would only accept the currency minted in Israel—the shekel. Therefore, foreign coins first needed to be converted to shekels. Of course, the agents of the priests would exchange the currency for an inflated rate that lined the pockets of the priestly family, corrupt to the core.

Beyond this, the Law of Moses stated that any animal offered to God had to be flawless. This gave an opportunity for the priests overseeing the temple to hold "outside animals" to an impossible standard of perfection. The inspector could arbitrarily find some blemish in an otherwise fine animal brought in by a worshiper. The inspector would reject it as unworthy of sacrifice and then direct the desperate worshiper to a stall where preapproved animals could be bought at multiple times the normal rate for such animals. Naturally, the priests took a cut of the exorbitant profits for the sale of the animals, leading to increased corruption and injustice. A. B. Bruce calls it "a grotesque and offensive combination of religion with shady morality."[79]

In light of these injustices, Jesus' dramatic response definitely fell under the category of righteous indignation. He drove out those corrupt profiteers, knocked over the tables of the money changers, and pushed over the chairs of those selling doves (21:12). Mark's Gospel adds that Jesus wouldn't let anyone "carry merchandise through the temple" (Mark 11:16). What should have been a holy place of reverence had become a consumerist's carnival!

To explain His actions, Jesus quoted from two Old Testament passages (Matt. 21:13). The first reminded His hearers what the temple was supposed to be: "My house will be called a house of prayer for all the peoples" (Isa. 56:7). The second was a snippet drawn from the prophet Jeremiah that accused the unholy hucksters of converting the temple of God into a "robbers' den." The context of the Jeremiah quotation reveals Jesus' mind-set:

> "Will you steal, murder, and commit adultery and swear falsely, and offer sacrifices to Baal and walk after other gods that you have not known, then come and stand before Me in this house, which is called by My name, and say, 'We are delivered!'—that you may do all these abominations? Has this house, which is called by My name, become a den of robbers in your sight? Behold, I, even I, have seen it," declares the LORD. (Jer. 7:9-11)

Just as Old Testament Israel had departed from their covenant-making God and turned to worldly pursuits and the worship of false gods, Israel's leadership in Jesus' day had replaced the right devotion of the temple with the worship of the almighty shekel!

— 21:14-17 —

Jesus' actions returned the temple to its rightful purpose, the prayerful worship of God—at least for the time being. As the dramatic scene unfolded, not a soul withstood Him. Why not? Perhaps those involved in the money-changing and price-gouging schemes knew that what they were doing wasn't ethical. The scriptural passages Jesus quoted may have pricked their consciences. The inerrant Word of God was on Jesus' side. Certainly, the poor customers who had been bamboozled by the cheats would have been on Jesus' side too. Remember that the Lord had ridden into the city with a large and growing crowd shouting the acclamation "Hosanna to the Son of David," and those resounding praises had followed Him even into the temple court (21:15). On top of this, Jesus immediately followed up His act of cleansing the temple with astonishing acts of healing toward the blind and lame (21:14). Because of all these things, Jesus was as safe in the temple as Daniel was in the lions' den.

Here the lions showed up to pace to and fro and to snarl from a distance. The chief priests and scribes saw all the commotion, as well as the miraculous things Jesus was doing. They heard children singing the roadside chorus, "Hosanna to the Son of David." In response to these things, the religious rulers "became indignant" (21:15). Here's a great example of *unrighteous* indignation, in direct contrast to Jesus' perfectly justified anger. What made those religious leaders so upset? Shouldn't they have been rejoicing? The blind saw, the lame walked, children sang praises, and the temple had been restored to a place of prayer! Why were the leaders so incensed?

They may have been thinking of the piles of money they were losing because of Jesus' actions. Maybe they were feeling embarrassed that He quoted Scripture that exposed them—and their racketeering—for what they really were. Perhaps they were thinking the people and the children should actually be singing praises about them! In fact, their sharpest criticism toward Jesus resulted from the children's song praising Jesus as the "Son of David." Jesus rebuked them by paraphrasing a line from Psalm 8:2: "Out of the mouth of infants and nursing babies You have prepared praise for Yourself" (Matt. 21:16).

This scene reminds us that Jesus was not the kind of Messiah those scholars and priests were looking for. They had no interest in personal righteousness; they were concerned only with political power. They had no time for national repentance; they were looking only for military might. They weren't longing for peace, justice, and mercy; they cared only about their own economic prosperity. If the Messiah came for anything other than their own personal gain, they weren't interested.

Jesus could have stood there and debated the priests and scribes for hours. Instead, He let Scripture have the last word. Having made His point that things weren't right with the religious and political heart of the nation of Israel, Jesus departed the way He had come and returned to Bethany (21:17).

— 21:18-22 —

The following morning, as Jesus was returning to Jerusalem, He longed for a snack from a roadside fig tree. Instead of finding edible fruit, He found the tree to be a disappointment: It had only leaves. On the surface, Jesus' extreme response may look like the impulsive action of a

A **fig tree**, perhaps similar to the one cursed by Jesus en route to Jerusalem

petulant child: "He said to it, 'No longer shall there ever be any fruit from you'" (21:18-19). But as we think about the scene in its context and recall Jesus' typical practice of teaching His disciples through illustrations and parables, we realize the great significance of His cursing the barren fig tree.

The fruitless fig tree was an illustration of the spiritual barrenness of the leaders of Israel. Having seen hypocrisy on parade the day before, Jesus pointed to the fig tree as a symbol of the tragedy of a life filled only with leaves—a life that appears to be healthy from a distance but proves to be fruitless upon closer examination. The fact that the tree immediately withered in response to Jesus' curse illustrates both the certainty and the suddenness with which God's judgment will befall those who don a false reputation of righteousness but lack true spiritual life. This act of Jesus may have reminded the disciples of the words of the prophet Micah:

> Woe is me! For I am
> Like the fruit pickers, like the grape gatherers.
> There is not a cluster of grapes to eat,
> Or a first-ripe fig which I crave.
> The godly person has perished from the land,
> And there is no upright person among men.
> All of them lie in wait for bloodshed;
> Each of them hunts the other with a net.

> Concerning evil, both hands do it well.
> The prince asks, also the judge, for a bribe,
> And a great man speaks the desire of his soul;
> So they weave it together.
> The best of them is like a briar,
> The most upright like a thorn hedge.
> The day when you post your watchmen,
> Your punishment will come.
> Then their confusion will occur. (Mic. 7:1-4)

We know that about forty years later, in the long shadow of Israel's unrepentant wickedness and refusal to accept Jesus as their King, the long-awaited Messiah, the Roman army would lay siege to Jerusalem and destroy the beautiful temple mount, casting its stones into the valley. Perhaps Jesus had one eye on the temple mount in the distance when He noted that those who have faith without doubt could not only curse a fig tree for its fruitlessness but also command a mountain to be rooted up and cast into the sea (Matt. 21:21). In any case, this hyperbolic (exaggerated) language was meant to paint a vivid picture of the power of faith. Jesus, as the incarnate God-man, is the only One who has the kind of infinite knowledge, wisdom, trust, and power to accomplish such an astonishing feat. Nevertheless, as the disciples learned to trust Him and to pray according to His will by the power of the Spirit, they, too, would find themselves figuratively "moving mountains."

The promise in 21:22 shouldn't be taken out of the context of the teaching in the Bible as a whole concerning faith, prayer, and the plan and purpose of God. The apostle John—who himself had been present when Jesus cursed the fig tree and uttered His promise about prayer—provides a clarifying perspective on the confidence we have in God answering our requests. Some sixty years after this event, John would write, "This is the confidence which we have before Him, that, if we ask anything according to His will, He hears us" (1 Jn. 5:14).

Where does a knowledge of God's will come from, so we know that what we pray will be answered? Colossians 1:9 gives us a hint: "We have not ceased to pray for you and to ask that you may be filled with the knowledge of His will in all spiritual wisdom and understanding." Such knowledge of God's will is a work of divine wisdom, which necessarily comes from the Spirit. As we learn and live the Spirit-breathed Word of God (2 Tim. 3:16), we will be equipped to pray according to His will.

APPLICATION: MATTHEW 21:12-22
Confidence to Act with Courage

Jesus wasn't afraid to act with courage and express angry displeasure with wickedness when the situation warranted it. He was completely confident that His actions were just and that they would bring about the intended effect. Yes, turning over the tables and driving out the buyers and sellers from the outer court of the temple attracted the ire of the scoundrels who stood to lose money. But that didn't dissuade the Lord from taking back His Father's house for its proper use.

When it comes to expressing anger, perhaps you find yourself at one of two extremes. At one extreme are those who exhibit anger either excessively or over matters where anger is unjustified. Do you get angry and throw a fit for illegitimate reasons? Is your rage out of control? Do little things set you off? That kind of anger is inappropriate, unfruitful, and sinful. Get control of yourself and seek the power of the Spirit to exhibit peace, patience, kindness, gentleness, and self-control. If you need outside help, such as counseling, get it. There is a kind of anger that's cowardly, not courageous—especially the kind of anger that manifests itself in verbal or physical abuse.

On the other extreme are those who back down in the face of true injustice. Do you stay silent when you see somebody being mistreated? Do you look the other way when you see wickedness? Do you try to make peace when the situation calls for intervention? Though we shouldn't seek conflict and controversy for its own sake, Jesus' example proves that sometimes it's necessary to step up and step in for the sake of truth and justice.

I've heard people say that Christians should never be angry. Clearly, this is incorrect. There are times when I would say that something's wrong with you if you don't feel anger. Don't be afraid of anger—just make sure it's for the right reason, expressed in the right way, at the right time. Again I point you to Paul's words: "Be angry, and yet do not sin" (Eph. 4:26). Passivity and neutrality aren't always the right stances. At times, the circumstances require you to size up a situation, determine that wrong is being done, and decide to act with confidence and courage.

Slugging It Out with Caustic Critics
MATTHEW 21:23-46

NASB

23 When He entered the temple, the chief priests and the elders of the people came to Him while He was teaching, and said, "By what authority are You doing these things, and who gave You this authority?" 24 Jesus said to them, "I will also ask you one ªthing, which if you tell Me, I will also tell you by what authority I do these things. 25 The baptism of John was from what *source,* from heaven or from men?" And they *began* reasoning among themselves, saying, "If we say, 'From heaven,' He will say to us, 'Then why did you not believe him?' 26 But if we say, 'From men,' we fear the ªpeople; for they all regard John as a prophet." 27 And answering Jesus, they said, "We do not know." He also said to them, "Neither will I tell you by what authority I do these things.

28 "But what do you think? A man had two ªsons, and he came to the first and said, 'ᵇSon, go work today in the vineyard.' 29 And he answered, 'I will not'; but afterward he regretted it and went. 30 The man came to the second and said the same thing; and he answered, 'I *will,* sir'; but he did not go. 31 Which of the two did the will of his father?" They said, "The first." Jesus said to them, "Truly I say to you that the tax collectors and prostitutes ªwill get into the kingdom of God before you. 32 For John came to you in the way of righteousness and you did not believe him; but the tax collectors and prostitutes did believe him; and you, seeing *this,* did not even feel remorse afterward so as to believe him.

33 "Listen to another parable. There

NLT

23 When Jesus returned to the Temple and began teaching, the leading priests and elders came up to him. They demanded, "By what authority are you doing all these things? Who gave you the right?"

24 "I'll tell you by what authority I do these things if you answer one question," Jesus replied. 25 "Did John's authority to baptize come from heaven, or was it merely human?"

They talked it over among themselves. "If we say it was from heaven, he will ask us why we didn't believe John. 26 But if we say it was merely human, we'll be mobbed because the people believe John was a prophet." 27 So they finally replied, "We don't know."

And Jesus responded, "Then I won't tell you by what authority I do these things.

28 "But what do you think about this? A man with two sons told the older boy, 'Son, go out and work in the vineyard today.' 29 The son answered, 'No, I won't go,' but later he changed his mind and went anyway. 30 Then the father told the other son, 'You go,' and he said, 'Yes, sir, I will.' But he didn't go.

31 "Which of the two obeyed his father?"

They replied, "The first."*

Then Jesus explained his meaning: "I tell you the truth, corrupt tax collectors and prostitutes will get into the Kingdom of God before you do. 32 For John the Baptist came and showed you the right way to live, but you didn't believe him, while tax collectors and prostitutes did. And even when you saw this happening, you refused to believe him and repent of your sins.

33 "Now listen to another story. A

was a ªlandowner who PLANTED A VINEYARD AND PUT A WALL AROUND IT AND DUG A WINE PRESS IN IT, AND BUILT A TOWER, and rented it out to ᵇvine-growers and went on a journey. ³⁴When the ªharvest time approached, he sent his slaves to the vine-growers to receive his produce. ³⁵The vine-growers took his slaves and beat one, and killed another, and stoned a third. ³⁶Again he sent another group of slaves larger than the first; and they did the same thing to them. ³⁷But afterward he sent his son to them, saying, 'They will respect my son.' ³⁸But when the vine-growers saw the son, they said among themselves, 'This is the heir; come, let us kill him and seize his inheritance.' ³⁹They took him, and threw him out of the vineyard and killed him. ⁴⁰Therefore when the ªowner of the vineyard comes, what will he do to those vine-growers?" ⁴¹They said to Him, "He will bring those wretches to a wretched end, and will rent out the vineyard to other vine-growers who will pay him the proceeds at the *proper* seasons." ⁴²Jesus said to them, "Did you never read in the Scriptures,

'THE STONE WHICH THE BUILDERS
  REJECTED,
THIS BECAME THE CHIEF CORNER
  stone;
THIS CAME ABOUT FROM THE
  LORD,
AND IT IS MARVELOUS IN OUR
  EYES'?

⁴³Therefore I say to you, the kingdom of God will be taken away from you and given to a ªpeople, producing the fruit of it. ⁴⁴And he who falls on this stone will be broken to pieces; but on whomever it falls, it will scatter him like dust."

⁴⁵When the chief priests and the Pharisees heard His parables, they understood that He was speaking

certain landowner planted a vineyard, built a wall around it, dug a pit for pressing out the grape juice, and built a lookout tower. Then he leased the vineyard to tenant farmers and moved to another country. ³⁴At the time of the grape harvest, he sent his servants to collect his share of the crop. ³⁵But the farmers grabbed his servants, beat one, killed one, and stoned another. ³⁶So the landowner sent a larger group of his servants to collect for him, but the results were the same.

³⁷"Finally, the owner sent his son, thinking, 'Surely they will respect my son.'

³⁸"But when the tenant farmers saw his son coming, they said to one another, 'Here comes the heir to this estate. Come on, let's kill him and get the estate for ourselves!' ³⁹So they grabbed him, dragged him out of the vineyard, and murdered him.

⁴⁰"When the owner of the vineyard returns," Jesus asked, "what do you think he will do to those farmers?"

⁴¹The religious leaders replied, "He will put the wicked men to a horrible death and lease the vineyard to others who will give him his share of the crop after each harvest."

⁴²Then Jesus asked them, "Didn't you ever read this in the Scriptures?

'The stone that the builders
  rejected
has now become the
  cornerstone.
This is the LORD's doing,
  and it is wonderful to see.'*

⁴³I tell you, the Kingdom of God will be taken away from you and given to a nation that will produce the proper fruit. ⁴⁴Anyone who stumbles over that stone will be broken to pieces, and it will crush anyone it falls on.*"

⁴⁵When the leading priests and Pharisees heard this parable, they realized he was telling the story

NASB

about them. ⁴⁶When they sought to seize Him, they feared the ᵃpeople, because they considered Him to be a prophet.

21:24 ᵃLit *word*   **21:26** ᵃLit *crowd*   **21:28** ᵃLit *children*   ᵇLit *Child*   **21:31** ᵃLit *are getting into*   **21:33** ᵃLit *a man, head of a household*   ᵇOr *tenant farmers*, also vv 34, 35, 38, 40   **21:34** ᵃLit *the fruit season*   **21:40** ᵃLit *lord*   **21:43** ᵃLit *nation*   **21:46** ᵃLit *crowds*

NLT

against them—they were the wicked farmers. ⁴⁶They wanted to arrest him, but they were afraid of the crowds, who considered Jesus to be a prophet.

21:29-31 Other manuscripts read *"The second."* In still other manuscripts the first son says "Yes" but does nothing, the second son says "No" but then repents and goes, and the answer to Jesus' question is that the second son obeyed his father.   **21:42** Ps 118:22-23.   **21:44** This verse is not included in some early manuscripts. Compare Luke 20:18.

The slugfest continued. In this final week of Jesus' earthly life and ministry, we see the religious leaders intensifying their criticisms. They moved into attack mode. A spirit of hostility replaced passive-aggressive confrontations, murmuring among the crowds, and plotting in the shadows. Judgmental statements that were once voiced as mere questions turned into harsh demands and public put-downs. It's obvious that the leaders' hatred of Jesus was growing with each encounter.

Rather than backing away and fleeing to His own turf in Galilee, Jesus "took off the gloves" and threw some strongly stated verbal punches. Typically, He did this in the form of stories called parables. These parables were meant to penetrate the thick armor of His opponents' hypocrisy, exposing the evil of the scribes, Pharisees, and priests. Though the religious leaders appeared to have the upper hand politically, Jesus stood His ground, refusing to budge an inch before their belligerence.

Speaking with great courage, Jesus stood toe to toe with His opponents and silenced them with strong words. As the verbal blows hit their mark, the leaders' rage toward Him reached a fevered pitch. By the time the dust began to settle after the next skirmish, they were trying to find a way to arrest Him (21:46). However, their fear of public disapproval and the potential for rioting crowds kept Jesus safe . . . for the time being.

Clearly, an intensifying battle was underway. It was getting ugly, and it was heading toward a climax.

— 21:23-27 —

The day after Jesus' controversial Triumphal Entry, He returned to the temple to teach the crowds that had gathered there. This time, though, "the chief priests and the elders of the people" were ready to pounce

(21:23). In their minds, Jesus had invaded their territory, and they were going to nail Him for it. As would be expected from men who cared only about their own religious, political, and social power, their first hostile question was related to authority, as they essentially asked, "Who do You think You are?" They wanted to know what kind of authority He thought He had to drive out the money changers and vendors.

We, as the readers, know the answer to this question. Jesus was acting with divine authority because He is the incarnate God-man. Besides that, He is the King, Israel's long-awaited Messiah. But the conniving leaders of the Jews weren't really interested in the truth. They were trying to trap Jesus into saying something that would firm up official opposition to Him or even draw the ire of the Romans. Getting Jesus to claim divine authority or kingship would do both.

Jesus wasn't having any of that. Drawing on a classic move in rabbinical debate, Jesus "answered" their question with a related question (21:24).[80] Yet it wasn't merely a bit of verbal swordplay. The answer to the question about the status of John the Baptizer—"The baptism of John was from what source, from heaven or from men?" (21:25)—was directly relevant to the Jewish leaders' question about Jesus' authority. Because John had pointed to the One after him, who would be greater than he (3:11-12), their answer to that question would answer their own.

Immediately the scheming minds of the critics began to whirl. If they answered, "From heaven," Jesus would call them out for rejecting John's message and failing to become John's followers—and ultimately followers of Jesus! But if they answered, "From men," their attempt to turn the mob against Jesus would backfire, because the masses regarded John as a heaven-sent prophet (21:25-26). So, weighing two bad options, they chose neither. Instead, they played stupid and said, "We do not know" (21:27).

Naturally, Jesus then refused to answer their question about His own authority. He knew their wicked motives. If He announced outright that His authority had come from God, He would be playing right into their hands. Jesus never lied, but neither did He feel compelled to answer every inquiry or meet everybody's expectations. He was in control of the timing of things, and this week would unfold according to His plan, not according to the plans of others. Thursday night was rapidly approaching, when He would be betrayed into the hands of the wicked men bent on His destruction, but until then, He would skillfully dodge their attempts at entrapment.

— 21:28-32 —

Jesus could have left it at that, but He didn't. He had His opponents on the defensive. Their mouths had been stopped; Jesus had forced them to feign ignorance about the authority of John the Baptizer. They were red-faced with embarrassment and anger. Like a boxer, Jesus had them on the ropes. The two stories that follow are like a one-two punch that continued to inflict damage on the Jewish leaders' egos.

The first story concerns two unnamed sons we'll call "I Won't" and "I Will." The scene is simple. Their father sent both of them into his vineyard to work. "I Won't" defiantly refused to work but felt bad and went to the vineyard as he had been told. "I Will" compliantly agreed to work but then failed to follow through on his commitment (21:28-30). Turning to His critics, Jesus asked them which son actually obeyed his father.

It was a simple, straightforward question, seemingly harmless to answer. Previously, when Jesus had thrown a fastball straight across home plate with the question regarding John the Baptizer, the Jewish leaders had failed to swing and had struck out. This time, when Jesus placed the ball on a tee, they didn't hesitate in trying to redeem themselves by answering. They weren't going to play stupid for such a simple and harmless multiple-choice question. They answered, "The first" (21:31)—the son who had promised nothing but fulfilled everything served his father obediently.

But then Jesus snatched up the ball and tagged them out. The father in the story clearly represented God the Father. The first son, "I Won't," represented the nonreligious, openly sinful tax collectors and prostitutes—the worst of the worst in the minds of religious Jews. These men and women heard John the Baptizer's message and defiantly turned away from it, but then, after thinking it over, they believed and repented. Meanwhile, the "I Will" son reflected those who appear obedient and faithful on the outside but prove to be wicked and disobedient. Specifically, he represented Israel's religious leaders who *professed* to believe, but who, deep within, didn't. Jesus declared that those deemed "sinners" by the religious authorities would enter the kingdom of God before them. Ouch! Jesus pulled no punches in this straightforward rebuke of His devious critics. If the religious leaders hadn't gotten the veiled references to their wickedness in His earlier parables, they certainly did now. Jesus directly pointed His finger at them and replayed their own rejection of John the Baptizer (21:32).

— 21:33-46 —

Jesus' sharp denouncement left the religious leaders reeling, stunned that He would publicly call them out and accuse them of faithlessness and disobedience. But Jesus wasn't finished with them yet. He followed the first jab with a second, taking a swing at them with a parable that outlines the big picture of God's offer of salvation (21:33-41). In this second story, the landowner of the vineyard represents God the Father. The vineyard is God's people, Israel—the nation He loves. Those taking care of the vineyard and farming the land are Israel's past and present leaders. As the story unfolds, the landowner takes a long journey, leaving the care of the vineyard in the hands of the custodians—the leaders of Israel (21:33). As harvest time approaches, the owner sends slaves—representing the Old Testament prophets—to make the collection, but the workers reject, mistreat, and kill them (21:34-36). So far, the story line closely follows the history of Israel as presented in the Old Testament and could even include what happened to John the Baptizer.

Finally, the owner sends his son—representing Jesus Himself—to whom total respect is owed. In a shocking act of defiance and rebellion, the farmers reject, mistreat, drag away, and brutally murder the son, hoping to leave the landowner without an heir, thus plotting to take over the vineyard for themselves (21:37-39). At this point, Jesus asked His listeners a crucial question: What would be the right response of the owner when he returns to his vineyard (21:40)?

Those present responded by pronouncing the just judgment on the rebellious workers in the vineyard: "Bring those wretches to a wretched end" (21:41). Those workers should be replaced by others who will faithfully farm the land and pay the owner what is rightfully his. In answering this way, though, Jesus' listeners had no idea they were announcing the just judgment on themselves for rejecting, mistreating, and soon condemning and killing the Son of God! Jesus knew they had murder in their hearts, but they were so blinded by their own sin that they failed to see they were on the wrong side of redemptive history.

In the last few verses of Matthew 21, Jesus lands the knockout punch. Seeing that He had them pinned in self-condemnation, He quoted Psalm 118 and called down the full force of the Word of God against them (Matt. 21:42):

> The stone which the builders rejected
> Has become the chief corner stone.
> This is the LORD's doing;
> It is marvelous in our eyes. (Ps. 118:22-23)

You may recall that some lines from Psalm 118 had already appeared in Matthew's account of the Holy Week. The crowd's "Hosanna" acclamation, including the words "Blessed is He who comes in the name of the Lord" (Matt. 21:9), came from Psalm 118:25-26. Just as Jesus had earlier accepted the application of that psalm to Himself, now He applied this part of the psalm to Himself as a testimony against His detractors and critics. The pertinent passage refers to the "stone which the builders rejected," which is now clearly understood as a reference to Christ. As a result of this rejection, the kingdom would be taken from Jesus' opponents and given to His true disciples—that ragtag bunch of relative nobodies, converted sinners, and, eventually, even clueless Gentiles—who would produce fruit fit for it (Matt. 21:43). Those who thumbed their noses at the Messiah would fall on the stone or be crushed by it, break to pieces, and be scattered like dust (21:44)—probably a reference to the judgment and scattering of the nation of Israel that would come about in the aftermath of the Jewish revolt of AD 66–70.

The message hit its target with full force. Up until that moment, the chief priests and Pharisees had been oblivious as to where they fit in Jesus' parables. After the one-two punch delivered in the stories of the two sons and the unfaithful tenants, Jesus got their attention. They now understood that He had been speaking about them (21:45). Though they fumed in rage, they could do nothing to Jesus in that public forum of the temple court. Because the people (rightly) believed that Jesus was a genuine prophet, the Jewish leaders feared openly arresting Him (21:46). They would have to wait for a more opportune moment.

APPLICATION: MATTHEW 21:23-46

Getting off Our Ringside Seats

As the battle begins to heat up between Jesus and the religious leaders who had a stranglehold on the people and institutions of Jerusalem, the disciples seem to recede into the background. And the crowd of exuberant followers seems to take a few steps back. Jesus and His detractors take center stage, like spotlighted contenders in a fight. In the midst of the verbal sparring, what was going through the minds of the onlookers—those who had ringside seats to the match? Were there brave supporters of Jesus cheering Him on when He scored polemical points against His opponents? Did the priests and Pharisees have their own disciples keeping score and feeding them advice from the sidelines? Did supporters of either side flip-flop as the debate intensified?

Today, when we hear people casting aspersions on Christ and attempting to bully Christians into silence, how do we respond? Do we sit back like spectators at a fight, waiting to see who lands the most punches and scores the most points? Or do we get off our seats and take sides? Jesus' response to the high priests and Pharisees shows that "turning the other cheek" doesn't apply to encounters with Christ-hating heresy. When the truth of Jesus' person and work is at stake, we, like Jesus, need to take a stand.

We must realize that we're not called to be spectators in the spiritual battles for the gospel but rather are called to "contend earnestly for the faith which was once for all handed down to the saints" (Jude 1:3). If this was true in Jesus' day and in the days of His brother Jude, it's certainly true today. In a post-Christian society increasingly hostile to truth and righteousness, we must be equipped to stand firm in the struggle—a struggle "not against flesh and blood, but against the rulers, against the powers, against the world forces of this darkness, against the spiritual forces of wickedness in the heavenly places" (Eph. 6:12). And we must remember that "the weapons of our warfare are not of the flesh, but divinely powerful for the destruction of fortresses" (2 Cor. 10:4). In God's power—not our own—we can take up the weapons of righteousness to counter falsehood with truth and wickedness with goodness until the King of Glory takes His throne and declares the battle to be over.

A Dialogue with Deceivers
MATTHEW 22:1-22

NASB

¹Jesus spoke to them again in parables, saying, ²"The kingdom of heaven ᵃmay be compared to ᵇa king who ᶜgave a wedding feast for his son. ³And he sent out his slaves to call those who had been invited to the wedding feast, and they were unwilling to come. ⁴Again he sent out other slaves saying, 'Tell those who

NLT

¹Jesus also told them other parables. He said, ²"The Kingdom of Heaven can be illustrated by the story of a king who prepared a great wedding feast for his son. ³When the banquet was ready, he sent his servants to notify those who were invited. But they all refused to come!

⁴"So he sent other servants to tell

have been invited, "Behold, I have prepared my dinner; my oxen and my fattened livestock are *all* butchered and everything is ready; come to the wedding feast.'" ⁵But they paid no attention and went their way, one to his own ᵃfarm, another to his business, ⁶and the rest seized his slaves and mistreated them and killed them. ⁷But the king was enraged, and he sent his armies and destroyed those murderers and set their city on fire. ⁸Then he said to his slaves, 'The wedding is ready, but those who were invited were not worthy. ⁹Go therefore to the main highways, and as many as you find *there*, invite to the wedding feast.' ¹⁰Those slaves went out into the streets and gathered together all they found, both evil and good; and the wedding hall was filled with ᵃdinner guests.

¹¹"But when the king came in to look over the dinner guests, he saw a man there who was not dressed in wedding clothes, ¹²and he said to him, 'Friend, how did you come in here without wedding clothes?' And the man was speechless. ¹³Then the king said to the servants, 'Bind him hand and foot, and throw him into the outer darkness; in that place there will be weeping and gnashing of teeth.' ¹⁴For many are ᵃcalled, but few *are* chosen."

¹⁵Then the Pharisees went and ᵃplotted together how they might trap Him ᵇin what He said. ¹⁶And they sent their disciples to Him, along with the Herodians, saying, "Teacher, we know that You are truthful and teach the way of God in truth, and ᵃdefer to no one; for You are not partial to any. ¹⁷Tell us then, what do You think? Is it ᵃlawful to give a poll-tax to Caesar, or not?" ¹⁸But Jesus perceived their ᵃmalice, and said, "Why are you testing Me, you hypocrites? ¹⁹Show Me the coin *used* for the poll-tax." And they

them, 'The feast has been prepared. The bulls and fattened cattle have been killed, and everything is ready. Come to the banquet!' ⁵But the guests he had invited ignored them and went their own way, one to his farm, another to his business. ⁶Others seized his messengers and insulted them and killed them.

⁷"The king was furious, and he sent out his army to destroy the murderers and burn their town. ⁸And he said to his servants, 'The wedding feast is ready, and the guests I invited aren't worthy of the honor. ⁹Now go out to the street corners and invite everyone you see.' ¹⁰So the servants brought in everyone they could find, good and bad alike, and the banquet hall was filled with guests.

¹¹"But when the king came in to meet the guests, he noticed a man who wasn't wearing the proper clothes for a wedding. ¹²'Friend,' he asked, 'how is it that you are here without wedding clothes?' But the man had no reply. ¹³Then the king said to his aides, 'Bind his hands and feet and throw him into the outer darkness, where there will be weeping and gnashing of teeth.'

¹⁴"For many are called, but few are chosen."

¹⁵Then the Pharisees met together to plot how to trap Jesus into saying something for which he could be arrested. ¹⁶They sent some of their disciples, along with the supporters of Herod, to meet with him. "Teacher," they said, "we know how honest you are. You teach the way of God truthfully. You are impartial and don't play favorites. ¹⁷Now tell us what you think about this: Is it right to pay taxes to Caesar or not?"

¹⁸But Jesus knew their evil motives. "You hypocrites!" he said. "Why are you trying to trap me? ¹⁹Here, show me the coin used for the tax." When they handed him a

brought Him a ªdenarius. ²⁰And He said to them, "Whose likeness and inscription is this?" ²¹They said to Him, "Caesar's." Then He said to them, "Then render to Caesar the things that are Caesar's; and to God the things that are God's." ²²And hearing *this*, they were amazed, and leaving Him, they went away.

22:2 ªLit *was compared to* ᵇLit *a man, a king* ᶜLit *made* 22:5 ªOr *field* 22:10 ªLit *those reclining* at the table 22:14 ªOr *invited* 22:15 ªLit *took counsel* ᵇLit *in word* 22:16 ªLit *it is not a concern to You about anyone;* i.e. You do not seek anyone's favor 22:17 ªOr *permissible* 22:18 ªOr *wickedness* 22:19 ªThe denarius was a day's wages

Roman coin,* ²⁰he asked, "Whose picture and title are stamped on it?"

²¹"Caesar's," they replied.

"Well, then," he said, "give to Caesar what belongs to Caesar, and give to God what belongs to God."

²²His reply amazed them, and they went away.

22:19 Greek *a denarius.*

Cloaked in deception, the Pharisees who hounded Jesus throughout His public ministry put on the outward appearance of morality while plotting to catch Him in a trap. While donning self-woven garments of righteousness, they tried to cast Jesus as a villain before both the common people and the religious and political establishment. If they could find a weak spot in Jesus' armor, they would lunge their dagger of deceit swiftly and mercilessly. Now that Jesus and His disciples were in Jerusalem for Passover, the Pharisees were on the prowl, sizing up their opponent, poking and prodding Him, trying to find that vulnerable place to strike.

Jesus knew exactly what they were up to. He saw through all their deception. Their ornate robes of religion didn't impress Him, and nothing they said or did fooled Him. Maybe they could get away with deceiving the crowds into believing they were truly pious inside and out, but Jesus knew they were masters of hypocrisy with murder on their minds. And though Jesus was treading on their home turf, He wasn't about to make a single misstep. Nor would He allow them to advance even one step in their desperate plot to snare Him by His words and actions. Instead, Jesus shifted into an aggressive mode, going on the offensive.

During that final week of His earthly ministry, Jesus' parables took on a sharp edge—pointed and penetrating. They cut through the hypocrisy of the religious elite. We've already seen two of those stories: the Parable of the Two Sons (21:28-32) and the Parable of the Wicked Vine-Growers (21:33-41). Upon hearing these stories, the chief priests and Pharisees "understood that He was speaking about them" (21:45). When Jesus told another parable—the story of the wedding feast and the unfit guests—the

Jewish leaders launched what they thought was a subtle counterattack to make Jesus discredit Himself by His own words. But their smooth talk and hypocritical approach couldn't fool Him for a second.

— 22:1-10 —

In His next parable, Jesus likened the invitation to the kingdom of heaven to being invited to a king's wedding feast held for his son (22:1-2). As is the case today, the people invited to a royal wedding would have included wealthy and influential dignitaries—political, social, and religious leaders of high standing. This would have been a VIP-only kind of event. However, in Jesus' telling of the story, the invitees snubbed the king, refusing to come even when personally invited several times (22:3-4). Some of those who refused to attend the wedding feast were indifferent, determined to go their own way (22:5). Others, however, were so belligerent that they attacked the messengers and killed them (22:6)!

The cast of characters reflected in this parable is easy to identify. The king represents God; the son stands for Jesus. The elite who were invited to the banquet presumably represent the Jewish leaders. The invitation includes the various ways that God had already called the elite to discipleship in the kingdom of God. John the Baptizer had extended the invitation to repent and believe. Jesus and His disciples had been beckoning them to come. Besides this, the Old Testament prophets had foretold of the Messiah, His miracles, and His mission. And the amazing signs and wonders performed through the Holy Spirit should have sealed the deal for anybody with eyes to see and ears to hear. However, the scribes, Pharisees, priests, and other leaders of the Jews either rudely ignored these invitations or actively attacked those who extended them.

In 22:7, Jesus described the angry response of the king. The Greek word translated "enraged" is a form of *orgizō* [3710], from the same root as the word for "wrath" (*orgē* [3709]). Though the king was eminently patient and gracious in his repeated attempts at urging his high-ranking subjects to attend the feast, his patience had a limit. When the response to his messengers turned violent, the king's patience gave way to justice—giving people what they deserved. The image of the king's armies destroying the city of the treasonous murderers was a prophetic allusion to the destruction of Jerusalem, which would occur in AD 70. Because of the repeated rejections by the Jewish leaders of God's gracious invitation to the kingdom, judgment was sure to come.

Because the first slate of names on the guest list proved unworthy

(22:8), the king broadened the invitation to include *everyone*—"both evil and good"—from the main highways and streets (22:9-10). In the interpretation of the parable, the recipients of this new broadcasted invitation certainly would have included the general population of Jews, regardless of social standing or perceived piety. However, it also would have included Gentiles who responded to the proclamation of the gospel of salvation by grace alone through faith alone in Christ alone. In his letter to the Romans, the apostle Paul alluded to this gracious opportunity for salvation that came because of the hardness of heart exhibited by the Jews: "By their transgression salvation has come to the Gentiles" (Rom. 11:11). In Matthew 22:9-10, then, we have an early reference to what has become known as the Great Commission, in which Jesus sent out His disciples to "make disciples of all the nations" (28:19). When the invitation was offered to Israel's leadership, they refused to accept it. But when God extended the invitation to all people everywhere, the banquet hall was filled with guests (22:10).

— 22:11-14 —

Jesus then took the opportunity, in connection with this parable, to teach an important lesson about the basis for acceptance into the kingdom of heaven. We've already seen that God is no respecter of social, economic, political, or religious status. The invitation is for anybody. However, when the king in the story examines the wedding guests, he finds an intruder "not dressed in wedding clothes" (22:11). If the banquet is a symbol of salvation—feasting in the Lord's presence—then the only garment appropriate for the feast is the righteousness of God that comes by grace through faith. If only a clean, pure robe is acceptable, then only the cleansing that comes through the shed blood of Christ can produce the attire that passes the test. One commentator notes, "The soiled garments of this guest were an insult to the host, especially since in God's grace the wedding garment is provided. For God clothes the redeemed (see Isa. 61:10; Zech. 3:1-4; Rev. 3:4-5, 18). God rejects those who try to enter the Kingdom without doing the will of the King."[81]

This is what theologians call the doctrine of imputed righteousness. One simple explanation of this doctrine states, "In salvation, our sin and guilt are credited to Christ, and His righteousness is credited to us."[82] The anonymous second-century writing *Letter to Diognetus* beautifully articulates this classic Christian teaching concerning the work of Christ for us:

> He himself gave his own son, a ransom on our behalf, the Holy
> for the lawless, the innocent for the guilty, the righteous for the

unrighteous, the incorruptible for the corruptible, the immortal for the mortal. For what else than that one's righteousness could cover up our sin? In who else than in the Son of God alone could our lawlessness and ungodliness possibly be justified? Oh, the sweet exchange! Oh, the fathomless creation! Oh, the unexpected benefits that the lawlessness of many should be concealed in the one righteous, and righteousness of the one should justify many lawless.[83]

In the original context of Jesus' parable, the one confronted by the king for not being dressed in proper wedding clothes corresponds to the Pharisees who had dressed themselves in their own works righteousness rather than in the righteousness of heaven given as a gift by Jesus Christ. They would have done well to recall the words of Isaiah the prophet: "For all of us have become like one who is unclean, and all our righteous deeds are like a filthy garment; and all of us wither like a leaf, and our iniquities, like the wind, take us away" (Isa. 64:6). Since Old Testament times, the offer of cleansing had been made known to any who would turn to God in repentance and faith: "'Come now, and let us reason together,' says the LORD, 'though your sins are as scarlet, they will be as white as snow; though they are red like crimson, they will be like wool'" (Isa. 1:18).

Because the unrighteous guest has no wedding clothes, he is excluded from the feast. This represents eternal separation from God, where there will be "weeping and gnashing of teeth" (Matt. 22:13). God freely offers forgiveness and eternal salvation to all, but only those who accept His invitation by grace alone through faith alone in Christ alone will be able to enter. In 22:14, a sobering message concludes Jesus' parable: "Many are called, but few are chosen." In this context, the "called" are the countless men and women of all backgrounds invited to the feast. The invitation of the gospel of salvation is broadcast to everybody without distinction. However, though all are invited, only some—the "chosen"—accept the gift of salvation and are clothed in the righteousness of Christ.

— 22:15-17 —

We shouldn't think for a second that the Pharisees missed the point. They recognized their place in the parable. They were those who rejected the king's invitation to the son's feast . . . and they were going to pay dearly for it. They were those who showed up without proper clothing for the wedding celebration . . . and they were going to be cast into outer darkness. But instead of responding to Christ's severe warning, the Pharisees proceeded with their deceptive plot to take down the One pointing the finger.

In 22:15-16, we see the trap being set. Notice that the Pharisees' motive was entirely deceptive and wicked: They "plotted together" to "trap Him" in His words. What followed wasn't a sincere question they were aching to have answered. They wanted Jesus to say something that would either anger the crowd or catch the attention of the Roman authorities. Also notice that the Pharisees themselves remained in the background. Instead of confronting Jesus themselves (which hadn't worked up to this point), they sent "their disciples" as well as "the Herodians."

This is the only time the Herodians are mentioned in Matthew's Gospel. The Herodians were a group of Jews loyal to Herod's family—specifically, Herod Antipas—and thus in support of the Roman occupation and control over Judea. As such, they would have been in support of Rome's right to exact taxes from the Jewish people. The disciples of the Pharisees, however, would have been opposed to Roman interference in the affairs of the Jews, God's chosen people. Here we have the unprecedented alliance of liberal and conservative, secular and religious—working side by side to snare Jesus in a diabolical trap.

The question these two groups posed to Jesus dripped with hypocritical flattery. They feigned respect for Jesus, calling Him "teacher" and pretending to honor His opinion as truthful, wise, and impartial. Then, imagining that Jesus would respond to their fawning by inserting His head into their noose, they tugged on the line by asking a question they thought would trap Jesus in an inescapable dilemma: "Is it lawful to give a poll-tax to Caesar, or not?" (22:17).

The question was admittedly clever and would have tripped up somebody who wasn't on guard. The term "lawful" here means "permissible"—that is, appropriate within Jewish Law. The tax in question was a tribute first imposed on the Jews by the Romans a few years after the death of Herod the Great. The poll-tax, which was based on a population census, was a constant reminder that Judea and the Jewish people were under the sovereign control of the emperor. This tax created a dilemma: By paying it, one obeyed Roman law but admitted subjection to a godless foreign power, but by refusing to pay it, one became a rebel in the eyes of Rome, subject to punishment.

Because the question was so controversial, it appeared to be a no-win for Jesus. A yes answer (pay the tax) would put Him on the side of the secular Herodians in favor of continued Roman oppression. Wasn't Jesus supposed to be the rightful King of the Jews? A no answer (don't pay the tax) would have landed Him squarely on the side of the masses, confirming the unspoken nationalistic sentiment simmering below the surface. But did Jesus want to become the voice of a movement that would lead to insurrection?

— 22:18-22 —

Jesus knew exactly what they were up to. He "perceived their malice" and confronted them directly: "Why are you testing Me, you hypocrites?" (22:18). While the Pharisees and Herodians dealt in deception and subtleties, Jesus hit them head-on. He wasn't about to step into their trap. Instead, He dismantled their argument with a clever show-and-tell presentation. He asked for somebody to show Him the coin used to pay the poll-tax (22:19). This coin, minted by the Romans, bore the image of Tiberius Caesar, the emperor at the time.

© Classical Numismatic Group, Inc./cngcoins.com

When Jesus was questioned about taxes (22:15-17), He was handed **a Roman coin**. It was likely a coin that looked like this one, bearing the image of Tiberius Caesar, who was the emperor of Rome during Jesus' ministry.

Taking the denarius in His hand, Jesus let the crowd answer the obvious question: "Whose likeness and inscription is this?" (22:20). Even an illiterate child would have known the answer: Caesar's. Then came Jesus' ingenious response that utterly defused the bomb the Pharisees and Herodians had dropped on Him: "Then render to Caesar the things that are Caesar's; and to God the things that are God's" (22:21).

Just as Caesar had minted coins with his likeness on them, God has placed His likeness on us (Gen. 1:26). As His image bearers, all humans owe Him our very selves. Physical, earthly treasures and powers are temporary. Why not give back to Caesar those trinkets of metal that have his image on them? God is much more concerned with what we do with the spiritual, eternal, heavenly dimensions of our lives. To give God the things that are God's means to render to Him our whole being—to "love the LORD your God with all your heart and with all your soul and with all your might" (Deut. 6:5).

Jesus' slimy opponents started the face-off certain they had Him dead to rights. They had thought their cleverly crafted question would be His downfall. How long, I wonder, had they connived to come up with the "poll-tax plot," only to have it thwarted with a flip of a coin and a single sentence? No wonder the deceivers went away amazed (Matt. 22:22). Once again, they had been caught in their own carefully spun web of deception.

APPLICATION: MATTHEW 22:1-22

Two Truths to Counter Deception

In Jesus' parable, and in the dialogue with the deceivers that follows, we see two important and related truths about God we would do well to remember. Keeping these truths front and center in our minds will help us counter the deception of religious phonies and false teachers.

First, *God is sovereign*. Therefore, it's His kingdom and His wedding feast. He sends out the invitations, makes the rules, and chooses the attire. Deceivers like to crash the party, set their own agendas, and clothe themselves in their own righteousness, which is really nothing but filthy rags. But God's sovereign plan of salvation is set according to His own will for the purpose of His own glory. It's a plan of sovereign grace, and He wants none to perish. But we must acknowledge that we are sinful and could never earn a place at His table. We accept the payment for sin—Christ's death in our place. And when we come to Him in simple faith, He takes our ragged garments of sin and replaces them with His own righteousness. That's the only way we can come to the feast.

Second, *God is King*. God isn't an elected official or a disinterested deity. God is King of the universe. We owe Him—and Him alone—our highest allegiance. No other do we worship. Our postmodern, pluralistic society tells us that all gods are simply metaphorical for the sense of the transcendent and all "good" religions are basically the same. This is patently false, for "there is one God, and one mediator also between God and men, the man Christ Jesus" (1 Tim. 2:5). We owe our greatest love, highest honor, and humblest obedience to God, not to a political leader, nation, boss, parent, or even church. Our appropriate respect for and honor toward those other authorities in our lives will only be enhanced by an acknowledgment of God alone as our King. To worship any other person, thing, or idea is idolatry. We must render to God what is God's—our whole selves!

Will We Be Married in the Resurrection?
MATTHEW 22:23-33

NASB

²³On that day *some* Sadducees (who say there is no resurrection) came to Jesus and questioned Him, ²⁴asking, "Teacher, Moses said, 'IF A MAN DIES HAVING NO CHILDREN, HIS BROTHER AS NEXT OF KIN SHALL MARRY HIS WIFE, AND RAISE UP CHILDREN FOR HIS BROTHER.' ²⁵Now there were seven brothers with us; and the first married and died, and having no children left his wife to his brother; ²⁶so also the second, and the third, down to the seventh. ²⁷Last of all, the woman died. ²⁸In the resurrection, therefore, whose wife of the seven will she be? For they all had *married* her."

²⁹But Jesus answered and said to them, "You are mistaken, not ᵃunderstanding the Scriptures nor the power of God. ³⁰For in the resurrection they neither marry nor are given in marriage, but are like angels in heaven. ³¹But regarding the resurrection of the dead, have you not read what was spoken to you by

NLT

²³That same day Jesus was approached by some Sadducees—religious leaders who say there is no resurrection from the dead. They posed this question: ²⁴"Teacher, Moses said, 'If a man dies without children, his brother should marry the widow and have a child who will carry on the brother's name.'* ²⁵Well, suppose there were seven brothers. The oldest one married and then died without children, so his brother married the widow. ²⁶But the second brother also died, and the third brother married her. This continued with all seven of them. ²⁷Last of all, the woman also died. ²⁸So tell us, whose wife will she be in the resurrection? For all seven were married to her."

²⁹Jesus replied, "Your mistake is that you don't know the Scriptures, and you don't know the power of God. ³⁰For when the dead rise, they will neither marry nor be given in marriage. In this respect they will be like the angels in heaven.

³¹"But now, as to whether there will be a resurrection of the dead— haven't you ever read about this in

God: ³²'I AM THE GOD OF ABRAHAM, AND THE GOD OF ISAAC, AND THE GOD OF JACOB'? He is not the God of the dead but of the living." ³³When the crowds heard *this,* they were astonished at His teaching.

22:29 ªOr *knowing*

the Scriptures? Long after Abraham, Isaac, and Jacob had died, God said,* ³²'I am the God of Abraham, the God of Isaac, and the God of Jacob.'* So he is the God of the living, not the dead."

³³When the crowds heard him, they were astounded at his teaching.

22:24 Deut 25:5-6. **22:31** Greek *read about this? God said.* **22:32** Exod 3:6.

Being presently earthbound creatures, our perspective is riveted to the created order outlined in Genesis 1: dirt and stone, water and air, drifting clouds and distant constellations. Experiencing these things day after day, year after year, we can't help but think of all reality in terms of earth, sky, and outer space. It's next to impossible for us to remove ourselves mentally from our earthly existence and really imagine what it would be like to dwell in another realm.

When the subject of the afterlife comes up, it's our natural tendency simply to transfer a picture of our earthbound lifestyle to our notion of heavenly existence. But we need to recognize the vast difference between the temporal life and eternal life, life on earth and life in heaven. For starters, our bodies won't be in their present, mortal condition. Rather, as we learn from the words of Jesus, we will be "like angels in heaven" (Matt. 22:30). But what does that mean? Does it mean we become angels? Or that angels are merely the souls of departed saints? Will we have no bodies? Will we have wings? Will we be neither male nor female? Will we even recognize each other?

As we tap into Jesus' teaching concerning resurrection and eternal life, we need to let Scripture challenge our unbiblical notions of heaven. Though the Bible doesn't answer every question we might have about our eternal home, what God does reveal will dispel a lot of superstitions, fanciful teachings, and outright deceptive doctrines floating around even in Christian circles.

— 22:23-28—

Having just dispensed with a plot of the Pharisees, Jesus had barely caught His breath when a group of Sadducees showed up. The pressure was mounting. Like a desperate military campaign to take a fortified city, Jesus' opponents were coming at Him from every angle with wave after wave of attacks. Little did the Messiah's enemies know that their unrelenting assaults were slamming against an immovable object. No political tricks or theological subtleties would be able to trap the One who could not only see through their devices but could also see into their hearts and minds. So when a small group of Sadducees came to question Jesus about His view on the doctrine of the resurrection, they had no way of knowing what they were up against.

Who were these Sadducees, and what did they believe? Matthew simply tells us that they denied the resurrection (22:23). Although the Hebrew Bible presents some notion of life after death (e.g., Job 14:14; Ps. 17:15) and even of a bodily resurrection (Job 19:26; Isa. 26:19; Dan. 12:2), it includes very few details about such matters. For example, there is virtually nothing about the spiritual existence between physical death and physical resurrection, or about the nature of the resurrection body.

In the centuries between the return of the Jews from Babylon (which began in the sixth century BC) and the birth of Christ, many wild speculations developed concerning the afterlife and resurrection, and some of these found their way into the popular beliefs of both the common people and the religious leaders. By the time of Christ, the Pharisees had developed a rich doctrine of the afterlife, including a bodily resurrection of the saved and unsaved, as well as teachings concerning rewards and punishments. Meanwhile, their theological rivals, the Sadducees, believed that the soul perished with the body and that the concept of resurrection was a myth. Since they accepted only the authority of the books of Moses, they rejected any teachings about the afterlife or resurrection that came from later prophets. They also denied the existence of angels and demons. Because they rejected the notion of life after death, they did not believe in heaven and hell or eternal judgment and rewards. They believed that obedience to God brought blessing in this life and that disobedience brought retribution in the here and now. They were worried far less about losing their eternal souls in heaven than about losing their temporal control of political power. We might compare the Sadducees of Jesus' day to the very secular, theologically liberal clergy of our own day. In the book of Acts, Luke briefly notes the differences between the Sadducees and the Pharisees this way: "The Sadducees say that there is no resurrection, nor an angel, nor a spirit, but the Pharisees acknowledge them all" (Acts 23:8).

On the matters of the conscious existence of the soul after death and the belief in a future bodily resurrection, Jesus and His disciples sided with the Pharisees. And the Sadducees knew it.

Now, even though the Sadducees didn't believe in life after death or the bodily resurrection, in their attempt to make a fool of Jesus, they concocted a far-fetched scenario that included both. Their question began with a paraphrase of a commandment from the Law of Moses, a section of the Hebrew Scriptures that they did accept as canonical: "When brothers live together and one of them dies and has no son, the wife of the deceased shall not be married outside the family to a strange man. Her husband's brother shall go in to her and take her to himself as wife and perform the duty of a husband's brother to her" (Deut. 25:5). So far, so good. But then came the hypothetical test case: What if this woman survived the deaths of seven brothers who each, in turn, had married her to fulfill the Law of Moses? In the afterlife, following the resurrection of the dead, whose wife would she be (Matt. 22:25-28)?

Those self-important, big-city Sadducees probably thought they were dealing with some country bumpkin who would easily be snagged in the twisted, tangled vines of their hypocritical hypothetical. I can picture them snickering with each other after posing that implausible riddle. They weren't sincerely seeking an answer from a respected rabbi. When they addressed Jesus as "teacher," it was just phony flattery. They thought they had harpooned Him with an unsolvable dilemma. All they had to do now was reel Him in and fillet Him before the crowds.

— 22:29-33 —

For a group of elitist snobs used to being feared by the people, Jesus' response—"You're wrong!"—would have come like a slap in the face. Jesus countered them by saying that they did not understand Scripture and that they were ignorant of God's great power (22:29). Jesus saw through their malicious intentions and instantly exposed their absolute ignorance. In the span of a few seconds, the tables turned, and the attacking Sadducees were put on the defensive. They were about to get schooled in Scripture by the One whose Spirit inspired it in the first place.

Like a specialist who can quickly disassemble the most complex machine, Jesus dismantled the trap they had set for Him. Regarding their ignorance, Jesus affirmed three theological truths that contrasted their heretical beliefs (22:30). First, the dead will indeed rise. Jesus simply asserted this as a fundamental theological truth—"in the resurrection . . ." There will be a physical resurrection of our bodies.

The second truth relates to the discontinuity between our present relationships and those in the afterlife. In the new world of resurrection

OUR RESURRECTION BODIES

MATTHEW 22:30

What will the resurrection be like? We know from Scripture that at the resurrection of believers, our earthly bodies, subject to sin, suffering, and death, will be miraculously transformed into perfect, immortal bodies like Christ's resurrection body (1 Cor. 15:51-54; Phil. 3:20-21; 1 Thes. 4:16-17). In our new, glorified state, nobody will be able to hold anything over our heads. We will be perfect and blameless before God (see Jude 1:24).

In 1 Corinthians 15:35-49, the apostle Paul goes into some detail describing the quality of our future resurrection bodies. The following chart summarizes the contrast he sets up between our present bodies and our future resurrection bodies:

PRESENT BODY	RESURRECTION BODY
Perishable	Imperishable
Dishonorable	Glorious
Weak	Powerful
Natural	Spiritual
Earthy	Heavenly

The most important detail to realize about our future resurrection bodies is that they will be "spiritual," not "natural" (1 Cor. 15:44-46). The word translated "natural" is the Greek word *psychikos* [5591], which means "pertaining to being material or physical."[84] It often refers to someone dominated by the desires of the natural person rather than the promptings of the Spirit (e.g., 1 Cor. 2:14; Jas. 3:15). In this "natural" life, we must constantly restrain the desires of the flesh (Rom. 7:14-25). But in our future, resurrected bodies, we'll encounter no temptations. Instead, we'll always be governed by the power of the Holy Spirit and will be able to live as Christ lives—in complete holiness and submission to the Father. By calling the resurrection body "spiritual," Paul wasn't implying that it will be "ghostly" or "immaterial." Remember, we will have resurrection bodies like Christ's (1 Jn. 3:2). We'll be able to do everything He did in His resurrected body (see Luke 24:33-43; John 20:19-29). And we'll be completely free from the weight of earthliness, the gravity of sin, and the downward pull of our fallen condition (Rev. 21:4).

life, there will be no marriage—neither marriages that carry over from the present world nor marriages that take place after the resurrection. This statement essentially sprang the trap set by the Sadducees. The whole basis for their unsolvable riddle was obliterated: In the afterlife, marriage is off! Before we go to extremes on this, though, listen to the clarifying words of Randy Alcorn: "Jesus said the institution of human marriage would end, having fulfilled its purpose. But he never hinted that deep relationships between married people would end. In our lives here, two people can be business partners, tennis partners, or pinochle partners. But when they're no longer partners, it doesn't mean their friendship ends."[85]

The third theological truth relates to the nature of the afterlife. Those who are resurrected will be "like angels in heaven" (22:30). Note that this doesn't say that departed saints will actually *become* angels. This is nowhere taught in the Bible. Rather, there will be something about us that will more closely resemble the angels in heaven than it will our present condition here on earth. The emphasis here seems to be on the idea that angelic beings do not marry. Other attributes of angels we will presumably share: They are ageless, tireless, and deathless, and they delight forever in the worship and service of their Creator.

In the course of His pointed rebuke of the Sadducees' bad theology concerning relationships after the resurrection, Jesus also took the opportunity to correct their unbiblical ideas concerning life after death in general. They had falsely rejected the notion of a conscious existence after death, believing that when our hearts stop, it's essentially "lights out." To counter this first error, Jesus took the Sadducees to a place in Scripture He knew they would accept—the book of Exodus. Remember, Sadducees accepted as inspired and authoritative only the first five books of the Bible, the books of Moses. By citing a Scripture passage from their own narrowly defined canon, Jesus demonstrated that even without the other Old Testament writings, He could make a case for continued existence after death.

The passage Jesus cited was Exodus 3:6, where God said to Moses, "I am the God of your father, the God of Abraham, the God of Isaac, and the God of Jacob." Even though Abraham, Isaac, and Jacob had been physically dead for centuries prior to the generation of Moses, God was still their God, and those patriarchs were still His people. Because God is not the God of the dead but the God of the living, Abraham, Isaac, and Jacob must still exist in an afterlife (Matt. 22:32).

Beyond their continued spiritual existence in the heavenly realm,

God also had a plan to fulfill His earthly promises to those patriarchs—in the physical realm. Here Jesus confronted the Sadducees' second error: rejecting the future physical resurrection. Christ had confirmed that in the coming kingdom "many will come from east and west, and recline at the table with Abraham, Isaac and Jacob" (8:11). God had promised Abraham that He would give the Promised Land "to you and to your descendants forever" (Gen. 13:15). The Sadducees thought the promises about the land applied only to the descendants of Israel, but Jesus took the promises of God literally—they were eternal promises not only to Abraham's descendants, but also to Abraham himself. The only way for God to keep His word, then, would be to resurrect the patriarchs to whom the promises had been given and fulfill those promises in the land.

Of course, regarding the resurrection, Jesus is the key to all of it. He said, "I am the resurrection and the life; he who believes in Me will live even if he dies, and everyone who lives and believes in Me will never die" (John 11:25-26). This statement by Jesus points to the fact that, for believers, eternal life begins in *this* life, and dying physically does not put an end to our conscious existence in the afterlife. Jesus is also the *source* of resurrection life: "An hour is coming, in which all who are in the tombs will hear His voice, and will come forth; those who did the good deeds to a resurrection of life, those who committed the evil deeds to a resurrection of judgment" (John 5:28-29). "Those who did the good deeds" are the saved, who are empowered by the Spirit to do so. "Those who committed the evil deeds" are the unsaved, who are dead in their trespasses and sins (see Eph. 2:1-10).

When Jesus finished His brief but powerful refutation of the Sadducees' errant teaching, the reaction of His detractors and those listening from the crowd was the same as earlier, when He had refuted the Pharisees (Matt. 22:22): They were "astonished at His teaching" (22:33).

APPLICATION: MATTHEW 22:23-33

The Keys to Self-Deception

If the Old Testament is so clear on the concepts of resurrection and life after death, how is it that the Sadducees were so deceived? What makes people so gullible, so easily led astray and caught up in their own ideas that they can't embrace basic truths like this one? In Matthew 22:29, Jesus put His finger on the two most common reasons people deceive themselves into rejecting truth and accepting false doctrines.

First, *not knowing the Word of God leads to self-deception.* Jesus said that the Sadducees were mistaken because they did not understand the Scriptures. Regarding their ignorance of Scripture, the Sadducees really had two problems. First, they failed to embrace the *whole* Bible as the Word of God by limiting themselves to just the five books of Moses. People today often do this by focusing only on the New Testament, or only on certain favorite books of the Bible. Instead of having this kind of self-selective "canon within the canon," we should maintain a program of Bible reading and study that exposes us to the whole of God's written revelation—the Old Testament and the New.

Second, the Sadducees obviously failed to read the Bible responsibly. They were not serious students of the Word. Perhaps they were so busy carrying out their administrative responsibilities or their work in the temple that they just didn't make time to devote to reading, studying, and memorizing Scripture. Maybe they thought the exposure they'd had to the Bible in their growing-up years was enough, or that the few lessons they received from their teachers were sufficient for their growth in knowledge. How wrong they were! And they paid the price in their lack of faith, love, and hope—especially the hope for a future in heaven and eternal life with glorious resurrection bodies.

Second, *not knowing the power of God leads to self-deception.* We know the power of God by having a personal relationship with Him. This knowledge first requires saving faith, given and received by God's grace. But then it requires a life over which God is continuously Lord. This includes being a person who practices regular, confident prayer. Let each day begin in time alone with the Lord, giving Him your day and declaring your total trust in Him, regardless of what may occur. A life like this also involves a minute-by-minute awareness that God is present in our lives, dwelling in us by the Holy Spirit and walking with us through everything. Such an awareness of the ever-present power of God in our lives will drive away fear, doubt, and temptation. It will keep us close to the source of truth and far away from deceptive false doctrine.

The Two Ultimate Questions
MATTHEW 22:34-46

NASB

34But when the Pharisees heard that Jesus had silenced the Sadducees, they gathered themselves together. 35One of them, [a]a lawyer, asked Him *a question*, testing Him, 36"Teacher, which is the great commandment in the Law?" 37And He said to him, "'YOU SHALL LOVE THE LORD YOUR GOD WITH ALL YOUR HEART, AND WITH ALL YOUR SOUL, AND WITH ALL YOUR MIND.' 38This is the great and [a]foremost commandment. 39The second is like it, 'YOU SHALL LOVE YOUR NEIGHBOR AS YOURSELF.' 40On these two commandments depend the whole Law and the Prophets."

41Now while the Pharisees were gathered together, Jesus asked them a question: 42"What do you think about [a]the Christ, whose son is He?" They said to Him, "*The son* of David." 43He said to them, "Then how does David [a]in the Spirit call Him 'Lord,' saying,

44 'THE LORD SAID TO MY LORD,
  "SIT AT MY RIGHT HAND,
  UNTIL I PUT YOUR ENEMIES
    BENEATH YOUR FEET"'?

45If David then calls Him 'Lord,' how is He his son?" 46No one was able to answer Him a word, nor did anyone dare from that day on to ask Him [a]another question.

22:35 [a]I.e. an expert in the Mosaic Law
22:38 [a]Or *first* 22:42 [a]I.e. the Messiah
22:43 [a]Or *by inspiration* 22:46 [a]Lit *any longer*

NLT

34But when the Pharisees heard that he had silenced the Sadducees with his reply, they met together to question him again. 35One of them, an expert in religious law, tried to trap him with this question: 36"Teacher, which is the most important commandment in the law of Moses?"

37Jesus replied, "'You must love the LORD your God with all your heart, all your soul, and all your mind.'* 38This is the first and greatest commandment. 39A second is equally important: 'Love your neighbor as yourself.'* 40The entire law and all the demands of the prophets are based on these two commandments."

41Then, surrounded by the Pharisees, Jesus asked them a question: 42"What do you think about the Messiah? Whose son is he?"

They replied, "He is the son of David."

43Jesus responded, "Then why does David, speaking under the inspiration of the Spirit, call the Messiah 'my Lord'? For David said,

44 'The LORD said to my Lord,
  Sit in the place of honor at my
    right hand
  until I humble your enemies
    beneath your feet.'*

45Since David called the Messiah 'my Lord,' how can the Messiah be his son?"

46No one could answer him. And after that, no one dared to ask him any more questions.

22:37 Deut 6:5.   22:39 Lev 19:18.   22:44 Ps 110:1.

Some questions are asked to make us think . . . not to be answered. In fact, some of life's best questions are those that leave us sitting in silence, pondering them, rather than rushing to an off-the-top-of-our-heads, quiz-show response. Some of the smartest and wisest people I know impress me not because they have all the right answers but because they know how to ask the right questions. My best mentors and teachers have been the ones who have driven me deeper into exploring the profound questions of life rather than making me jot down their bullet-point lists of answers.

Maybe this is why I'm so intrigued by this particular chapter of Matthew, in which the question-and-answer interrogation of Jesus reveals such profound, deep truths. As His enemies pummeled Him repeatedly with what they believed to be "Gotcha!" questions, Jesus responded either by turning their questions around or by asking better questions of His own. Remember Jesus' clever question about whose image was impressed upon the denarius (22:20)? That one left the questioners "amazed" (22:22). Or the question about the resurrection—whether the God of Abraham, Isaac, and Jacob was the God of the living or the dead (22:31-32)? In response to that, the crowds were "astonished" (22:33).

But the questioning wasn't over. The first attack had come from Pharisees in cahoots with the Herodians (22:15-16). The second attack came from the Sadducees (22:23). The third—and final—attack came again from the Pharisees, who had regrouped and decided to face Jesus head-on with one of their star experts in the Law.

— 22:34-36 —

This final episode in the dramatic rhetorical clash between Jesus and His critics begins with a connection to the previous interaction with the Sadducees concerning the resurrection and life after death (22:23-33). Matthew reports that Jesus had "silenced" the Sadducees (22:34)—and that silence was deafening. The verb Matthew uses is *phimoō* [5392], which literally means to "tie shut," especially in the sense of shutting the mouth of an animal with a muzzle.[86]

In Jesus' muzzling of the Sadducees, the opposing party of the Pharisees saw an opportunity to kill two birds with one stone. If they could swoop in and deal a blow to Jesus, they would not only put that rabble-rousing rabbi in His place, but they would also demonstrate their intellectual superiority over the Sadducees. A. T. Robertson even suggests that the Pharisees "could not restrain their glee" at the opportunity handed to them by the circumstances, as if on a silver platter.[87]

But the Pharisees couldn't afford to mess this up. If they, too, were soundly defeated by Jesus' uncanny ability to deflect His opponents' attacks, the end would be worse than the beginning. Remember, they were still licking their wounds after the "render to Caesar the things that are Caesar's" defeat, in which their disciples had gone away in amazement at Jesus' teaching (22:21-22). This time they had to hit Jesus as hard as they could and make it hurt.

So, after gathering together, the Pharisees determined to send one of their experts in the Law, whom the NASB calls "a lawyer" and the NLT calls "an expert in religious law" (22:35). The Greek word here is *nomikos* [3544], literally, "a man of the law." These "lawyers" were usually scribes, men who dedicated their lives to meticulously copying the Hebrew Scriptures to preserve them from decay or corruption. Consequently, their constant contact with God's Word made them extremely knowledgeable, and they would be called upon to explain and apply the Law. We can imagine that the Pharisees, desirous of dealing Jesus a rhetorical death blow, found the best trained, most brilliant scholar they could. It wouldn't have been difficult, considering that they were in Jerusalem, the center of the study of the Torah.

Interestingly, the first question of the Pharisees and Herodians had been a yes-or-no question: whether it was right to pay the poll-tax to Caesar (22:17). The next question, by the Sadducees, had been similarly straightforward: To which deceased husband did the wife belong in the resurrection? (22:28). But the expert in the Law who was conscripted into a public showdown with Jesus assailed Him with an open-ended question that could have gone in hundreds of different directions: "Which is the great commandment in the Law?" (22:36). Once again, this wasn't a sincere question but a trap (22:35).

We might imagine that Jesus had ten options to choose from—one of the "Top Ten" from the tablets of the Law given at Sinai. However, as R. T. France notes, "The scribes distinguished 613 commands in the Old Testament law" that were "equally binding."[88] The question was not only a test of Jesus' ability to skillfully nuance His answer in order to keep from sounding like a breaker of the Law (by annulling 612 commandments), but it was also a test to see if He was aware of the ongoing scholarly debates concerning the proper ranking and ordering of the commandments. D. A. Carson explains,

> The Jews quite commonly drew distinctions among the laws of Scripture—great and small, light and heavy. . . . Verse 36 shows that the question of the expert was probably a hotly debated one. . . . The scene is like an ordination council, where the candidate is doing so well that some of the most learned ministers ask him questions they themselves have been unable to answer—in the hope of tripping him up or of finding answers.[89]

How would Jesus weigh in on the scholarly discussion? Would He even have the faintest awareness that there was a debate? We should probably picture this encounter as the ivory-tower scholar with the first-century equivalent of a PhD trying to show just how ignorant the amateur from Nazareth really was.

— 22:37-40 —

Without a moment's hesitation, Jesus quoted directly from Deuteronomy 6:4-9, which is commonly referred to as the *Shema* (from the Hebrew word for "hear" [H8085], which is the first word of the passage). By far, this was the single most familiar, most quoted, and most copied portion of Scripture in all of Judaism. The *Shema* constituted the foundational "creed" of the Jews, who quoted it twice a day. It begins, "Hear, O Israel! The LORD is our God, the LORD is one!" (Deut. 6:4). Following that affirmation of the absolute uniqueness of the one true God of Israel came what Jesus insisted was the "great and foremost commandment": "'You shall love the LORD your God with all your heart, and with all your soul, and with all your mind'" (Matt. 22:37-38).

Note that Jesus didn't couch His response in carefully crafted qualifications. He didn't have to deliberate, didn't have to ponder, didn't have to wrack His brain evaluating each of the 613 commandments in the Law and weighing each one. Jesus gave a straightforward, immediate, and unequivocal answer to the scholar's question. But He didn't stop there. He also added the second most important command, quoting Leviticus 19:18: "You shall love your neighbor as yourself" (Matt. 22:39). Jesus thus placed the vertical love of God and the horizontal love of fellow men and women as the foundation and structure of the entire Law (22:40).

Jesus' response left the teacher of the Law with nowhere to go. The parallel account in the Gospel of Mark records that the lawyer was forced to agree with Jesus, essentially admitting that the rabbi from Nazareth had passed the test with flying colors: "The scribe said to Him, 'Right, Teacher; You have truly stated that He is One, and there is no one else besides Him; and to love Him with all the heart and with all the understanding and with all the strength, and to love one's neighbor as himself, is much more than all burnt offerings and sacrifices'" (Mark 12:32-33). Then Mark adds an interesting detail. While the lawyer had originally approached Jesus with an attitude of condescension in order to test Him, Jesus concluded by actually commending the scribe: "You are not far from the kingdom of God" (Mark 12:34). Note that the tables had turned. By the end of the encounter, Jesus stood in the place of religious authority giving *the scribe* the grade!

— 22:41-46 —

Jesus' swift and sound defeat of their star legal scholar surely infuriated the Pharisees. In the very next verse we see them "gathered together," probably wallowing in the mire of disappointment and defeat (22:41). Jesus took the opportunity of having an audience of Pharisees, lingering Sadducees, and a large crowd of onlookers and eavesdroppers to ask His own question. The Pharisees had asked Jesus about politics; the Sadducees had asked about the afterlife; the lawyer had asked about the Law. Now Jesus took a dive into the waters of deep theology. He asked the Pharisees what they believed about the identity of the Messiah: "Whose son is He?" (22:42).

Don't miss what's really going on here. This wasn't just a random inquiry or a light afternoon game of theological trivia. Commenting on this passage, a great preacher of the early church named John Chrysostom, wrote, "He asks these questions, secretly leading them on to confess Him also to be God."[90]

The simple question called for a simple answer, and they answered correctly: The Messiah is "the son of David." That is, the Christ was rightly expected to be a descendant of David. This fact was well established in the Old Testament messianic prophecies. In the covenant established with David, the Lord had promised, "When your days are complete and you lie down with your fathers, I will raise up your descendant after you, who will come forth from you, and I will establish his kingdom. . . . Your house and your kingdom shall endure before Me forever; your throne shall be established forever" (2 Sam. 7:12, 16). Centuries later, as the prophet Isaiah peered ahead to the coming of the Messiah, he wrote, "For a child will be born to us, a son will be given to us; and the government will rest on His shoulders. . . . There will be no end to the increase of His government or of peace, on the throne of David and over his kingdom, to establish it and to uphold it with justice and righteousness from then on and forevermore" (Isa. 9:6-7).

The Pharisees' response was correct. But it was also incomplete. The same prophecy of Isaiah that announced the "son" who would be born from the lineage of David also said that He would be called "Mighty God" (Isa. 9:6). Was that just a metaphor, a title, or a name of honor? Or was it literally the case that the Messiah was to be both son of David and Son of God, fully human and fully divine? In a moment of profound teaching, Jesus led the Pharisees—and all those listening in on the conversation—to a more complete understanding of the true identity of the Christ.

To do this, Jesus quoted from David's writing in Psalm 110:1, long regarded by the rabbis in Jesus' day as applying to the Messiah.[91] Psalm 110:1 reads, "The LORD says to my Lord: 'Sit at My right hand until I make Your enemies a footstool for Your feet.'" Jesus affirmed that David wrote the psalm "in the Spirit" (Matt. 22:43)—that is, by the inspiration of the Holy Spirit. Thus, not only was the psalm a song of praise for God's Davidic covenant and the promise of a coming king, but it was also a prophetic revelation of the true nature of the Messiah. By the insight of the Holy Spirit, David had called the coming Messiah—his own descendant—"Lord."

Jesus' question, based on this reading of Psalm 110, was pointed: If the Messiah were merely a physical descendant of David, why did David prophetically call Him "Lord" (Matt. 22:43, 45)? Warren Wiersbe writes, "There is only one answer to this question. As God, Messiah is David's Lord; as man, He is David's Son. He is both 'the root and the offspring of David' (Rev. 22:16). Psalm 110:1 teaches the deity and the humanity of Messiah. He is David's Lord and He is David's Son."[92] Sometime later, Paul—himself a convert from among the strict sect of the Pharisees—would put it simply: "Jesus Christ our Lord" was "born of a descendant of David according to the flesh" and "declared the Son of God with power by the resurrection from the dead, according to the Spirit of holiness" (Rom. 1:3-4).

William Barclay beautifully characterizes the response of the crowd: "There would be few that day who caught anything like all that Jesus meant; but when Jesus spoke these words, even the densest of them felt a shiver in the presence of the eternal mystery. They had the awed and uncomfortable feeling that they had heard the voice of God; and for a moment, in this man Jesus, they glimpsed God's very face."[93] Is it any wonder that Jesus' claim that the Messiah was the divine Lord rendered the crowd speechless—not only on that day, but from that time forward? Neither Pharisee nor Sadducee, scholar nor politician, dared to ask Jesus another question.

APPLICATION: MATTHEW 22:34-46

Loving God, Loving Others

We live in an era that exalts the god of Self. We're told to be ourselves, respect ourselves, live for ourselves, indulge ourselves, look out for ourselves, and adore ourselves. Of course, we shouldn't *hate* ourselves. We should take care of our health and well-being. But we shouldn't adore ourselves above everything else, including the Lord God and other people.

In light of Christ's emphasis on the foremost commandment—"You shall love the LORD your God with all your heart, and with all your soul, and with all your mind"—and its close second—"You shall love your neighbor as yourself" (22:37-39)—let's pause and ask some important questions.

First, *do you love the Lord with everything you are, everything you do, and everything you have?* If a person close to you were to scrutinize your life, would they conclude that your number-one love is the Lord God? Do you spend more of your time, energy, and money on the Lord's priorities, or on your own? Do you make time with Him, listening to His voice through His Word and talking to Him in prayer and praise? And in the things you enjoy daily, do you give Him thanks, acknowledging with gratitude that all good things come from Him?

Second, *do you love others as yourself?* Do you pray for others, build up others in your local church, and provide for the needs of others when you can? Or do you have a kind of blacklist of people you never want to see again? Loving others means anointing our interpersonal relationships with the fruit of the Holy Spirit: "love, joy, peace, patience, kindness, goodness, faithfulness, gentleness, self-control" (Gal. 5:22-23). It means treating people the same way we would want to be treated (Matt. 7:12). And it means pursuing peace and building up one another (Rom. 14:19). In all honesty, are you doing these things?

Jesus not only gave us clear teaching on loving God and others, but He also gave us a clear example in His words and works (Phil. 2:5-11). Beyond that, He gave us His Spirit to make us both willing and able to live lives that are pleasing to God (Phil. 2:12-13). Therefore, we are without excuse. Loving God and loving others are not just nice suggestions. They are clear commands. And a world of increasing anger and hatred needs these kinds of divine love more than ever.

Woes for Religious Phonies
MATTHEW 23:1-39

NASB

¹Then Jesus spoke to the crowds and to His disciples, ²saying: "The scribes and the Pharisees have seated themselves in the chair of Moses; ³therefore all that they tell you, do and observe, but do not do according to their deeds; for they say *things* and do not do *them*. ⁴They tie up heavy burdens and lay them on men's shoulders, but they themselves are unwilling to move them with *so much as* a finger. ⁵But they do all their deeds to be noticed by men; for they broaden their ªphylacteries and lengthen the tassels *of their garments*. ⁶They love the place of honor at banquets and the chief seats in the synagogues, ⁷and respectful greetings in the market places, and being called Rabbi by men. ⁸But do not be called Rabbi; for One is your Teacher, and you are all brothers. ⁹Do not call *anyone* on earth your father; for One is your Father, He who is in heaven. ¹⁰Do not be called ªleaders; for One is your Leader, *that is*, Christ. ¹¹But the greatest among you shall be your servant. ¹²Whoever exalts himself shall be humbled; and whoever humbles himself shall be exalted.

¹³"But woe to you, scribes and Pharisees, hypocrites, because you shut off the kingdom of heaven ªfrom ᵇpeople; for you do not enter in yourselves, nor do you allow those who are entering to go in. ¹⁴[ªWoe to you, scribes and Pharisees, hypocrites, because you devour widows' houses, and for a pretense you make long prayers; therefore you will receive greater condemnation.]

¹⁵"Woe to you, scribes and Pharisees, hypocrites, because you travel around on sea and land to make one

NLT

¹Then Jesus said to the crowds and to his disciples, ²"The teachers of religious law and the Pharisees are the official interpreters of the law of Moses.* ³So practice and obey whatever they tell you, but don't follow their example. For they don't practice what they teach. ⁴They crush people with unbearable religious demands and never lift a finger to ease the burden.

⁵"Everything they do is for show. On their arms they wear extra wide prayer boxes with Scripture verses inside, and they wear robes with extra long tassels.* ⁶And they love to sit at the head table at banquets and in the seats of honor in the synagogues. ⁷They love to receive respectful greetings as they walk in the marketplaces, and to be called 'Rabbi.'*

⁸"Don't let anyone call you 'Rabbi,' for you have only one teacher, and all of you are equal as brothers and sisters.* ⁹And don't address anyone here on earth as 'Father,' for only God in heaven is your Father. ¹⁰And don't let anyone call you 'Teacher,' for you have only one teacher, the Messiah. ¹¹The greatest among you must be a servant. ¹²But those who exalt themselves will be humbled, and those who humble themselves will be exalted.

¹³"What sorrow awaits you teachers of religious law and you Pharisees. Hypocrites! For you shut the door of the Kingdom of Heaven in people's faces. You won't go in yourselves, and you don't let others enter either.*

¹⁵"What sorrow awaits you teachers of religious law and you Pharisees. Hypocrites! For you cross land

NASB

ᵃproselyte; and when he becomes one, you make him twice as much a son of ᵇhell as yourselves.

¹⁶"Woe to you, blind guides, who say, 'Whoever swears by the ᵃtemple, *that* is nothing; but whoever swears by the gold of the ᵃtemple is obligated.' ¹⁷You fools and blind men! Which is ᵃmore important, the gold or the ᵇtemple that sanctified the gold? ¹⁸And, 'Whoever swears by the altar, *that* is nothing, but whoever swears by the ᵃoffering on it, he is obligated.' ¹⁹You blind men, which is ᵃmore important, the ᵇoffering, or the altar that sanctifies the ᵇoffering? ²⁰Therefore, ᵃwhoever swears by the altar, swears *both* by ᵇthe altar and by everything on it. ²¹And ᵃwhoever swears by the ᵇtemple, swears *both* by ᶜthe temple and by Him who dwells within it. ²²And ᵃwhoever swears by heaven, swears *both* by the throne of God and by Him who sits upon it.

²³"Woe to you, scribes and Pharisees, hypocrites! For you tithe mint and dill and ᵃcummin, and have neglected the weightier provisions of the law: justice and mercy and faithfulness; but these are the things you should have done without neglecting the others. ²⁴You blind guides, who strain out a gnat and swallow a camel!

²⁵"Woe to you, scribes and Pharisees, hypocrites! For you clean the outside of the cup and of the dish, but inside they are full ᵃof robbery and self-indulgence. ²⁶You blind Pharisee, first clean the inside of the cup and of the dish, so that the outside of it may become clean also.

²⁷"Woe to you, scribes and Pharisees, hypocrites! For you are like

NLT

and sea to make one convert, and then you turn that person into twice the child of hell* you yourselves are!

¹⁶"Blind guides! What sorrow awaits you! For you say that it means nothing to swear 'by God's Temple,' but that it is binding to swear 'by the gold in the Temple.' ¹⁷Blind fools! Which is more important—the gold or the Temple that makes the gold sacred? ¹⁸And you say that to swear 'by the altar' is not binding, but to swear 'by the gifts on the altar' is binding. ¹⁹How blind! For which is more important—the gift on the altar or the altar that makes the gift sacred? ²⁰When you swear 'by the altar,' you are swearing by it and by everything on it. ²¹And when you swear 'by the Temple,' you are swearing by it and by God, who lives in it. ²²And when you swear 'by heaven,' you are swearing by the throne of God and by God, who sits on the throne.

²³"What sorrow awaits you teachers of religious law and you Pharisees. Hypocrites! For you are careful to tithe even the tiniest income from your herb gardens,* but you ignore the more important aspects of the law—justice, mercy, and faith. You should tithe, yes, but do not neglect the more important things. ²⁴Blind guides! You strain your water so you won't accidentally swallow a gnat, but you swallow a camel!*

²⁵"What sorrow awaits you teachers of religious law and you Pharisees. Hypocrites! For you are so careful to clean the outside of the cup and the dish, but inside you are filthy—full of greed and self-indulgence! ²⁶You blind Pharisee! First wash the inside of the cup and the dish,* and then the outside will become clean, too.

²⁷"What sorrow awaits you teachers of religious law and you Pharisees. Hypocrites! For you are like

whitewashed tombs which on the outside appear beautiful, but inside they are full of dead men's bones and all uncleanness. ²⁸So you, too, outwardly appear righteous to men, but inwardly you are full of hypocrisy and lawlessness.

²⁹"Woe to you, scribes and Pharisees, hypocrites! For you build the tombs of the prophets and adorn the monuments of the righteous, ³⁰and say, 'If we had been *living* in the days of our fathers, we would not have been partners with them in *shedding* the blood of the prophets.' ³¹So you testify against yourselves, that you are ᵃsons of those who murdered the prophets. ³²Fill up, then, the measure *of the guilt* of your fathers. ³³You serpents, you brood of vipers, how ᵃwill you escape the ᵇsentence of ᶜhell?

³⁴"Therefore, behold, I am sending you prophets and wise men and scribes; some of them you will kill and crucify, and some of them you will scourge in your synagogues, and persecute from city to city, ³⁵so that upon you may fall *the guilt of* all the righteous blood shed on earth, from the blood of righteous Abel to the blood of Zechariah, the son of Berechiah, whom you murdered between the ᵃtemple and the altar. ³⁶Truly I say to you, all these things will come upon this generation.

³⁷"Jerusalem, Jerusalem, who kills the prophets and stones those who are sent to her! How often I wanted to gather your children together, the way a hen gathers her chicks under her wings, and you were unwilling. ³⁸Behold, your house is being left to you desolate! ³⁹For I say to you, from now on you will not see Me until you

whitewashed tombs—beautiful on the outside but filled on the inside with dead people's bones and all sorts of impurity. ²⁸Outwardly you look like righteous people, but inwardly your hearts are filled with hypocrisy and lawlessness.

²⁹"What sorrow awaits you teachers of religious law and you Pharisees. Hypocrites! For you build tombs for the prophets your ancestors killed, and you decorate the monuments of the godly people your ancestors destroyed. ³⁰Then you say, 'If we had lived in the days of our ancestors, we would never have joined them in killing the prophets.'

³¹"But in saying that, you testify against yourselves that you are indeed the descendants of those who murdered the prophets. ³²Go ahead and finish what your ancestors started. ³³Snakes! Sons of vipers! How will you escape the judgment of hell?

³⁴"Therefore, I am sending you prophets and wise men and teachers of religious law. But you will kill some by crucifixion, and you will flog others with whips in your synagogues, chasing them from city to city. ³⁵As a result, you will be held responsible for the murder of all godly people of all time—from the murder of righteous Abel to the murder of Zechariah son of Berekiah, whom you killed in the Temple between the sanctuary and the altar. ³⁶I tell you the truth, this judgment will fall on this very generation.

³⁷"O Jerusalem, Jerusalem, the city that kills the prophets and stones God's messengers! How often I have wanted to gather your children together as a hen protects her chicks beneath her wings, but you wouldn't let me. ³⁸And now, look, your house is abandoned and desolate.* ³⁹For I tell you this, you will never see me again until you say, 'Blessings on the

NASB

say, 'BLESSED IS HE WHO COMES IN THE NAME OF THE LORD!'"

23:5 ªI.e. small cases containing Scripture texts worn on the left arm and forehead for religious purposes 23:10 ªOr *teachers* 23:13 ªLit *in front of* ᵇGr *anthropoi* 23:14 ªThis v not found in early mss 23:15 ªOr *convert* ᵇGr *Gehenna* 23:16 ªOr *sanctuary* 23:17 ªLit *greater* ᵇOr *sanctuary* 23:18 ªOr *gift* 23:19 ªLit *greater* ᵇOr *gift* 23:20 ªLit *he who* ᵇLit *it* 23:21 ªLit *he who* ᵇOr *sanctuary* ᶜLit *it* 23:22 ªLit *he who* 23:23 ªSimilar to caraway seeds 23:25 ªOr *as a result of* 23:31 ªOr *descendants* 23:33 ªLit *would* ᵇOr *judgment* ᶜGr *Gehenna* 23:35 ªOr *sanctuary*

NLT

one who comes in the name of the LORD!'*"

23:2 Greek *and the Pharisees sit in the seat of Moses.* 23:5 Greek *They enlarge their phylacteries and lengthen their tassels.* 23:7 *Rabbi,* from Aramaic, means "master" or "teacher." 23:8 Greek *brothers.* 23:13 Some manuscripts add verse 14, *What sorrow awaits you teachers of religious law and you Pharisees. Hypocrites! You shamelessly cheat widows out of their property and then pretend to be pious by making long prayers in public. Because of this, you will be severely punished.* Compare Mark 12:40 and Luke 20:47. 23:15 Greek *of Gehenna;* also in 23:33. 23:23 Greek *tithe the mint, the dill, and the cumin.* 23:24 See Lev 11:4, 23, where gnats and camels are both forbidden as food. 23:26 Some manuscripts do not include *and the dish.* 23:38 Some manuscripts do not include *and desolate.* 23:39 Ps 118:26.

Anyone who has the mistaken idea that Jesus was always a soft-spoken, meek-and-mild soul who uttered only affirming words in tender tones has never read Matthew 23. Here He boldly unleashed a tirade of righteous and true judgments against the most deceptive and dangerous people in Jewish society. Not the defeated sinners. Not the confused commoners. Not even the godless Gentiles in Roman garb. Jesus reserved His strongest and most critical words for the religious elites!

Knowing His time was short and that unreliable, hypocritical leaders were in charge of the religious world of the Jews, Jesus held nothing back. He exposed the pretense and pride of the scribes and Pharisees, whose ostentatious lifestyle was the furthest thing from true godliness and pure religion. They displayed their pious theatrics for all to see—until Jesus called out what they were doing for what it was: putting on appearances to impress people (23:5). Refusing to look the other way, Jesus openly exposed it all, right down to where they chose to sit at banquets, the titles by which they loved to be addressed, and how they craved being seen in the eyes of the public.

This bold confrontation with His enemies climaxed in a litany of "woes," warning of the direst consequences for their hypocrisy and abuse of power (23:13-33). His speech concluded with an emotional lament over Jerusalem's rejection of the King, Israel's long-awaited Messiah (23:37-39). Matthew 23 relays the last sermon Jesus preached publicly. There would be other important things to say, but those were reserved for His close disciples.

— 23:1-12 —

Before Jesus unleashed His rebuke on the religious deceivers (beginning in 23:13), He spoke both to the crowds of committed followers (23:1-7) and to His closest disciples (23:8-12).

Addressing the crowds, Jesus attempted to inoculate them from the deadly infection of pharisaical hypocrisy. First, He urged them to follow the pure teachings of Scripture rather than the putrid examples of the Pharisees. Here Jesus acknowledged that the scribes and Pharisees did, in fact, serve an important function in reading and proclaiming the Law of Moses to the people from their seats of authority, the "chair of Moses" (23:2). R. V. G. Tasker puts it this way: "Jesus recognizes the rightful claims of the scribes, the legal experts of the Pharisaic party, to be exponents of the law; and so long as they confine themselves to that task, their words, He insists, are to be respected, even if the conduct of some of them is inconsistent with their teaching."[94]

Remember, the scribes and Pharisees strove for an orthodox approach to faith and practice. Their theological views tended to be much closer to Scripture than those of the Sadducees. However, for many scribes, the Bible had become just a textbook of information rather than a means of personal transformation. On one extreme, the scribes' academic approach to Scripture could result in a head full of knowledge without a lifestyle that matched. On the other extreme, the Pharisees' obsession with outward purity and perfection could result in an excessive number of man-made rules that nobody could live up to.

In the first century, the common people had very little access to the Word of God themselves and would have had to rely on the scribes to hear the reading of the Law and its explanation. So, Jesus affirmed, what they heard from Scripture must be obeyed (23:3). God's pure, unadulterated Word is true and reliable. But as soon as those scribes and Pharisees began applying Scripture or going beyond what it said, their interpretations should be held in suspicion.

In the second half of 23:3, Jesus shifted gears and began spelling out some important points the unsuspecting crowds needed to be aware of. First, the scribes and Pharisees didn't practice what they preached. They lacked integrity and modeled hypocrisy. When the scribes were the ones holding the Scriptures and reading to the people, the only way to keep from falling into their trap of hypocrisy was to listen attentively to the Word of God as it was being read, then pay little attention to the way the scribes and Pharisees interpreted it and applied it.

Second, the scribes and Pharisees crushed common people with

PHYLACTERIES AND TASSELS

MATTHEW 23:5

Beginning about a century before Christ, pious Jewish men wore on their left forearms and foreheads small leather pouches known as *phylacteries*. These boxes contained selected texts from the Torah (see Exod. 13:1-16; Deut. 6:4-9; 11:13-21). They did this in obedience to God's command in Deuteronomy 6:8, which they took literally: "You shall bind [My words] as a sign on your hand and they shall be as frontals on your forehead." The idea was that this would keep the Law foremost in their minds during times of prayer.[95]

Jews also wore outer tunics with four tassels hanging from their hems in obedience to the Lord's command in Deuteronomy 22:12: "You shall make yourself tassels on the four corners of your garment with which you cover yourself." The purpose of this practice is spelled out in Numbers 15:38-40:

> "Speak to the sons of Israel, and tell them that they shall make for themselves tassels on the corners of their garments throughout their generations, and that they shall put on the tassel of each corner a cord of blue. It shall be a tassel for you to look at and remember all the commandments of the LORD, so as to do them and not follow after your own heart and your own eyes, after which you played the harlot, so that you may remember to do all My commandments and be holy to your God."

© Mark Neyman/Government Press Office/Israel

A Jewish man praying with a **phylactery** on his forehead (left), and the **tassels** worn on the outermost garments (right)

In Matthew 23:5, Jesus wasn't complaining about phylacteries and tassels. In fact, Jesus Himself wore the prescribed outer garment with the tassels on the four corners (see 9:20-21). What Jesus was objecting to was the Pharisees' practice of enlarging the phylacteries and lengthening the tassels so as to be noticed by the people around them.

unbearable demands (23:4). They lacked sympathy and modeled cruelty. As consummate taskmasters, the religious phonies established unreachable standards of manufactured "holiness" that nobody could live up to. This produced only guilt and shame among the people, who should have been able to respond to the Law with joy and peace.

Third, the scribes and Pharisees did everything for show (23:5). They lacked humility, and they modeled self-importance and conceit. It was all fake. When in public, they paraded their piety to be seen by the masses. They made a production of "glorifying God" when people were watching. Everything they wore, everywhere they sat, every word they uttered, every act they performed, and every title they took was actually to glorify themselves (23:5-7). In short, the religion of the scribes and Pharisees was nothing more than an outrageous display of over-the-top ostentation. They went out of their way to call attention to themselves.

In 23:8-12, Jesus seems to have shifted from addressing the crowd to instead speaking with His disciples, transitioning to this more private conversation by continuing to use the hypocrisy of the Pharisees as a negative example to avoid. His words apply to our lives just as they did to the lives of His first disciples. First, we should shun pretentious titles (23:8, 10). Seeking honorifics like "Rabbi" (literally, "my lord"), "Teacher," "Leader," and the like represents an attempt to place oneself above others. Jesus reminded His followers that we have one true Teacher and one true Leader—Christ Himself. Instead of seeking to pull rank on each other, the disciples of Jesus must remember that we are all "brothers" in Christ (23:8).

Second, just as we should reject being placed on a pedestal by others, we should resist placing others on a pedestal (23:9). Granting teachers and leaders the revered title "Father" can essentially cross the line from admiration and appreciation to exaltation and worship. The more we exalt a human to a position of unparalleled honor like that, the more we rob our heavenly Father of that unique position in our hearts and minds.

Third, we should cultivate a servant's heart and model genuine humility (23:11-12). True greatness comes by putting others above ourselves, humbling ourselves before others, and thus following the example of Christ. The apostle Paul wrote, "Do nothing from selfishness or empty conceit, but with humility of mind regard one another as more important than yourselves; do not merely look out for your own personal interests, but also for the interests of others" (Phil. 2:3-4).

Does this mean we should abolish all leadership positions and re-move from authority all of our pastors, teachers, and leaders? Doesn't the New Testament establish leadership roles in churches "for the equipping of the saints for the work of service" (Eph. 4:11-12)? Jesus wasn't condemning the shepherds in the churches who teach, preach, train, and lead "with eagerness . . . proving to be examples to the flock"—He was condemning the attitudes of the Pharisees who sought out the prestige of the pedestal for themselves "for sordid gain . . . lord-ing it over those" under them (1 Pet. 5:2-3). As one commentator states, "Leadership positions should never be a goal in and of themselves, but should always be viewed as opportunities to serve others."[96]

— 23:13-36 —

After warning the crowds and the disciples regarding the dangerous deception of the religious phonies of His day (23:1-12), Jesus took direct aim at the scribes and Pharisees themselves. Because of their tendency to hang out in the crowds and drop in on Jesus' teaching to find an opportunity to entrap Him, we can be sure that at least some repre-sentatives of these groups were present to hear the Messiah's thun-derous rebukes. Jesus directed the remainder of His scorching sermon at those self-important scholars and self-righteous sages. Every one of the woeful warnings, and each reference to "you" and "your" and "yourselves," was addressed to them. Because their influence over the people was so demoralizing and destructive, Jesus didn't hold back. It was time to put them in their place.

Jesus punctuated His sharp reproach with seven "woes," beginning each scathing rebuke with the exclamation *ouai* [3759], a word that intends to mimic a cry of anguish. These outcries aimed at the reli-gious leaders were part reproof and part lament. Jesus' seven "woes" in Matthew 23:13-36 were both cries of anguish for their stubborn, wicked hearts and cries of sorrow for the judgments they and their followers would suffer because of their rejection of the Messiah. William Barclay puts it well: "[*Ouai*] includes not only *wrath* but also *sorrow*. There is righteous anger here, but it is the anger of the heart of love, broken by stubborn human blindness. There is not only an air of savage denuncia-tion; there is also an atmosphere of poignant tragedy."[97]

To make the rebuke even more severe, in six of the seven instances in which Jesus declared, "Woe to you," He added an apt descriptive term that exposed the religious leaders' deception: "hypocrites!" The Greek word *hypokritēs* [5273] was often used of actors in a staged play. In a

"It's DOCTOR Schlock!"

MATTHEW 23:6-7

As I read Jesus' warnings about those religious phonies strutting their stuff in the streets, seeking the best seats at the synagogue, and insisting on being called "Rabbi" by all the unworthy underlings, my mind goes back many, many years ago to when I had an encounter with a Christian version of what Jesus described in Matthew 23:6-7. I had a friend back in California who produced an excellent television broadcast. He wanted to put together a Christian talk show with four individuals from different walks of life. He invited me, a friend of mine who was also in ministry, a layperson, and a fourth man none of us had ever met who was president of a little Christian college. Let's just call him "Sam Schlock."

The television show was to be filmed in Dallas, so we all caught our flights to meet up the night before and discuss some details of the next day. The producer of the show asked my friend and me if we would stick around the airport and meet Sam Schlock at his plane. He was flying in from another part of the country. This was way before the Internet and smartphones, so we couldn't Google "Schlock" and get a picture of him. So I asked my producer friend, "How will we know who he is?"

"Oh, you'll know," he said. "You can't miss him."

This was back in the day (pre-9/11) when you could meet people at the gate. So, we went all the way to the gate and waited until everybody had deplaned. Unfortunately, we failed to notice the man we were waiting for. So I said to my buddy, "Well, we'd better go down to the baggage claim and meet him there." On the way down, we saw a guy with his hat pulled down tight, his tie cinched up tight, and his shirt starched stiff as a board, all decked out in a three-piece suit. I nudged my friend and said, "That's gotta be him." My friend and I hesitated a moment, looked at each other, then made our way to the man.

(continued on next page)

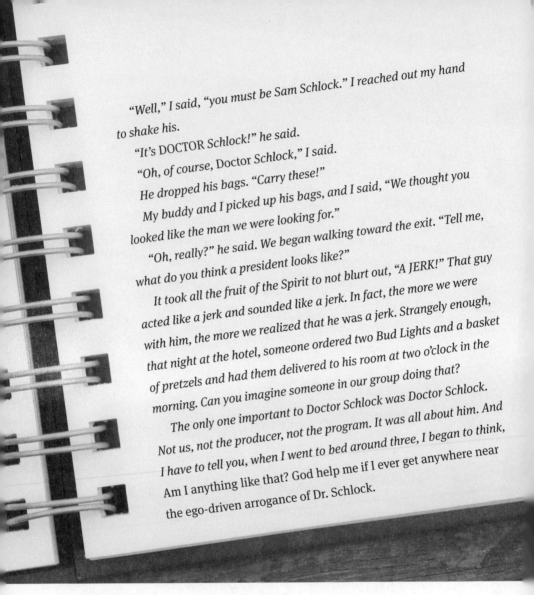

"Well," I said, "you must be Sam Schlock." I reached out my hand to shake his.

"It's DOCTOR Schlock!" he said.

"Oh, of course, Doctor Schlock," I said.

He dropped his bags. "Carry these!"

My buddy and I picked up his bags, and I said, "We thought you looked like the man we were looking for."

"Oh, really?" he said. We began walking toward the exit. "Tell me, what do you think a president looks like?"

It took all the fruit of the Spirit to not blurt out, "A JERK!" That guy acted like a jerk and sounded like a jerk. In fact, the more we were with him, the more we realized that he was a jerk. Strangely enough, that night at the hotel, someone ordered two Bud Lights and a basket of pretzels and had them delivered to his room at two o'clock in the morning. Can you imagine someone in our group doing that?

The only one important to Doctor Schlock was Doctor Schlock. Not us, not the producer, not the program. It was all about him. And I have to tell you, when I went to bed around three, I began to think, Am I anything like that? God help me if I ever get anywhere near the ego-driven arrogance of Dr. Schlock.

negative sense of the term, "the stage is a sham world and actors are deceivers."[98] It's in this sense that Matthew's Gospel uses it. The whole idea of religion for the scribes and Pharisees was something done for show—performing outward observances, wearing elaborate garb, and keeping tedious rules and regulations when people were watching. But in their hearts—behind the mask—they harbored bitterness, envy, hatred, pride, arrogance . . . even murder!

Realizing that this would be His last opportunity to lay it on the line, Jesus castigated His opponents, repeatedly condemning them for their wanton deception and shameless hypocrisy. Let's summarize Jesus' seven woes in the form of a chart.[99]

CHARGE	VERSE(S)	MEANING
Exclusion	23:13	Rather than drawing others into God's kingdom life with the glorious message of forgiveness and hope, they intentionally resisted the truth themselves and stood in the way of others.
Subversion	23:15	They had become "missionaries of evil," multiplying their numbers by spreading legalism like a disease. Their way included zeal without knowledge, capturing unsuspecting converts in deceptive, destructive false piety.
Deception	23:16-22	They went to great lengths to accommodate the Scriptures to their own desires. Their self-serving interpretations led to disobedience of the clear teaching of the Law. So twisted was their thinking, though, that they were blind to their own deceptions.
Majoring on Minors	23:23-24	They had made an art of obsessing over tiny details while neglecting vital matters. They counted seeds and tiny leaves for offering their tithes with precision, but they were neglecting basic virtues, like justice, mercy, and faithfulness. Jesus compared this tendency to straining out a tiny gnat from a drink while swallowing a whole camel!
Emphasizing External Rituals	23:25-26	While agonizing over the purity of the things around them, they cared nothing for the purity of their hearts. Just as it doesn't matter how spotless cups or dishes are on the outside if they are dirty within, the religious leaders' emphasis on external purity was pointless if their hearts were filled with robbery and selfishness.
Spiritual Death	23:27-28	To those on the outside, they looked spotless, clean, pure, and holy. Their clothes no doubt gleamed in the light. However, like tombs painted with bright white paint, inside they were filled with the stench of death and corruption.
Hearts of Murder	23:29-36	They were poisonous and dangerous, like vipers ready to strike their unsuspecting prey. Specifically, they hypocritically praised the prophets of old, while in reality they would have been among those who persecuted and killed the prophets, just as they were plotting to murder Jesus in just a few days.

These are the strongest words Jesus ever delivered during His three-year ministry—and for good reason. He was dealing with those whose influence reached well beyond their own number. Men and women in the crowds had been intimidated by the high-bar spirituality of the scribes and Pharisees. They had been bullied all their lives by the man-made rules enforced by guilt and shame. Through these religious leaders, people were learning to hate rather than love the things of God. People dreaded spiritual disciplines rather than longing for them. So Jesus unleashed His sharpest rebukes on these leaders, not simply in a fit of rage, but with a broken heart over the negative influence they had.

— 23:37-39 —

Jesus concluded His denunciation of the scribes and Pharisees with a lament against Jerusalem. In these last lines, Jesus used the city of Jerusalem as a representation of its political and religious leaders as well as the mob of men and women who cared nothing for the coming kingdom. While Jesus had hundreds of followers who believed His message and accepted Him as their long-awaited King, the great majority of Jews rejected Him entirely, just as they had rejected the preaching of the prophets who had gone before Him. They had stoned and killed them, and Jesus Himself would soon fall under the unjust sentence of death at their hands.

Because of their stubborn unwillingness to repent and believe, Jesus did not fulfill His deep desire to gather the people of Israel and restore the nation's blessing as their Messiah (23:37). Instead of blessing Israel and judging the nations that were oppressing it, God would leave the nation of Israel and the city of Jerusalem "desolate" (23:38). The patience of the Lord would continue, however, even after the leaders of Jerusalem had their Messiah crucified. For a whole generation (about forty years), judgment was delayed, until the Roman army swept through Judea, laid siege to Jerusalem, and destroyed the city and the temple in AD 70.

Yet even in spite of the just judgment of the people of Jerusalem, sent on account of their hardness of heart, Jesus never ceases to reach out His hands to gather them into His embrace. Matthew 23:39 looks forward to a day when the hearts of the Jewish people will be softened, and they will say, "Blessed is He who comes in the name of the LORD!" The apostle Paul echoed this same hope for the future restoration of Israel when he wrote, "A partial hardening has happened to Israel until the fullness of the Gentiles has come in; and so all Israel will be saved" (Rom. 11:25-26). This is certain because "the gifts and the calling of God are irrevocable" (Rom. 11:29).

APPLICATION: MATTHEW 23:1-39

Putting on a Show

No one was ever more "religious" than the scribes and Pharisees, who placed their confidence in their own abilities to put on a show of righteousness that would not only impress their neighbors but even please God! Prior to his conversion to being a follower of Jesus, the crucified and resurrected Messiah, the apostle Paul was one of those Pharisees who placed all his trust in his own good deeds. He wrote: "If anyone else has a mind to put confidence in the flesh, I far more: circumcised the eighth day, of the nation of Israel, of the tribe of Benjamin, a Hebrew of Hebrews; as to the Law, a Pharisee; as to zeal, a persecutor of the church; as to the righteousness which is in the Law, found blameless" (Phil. 3:4-6).

So many people believe like Paul did—that good deeds, good intentions, good words, and religious acts are enough to get them into heaven. Many think God would never judge the sincere, pious acts of people but will only condemn the overtly wicked, the irreligious, the obviously sinful people. But Jesus' castigation of the Pharisees in Matthew 23 completely destroys this kind of thinking. Who was it whom Jesus was judging?

- those who regularly attended worship
- those who made religious vows
- those who consistently tithed
- those who meticulously strove to obey God's commands
- those who enforced the rules on those around them
- those who built monuments to biblical heroes of the faith

In God's eyes, none of these things matter apart from a genuine relationship with Him through Jesus Christ by the life-giving power of the Holy Spirit. Those sad words "Jerusalem, Jerusalem" (23:37) were personalized when the risen Lord met Saul of Tarsus on the road to Damascus at the climax of his venomous hatred toward Christ and the believers:

"Saul, Saul, why are you persecuting Me?" (Acts 9:4). And they can be repeated for anybody who believes their religious zeal can get them even one inch closer to heaven without a personal relationship with Christ: "John, John" . . . "Shirley, Shirley" . . . "Linda, Linda" . . . "Steve, Steve" . . .

Going to church, studying the Bible, being baptized, paying your bills, living a moral life, obeying the Ten Commandments—these won't win God's favor. God requires internal righteousness that can only come from grace through faith in the person and work of Christ. Putting on a show won't impress Him. So, if you're a believer in Jesus, put the mask down and stop performing. God's not fooled by a fake external. He's interested in a humble, repentant heart that comes to Him like a broken, needy child. Putting on a performance for others is not only deceptive—it's destructive. It gives people a false sense of guilt and shame when they try to measure up to a phony spirituality. Instead of performing, point people to Jesus as the source of grace and mercy, forgiveness and restoration. The righteousness that brings eternal life comes from Jesus Christ and from Him alone.

First Glimpses of the Last Days
MATTHEW 24:1-28

NASB

¹Jesus came out from the temple and was going away ªwhen His disciples came up to point out the temple buildings to Him. ²And He said to them, "Do you not see all these things? Truly I say to you, not one stone here will be left upon another, which will not be torn down."

³As He was sitting on the Mount of Olives, the disciples came to Him privately, saying, "Tell us, when will these things happen, and what *will be* the sign of Your coming, and of the ªend of the age?"

⁴And Jesus answered and said to them, "See to it that no one misleads you. ⁵For many will come in My name, saying, 'I am the ªChrist,' and will mislead many. ⁶You will be

NLT

¹As Jesus was leaving the Temple grounds, his disciples pointed out to him the various Temple buildings. ²But he responded, "Do you see all these buildings? I tell you the truth, they will be completely demolished. Not one stone will be left on top of another!"

³Later, Jesus sat on the Mount of Olives. His disciples came to him privately and said, "Tell us, when will all this happen? What sign will signal your return and the end of the world?*"

⁴Jesus told them, "Don't let anyone mislead you, ⁵for many will come in my name, claiming, 'I am the Messiah.' They will deceive many. ⁶And you will hear of wars and threats

hearing of wars and rumors of wars. See that you are not frightened, for *those things* must take place, but *that* is not yet the end. ⁷For nation will rise against nation, and kingdom against kingdom, and in various places there will be famines and earthquakes. ⁸But all these things are *merely* the beginning of birth pangs.

⁹"Then they will deliver you to tribulation, and will kill you, and you will be hated by all nations because of My name. ¹⁰At that time many will ᵃfall away and will ᵇbetray one another and hate one another. ¹¹Many false prophets will arise and will mislead many. ¹²Because lawlessness is increased, ᵃmost people's love will grow cold. ¹³But the one who endures to the end, he will be saved. ¹⁴This gospel of the kingdom shall be preached in the whole ᵃworld as a testimony to all the nations, and then the end will come.

¹⁵"Therefore when you see the ABOMINATION OF DESOLATION which was spoken of through Daniel the prophet, standing in the holy place (let the reader understand), ¹⁶then those who are in Judea must flee to the mountains. ¹⁷ᵃWhoever is on the housetop must not go down to get the things out that are in his house. ¹⁸ᵃWhoever is in the field must not turn back to get his cloak. ¹⁹But woe to those who are pregnant and to those who are nursing babies in those days! ²⁰But pray that your flight will not be in the winter, or on a Sabbath. ²¹For then there will be a great tribulation, such as has not occurred since the beginning of the world until now, nor ever will. ²²Unless those days had been cut short, no ᵃlife would have been saved; but for the sake of the ᵇelect those days will be cut short. ²³Then if anyone says to you, 'Behold, here is

of wars, but don't panic. Yes, these things must take place, but the end won't follow immediately. ⁷Nation will go to war against nation, and kingdom against kingdom. There will be famines and earthquakes in many parts of the world. ⁸But all this is only the first of the birth pains, with more to come.

⁹"Then you will be arrested, persecuted, and killed. You will be hated all over the world because you are my followers.* ¹⁰And many will turn away from me and betray and hate each other. ¹¹And many false prophets will appear and will deceive many people. ¹²Sin will be rampant everywhere, and the love of many will grow cold. ¹³But the one who endures to the end will be saved. ¹⁴And the Good News about the Kingdom will be preached throughout the whole world, so that all nations* will hear it; and then the end will come.

¹⁵"The day is coming when you will see what Daniel the prophet spoke about—the sacrilegious object that causes desecration* standing in the Holy Place." (Reader, pay attention!) ¹⁶"Then those in Judea must flee to the hills. ¹⁷A person out on the deck of a roof must not go down into the house to pack. ¹⁸A person out in the field must not return even to get a coat. ¹⁹How terrible it will be for pregnant women and for nursing mothers in those days. ²⁰And pray that your flight will not be in winter or on the Sabbath. ²¹For there will be greater anguish than at any time since the world began. And it will never be so great again. ²²In fact, unless that time of calamity is shortened, not a single person will survive. But it will be shortened for the sake of God's chosen ones.

²³"Then if anyone tells you, 'Look, here is the Messiah,' or 'There he is,'

the ªChrist,' or ᵇ'There *He is*,' do not believe *him*. ²⁴For false Christs and false prophets will arise and will ªshow great ᵇsigns and wonders, so as to mislead, if possible, even the ᶜelect. ²⁵Behold, I have told you in advance. ²⁶So if they say to you, 'Behold, He is in the wilderness,' do not go out, *or,* 'Behold, He is in the inner rooms,' do not believe *them*. ²⁷For just as the lightning comes from the east and flashes even to the west, so will the coming of the Son of Man be. ²⁸Wherever the corpse is, there the ªvultures will gather.

24:1 ªLit *and*   24:3 ªOr *consummation*   24:5 ªI.e. the Messiah   24:10 ªLit *be caused to stumble* ᵇOr *hand over*   24:12 ªLit *the love of many*   24:14 ªLit *inhabited earth*   24:17 ªLit *He who*   24:18 ªLit *He who*   24:22 ªLit *flesh* ᵇOr *chosen ones*   24:23 ªI.e. Messiah ᵇLit *here*   24:24 ªLit *give* ᵇOr *attesting miracles* ᶜOr *chosen ones*   24:28 ªOr *eagles*

don't believe it. ²⁴For false messiahs and false prophets will rise up and perform great signs and wonders so as to deceive, if possible, even God's chosen ones. ²⁵See, I have warned you about this ahead of time.

²⁶"So if someone tells you, 'Look, the Messiah is out in the desert,' don't bother to go and look. Or, 'Look, he is hiding here,' don't believe it! ²⁷For as the lightning flashes in the east and shines to the west, so it will be when the Son of Man* comes. ²⁸Just as the gathering of vultures shows there is a carcass nearby, so these signs indicate that the end is near.*

24:3 Or *the age?*   24:9 Greek *on account of my name.*   24:14 Or *all peoples.*   24:15 Greek *the abomination of desolation.* See Dan 9:27; 11:31; 12:11.   24:27 "Son of Man" is a title Jesus used for himself.   24:28 Greek *Wherever the carcass is, the vultures gather.*

The subject of biblical prophecy is like one magnet interacting with another. For many people, it pulls them in. For others, it drives them away. Those drawn to prophecy long to know about the future. They speculate about how current events might relate to their future and how their own lives may be affected by both. Those repelled by the subject of prophecy often fear the implications of coming judgment, find the biblical language and imagery confusing, or don't believe the future has any practical application for their everyday lives.

It's easy to see how people can go to extremes regarding Bible prophecy—despising it or obsessing over it. Even in the first century we have evidence of these extremes. On the one hand, Peter noted that some people mocked the notion of coming judgment (2 Pet. 3:3-4); on the other, Paul had to correct some who mistakenly believed they were already in the midst of the end-times events (2 Thes. 2:1-2). Jesus' words on the Mount of Olives during that last week of His earthly ministry helped set the record straight—for His original disciples and for us.

— 24:1-3 —

After Jesus finished giving His heated and forceful warnings to the scribes and Pharisees (Matt. 23), He and His disciples left the temple and started the roughly 2-mile journey to Bethany by way of the Mount of Olives. As their path snaked down into the Kidron Valley and then up the slope of the steep Mount of Olives, some of the disciples stared back at the temple and observed its majestic structures (24:1). The Gospels of Mark and Luke both inform us that the disciples were marveling at the beautiful, ornate stonework of the temple complex (Mark 13:1; Luke 21:5).

It's easy to understand why the disciples felt great pride in the handiwork of Herod the Great, who had funded an ambitious reconstruction program on the temple mount that involved the construction of a massive retaining wall to expand the hill itself. To this day, the western side of that original retaining wall (sometimes called the Wailing Wall) can still be seen. Nearly two millennia after the time of Jesus, it's still a marvelous sight to behold! Upon this enlarged base, Herod completely reconstructed and beautified the temple area, giving it an awe-inspiring majesty. From a purely human perspective, the disciples' fixation on the temple was not misplaced. As one writer explains, "All speak of the grandeur of the building, which was of white marble, its eastern front covered with plates of gold that reflected the rays of the rising sun."[100] It was this glorious eastern face of the temple that held the disciples' gaze as they crossed the Kidron Valley.

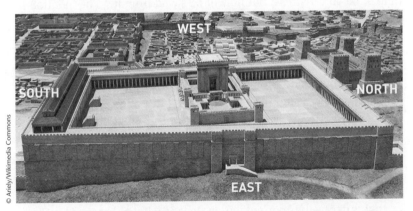

A model of **Herod's expanded temple mount** with the temple itself facing to the east and the impressive eastern wall standing in the foreground. The disciples were looking at this eastern side of the temple complex when they marveled at the beautiful stones.

In response to their admiration of the temple and its man-made splendor, Jesus replied, "Do you not see all these things? Truly I say to you, not one stone here will be left upon another, which will not be torn down" (Matt. 24:2). This unexpected response to their enthusiasm over the temple complex may have felt like a slap in the face, but it was a necessary correction to their fixation on the physical and their obsession with the opulent.

Following Jesus' prophetic statement concerning the future destruction of the temple complex, Peter, James, John, and Andrew approached Jesus privately as He sat on the Mount of Olives, staring across the valley at the temple (24:3; Mark 13:3). I imagine the sun descending in the west, enshrouding the temple in an orange glow and casting an ominous shadow into the valley below. These disciples, obviously concerned about Jesus' prophecy, asked two questions: "When will these things happen, and what will be the sign of Your coming, and of the end of the age?" (Matt. 24:3).

The phrase "these things" in the first question refers to the tragic event Jesus mentioned: the destruction of the temple, in which no stone would be left upon another (24:2). The second question makes it clear that the disciples assumed that the destruction of the glorious temple would somehow be associated with the coming of the Messiah as Judge and King and the "end of the age"—that is, the great period of tribulation leading to the restoration of the nation of Israel under the Messiah. The disciples would have been quite familiar with the prophecy of Jeremiah 30:7: "Alas! for that day is great, there is none like it; and it is the time of Jacob's distress, but he will be saved from it." The mention of the temple's destruction would have also brought to mind the prophecy of Daniel 9:26-27, which says,

> "Then after the sixty-two weeks the Messiah will be cut off and have nothing, and the people of the prince who is to come will destroy the city and the sanctuary. And its end will come with a flood; even to the end there will be war; desolations are determined. And he will make a firm covenant with the many for one week, but in the middle of the week he will put a stop to sacrifice and grain offering; and on the wing of abominations will come one who makes desolate, even until a complete destruction, one that is decreed, is poured out on the one who makes desolate."

With these Old Testament "end of the age" passages in the background, the disciples' questions made sense. However, their understanding of the chronology of events was not quite accurate. Though the utter destruction of the temple would happen only a few decades later, in AD 70, the coming of the Messiah as Judge and King and the end of the rule of unrighteous nations would not occur until after a span of time known to us as the church age. As such, Jesus' answers to the disciples' jumbled questions involve both near fulfillments and far fulfillments, some that occurred in the first century and others that will not occur until the second coming of Christ.

— 24:4-14 —

That day on the Mount of Olives, Jesus set before the disciples a survey of the events that would take place in the future. He first addressed the *what* question: the sign of the coming of the Messiah and the end of the age. Then He briefly addressed the *when* question. Regarding the end of the age, the "time of Jacob's distress" (Jer. 30:7), Jesus gave six signs that would be associated with the last generation of people prior to Christ's return to establish His earthly kingdom.

Remember, though, that some of the events Jesus described have already come to pass from our perspective; they were fulfilled in the first-century Roman invasion and destruction of Jerusalem. Some events are still future to us. And some of Jesus' words may even play double duty, having a near reference in the first century that then becomes a type or foreshadowing of a future, ultimate fulfillment in the end times. Determining which events are near, far, or both has been a subject of great debate for centuries. So, as we quickly walk through these "signs of the times," we need to tread lightly, keeping our focus on the big picture rather than falling into speculations or dogmatic declarations regarding the details.

The first sign of the end is widespread deception by a growing number of false Christs (Matt. 24:4-5). The deception in future days will intensify and escalate as never before, eventually culminating in the arrival of the ultimate, individual Antichrist figure and his False Prophet, who will personally embody worldwide satanic deception (see Rev. 13). Because the Holy Spirit will have withdrawn His restraining power during the time of the Tribulation (see 2 Thes. 2:6-7), an unprecedented era of spiritual, moral, and political turmoil will ensue.

Today, the Holy Spirit restrains the world's lawlessness chiefly through the Spirit-empowered church. His presence in believers allows us to shine as the light of the world and to permeate secular culture as the salt of the earth (Matt. 5:13-16). When the church is raptured to be with Christ prior to the seven-year Tribulation (1 Thes. 4:16-17), also known as the "time of Jacob's distress" or the great "Day of the Lord," the children of light will be removed from the world of darkness (cf. 1 Thes. 5:1-8). In the resulting spiritual "night" of the Tribulation period, truth will be twisted like never before. And, what's worse, the man of lawlessness, the Antichrist, will take center stage. F. F. Bruce sums it up this way: "The restrainer has not yet been removed, therefore the man of lawlessness has not yet appeared, and *a fortiori* the Day of the Lord has not yet arrived."[101]

Yet this warning still has application for us today. Paul reminded the Thessalonians that the "mystery of lawlessness" is already at work in the world (2 Thes. 2:7), just as John warned that the "spirit of the antichrist" is already present (1 Jn. 4:3), inspiring many little "antichrists" (1 Jn. 2:18). We, too, should be alert to the fact that false prophets, false teachers, and false messiahs are currently and constantly peddling their false spirituality, even as Jesus' words in the Olivet discourse point to a future, definitive manifestation of this satanic deception. In our age, prior to the rapture of the church, spiritual wickedness is restrained—not absent, but unable to take complete control. During the Tribulation, that restraint will be removed.

The second sign of the end is international dispute (often leading to warfare) that will intensify among the nations of the world (Matt. 24:6-7). In the future, before Christ physically returns to the earth as Judge and King, there will be massive world wars among the kingdoms of this world. Though the book of Revelation suggests that the Middle East will be the epicenter of this global conflict, the interconnection of the world's political and economic structures will mean that everybody will likely be dragged into war. We see the ultimate expression of this in Revelation 13, where the beast from the sea exercises unchecked military power, waging war against the saints and subduing "every tribe and people and tongue and nation" under his authority (Rev. 13:3-7). Similar to how the birth pangs of a pregnant woman intensify as labor progresses and delivery approaches, warfare will increase throughout the world as the end nears, culminating in full-on global conflict.

The third sign of the end involves the proliferation of famines, earthquakes, and other natural disasters (Matt. 24:7-8). Geological disturbances will coincide with spiritual deception and political turmoil, adding further panic and widespread desperation. Starvation and the spread of diseases will add to the misery. We can imagine that the disasters will include the decimation of crops and livestock, the drying up of streams, wells, and reservoirs, and the destruction of natural and man-made infrastructures necessary for delivering vital resources, like food, water, and electricity. Supply lines will be disrupted, and lives will be lost. Today, on a limited scale, we can already observe the effects of natural disasters on cities and nations. These things are merely a foreshadowing of the intensification of catastrophes associated with the Tribulation period.

The fourth sign of the end is that believers will experience severe persecution from those who hate Christ (24:9). Those who will come to faith in Christ after the rapture of the church—often referred to as "Tribulation saints"—will become the targets of persecution and execution. Because those believers will identify themselves with Jesus Christ at a time when the rest of the world worships the Antichrist, the seething hatred of the unsaved will rise up against them. Many will be hunted down, arrested, tried, and killed. Martyrdom will greatly increase, but those believers will be heirs to an eternal reward. The book of Revelation describes a great multitude of believers "from every nation and all tribes and peoples and tongues" who will "come out of the great tribulation" (Rev. 7:9-17). These are people who will have suffered martyrdom at the hands of the Antichrist and his wicked empire (Rev. 6:9-11; 13:7-10).

The fifth sign of the end is that many supposed Christians will defect (Matt. 24:10-13). End-times spiritual deception and physical persecution will result in a sifting of the truly saved from those who only claimed to be saved. Some who had acted as if they were followers of Jesus Christ will show their true colors by following the deception and by denying Christ under threat of bodily harm. Instead of standing strong in their faith, they will turn away from the truth, betray their fellow believers, and demonstrate hatred rather than love toward the brethren. Today—as throughout history—persecution weeds out phony followers of Jesus. It's always been that way. The truly regenerate and genuinely saved will endure to the end by the power of the Holy Spirit.

The sixth sign of the end is a worldwide declaration of the gospel (24:14). Despite the global horrors growing toward an unspeakable crescendo—with false Christs, destructive warfare, natural disasters, and persecution—the message of the saving gospel of Jesus Christ will still be proclaimed. All nations will hear the gospel, giving everybody an opportunity to believe unto eternal life. How will such an ambitious worldwide mission occur during the short time of the future seven-year Tribulation period? Perhaps God will use angelic messengers to bring the good news, as He did in the very first proclamation of the Resurrection, at the empty tomb (28:5-7). The book of Revelation suggests such a future angelic proclamation:

> I saw another angel flying in midheaven, having an eternal gospel to preach to those who live on the earth, and to every nation

and tribe and tongue and people; and he said with a loud voice, "Fear God, and give Him glory, because the hour of His judgment has come; worship Him who made the heaven and the earth and sea and springs of waters." (Rev. 14:6-7)

It is also likely that God will work through the 144,000 converts from the twelve tribes of Israel described in Revelation 7:1-8. These Hebrews will serve as faithful, courageous, and diligent witnesses for Christ during the darkest period of the earth's history. God will preserve them from harm during the Tribulation and use them to fulfill the ancient Old Testament calling of Israel to be God's witnesses among the nations (see Isa. 43:1-13). God's plan for Israel was always that they would serve as the light of truth for the Gentiles. During the Tribulation, they will finally fulfill this global mission. This believing remnant from ethnic Israel will not only be sealed for power and protection, but they will also survive the Tribulation period and become the first fruits of the nation of Israel when it is restored to the land during the coming millennial kingdom.

— 24:15-28 —

Jesus employed some disturbing and dreadful imagery to describe the conditions of the world leading up to His return to earth as Judge and King. Just as a woman suffers from intensifying birth pains, so the inhabitants of the earth during that period will be caught in the throes of intensifying calamities (24:8). These will eventually culminate in the judgment of the Antichrist and all his followers, as well as the deliverance of God's people. With this revelation, Jesus partly answered the disciples' second question: "What will be the sign of Your coming, and of the end of the age?" (24:3). Yet there's much more to tell.

While describing these signals of the end times, Jesus suddenly inserted a comment regarding the "abomination of desolation" (24:15), something to which the prophet Daniel referred three times (Dan. 9:27; 11:31; 12:11). This phrase can also be rendered "the abomination that causes desolation." As R. V. G. Tasker notes, "The desecration of the Temple by Antiochus Epiphanes who set up a heathen altar within the sacred precincts in 168 BC was such an abomination."[102] A similarly abhorrent desecration—and related desolation—occurred in AD 70, when "the Romans burned the temple and offered sacrifices to their ensigns placed by the eastern gate when they proclaimed Titus as Emperor."[103]

Here we arrive at an element of the Olivet discourse that seems to

Timeline of Future Events

CHURCH AGE	SEVEN-YEAR TRIBULATION		MILLENNIAL KINGDOM	ETERNITY

Rapture of Believers — 1 Thes. 4:13-18

Judgment Seat of Christ — 2 Cor. 5:10

Second Coming of Christ — Rev. 19:11-21; Matt. 25:31-46

Great White Throne Judgment — Rev. 20:11-15

Divine Judgments — Seals, Trumpets, Bowls

Israel's Restoration

New Heaven and New Earth — Rev. 21–22

Abomination of Desolation   **Armageddon** — Rev. 16:13-16

Gospel preached to the nations | 3½ years of deception | 3½ years of Antichrist's reign | Christ reigns on the Earth

CHURCH AGE — from the Day of Pentecost to the Rapture

SEVEN-YEAR TRIBULATION — Dan. 9:27; 11:36-39; Matt. 24:15; 2 Thes. 2:1-8; Rev. 4–19

MILLENNIAL KINGDOM — 1,000 years of peace on Earth — Rev. 20:1-8

ETERNITY — ∞

Many of Jesus' words in Matthew 24 and 25 refer to the future period of the seven-year Tribulation that will follow the church age and precede the millennial kingdom. This chart pulls together various Old and New Testament passages related to these future events.

have in view both a near fulfillment and a far fulfillment. Luke's parallel account of Jesus' teaching appears to emphasize the nearer application, which occurred at the hands of the Romans nearly forty years after Jesus' words: "But when you see Jerusalem surrounded by armies, then recognize that her desolation is near. Then those who are in Judea must flee to the mountains" (Luke 21:20-21). Mark mentions the abomination of desolation but does not specify that he is citing Daniel (Mark 13:14). When Matthew points the readers specifically to Daniel's prophecy, he clearly pushes the ultimate fulfillment of this prophecy into the future, leading up to the return of Christ. Matthew's emphasis doesn't reject the idea of a near fulfillment in AD 70. Rather, that partial, historical fulfillment now serves as a type or a foreshadowing of future end-times events, just as the earlier abomination of desolation by Antiochus Epiphanes in 168 BC may also be seen as a partial fulfillment of Daniel's words, at least in a limited sense.

Like a stone skipped across the waters of history, Daniel's prophecy of the abomination of desolation sees a number of partial "rehearsals" prior to the final event in the future Tribulation period under the Antichrist. This final event is confirmed by the vision of the beast in Revelation 13—written decades after the destruction of the temple in AD 70—in which John sees the rise of the Antichrist and his worldwide kingdom, which presumably tramples the future temple of the Tribulation (Rev. 13:1-10; cf. Rev. 11:1-2). Likewise, the apostle Paul affirms that the Day of the Lord (the Tribulation period) will not occur until "the man of lawlessness is revealed, the son of destruction, who opposes and exalts himself above every so-called god or object of worship, so that he takes his seat in the temple of God, displaying himself as being God" (2 Thes. 2:3-4). Taking these passages together, we can see that the ultimate manifestation of the abomination of desolation is the Antichrist himself!

When the residents of Judea—whether the immediate generation of the first century or the remote generation who will be alive during the Tribulation—see such events unfolding in their midst, they are to take immediate action for escape (Matt. 24:15-20). It doesn't take a Bible scholar with a doctorate to put two and two together and recognize the urgency needed for "getting out of Dodge." They will be like evacuees exiting a burning building. No material possessions will be worth the risk of hanging back. All haste must be taken to flee to safety.

Within the last century, we've seen numerous examples of natural catastrophes and political crises that have required urgent responses like this. As the relentless Nazi regime closed in on one European country after another, Jews fled for survival. Those who stayed behind suffered not only the loss of their livelihoods but in most cases their lives. As the Viet Cong invaded the city of Saigon and the last helicopters took on as many as they could carry, the Vietnamese living there fled from their homeland to survive. And as countless hurricanes have approached landfall, residents of the coastal cities in the storms' paths have fled inland to avoid destruction and death. Although we are familiar with such disasters, Jesus' ominous words on the Mount of Olives that evening convey a sobering truth about the last days: "Then there will be a great tribulation, such as has not occurred since the beginning of the world until now, nor ever will" (24:21). So horrifying will those days be that if the destruction was not to be stopped by the glorious return of Christ, "no life would have been saved" (24:22). Jesus' words at this point clearly look to the distant future, to the last great period of judgment and wrath upon this earth.

In Matthew 24:23-28, we return to where Jesus began at 24:4—a warning against deceptive words and equally deceptive signs and wonders. For the believing Jewish refugees fleeing Jerusalem and Judea when the Antichrist takes his place in the temple, these words would be a reminder. They must still be on the alert for false Christs and false prophets who would "show great signs and wonders" not only to deceive the unsaved into believing their lies but also to coax the elect from their places of safety (24:23-26). To the implied question "How will we know, then, that the true Messiah and His heavenly army have arrived?"—or "How will we know the coast is clear?"—Jesus gave this answer: "For just as the lightning comes from the east and flashes even to the west, so will the coming of the Son of Man be" (24:27). In other words, the real coming of Christ in glory will be unmistakable. Nobody will confuse it with even the most astonishing "signs and wonders" of the false Christs and false prophets populating the end times.

The obscure saying in Matthew 24:28 has puzzled many commentators throughout history.[104] The statement certainly has an ominous tone. In a parallel of this saying at Luke 17:37, the context indicates a direct connection with coming judgment. In that account of this discourse, Jesus mentions that just as in the days of Noah and Lot, people will be going about their business until judgment suddenly comes upon them (Luke 17:26-36; cf. Matt. 24:36-41). During that time of judgment, a separation between the saved and unsaved will occur as "one will be taken and the other will be left" (Luke 17:34-35; cf. Matt. 24:40-41). In response to this statement, the disciples asked, "Where, Lord?" (Luke 17:37). It's not clear whether the question relates to those taken or to those left behind (or both). And it isn't completely clear which group is to be judged and which is to be saved. What is clear, though, is that a definite, unequivocal distinction will be made between believers and unbelievers.

In light of the menacing vision in Revelation 19:21 of birds gorging on the flesh of those slain at the return of Christ, it seems best to understand Jesus' use of these words as foretelling the certainty of the future judgment of the wicked. His cryptic statement points to the earth as the place of judgment, as evidenced by the birds feasting on carrion. Evil and death tend to be found in the same places. Those separated from the righteous will be consigned to judgment because they did not find salvation by grace alone through faith alone in Christ alone.

APPLICATION: MATTHEW 24:1-28

Living *Now* in Light of *Then*

After reading Jesus' prophetic words in the first part of the Olivet discourse, we could start to "run scared." We could allow the future realities to make us paranoid, constantly scouring news sources for current events around the world that look like fulfillments of these judgments. Some have done this. They've pointed at world events and declared, "This is it!" Or they've started a countdown to the return of Christ after learning of alarming developments in global politics. This is no way to live now in light of then. Let me instead give you three suggestions for living confidently (not fearfully) and hopefully (not suspiciously) in light of Christ's prophetic picture of end-times events. With each of these suggestions, I'll add a promise from the Old Testament and another from the New Testament.

First, *reject every temptation to live in fear.* Jesus' words in the Olivet discourse weren't meant to frighten true believers who find salvation in Jesus Christ. These were warnings for those who wallowed in unbelief and unrighteousness and therefore stood in danger of entering into earthly and eternal judgment. Believers in Christ need not be afraid. Isaiah 41:10 says, "'Do not fear, for I am with you; do not anxiously look about you, for I am your God. I will strengthen you, surely I will help you, surely I will uphold you with My righteous right hand." Paul wrote to his disciple Timothy that "God has not given us a spirit of timidity, but of power and love and discipline" (2 Tim. 1:7).

Second, *remember that God is completely sovereign.* He's not *almost* sovereign or *mostly* sovereign or *partly* sovereign. We believe in, love, and serve a God who is *completely* sovereign both over world events and over our personal life events. Nothing transpires outside of His plan. This means that the timing of everything present and future is in His hands. We don't need to worry one bit. Psalm 115:3 says, "But our God is in the heavens; He does whatever He pleases." Because He's all-good and all-wise, we can trust Him in whatever He does, as Paul writes: "And we know that God causes all things to work together for good to those who love God, to those who are called according to His purpose" (Rom. 8:28).

Finally, *rely on God's Word whenever you feel uncertain or insecure.* His inspired, inerrant Word takes precedence over every merely human word. News reports can work people into a frenzy; God's Word settles our hearts and relieves our worries. People like to emphasize the negative and project a dismal future; God's Word points us to the hope we have in Jesus Christ: When He comes, He will come as the Savior of believers and the just Judge of unbelievers. When something worrisome occurs, we should turn to the Word of God first. Hear the words of Psalm 119:105: "Your word is a lamp to my feet and a light to my path." Scripture will never lead you astray or drive you into despair. In fact, Paul wrote in Romans 15:4, "For whatever was written in earlier times was written for our instruction, so that through perseverance and the encouragement of the Scriptures we might have hope." Not uncertainty, not insecurity, not dread of the future, but perseverance, encouragement, and hope.

Ready or Not, Here He Comes
MATTHEW 24:29–25:46

NASB

29 "But immediately after the tribulation of those days THE SUN WILL BE DARKENED, AND THE MOON WILL NOT GIVE ITS LIGHT, AND THE STARS WILL FALL from ªthe sky, and the powers of ªthe heavens will be shaken. 30 And then the sign of the Son of Man will appear in the sky, and then all the tribes of the earth will mourn, and they will see the SON OF MAN COMING ON THE CLOUDS OF THE SKY with power and great glory. 31 And He will send forth His angels with A GREAT TRUMPET and THEY WILL GATHER TOGETHER His ªelect from the four winds, from one end of the sky to the other.

32 "Now learn the parable from the fig tree: when its branch has already become tender and puts forth its leaves, you know that summer is near; 33 so, you too, when you see all these things, ªrecognize that ᵇHe

NLT

29 "Immediately after the anguish of those days,

the sun will be darkened,
the moon will give no light,
the stars will fall from the sky,
and the powers in the heavens
will be shaken.*

30 And then at last, the sign that the Son of Man is coming will appear in the heavens, and there will be deep mourning among all the peoples of the earth. And they will see the Son of Man coming on the clouds of heaven with power and great glory.* 31 And he will send out his angels with the mighty blast of a trumpet, and they will gather his chosen ones from all over the world*—from the farthest ends of the earth and heaven.

32 "Now learn a lesson from the fig tree. When its branches bud and its leaves begin to sprout, you know that summer is near. 33 In the same way, when you see all these things, you can know his return is very near,

NASB

is near, *right* at the ^cdoor. ³⁴Truly I say to you, this ^ageneration will not pass away until all these things take place. ³⁵Heaven and earth will pass away, but My words will not pass away.

³⁶"But of that day and hour no one knows, not even the angels of heaven, nor the Son, but the Father alone. ³⁷For ^athe coming of the Son of Man will be just like the days of Noah. ³⁸For as in those days before the flood they were eating and drinking, marrying and giving in marriage, until the day that Noah entered the ark, ³⁹and they did not ^aunderstand until the flood came and took them all away; so will the coming of the Son of Man be. ⁴⁰Then there will be two men in the field; one ^awill be taken and one ^awill be left. ⁴¹Two women *will be* grinding at the ^amill; one ^bwill be taken and one ^bwill be left.

⁴²"Therefore be on the alert, for you do not know which day your Lord is coming. ⁴³But ^abe sure of this, that if the head of the house had known at what time of the night the thief was coming, he would have been on the alert and would not have allowed his house to be ^bbroken into. ⁴⁴For this reason you also must be ready; for the Son of Man is coming at an hour when you do not think *He will.*

⁴⁵"Who then is the faithful and sensible slave whom his ^amaster put in charge of his household to give them their food at the proper time? ⁴⁶Blessed is that slave whom his ^amaster finds so doing when he comes. ⁴⁷Truly I say to you that he will put him in charge of all his possessions. ⁴⁸But if that evil slave says in his heart, 'My ^amaster ^bis not coming for a long time,' ⁴⁹and begins to beat his fellow slaves and eat and drink with drunkards; ⁵⁰the ^amaster of that slave will come on a day when

NLT

right at the door. ³⁴I tell you the truth, this generation* will not pass from the scene until all these things take place. ³⁵Heaven and earth will disappear, but my words will never disappear.

³⁶"However, no one knows the day or hour when these things will happen, not even the angels in heaven or the Son himself.* Only the Father knows.

³⁷"When the Son of Man returns, it will be like it was in Noah's day. ³⁸In those days before the flood, the people were enjoying banquets and parties and weddings right up to the time Noah entered his boat. ³⁹People didn't realize what was going to happen until the flood came and swept them all away. That is the way it will be when the Son of Man comes.

⁴⁰"Two men will be working together in the field; one will be taken, the other left. ⁴¹Two women will be grinding flour at the mill; one will be taken, the other left.

⁴²"So you, too, must keep watch! For you don't know what day your Lord is coming. ⁴³Understand this: If a homeowner knew exactly when a burglar was coming, he would keep watch and not permit his house to be broken into. ⁴⁴You also must be ready all the time, for the Son of Man will come when least expected.

⁴⁵"A faithful, sensible servant is one to whom the master can give the responsibility of managing his other household servants and feeding them. ⁴⁶If the master returns and finds that the servant has done a good job, there will be a reward. ⁴⁷I tell you the truth, the master will put that servant in charge of all he owns. ⁴⁸But what if the servant is evil and thinks, 'My master won't be back for a while,' ⁴⁹and he begins beating the other servants, partying, and getting drunk? ⁵⁰The master

READY OR NOT, HERE HE COMES | MATTHEW 24:29–25:46

he does not expect *him* and at an hour which he does not know, ⁵¹and will ᵃcut him in pieces and ᵇassign him a place with the hypocrites; in that place there will be weeping and gnashing of teeth.

²⁵:¹"Then the kingdom of heaven will be comparable to ten virgins, who took their lamps and went out to meet the bridegroom. ²Five of them were foolish, and five were prudent. ³For when the foolish took their lamps, they took no oil with them, ⁴but the prudent took oil in flasks along with their lamps. ⁵Now while the bridegroom was delaying, they all got drowsy and *began* to sleep. ⁶But at midnight there was a shout, 'Behold, the bridegroom! Come out to meet *him*.' ⁷Then all those virgins rose and trimmed their lamps. ⁸The foolish said to the prudent, 'Give us some of your oil, for our lamps are going out.' ⁹But the prudent answered, 'No, there will not be enough for us and you *too;* go instead to the dealers and buy *some* for yourselves.' ¹⁰And while they were going away to make the purchase, the bridegroom came, and those who were ready went in with him to the wedding feast; and the door was shut. ¹¹Later the other virgins also came, saying, 'Lord, lord, open up for us.' ¹²But he answered, 'Truly I say to you, I do not know you.' ¹³Be on the alert then, for you do not know the day nor the hour.

¹⁴"For *it is* just like a man *about* to go on a journey, who called his own slaves and entrusted his possessions to them. ¹⁵To one he gave five ᵃtalents, to another, two, and to another, one, each according to his

will return unannounced and unexpected, ⁵¹and he will cut the servant to pieces and assign him a place with the hypocrites. In that place there will be weeping and gnashing of teeth.

²⁵:¹"Then the Kingdom of Heaven will be like ten bridesmaids* who took their lamps and went to meet the bridegroom. ²Five of them were foolish, and five were wise. ³The five who were foolish didn't take enough olive oil for their lamps, ⁴but the other five were wise enough to take along extra oil. ⁵When the bridegroom was delayed, they all became drowsy and fell asleep.

⁶"At midnight they were roused by the shout, 'Look, the bridegroom is coming! Come out and meet him!'

⁷"All the bridesmaids got up and prepared their lamps. ⁸Then the five foolish ones asked the others, 'Please give us some of your oil because our lamps are going out.'

⁹"But the others replied, 'We don't have enough for all of us. Go to a shop and buy some for yourselves.'

¹⁰"But while they were gone to buy oil, the bridegroom came. Then those who were ready went in with him to the marriage feast, and the door was locked. ¹¹Later, when the other five bridesmaids returned, they stood outside, calling, 'Lord! Lord! Open the door for us!'

¹²"But he called back, 'Believe me, I don't know you!'

¹³"So you, too, must keep watch! For you do not know the day or hour of my return.

¹⁴"Again, the Kingdom of Heaven can be illustrated by the story of a man going on a long trip. He called together his servants and entrusted his money to them while he was gone. ¹⁵He gave five bags of silver* to one, two bags of silver to another, and one bag of silver to the last—dividing it in

own ability; and he went on his journey. [16]Immediately the one who had received the five talents went and traded with them, and gained five more talents. [17]In the same manner the one who *had received* the two *talents* gained two more. [18]But he who received the one *talent* went away, and dug *a hole* in the ground and hid his [a]master's money.

[19]"Now after a long time the master of those slaves came and settled accounts with them. [20]The one who had received the five talents came up and brought five more talents, saying, 'Master, you entrusted five talents to me. See, I have gained five more talents.' [21]His master said to him, 'Well done, good and faithful slave. You were faithful with a few things, I will put you in charge of many things; enter into the joy of your [a]master.'

[22]"Also the one who *had received* the two talents came up and said, 'Master, you entrusted two talents to me. See, I have gained two more talents.' [23]His master said to him, 'Well done, good and faithful slave. You were faithful with a few things, I will put you in charge of many things; enter into the joy of your master.'

[24]"And the one also who had received the one talent came up and said, 'Master, I knew you to be a hard man, reaping where you did not sow and gathering where you scattered no *seed*. [25]And I was afraid, and went away and hid your talent in the ground. See, you have what is yours.'

[26]"But his master answered and said to him, 'You wicked, lazy slave, you knew that I reap where I did not sow and gather where I scattered no *seed*. [27]Then you ought to have put my money [a]in the bank, and on my

proportion to their abilities. He then left on his trip.

[16]"The servant who received the five bags of silver began to invest the money and earned five more. [17]The servant with two bags of silver also went to work and earned two more. [18]But the servant who received the one bag of silver dug a hole in the ground and hid the master's money.

[19]"After a long time their master returned from his trip and called them to give an account of how they had used his money. [20]The servant to whom he had entrusted the five bags of silver came forward with five more and said, 'Master, you gave me five bags of silver to invest, and I have earned five more.'

[21]"The master was full of praise. 'Well done, my good and faithful servant. You have been faithful in handling this small amount, so now I will give you many more responsibilities. Let's celebrate together!*'

[22]"The servant who had received the two bags of silver came forward and said, 'Master, you gave me two bags of silver to invest, and I have earned two more.'

[23]"The master said, 'Well done, my good and faithful servant. You have been faithful in handling this small amount, so now I will give you many more responsibilities. Let's celebrate together!'

[24]"Then the servant with the one bag of silver came and said, 'Master, I knew you were a harsh man, harvesting crops you didn't plant and gathering crops you didn't cultivate. [25]I was afraid I would lose your money, so I hid it in the earth. Look, here is your money back.'

[26]"But the master replied, 'You wicked and lazy servant! If you knew I harvested crops I didn't plant and gathered crops I didn't cultivate, [27]why didn't you deposit my money

arrival I would have received my *money* back with interest. 28 Therefore take away the talent from him, and give it to the one who has the ten talents.'

29 "For to everyone who has, *more* shall be given, and he will have an abundance; but from the one who does not have, even what he does have shall be taken away. 30 Throw out the worthless slave into the outer darkness; in that place there will be weeping and gnashing of teeth.

31 "But when the Son of Man comes in His glory, and all the angels with Him, then He will sit on His glorious throne. 32 All the nations will be gathered before Him; and He will separate them from one another, as the shepherd separates the sheep from the goats; 33 and He will put the sheep on His right, and the goats on the left.

34 "Then the King will say to those on His right, 'Come, you who are blessed of My Father, inherit the kingdom prepared for you from the foundation of the world. 35 For I was hungry, and you gave Me *something* to eat; I was thirsty, and you gave Me *something* to drink; I was a stranger, and you invited Me in; 36 naked, and you clothed Me; I was sick, and you visited Me; I was in prison, and you came to Me.' 37 Then the righteous will answer Him, 'Lord, when did we see You hungry, and feed You, or thirsty, and give You *something* to drink? 38 And when did we see You a stranger, and invite You in, or naked, and clothe You? 39 When did we see You sick, or in prison, and come to You?' 40 The King will answer and say to them, 'Truly I say to you, to the extent that you did it to one of these brothers of Mine, *even* the least *of them,* you did it to Me.'

41 "Then He will also say to those on His left, 'Depart from Me, accursed ones, into the eternal fire

in the bank? At least I could have gotten some interest on it.'

28 "Then he ordered, 'Take the money from this servant, and give it to the one with the ten bags of silver. 29 To those who use well what they are given, even more will be given, and they will have an abundance. But from those who do nothing, even what little they have will be taken away. 30 Now throw this useless servant into outer darkness, where there will be weeping and gnashing of teeth.'

31 "But when the Son of Man* comes in his glory, and all the angels with him, then he will sit upon his glorious throne. 32 All the nations* will be gathered in his presence, and he will separate the people as a shepherd separates the sheep from the goats. 33 He will place the sheep at his right hand and the goats at his left.

34 "Then the King will say to those on his right, 'Come, you who are blessed by my Father, inherit the Kingdom prepared for you from the creation of the world. 35 For I was hungry, and you fed me. I was thirsty, and you gave me a drink. I was a stranger, and you invited me into your home. 36 I was naked, and you gave me clothing. I was sick, and you cared for me. I was in prison, and you visited me.'

37 "Then these righteous ones will reply, 'Lord, when did we ever see you hungry and feed you? Or thirsty and give you something to drink? 38 Or a stranger and show you hospitality? Or naked and give you clothing? 39 When did we ever see you sick or in prison and visit you?'

40 "And the King will say, 'I tell you the truth, when you did it to one of the least of these my brothers and sisters,* you were doing it to me!'

41 "Then the King will turn to those on the left and say, 'Away with you, you cursed ones, into the eternal fire

NASB

which has been prepared for the devil and his angels; [42]for I was hungry, and you gave Me *nothing* to eat; I was thirsty, and you gave Me nothing to drink; [43]I was a stranger, and you did not invite Me in; naked, and you did not clothe Me; sick, and in prison, and you did not visit Me.' [44]Then they themselves also will answer, 'Lord, when did we see You hungry, or thirsty, or a stranger, or naked, or sick, or in prison, and did not [a]take care of You?' [45]Then He will answer them, 'Truly I say to you, to the extent that you did not do it to one of the least of these, you did not do it to Me.' [46]These will go away into eternal punishment, but the righteous into eternal life."

24:29 [a]Or *heaven* 24:31 [a]Or *chosen ones* 24:33 [a]Or *know* [b]Or *it* [c]Lit *doors* 24:34 [a]Or *race* 24:37 [a]Lit *just as...were the days* 24:39 [a]Lit *know* 24:40 [a]Lit *is* 24:41 [a]I.e. handmill [b]Lit *is* 24:43 [a]Lit *know this* [b]Lit *dug through* 24:45 [a]Or *lord* 24:46 [a]Or *lord* 24:48 [a]Or *lord* [b]Lit *lingers* 24:50 [a]Or *lord* 24:51 [a]Or *severely scourge him* [b]Lit *appoint his portion* 25:15 [a]A talent was worth about fifteen years' wages of a laborer 25:18 [a]Or *lord's* 25:21 [a]Or *lord* 25:27 [a]Lit *to the bankers* 25:44 [a]Or *serve*

NLT

prepared for the devil and his demons.* [42]For I was hungry, and you didn't feed me. I was thirsty, and you didn't give me a drink. [43]I was a stranger, and you didn't invite me into your home. I was naked, and you didn't give me clothing. I was sick and in prison, and you didn't visit me.'

[44]"Then they will reply, 'Lord, when did we ever see you hungry or thirsty or a stranger or naked or sick or in prison, and not help you?'

[45]"And he will answer, 'I tell you the truth, when you refused to help the least of these my brothers and sisters, you were refusing to help me.'

[46]"And they will go away into eternal punishment, but the righteous will go into eternal life."

24:29 See Isa 13:10; 34:4; Joel 2:10. 24:30 See Dan 7:13. 24:31 Greek *from the four winds*. 24:34 Or *this age*, or *this nation*. 24:36 Some manuscripts do not include *or the Son himself*. 25:1 Or *virgins*; also in 25:7, 11. 25:15 Greek *talents*; also throughout the story. A talent is equal to 75 pounds or 34 kilograms. 25:21 Greek *Enter into the joy of your master* [or *your Lord*]; also in 25:23. 25:31 "Son of Man" is a title Jesus used for himself. 25:32 Or *peoples*. 25:40 Greek *my brothers*. 25:41 Greek *his angels*.

Biblical prophecy has always been a target of critics. Throughout history, skeptics have had a field day in relation to prophetic Scripture—poking fun, making jokes, and picking apart prophecies. This perennial pastime of scoffers will be especially prevalent as the world gets closer to the last days. The apostle Peter wrote about this near the end of his second letter: "Know this first of all, that in the last days mockers will come with their mocking, following after their own lusts, and saying, 'Where is the promise of His coming? For ever since the fathers fell asleep, all continues just as it was from the beginning of creation'" (2 Pet. 3:3-4).

Sounds familiar, doesn't it? It's easy to think like that if you choose to ignore cataclysmic events like the Flood, when God judged the ungodly people of the world back in the days of Noah. Or it's easy to tease those who believe in biblical prophecy if you think the story of God's judgment of Sodom and Gomorrah and the rescue of Lot was just a

You Better Git Ready!

MATTHEW 24–25

I have a good friend—we'll just call him Bruce—who was a skeptic before he became a believer. During his years of stubborn unbelief, Bruce kept all things religious at a nice, safe, comfortable distance. He either never thought about spiritual things, or if they came up in conversation, would quickly change the subject.

Well, Bruce was hitchhiking across America a number of years ago. As night began to fall, dark clouds formed overhead, and distant thunder began to rumble. He started to get desperate for a ride, not only to get where he was going but also to avoid the impending storm. Just as the drops of rain began to fall, a car pulled over, a door flew open, and a driver yelled, "Hop in!" Bruce didn't hesitate. He was delighted to get out of the rain. As soon as he got in, the rain started pounding violently on the car. So, he just settled into the seat. He was suddenly shocked when he saw a small card taped to the glove box right in front of him that read,

WARNING!

IN THE EVENT OF CHRIST'S RETURN THIS DRIVER WILL SUDDENLY DISAPPEAR AND THIS CAR WILL SELF-DESTRUCT!

YOU BETTER GIT READY!

I once asked Bruce how that made him feel—rain falling, now close to nightfall, stuck in a car with a person he regarded as a religious nut. He responded, "I didn't know whether to write my will, pray, or jump. So, the first thing I did was unlock my door, just in case. The guy kept wanting to bring our conversation back to Jesus, and I kept wanting to talk about anything but Jesus." All the while that sign with its bold believe-it-or-not message kept staring at Bruce from the dash.

(continued on next page)

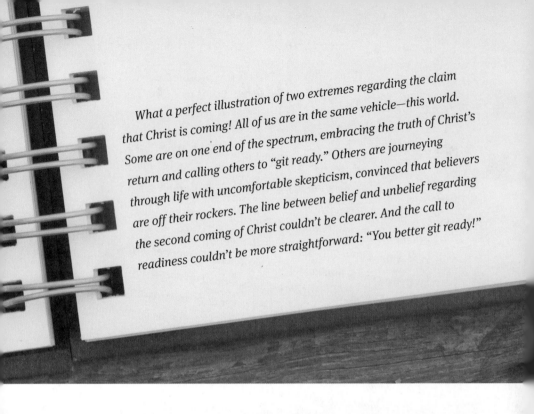

What a perfect illustration of two extremes regarding the claim that Christ is coming! All of us are in the same vehicle—this world. Some are on one end of the spectrum, embracing the truth of Christ's return and calling others to "git ready." Others are journeying through life with uncomfortable skepticism, convinced that believers are off their rockers. The line between belief and unbelief regarding the second coming of Christ couldn't be clearer. And the call to readiness couldn't be more straightforward: "You better git ready!"

myth to scare people into believing. But as it happened in the days of Noah and Lot, so it will be in the future when Christ returns. Those who are unprepared will suddenly find themselves overcome by a period of worldwide judgment. Ready or not, Jesus is coming!

Teaching concerning the return of Christ never fails to create mixed feelings. For those who are ready for it, there's a mixture of comfort, relief, and eager expectation. For those *not* ready because of unbelief, disobedience, or rebellion, the range of emotions runs from ignorant indifference to contemptuous scorn. Yet just like it's impossible to remain neutral in our response to the gospel of the saving person and work of Jesus Christ, so it is with regard to the Second Coming. Even when we're not thinking about it, God's clock is ticking, moving toward that moment when the true believers will be snatched from this earth and the rest of the world will face the great Day of the Lord—the seven-year Tribulation (1 Thes. 4:16–5:3).

— 24:29–25:46 —

Though we could spend volumes exploring the details of end-times events, I've decided to focus attention on the big picture by drawing seven principles (often with related applications) from Jesus' discourse concerning the days leading up to and including His glorious return.

These principles will be based largely on the prophecies of Matthew 24:29-51 and 25:31-46, though some insights will also be drawn from the two related parables in Matthew 25:1-30. I won't offer a point-by-point explanation of what each verse means, nor am I going to wade deeply into the murky waters of speculation. I offer a fuller explanation of the details of end-times events in my commentary on the book of Revelation.[105] Basically, I'd like to offer a concise overview of Jesus' main points in this section, along with a few practical words pertaining to our response.

First, *Christ's delay may be lengthy, so let's wait with patient anticipation.* As is now clear, from the time Jesus spoke the words in the Olivet discourse until His return, many centuries would pass. The original disciples sitting with Him on the Mount of Olives had no idea there would be such a long delay. Nor did the next several generations of the early church, who were living through intense persecution. Nor did the faithful remnant of true believers keeping the flame of hope alive during the Dark Ages. Nor did the Reformers, who saw their movement as a restoration of the gospel prior to the Second Coming. Nor do many prophecy enthusiasts today, who have convinced themselves and others that we are certainly the generation who will experience the rapture of the church.

Yet Jesus clearly said that no one can know when the end-times events will begin to take place (24:36). In fact, in the Parable of the Ten Virgins, the figure of the bridegroom (representing Christ) delayed his coming (25:5). Similarly, when telling the Parable of the Talents, Jesus made the point that the master returned to settle accounts "after a long time" (25:19). The fact is, the gap between His first coming and His second coming is a delay only from our human perspective. We must not forget 2 Peter 3:8: "With the Lord one day is like a thousand years, and a thousand years like one day." God's timing is different from our timing. Therefore, we should be ever alert, patiently waiting while diligently working.

Second, *Christ's return will be sudden and unexpected.* Though we are to be faithful in our waiting and fruitful in our service, we should never get too comfortable in the world. In Matthew 24:37-39, Jesus likened the context of His future coming to the days of Noah and Lot: People were living normal lives, oblivious to the fact that their wickedness was about to be judged. Similarly, the last generation on this earth will not expect the sudden onset of judgments at the Tribulation (24:39, 42-44, 50). In light of the fact that He will come as unexpectedly as a thief (24:43), our responsibility is clear: "Be ready; for the Son of Man is coming at an hour when you do not think He will" (24:44). In the Parable of the Ten Virgins, the wise virgins were prepared for the sudden, unexpected arrival of the bridegroom, and these women were welcomed into the wedding feast (25:6-10). However, the foolish virgins were caught off guard. They were shut outside with no hope of entering (25:10-12). The application: "Be on the alert then, for you do not know the day nor the hour" (25:13).

Third, *Christ's judgment will be irreversible.* People need to learn to take God and His Word seriously. He doesn't waffle in His will or stutter in His utterances. Woven throughout Matthew 24 and 25 are warnings against delaying decisions, being unprepared, and hoping for second chances. When God's time of testing arrives, He doesn't grade on a curve, nor does He offer retakes or extra credit. The serious and sudden judgments at the return of Christ are not just metaphorical, designed to move people to repentance; they are real and irreversible. We only get one opportunity to believe as long as we're alive: "It is appointed for men to die once and after this comes judgment" (Heb. 9:27).

Fourth, *when Christ returns, the truth will be revealed.* In the Parable of the Ten Virgins, the foolish virgins, who were unprepared for the coming of the bridegroom, found themselves locked outside the wedding party, unable to enter (Matt. 25:8-11). When they knocked and asked to be let in, the bridegroom replied, "Truly I say to you, I do not know you" (25:12). Though pretenders can play the part of faithful friends and put on appearances for a while, in the end, the truth will be manifest. It's certainly possible to live the life of a hypocrite and get away with it for a long time. Some Christians act one way in public but behave another way in private. Often, family and close friends know the truth, but sometimes even they are fooled. In the end, however, not even the best charlatan or most experienced hypocrite will be able to pull one over on the all-knowing Judge. The truth will be revealed.

Fifth, *each individual will be personally accountable at the return of Christ.* The mysterious description in Matthew 24:40-41 tells us that at the coming of Christ two people will be working together in the same occupation, but one will be taken and the other left. Some understand this to mean that those taken will be rescued from the coming judgment and thus removed to a safe place.[106] However, I think it's best to understand those taken as the ones who are swept away in judgment—parallel to the wicked at the time of Noah, mentioned in 24:38-39,

THE TWO ADVENTS OF CHRIST CONTRASTED

At His First Coming . . .	At His Second Coming . . .
He came in meekness as a servant (Matt. 20:28).	He will come in power as a judge (Matt. 24:30-31; 25:31-46; John 5:26-29).
He came in humility and gentleness (Matt. 11:29; John 5:41).	He will come in majesty and splendor (1 Thes. 4:16; Rev. 1:7).
He came to seek and save the lost (Matt. 18:11; Luke 19:10; John 3:17).	He will come to judge and reign (Acts 10:40-42; 2 Cor. 5:10; Rev. 11:15).
He came as a servant to suffer wrath for sinners (Matt. 16:21; 17:12; Mark 9:12).	He will come as a conqueror to rescue the righteous from wrath (1 Cor. 15:51-52; 1 Thes. 4:15-17).
He came to sow the seed of the gospel (Matt. 13:3-9; Luke 8:11).	He will come to reap the harvest (Matt. 13:37-43).

where Jesus said that "the flood came and took them all away."[107] But in either case, the point stands: Each individual will be accountable for his or her own faith or unbelief. You won't be able to stand behind your wife or husband, claim for yourself the faith of your parents, or plead innocent on the grounds of your family name, church membership, or ministry involvement. One will be taken in judgment, the other left to inherit the rewards of the kingdom of God.

Sixth, *the future of the faithful will be joyful.* God's promises will be fulfilled, and He will never forget His own children. Matthew 24:31 tells us that at the end of the Tribulation, the Son of Man will send His angels with a trumpet sound to gather His elect from "the four winds," or, as Mark has it, "from the farthest end of the earth to the farthest end of heaven" (Mark 13:27). In other words, from the north, south, east, and west—as far as the eye can see—believers will be gathered into the earthly messianic kingdom. Some have mistakenly identified this event as the rapture of the church mentioned in 1 Thessalonians 4:16-17, but the quotation from the Old Testament in Matthew 24:31 points to a different gathering of a different elect. Isaiah 11:12 says that God "will lift up a standard for the nations and assemble the banished ones of Israel, and will gather the dispersed of Judah from the four corners of the earth." This gathering will occur at the second coming of Christ, when He comes in glory (see Matt. 19:28)—after the Tribulation (see 24:29). As one commentator explains, "This involves the gathering of those who will have become believers during the Seventieth Week of

NOBODY KNOWS THE DAY OR THE HOUR

From Jesus to Paul, from Peter to the entire early church, all agreed that nobody knows when the Day of the Lord will begin or when the Lord will return. Consider these clear biblical texts:

- "But of that day and hour no one knows, not even the angels of heaven, nor the Son, but the Father alone." (Matt. 24:36)
- "Therefore be on the alert, for you do not know which day your Lord is coming." (Matt. 24:42)
- "Take heed, keep on the alert; for you do not know when the appointed time will come." (Mark 13:33)
- "So when they had come together, they were asking Him, saying, 'Lord, is it at this time You are restoring the kingdom to Israel?' He said to them, 'It is not for you to know times or epochs which the Father has fixed by His own authority.'" (Acts 1:6-7)
- "Now as to the times and the epochs, brethren, you have no need of anything to be written to you. For you yourselves know full well that the day of the Lord will come just like a thief in the night." (1 Thes. 5:1-2)
- "But the day of the Lord will come like a thief." (2 Pet. 3:10)
- "I will come like a thief, and you will not know at what hour I will come to you." (Rev. 3:3)
- "Behold, I am coming like a thief. Blessed is the one who stays awake and keeps his clothes, so that he will not walk about naked and men will not see his shame." (Rev. 16:15)

Daniel and who will have been scattered into various parts of the world because of persecution (cf. Matt. 24:16)."[108]

This gathering of the elect into the kingdom is also pictured in the great judgment of "the sheep and the goats" in Matthew 25:31-46, in which the Messiah invites the sheep standing on His right—the righteous—to "inherit the kingdom" (25:34-36). Though this promise is written regarding the remnant of faithful saints who will be on the earth during the final days of the Tribulation, prior to Christ's second coming, there's an application for us as well: God honors the life of faith and obedience. He even promises specific rewards in the future kingdom for acts of faithfulness in this life (25:21). And, similar to the way the believers surviving at the end of the Tribulation will be gathered together and rewarded with life in the kingdom, so believers today—during the church age—will be raptured to heaven to meet the Lord in the air, based solely on our position in Christ (1 Thes. 4:16-17).

Finally, *the destiny of the lost will be dreadful.* There's no way to downplay this. The unbelievers, those unprepared for the return of Christ, the hypocrites and wicked revilers, will be consigned to a place where there will be "weeping and gnashing of teeth" (Matt. 24:51). The Parable of the Talents describes this place as "the outer darkness" (25:30). Elsewhere, it's referred to as a place of "eternal punishment" (25:46). Changing our eternal destination is something that must take place in this life. The only way to be assured of eternal life is to accept Christ's sacrificial, atoning death for us and His miraculous, bodily resurrection (1 Cor. 15:1-5). We are saved by grace alone through faith alone in Christ alone, or we are not saved at all.

APPLICATION: MATTHEW 24:29-25:46

Three Questions Only You Can Answer

In this section, I took an unusual approach. Rather than going through each verse explaining details and answering some of the knotty questions, I chose to present the big picture and to focus on the practical implications for all of us. Why? Because when we stand before our Lord one day to give an account of our lives, He won't give us a theological exam on the doctrine of the end times or a Bible quiz on key passages about the Rapture or the Second Coming. He won't give us a blank sheet and ask us to draw an end-times chart with all the events in the right chronological order. Rather, we will be evaluated based on how we answer three vital questions.

First, *how did I respond to what I heard?* Some will continue to ignore the truth throughout their lives, delaying a decision for Christ day after day, year after year. Yet, to enter eternal life, the gospel of salvation through Christ alone must be received—by faith. This requires a decisive, unambiguous embrace of who He is (the God-man) and what He did for us (died and rose again). I believe the end-times events described in Matthew 24 and 25 are set forth thematically, not strictly chronologically, for a reason: to draw our attention away from the *chart* and toward the *heart*.

Second, *am I able to stand before Christ in full assurance?* We must trust in Christ *and Christ alone* for our salvation. This is not a

"BEHOLD, THE BRIDEGROOM!"

MATTHEW 25:1-13

When we see the New Testament comparing Christ's relationship with the church to a groom's relationship with his bride (e.g., 9:15; 25:1-13), we need to understand the historical and cultural context of this analogy. The marriage traditions of the ancient Near East were quite different from those of our twenty-first-century Western culture. Rather than there being a single celebration, in Jewish marriage traditions, there are several distinct stages.

The betrothal. This was much more official and legally binding than a modern engagement. The parents of both the bride and the groom sealed a contract. Then they began making arrangements for the ceremony, which often took place a year or more later. During this betrothal period, the man and woman were considered legally married—though they didn't live together—and a betrothal could only be broken by a writ of divorce.

The presentation. After the preparations of the couple's future home were finished and the arrangements were finalized, the next stage in the marriage could commence. Leading up to the festivities of the actual wedding ceremony, the groom would leave his home and travel to the bride's home, where she would be waiting with her friends, the bridesmaids. The groom would then claim her as his own beloved bride.

The ceremony. The presentation of the bride would initiate a lengthy festivity known as the wedding supper, which could last several days. The new bride and groom would depart the marriage supper with the full rights, privileges, and responsibilities of husband and wife.[109]

The analogy of the church's marriage to Christ reflects these ancient Jewish wedding customs. In God the Father's foresight, He chose the church "before the foundation of the world" (Eph. 1:4). So, when sinners are saved, they are betrothed to Christ, a binding relationship that still awaits its complete realization. At the presentation, the church will be raptured to meet the Lord in the air (1 Thes. 4:17; cf. Matt. 25:1-13). Then, at the wedding feast of the Lamb (Rev. 19:7-9), the marriage will be finalized, and Christ and His people will take their places to reign over the earth (Rev. 20:4-6).[110]

cooperative effort, in which Jesus does His part and we do ours. Our own efforts are an affront to the absolutely free, unmerited grace that we receive through simple faith. Just as we will contribute absolutely nothing to our future bodily resurrection at Christ's return, so we are able to contribute nothing to the power that raises us from spiritual death when we accept Christ by faith. Our assurance of salvation will wobble and waffle if we place even an ounce of trust for that salvation in anything other than the God-man, who died, rose, and ascended, and who will one day return as Judge and King.

Third, *have I been living my life as if He might call me home this very moment?* None of us know how many minutes, hours, days, or years we have ahead of us. But we do know that we all have one second less than we had one second ago. Our lives are ticking away, and so are the opportunities to serve the Lord and to love others with everything we have. Those of us who have been saved by faith are called to faithfulness—not because loving God and loving others through our words and works saves us but because we are indwelled and compelled by the Holy Spirit to live a new life in Christ. Jesus' words in the Olivet discourse remind us repeatedly that with faithfulness comes reward when He returns as our long-expected King.

PASSION AND TRIUMPH OF THE KING (MATTHEW 26:1–28:20)

As we transition from Jesus' discourse on the end times and the Second Coming (Matt. 24–25), we leave powerful scenes of victory and vindication, and Matthew's Gospel suddenly cuts to scenes of weakness and apparent—*but only apparent*—defeat. At the end of Matthew 25, we hear of the Son of Man coming in glory with His angels, taking a seat on His glorious throne and judging the nations as the King, Israel's long-awaited Messiah (25:31-46). But with His next breath, we hear of the Son of Man being "handed over for crucifixion" (26:2). I can only imagine the jolt the disciples must have felt as they were shaken from their visions of regal glory as crowned co-regents with Christ and were sharply forced to reckon with the startling prospect that the heir to the throne was about to be arrested, tortured, and executed.

I've titled this section on the final three chapters of Matthew *Passion and Triumph of the King*. Leading up to the crucial climax of this Gospel, we witness the unfolding plot of certain Jewish leaders to have Jesus executed (26:1-16). In the meantime, Jesus somberly celebrates a last Passover meal with His disciples and institutes the Lord's Supper (26:17-30). In a matter of hours, Judas betrays Jesus, and the authorities arrest Him, just as Jesus Himself had predicted (26:31-56). Abandoned by most of His disciples, Jesus is railroaded through an unjust series of sham trials (26:57–27:26). Then, at the hands of both Jews and Gentiles, Jesus is executed on a Roman cross. Both heaven and earth shake at the crucifixion of the rightful King of Israel, the long-awaited Messiah (27:27-66).

But profound tragedy transforms into resounding triumph as Jesus is miraculously and gloriously raised—bodily—from the dead on the third day. He steps from the tomb victorious, even as those responsible for His death continue to connive against Him (28:1-15). Having conquered death and the grave, the Lord Jesus presents Himself alive to His disciples, commissioning them as His ambassadors of the coming kingdom. Their new mission—which is also ours—is to make disciples from among all the nations by proclaiming the gospel of the saving death and resurrection of Jesus, baptizing them into the faith through the name of the Father, Son, and Holy Spirit, and instructing them to live faithful lives as heavenly citizens until He comes again in glory (28:16-20).

Yes, Jesus was to endure suffering—betrayal by friends, torture by enemies, anguish in body and soul, experiencing the public death of a criminal and a hasty burial in a borrowed tomb. Yet such a humiliating death would give way to triumph when His glorious resurrection proved that He was who He had claimed to be in word and deed: the one true King, Israel's long-awaited Messiah.

KEY TERMS IN MATTHEW 26:1-28:20

paradidōmi **(παραδίδωμι)** [3860] "to hand over," "to surrender," "to transfer possession"

Based on the verb meaning "to give" (*didōmi* [1325]), this term carries the idea of surrendering possession of something to the control of another. Depending on the context, some translators render the term as "betray" (see, e.g., 24:10 and 26:16 in the NASB), but the Greek word itself does not suggest whether the motivation is good or evil (see 11:27; 25:20). The term is used extensively in the Passion narrative, in which Jesus is "handed over" to the authorities (27:2, 18, 26). Earlier, Jesus had prepared His followers for this, telling them that He would be "delivered" into the hands of men who would condemn Him to suffering and death (17:22; 20:18, 19; 26:2, 45).

paschō **(πάσχω)** [3958] "to suffer," "to endure pain"

In Matthew 16 Jesus began to announce to His disciples that He would soon "suffer" at the hands of His enemies (16:21). This period of suffering has come to be called the "passion" of Christ. The English word *passion* is derived from the Greek term *paschō*. This verb can refer to suffering death (17:12), suffering from sickness (17:15), suffering from trials or temptations (Heb. 2:18), or suffering from mental or emotional anguish (Matt. 27:19). Very early on, Christians began to refer to the entirety of Jesus' experiences from His arrest to His crucifixion as "His suffering" (Acts 1:3). In fact, the two crucial rites of the Christian faith, baptism and the Lord's Supper, both commemorate the events of the Passion.

Countdown to Betrayal
MATTHEW 26:1-16

NASB

¹When Jesus had finished all these words, He said to His disciples, ²"You know that after two days the Passover is coming, and the Son of Man is *to be* handed over for crucifixion."

³Then the chief priests and the elders of the people were gathered together in the court of the high priest, named Caiaphas; ⁴and they plotted together to seize Jesus by stealth and kill Him. ⁵But they were saying, "Not during the festival, otherwise a riot might occur among the people."

⁶Now when Jesus was in Bethany, at the home of Simon the leper, ⁷a woman came to Him with an alabaster vial of very costly perfume, and she poured it on His head as He reclined *at the table.* ⁸But the disciples were indignant when they saw *this*, and said, "Why this waste? ⁹For this *perfume* might have been sold for a high price and *the money* given to the poor." ¹⁰But Jesus, aware of this, said to them, "Why do you bother the woman? For she has done a good deed to Me. ¹¹For you always have the poor with you; but you do not always have Me. ¹²For when she poured this perfume on My body, she did it to prepare Me for burial. ¹³Truly I say to you, wherever this gospel is preached in the whole world, what this woman has done will also be spoken of in memory of her."

¹⁴Then one of the twelve, named Judas Iscariot, went to the chief priests ¹⁵and said, "What are you willing to give me ᵃto ᵇbetray Him to you?" And they weighed out thirty ᶜpieces of silver to him. ¹⁶From then on he *began* looking for a good opportunity to ᵃbetray ᵇJesus.

26:15 ᵃLit *and I will* ᵇOr *deliver* ᶜI.e. silver shekels
26:16 ᵃOr *deliver* ᵇLit *Him*

NLT

¹When Jesus had finished saying all these things, he said to his disciples, ²"As you know, Passover begins in two days, and the Son of Man* will be handed over to be crucified."

³At that same time the leading priests and elders were meeting at the residence of Caiaphas, the high priest, ⁴plotting how to capture Jesus secretly and kill him. ⁵"But not during the Passover celebration," they agreed, "or the people may riot."

⁶Meanwhile, Jesus was in Bethany at the home of Simon, a man who had previously had leprosy. ⁷While he was eating,* a woman came in with a beautiful alabaster jar of expensive perfume and poured it over his head.

⁸The disciples were indignant when they saw this. "What a waste!" they said. ⁹"It could have been sold for a high price and the money given to the poor."

¹⁰But Jesus, aware of this, replied, "Why criticize this woman for doing such a good thing to me? ¹¹You will always have the poor among you, but you will not always have me. ¹²She has poured this perfume on me to prepare my body for burial. ¹³I tell you the truth, wherever the Good News is preached throughout the world, this woman's deed will be remembered and discussed."

¹⁴Then Judas Iscariot, one of the twelve disciples, went to the leading priests ¹⁵and asked, "How much will you pay me to betray Jesus to you?" And they gave him thirty pieces of silver. ¹⁶From that time on, Judas began looking for an opportunity to betray Jesus.

26:2 "Son of Man" is a title Jesus used for himself.
26:7 Or *reclining.*

As Matthew 26 begins, we can almost hear the throbbing drumbeat of death. Several significant events follow each other in sequence as the cross of Calvary casts its ominous shadow over every scene. Shortly after finishing His discourse on the Mount of Olives, Jesus turned His disciples' attention to the reality of what would soon transpire. He wasted no time in telling them: "The Son of Man is to be handed over for crucifixion" (26:2).

Place yourself for a moment in the position of those disciples. It wasn't the first time they had heard their revered rabbi utter such things (e.g., 20:19). But this time the words came on the heels of some earth-shattering prophecies of the end of the age and the ushering in of Christ's kingdom. Was Jesus speaking in some kind of code? Was "Son of Man" a reference to somebody else who would suffer these things? Or maybe He would be handed over for crucifixion but would then escape from the grasp of His enemies and turn the tables on their plot. Maybe this chain of events would culminate in the great overthrow of Rome and the establishment of the Messiah's kingdom. Whatever was going through the disciples' minds, the last thing they could imagine was what was about to actually take place.

While Jesus tried to mentally prepare His closest followers for what was coming, His archenemies were on the move in the shadows and behind closed doors, plotting a seek-and-destroy mission against the Messiah (26:4). He had ruffled their feathers of self-righteousness and riled them up by His bold proclamation of truth against their hypocritical falsehoods. Now they wanted to put an end to Him once and for all.

— 26:1-2 —

Between chapters 25 and 26, Matthew turns his readers' attention from the crown to the cross, from future glory to imminent suffering. Once he pulls the camera away from his long-range shot to focus on the cross peeking over the horizon, the narrative slows down, closing in on Calvary over the span of two lengthy chapters. In the early scenes of chapter 26, Matthew takes the first steps in leading us—from the point of view of the disciples—toward the betrayal, arrest, trials, and crucifixion of Christ.

These verses remind me of Winston Churchill's multivolume work on World War II, in which he provided background information from earlier events that set the stage for and made sense of what was to come. His first volume, titled *The Gathering Storm*, describes what transpired in the dark, twisted, and depraved mind of Adolf Hitler and in the burgeoning Nazi party. Similarly, Matthew relays certain scenes that, placed together, give us a glimpse of the gathering storm rolling in over Jerusalem—a storm of jealousy, deception, betrayal, and brutality.

In 26:1, Matthew reminds us that Jesus had just finished His lengthy discourse answering the disciples' questions "When will these things happen, and what will be the sign of Your coming, and of the end of the age?" (24:3). While His followers were still mulling over the barrage of images He had shared pertaining to the distant future, Jesus pulled them back to the here and now with a reminder that the Passover was just two days away. Then He added, "And the Son of Man is to be handed over for crucifixion" (26:2). No fewer than six times, Jesus had already mentioned—either directly or indirectly—the fact of His coming suffering and death at the hands of men (16:21; 17:12, 22-23; 20:18-19, 22-23; 21:38-39). The fact that Jesus knew of His impending death and resurrection in detail demonstrates an important theological truth: Though the perpetrators engaged in wicked plotting for their own twisted purposes, nothing transpired outside of God's sovereign will or contrary to His own timetable. Jesus Himself declared, "I lay down My life so that I may take it again. No one has taken it away from Me, but I lay it down on My own initiative. I have authority to lay it down, and I have authority to take it up again. This commandment I received from My Father" (John 10:17-18).

— 26:3-5 —

With the foretelling of Jesus' impending crucifixion hanging in the air, Matthew suddenly cuts to a room inside the high priest's home southwest of the temple mount. We're dropped into the middle of a conspiracy in motion, with several of the chief priests and elders having gathered to plot Jesus' demise (26:3-4). Caiaphas, the high priest, becomes the leading antagonist, embodying all the forces of the religious elites bent on protecting their power and promoting their personal interests. Caiaphas may have been behind many of the previous attempts to hinder or trap Jesus, to question His integrity, and to weaken His influence. Now, after the numerous, multipronged efforts to foil Christ's mission and resist His message have come up empty, the high priest and his wicked cabal have murder on their minds: "They plotted together to seize Jesus by stealth and kill Him" (26:4).

Acknowledging that Jesus' popularity with the people was at an all-time high, the members of the conspiracy deemed it unwise to attempt an obvious, direct assault on their enemy. Because of the Passover

THE GANGSTERS OF JERUSALEM

MATTHEW 26:3

At the time of Christ, the office of high priest in Jerusalem carried a lot of clout. Not only was the high priest the head of the temple proceedings, but he was also the ruler over many civil, social, and political affairs. Those of the priestly class "were the real rulers of the nation, although they did not claim for themselves the title of king."[1] Since the Jews were under the thumb of the Roman Empire, the appointment of the high priest had to be undertaken by Rome, and the high priest operated under the authority of the Roman procurator.

At the time of Jesus' trial, Caiaphas officially held the office (26:3), having been appointed by the Romans, but many recognized Caiaphas's father-in-law, Annas, as the real power behind the throne. Annas had been appointed high priest in AD 6, but he was deposed nine years later. However, he remained the powerful head of an elite family, not unlike figures we see in modern organized crime syndicates. After his removal from office, he continued to wield power behind the scenes, first through his son Eleazar and then through his son-in-law Caiaphas, which explains his presence in the trials of Jesus.

Meanwhile, Caiaphas's long tenure as high priest indicates that he was skilled in the underhanded dealings of Jerusalem politics. One commentator notes that "between 37 BC and AD 67 . . . there were no fewer than twenty-eight high priests," yet "Caiaphas was high priest from AD 18–36. This was an extraordinarily long time for a high priest to last, and Caiaphas must have brought the technique of co-operating with the Romans to a fine art."[2]

So, as we visualize the plot to kill Jesus, we should not imagine an aboveboard deliberation among otherwise law-abiding rulers who simply made mistakes because of a lack of spiritual insight. Rather, we should picture the kind of backroom scheming we might see in a movie about the Mafia, in which unscrupulous thugs plot how to take out an adversary who is treading on their territory. Members of the high priestly family were in many respects the gangsters of Jerusalem who felt their unchallenged power squeezed by Jesus' words and deeds. And in order to maintain the status quo of deep corruption, they were willing to commit murder.

celebration, the number of visitors to Jerusalem had swelled, and just a few days earlier, Jesus had ridden a donkey into Jerusalem with cries of "Hosanna to the Son of David!" (21:6-11). The leaders of Jerusalem had seen the large crowds enamored with His teaching. They knew a public arrest would certainly result in a riot (26:5). On top of that, they seemed to have no idea where Jesus and His small band of disciples went when they retired for the evening (cf. John 18:1-2). That is, their secret hideout remained hidden. So, Caiaphas and his clan decided to lie low and take a more prudent approach: wait until after the festival, when the throngs of Jews had departed Jerusalem and returned to their homes. Then, when the right moment presented itself, Jesus—and perhaps some of His closest companions—would simply "disappear."

But as we will see, behind the scenes there were even darker forces at work that would provide a more immediate opportunity for the chief priests to do away with Jesus of Nazareth.

— 26:6-13 —

We should probably not picture the next scene as a sudden cutaway from the behind-closed-doors conspiracy of the chief priests to an event happening concurrently at an evening dinner. If we look closely, Matthew doesn't actually say that the event described in 26:6-13 occurred at the same time or even next chronologically. We see no "then" or "after this" or "at that time." Rather, he simply says, "Now when Jesus was in Bethany . . ." (26:6). In fact, when we look at the parallel account of this event in the Gospel of John (John 12:2-11), we discover that it actually took place about four days earlier—the Saturday before the Triumphal Entry, six days before the Passover (John 12:1). Why would Matthew push the pause button on the story line to provide this flashback here in the midst of the narrative? The answer is simple: The scene provides the motivation for Judas Iscariot's betrayal, which would give the Jewish leaders an opportunity to apprehend Jesus during the festival rather than having to wait until its conclusion.

Matthew and Mark don't give details of the specific people involved at the dinner in Bethany except that it took place at the home of "Simon the leper" (Matt. 26:6; Mark 14:3). While everyone was dining, a woman entered with a vial of extremely expensive perfume (Matt. 26:7). The Gospel of John identifies the woman as none other than Mary, the sister of Lazarus and Martha (John 12:3). Matthew isn't concerned about her identity as much as the controversial nature of her actions. While Jesus was reclining at the table in the traditional manner, Mary broke the alabaster jar of perfume and poured it on Jesus' head (Matt. 26:7). John tells us that she also anointed His feet with it, wiping His feet with her hair (John 12:3). Thus Jesus, who was the Christ—meaning "anointed one"—had been anointed with costly oil from head to toe.

Though this act of sacrifice and service demonstrated Mary's devotion to Jesus, to the onlookers the quality and quantity of the perfume used in the anointing seemed to be an incredible waste of such a valuable commodity. John and Mark tell us that the perfume was made from "pure nard" (Mark 14:3; John 12:3). Nard, or spikenard, originated in India and had to be imported from the Himalaya region.[3] Given the exotic nature and remote source of the perfume, the quantity used in the anointing of Jesus was shocking—a pound undiluted (John 12:3). Matthew reports that in response to this luxurious action to anoint Jesus' head and feet, "the disciples were indignant." They saw it as a great waste and complained that the perfume could have been sold and the money given to the poor (Matt. 26:8-9).

John's Gospel gives us an illuminating detail about the disciples' complaint. It originated from Judas Iscariot: "Judas Iscariot, one of His disciples, who was intending to betray Him, said, 'Why was this perfume not sold for three hundred denarii and given to poor people?' Now he said this, not because he was concerned about the poor, but because he was a thief, and as he had the money box, he used to pilfer what was put into it" (John 12:4-6).[4]

Having stirred up the disciples to pass judgment on Mary's act of unfettered devotion, Judas probably wondered how Jesus would respond. But instead of joining in on the scolding, Jesus rebuked the scolders! His response must have stung those shortsighted disciples, so easily manipulated by Judas's self-serving spin on Mary's worshipful action. Jesus highly commended her for her good deed (Matt. 26:10), promising, in fact, that wherever the gospel would be preached throughout the world, it would be accompanied by an account of her act of devotion (26:13). He also clarified that His disciples would always have opportunities to show kindness and generosity toward the poor, but they would not always be able to worship their King in person (26:11).

As the overpowering fragrance wafted through the entire house (John 12:3), it would have brought to mind the strong odor associated with the anointing of dead bodies for burial (cf. Mark 16:1; Luke 24:1; John 19:40). Mary likely intended the anointing of Jesus' head and feet to be an act of worship and a confession that He was the true Messiah ("anointed one"). Yet Jesus provided a more profound interpretation of her act: "When she poured this perfume on My body, she did it to prepare Me for burial" (Matt. 26:12).

— 26:14-16 —

If a filmmaker were editing this flashback that appears in the flow of Matthew's account of Jesus' last days, no doubt the camera would slowly pan across the puzzled faces of the disciples at that table and settle on a shifty-eyed figure visibly fuming at Jesus' rebuke: Judas Iscariot. In his lust for money and his presumably growing frustration with Jesus' frequent talk about His own death—instead of a plan to overthrow the enemies of Israel—Judas lost all confidence in the messiahship of the carpenter's son from Nazareth. The absurdity (from Judas's perspective) of Mary's anointing of Jesus and Jesus' praising acceptance of it pushed him over the edge. Again, this is why Matthew included the flashback: to explain Judas's actions recorded in 26:14-16.

As the chief priests and elders discussed how to best corner Jesus, the answer to their dilemma was already developing. Judas, who couldn't abide such extravagant adoration of the Savior, joined in the conspiracy of those men who had assassination in their hearts. He snuck away from the disciples, went to the chief priests, and asked, "What are you willing to give me to betray Him to you?" (26:14-15).

What a shocking question! The divine words that had flowed from Jesus' lips had done nothing to penetrate Judas's hard heart. The stunning miracles that Jesus had done, in which Judas himself had participated, didn't seem to make a dent in his conscience. With a feigned faith and a treacherous disposition that seemed only to calcify all the more when exposed to the light of Christ's divinity, Judas betrayed his Lord for thirty pieces of silver. And from the moment Judas took the money from the Jerusalem gangsters, he began looking for the right opportunity to lead them to Jesus.

APPLICATION: MATTHEW 26:1-16

Self-Sacrificial Worship vs. Self-Serving Betrayal

Matthew strategically placed the scene of Mary's self-sacrificial worship of her King between two scenes of self-serving betrayal. This was no accident. It reveals a profound truth and calls each of us to consider our own relationship with the Lord Jesus. The first group of self-serving betrayers—the chief priests and elders—had always been far from Jesus. They were outsiders, critics, enemies from the start. Their desire to silence the Savior makes sense at the human level: They had a history of betrayal in how they treated the prophets and the people they were supposed to lead in righteousness and truth.

Meanwhile, Judas enjoyed a close, intimate relationship with Jesus as one of the Twelve. He saw what nobody on the outside got to see. He heard things nobody but the inner circle got to hear. Yet he spent his days and nights slithering like a venomous snake, seeking an opportunity to strike. His betrayal makes no sense even from a human perspective. Yet it makes sense when we realize that "the heart is more deceitful than all else and is desperately sick" (Jer. 17:9). Judas had a spiritual problem. Without the illumination and regeneration of the Spirit of God, all of us would be in a similar state, regardless of how well we know God's Word or how close we are to His people.

Notice how quiet and secretive Judas was. He didn't announce his plans to those closest to him. In fact, I suspect that by this point he may have been much closer to the enemies of Christ than he ever had been to his fellow disciples. And isn't it amazing how this betrayal happened despite Judas's exceptional knowledge about Christ? He knew the songs. He knew the prayers. He could describe to you the settings when the lame were healed and the dead were raised. But these things never touched his heart.

Throughout life, events have occurred that have moved you either toward or away from the claims of Christ. Everyone is either for Christ or against Him. Are you for Him, like Mary, who gave up a year's wages' worth of precious ointment to demonstrate her worship and devotion? Have you told Him? Have you showed Him? Does your life reveal it? Or do you give off the appearance of a disciple to those on the sidelines when in fact you're nothing of the sort? I urge you to move in the right direction of the "good deed" of Mary—devoting yourself to Jesus afresh as the anointed Lord of your life. Lay before Him all the things that have competed for your allegiance. And worship Him!

Soul Searching during Supper
MATTHEW 26:17-30

NASB

17 Now on the first *day* of Unleavened Bread the disciples came to Jesus and asked, "Where do You want us to prepare for You to eat the Passover?" 18 And He said, "Go into the city to a certain man, and say to him, 'The

NLT

17 On the first day of the Festival of Unleavened Bread, the disciples came to Jesus and asked, "Where do you want us to prepare the Passover meal for you?"

18 "As you go into the city," he told them, "you will see a certain man. Tell him, 'The Teacher says: My

NASB

Teacher says, "My time is near; I *am to* keep the Passover at your house with My disciples."'" [19]The disciples did as Jesus had directed them; and they prepared the Passover.

[20]Now when evening came, Jesus was reclining *at the table* with the twelve disciples. [21]As they were eating, He said, "Truly I say to you that one of you will betray Me." [22]Being deeply grieved, they [a]each one began to say to Him, "Surely not I, Lord?" [23]And He answered, "He who dipped his hand with Me in the bowl is the one who will betray Me. [24]The Son of Man *is to* go, just as it is written of Him; but woe to that man by whom the Son of Man is betrayed! It would have been good [a]for that man if he had not been born." [25]And Judas, who was betraying Him, said, "Surely it is not I, Rabbi?" Jesus said to him, "You have said *it* yourself."

[26]While they were eating, Jesus took *some* bread, and [a]after a blessing, He broke *it* and gave *it* to the disciples, and said, "Take, eat; this is My body." [27]And when He had taken a cup and given thanks, He gave *it* to them, saying, "Drink from it, all of you; [28]for this is My blood of the covenant, which is poured out for many for forgiveness of sins. [29]But I say to you, I will not drink of this fruit of the vine from now on until that day when I drink it new with you in My Father's kingdom."

[30]After singing a hymn, they went out to the Mount of Olives.

26:22 [a]Or *one after another* 26:24 [a]Lit *for him if that man had not been born* 26:26 [a]Lit *having blessed*

NLT

time has come, and I will eat the Passover meal with my disciples at your house.'" [19]So the disciples did as Jesus told them and prepared the Passover meal there.

[20]When it was evening, Jesus sat down at the table* with the Twelve. [21]While they were eating, he said, "I tell you the truth, one of you will betray me."

[22]Greatly distressed, each one asked in turn, "Am I the one, Lord?"

[23]He replied, "One of you who has just eaten from this bowl with me will betray me. [24]For the Son of Man must die, as the Scriptures declared long ago. But how terrible it will be for the one who betrays him. It would be far better for that man if he had never been born!"

[25]Judas, the one who would betray him, also asked, "Rabbi, am I the one?"

And Jesus told him, "You have said it."

[26]As they were eating, Jesus took some bread and blessed it. Then he broke it in pieces and gave it to the disciples, saying, "Take this and eat it, for this is my body."

[27]And he took a cup of wine and gave thanks to God for it. He gave it to them and said, "Each of you drink from it, [28]for this is my blood, which confirms the covenant* between God and his people. It is poured out as a sacrifice to forgive the sins of many. [29]Mark my words—I will not drink wine again until the day I drink it new with you in my Father's Kingdom."

[30]Then they sang a hymn and went out to the Mount of Olives.

26:20 Or *Jesus reclined.* 26:28 Some manuscripts read *the new covenant.*

In the Swindoll home, we occasionally imagine what it would have been like to be a "bug on the wall" during certain important historical events—in the lab when Edison made the first voice recording . . . in the war room when Eisenhower gave the order for the invasion of

Normandy . . . in Mission Control when men first landed on the moon—the list could go on and on. Although it would be difficult to select from among the countless profound biblical scenes in God's unfolding plan of redemption, several events particularly invite a bug-on-the-wall reflection: when Adam and Eve were kicked out of the Garden, when God split the Red Sea, or when Mary and Joseph first looked into the face of Jesus. But I would have especially liked being a bug on the wall at the Last Supper when the Twelve and their Master reclined at the table to celebrate Passover together.

At this point in Matthew's account, everything is moving inexorably toward Christ's crucifixion. The Last Supper is the calm before the storm. Within a matter of hours, He would be betrayed by Judas, arrested at Gethsemane, pushed through a series of unjust trials by both Jews and Romans, scourged severely, mocked, and nailed to a cross by heartless soldiers, where He would die a slow, excruciating death. But before all this, He and His twelve disciples gathered around a common table for the Passover meal—their last supper together.

As Matthew recalled and recorded these events, he methodically outlined the relevant details of the supper. At one particular moment, Jesus' mysterious words—"One of you will betray Me" (26:21)—put everybody on the defensive. Though the conspirator, Judas Iscariot, slinked silently in the shadows, hiding behind a wall of hypocrisy, he couldn't escape the probing insight of the Light of the World. Yet even Judas sat at the table with the Savior, partaking of the Passover. It's unfathomable to imagine how deep-seated was Judas' depravity that it could lead to such bald-faced betrayal . . . until we realize that the fallen human heart that led to his rock-bottom treachery beats in our chests too.

— 26:17-19 —

The Jewish observance of the Feast of Unleavened Bread recalled the unleavened cakes baked prior to the exodus from Egypt (Exod. 12:39). The festival began with the offering of the Passover lamb. Preparations for the special meal "came during the daylight hours on Thursday, the fourteenth of Nisan" when lambs were offered in the afternoon and prepared to be eaten in the evening—Thursday night.[5] That meal was called the Passover. The rest of the Feast of Unleavened Bread then extended for seven more days.[6]

As the day of Passover dawned, the disciples were naturally becoming concerned about where they would observe the annual meal. To forsake the meal would have been a violation of the Law, which required

PASSOVER AND THE FEAST OF UNLEAVENED BREAD

MATTHEW 26:17-19

The first—and most important—of the annual feasts in the ancient Jewish calendar was the seven-day Feast of Unleavened Bread. It began with the commemoration of the Passover. Each family was responsible for offering an unblemished lamb at the temple in the afternoon on the fourteenth day of Nisan, the day of preparation. At midafternoon, the priests would blow a ram's horn, and representatives of the families would flood into the temple to offer their lambs. The animals were killed and skinned, and the blood was drained into a basin. A priest then splashed the blood against the base of the altar to signify atonement for sin. Inner organs and fat were burned on the altar as part of the offering. The rest of the sacrificial lamb was then brought home before sunset and roasted for the Passover meal. Passover technically began when the sun set at the end of the fourteenth day of Nisan (also considered the beginning of the fifteenth day).

Though many elements of the modern Jewish Passover *seder* (or "order") stem from developments that have occurred over the centuries since the destruction of the temple in AD 70, scholars can discern the basic outline of the celebration as Jesus and His disciples would have likely observed it in the first century.[7] The head of the household (or, in the case of the disciples, Jesus) would raise a first cup of wine and recite a standard prayer of blessing. Then the *matzah* (unleavened bread), *maror* (bitter herbs, perhaps a tart leafy vegetable like lettuce), *haroset* (a thick, fruity relish), and *pesach* (roasted lamb) would be presented for the meal.

Early rabbis described the significance of the elements of the meal in various ways. Eventually, a script—or liturgy—of questions and answers became part of the *seder* ritual. The bitter herbs were dipped in the *haroset*, which some say had the consistency of clay. This reminded the Jews of their bitter bondage in Egypt where they worked to make bricks from clay. It's also thought that the *haroset* had a reddish color, reminding Jews of the blood that was shed under the oppression of Pharaoh.

During the meal, the host would pour a second cup and would rehearse the story of the Hebrews' delivery from bondage in Egypt. This included details of the first Passover itself, when God struck down the firstborn of Egypt but passed over the children of Israel because blood had been applied to their doorposts. The red wine associated with the second blessing was a vivid reminder of the blood of the sacrificial lamb that marked their deliverance. After the commemorative meal, a third cup of blessing would accompany a prayer of thanksgiving that typically followed Jewish meals. A final cup concluded the entire service, during which the host would lead in a closing prayer and song.

particular feasts to be observed annually (Lev. 23). Undoubtedly, they assumed that their rabbi had arranged for the meal somewhere in Jerusalem, since they were from Galilee. The disciples were more than willing to make the necessary preparations for the meal; they just needed to know the venue (Matt. 26:17).

While Matthew presents a very brief, to-the-point account of the events that led to the location of the supper (26:18-19), the Gospels of Mark and Luke fill in additional details (see Mark 14:12-16; Luke 22:7-13). Evidently, Jesus had already made initial contact with some of His followers in Jerusalem. Some scholars believe it was the family of John Mark, and that the location was perhaps the same upper room where, as recorded in the early chapters of Acts, the disciples would gather to await the coming of the Spirit (Acts 1:13) and the church of Jerusalem would continue to gather later on (Acts 12:12).[8] However, we can't be sure.

If the Passover meal was to be observed at the home of somebody known by the disciples, why didn't Jesus simply tell the disciples outright? Some have suggested that because Jesus knew Judas had set in motion a plot to betray Him (Matt. 26:16), He had to make the arrangements for the Passover meal behind the traitor's back.[9] This could be the reason He didn't observe the feast at the home in Bethany where He was staying. That would have been an obvious place for an arrest, and the meal would have provided a great opportunity for Judas, as the streets of the city would have been mostly empty while families remained indoors to observe the Passover. But Jesus wasn't about to let Himself be caught in Judas's diabolical web until it was time. Though His time was "near" (26:18), the moment for His arrest had not yet come.

— 26:20-25 —

Once Peter and John completed the preparations (see Luke 22:8) and the time for the Passover meal arrived, Jesus and the disciples assembled at the planned location. I can just imagine Judas following Jesus and the other disciples as they wound through the crowded Jerusalem streets, unsure of where they were going, his eyes shifting back and forth as his brain went into overdrive searching for the best moment to report Jesus' secret itinerary to the Jewish authorities. Yet by the time they arrived at the prearranged room, any opportunity for immediate betrayal had slipped away. He would have to wait for the right moment.

With the table set and the meal prepared, Jesus and the Twelve gathered according to the Jewish custom at the time (Matt. 26:20). Throughout the entire meal, the participants would have reclined (not sat) at the table. William Barclay notes, "The table was a low solid block, with couches round it. It was shaped like a U and the place of the host was at the centre. They reclined on their left side, resting on the left elbow, thus leaving the right hand free to deal with the food."[10]

After the opening blessing and first cup of wine, the meal of un-leavened bread, roasted lamb, bitter leafy herbs, and sweet relish was served. During the meal Jesus would have rehearsed the experience of the Hebrews during their liberation from slavery in Egypt. It was some-time during this traditional instruction that Jesus got up from supper and washed the disciples' feet, giving them an example of utter humil-ity and self-sacrificial service toward one another—an act recorded only in the Gospel of John (John 13:3-20).

Then, at another point in the traditional service, Jesus went "off script" again. He announced, "Truly I say to you that one of you will betray Me" (Matt. 26:21). This shocking statement not only jarred them from the recollection of redemption at the Passover but also put every-body at the table on the defensive. I can imagine that Judas turned pale and that the hair raised on the back of his neck. Perhaps he went numb and began to fumble and stammer. He'd been found out for sure.

When all the disciples at the table protested (26:22), Jesus replied that the one who dipped his hand with Him in the bowl was the one who would betray Him (26:23). Mark's version includes the statement "one who is eating with Me" (Mark 14:18). In speaking of the one "dip-ping his hand" in the bowl, Jesus wasn't talking about washing hands at the table. He was referring to the dipping of the herbs or the bread in the *haroset* (relish) as part of the Passover meal. He was also alluding to Psalm 41:9, which says, "Even my close friend in whom I trusted, who ate my bread, has lifted up his heel against me." It's unlikely that those at the table would have singled out Judas at this point. The fact is, during the Passover meal, everybody at the table at some point or another had dipped into the *haroset* with Jesus. It may be that Judas was the last to do so—an act that had gone unnoticed to the others but would have been known by Judas himself. In any case, to a couple of people present, it would be clear who it was that Jesus had in mind.

Jesus immediately followed up his cryptic statement about betrayal with a stern warning that would have caused Judas's heart to skip a beat. Jesus said that though the Messiah was to go to His death just as predicted in Scripture, the one who would betray Him would still be guilty of a heinous sin. So terrible was such a betrayal, in fact, that it would have been better if that person had never been born (Matt. 26:24)!

While Jesus spoke concerning His betrayal, the disciples continued to insist that they would never turn on Him. And like the others, Judas asked, "Surely it is not I, Rabbi?" (26:25). But to Judas, Jesus replied, "You have said it yourself." The interaction between Jesus and Judas at that point would likely have been private, perhaps held in whispers. Judas probably occupied a place at the table to Jesus' left (cf. John 13:26).[11] Jesus' cryptic, indirect response to Judas's question was an idiom similar to our English phrases "You got it!" or "Bingo!"[12] The point was at least clear to Judas: "You're the one I'm talking about, and you and I both know it."

Judas went silent.

The Gospel of John informs us that at Peter's prompting from across the table, John, who was sitting immediately beside Jesus on his right, leaned over and whispered, "Lord, who is it?" (John 13:23-25). Seemingly in an aside, spoken quietly to prevent everybody from hearing, Jesus informed John, "That is the one for whom I shall dip the morsel and give it to him" (John 13:26). In John's Gospel it appears as though Jesus immediately took the morsel of bread, dipped it in the relish, and handed it to Judas. However, another possible scenario is worth mentioning.

At first glance, it appears that the institution of the Lord's Supper is conspicuously left out of the Gospel of John. However, it may be that the mention of Jesus' sharing of the morsel is an allusion to the event of the Lord's Supper itself.[13] If so, instead of picturing Jesus whispering to John and then immediately turning to hand a piece of bread to Judas, we might picture Jesus whispering to John and then transitioning to the institution of the Lord's Supper. In this alternative scenario, during that profound observance, Jesus shared the bread with Judas as well as the others (see Luke 22:19-21). But with respect to Judas, Jesus dipped his morsel of bread in the relish before giving it to him. This would have served as a signal to John that Judas was the one who would betray Him. This event likely would have also served as an example with respect to those who might partake of the Lord's Supper in an unworthy manner (1 Cor. 11:27).

— 26:26-30 —

This leads us to Matthew's account of the institution of the Lord's Supper. The event is recorded not only in Matthew 26:26-29, but also in Mark 14:22-25; Luke 22:17-20; and 1 Corinthians 11:23-26. (As I have suggested, it is also possible that John indirectly referred to the observance of the Lord's Supper when he mentioned that Jesus gave Judas a morsel of bread dipped in the relish [John 13:26], though that scenario is uncertain.) From Matthew's brief account we know that while they were eating, Jesus took bread from the table, blessed it, and broke it into pieces to distribute to the disciples. In doing so, He famously proclaimed, "Take, eat; this is My body" (Matt. 26:26). He also took a cup of the wine from the table, gave thanks, and said, "Drink from it, all of you; for this is My blood of the covenant, which is poured out for many for forgiveness of sins" (26:27-28). Jesus' words then took a sudden turn to refer to the distant future, when He would reign eternally. He noted that this would be the last sip of wine He would have "until that day when I drink it new with you in My Father's kingdom" (26:29).

Note that in the midst of a commemoration of the Passover—a central rite of the old covenant—Jesus abruptly introduced a completely new explanation of the symbolism of the bread and wine. When He said of the bread, "This is My body," and of the wine, "This is My blood," Jesus was not speaking literally, but figuratively. His words didn't miraculously transform the very physical essence of the bread and wine into His actual fleshly body and blood. But His words do affirm that He had a real body (He was not merely a spiritual or angelic being), and it was that very real body that would be broken and His very real blood that would be shed for the sins of the world.

The Gospel of John informs us that around this point in the meal Satan entered into Judas, taking possession of that vessel devoid of true salvation (John 13:27). Jesus then said to Judas, "What you do, do quickly." Immediately Judas rose from the table and departed into the night (John 13:30). Though puzzled, most of the disciples thought nothing of it. They assumed that as the keeper of the money among the group, Judas had to take care of some financial obligation—paying expenses for the feast or giving an offering to the poor (John 13:28-29).

Matthew concludes his account of the Passover *seder*–turned– Lord's Supper with a brief summary statement alluding to a practice that would have been familiar to Jews living at the time—the singing of a hymn. The "hymn" was probably one of the *Hallel* Psalms (psalms of praise)—perhaps the "Great Hallel," Psalm 136, typically recited as part of the Passover meal. Whatever song they sang, the disciples' supper had concluded, and they began the short trip through the city, across the Kidron Valley, to the Mount of Olives (Matt. 26:30). As they did, they stepped into the same dark night that Judas had slithered into earlier. And while they ascended the hill to continue fellowshiping with the

EXCURSUS: "THIS IS MY BODY; THIS IS MY BLOOD"

MATTHEW 26:26-29

Regarding Jesus' words instituting the Lord's Supper, many Christians have gone to one of two extremes. Some have taken Jesus too literally, believing His words miraculously transformed (and continue to transform) the elements into the actual body and blood of Christ. Others swing to the other extreme, believing that the symbolic nature of the words renders the whole Lord's Supper unimportant. A proper understanding of the nature of the signs, the realities they signify, and their significance will help us avoid these extremes.

With respect to the first extreme, let me give you an illustration. Sitting on my desk in my office is my favorite framed picture of my wife, Cynthia. When I look at that photo, it reminds me of her. Imagine if somebody were to visit me in my study, point at the photo, and ask, "Who's this?" I would immediately answer, "Oh, this is my wife." I'm pretty certain the visitor would not conclude that I married a framed photo! He would know that when I said, "This is my wife," I meant "This is a visual representation of my wife." That should go without saying. The same is true about the representation of the body and blood of Christ in the bread and wine of the Lord's Supper. Even though the sign takes the name of the thing signified—"This is My body" and "This is My blood"—it's evident that Jesus meant that these are *pictures* that represent His body and blood.

Pertaining to the other extreme, the symbolic nature of the bread and wine of the Lord's Supper doesn't suggest that we are to downplay their significance or fail to treat the observance of the Lord's Supper with thanksgiving and due reverence.

Rather, we should value the symbols because of the high regard we have for what they represent. Let's go back to that photo of Cynthia on my desk. Imagine if the visitor in my office were to take the photo of my wife from my desk and smash it. Or throw it to the ground and jump on it. Or fling it across the room in anger. Or spit on it. I guarantee that I wouldn't lean back in my chair and say, "Oh, go ahead, it's just a picture. A mere symbol. It doesn't matter how you treat it. Burn it, for all I care." Unthinkable! Because I value my wife more than any person in this world, that likeness of Cynthia has tremendous value to me. To show disrespect toward the representation would show disrespect for the reality. This is the same reason I and many others can't stand to see people trampling on, burning, or disrespecting the United States flag. Of course, the flag is a symbol—there's nothing magical about the red, white, and blue cloth from which it's made. But we show honor for the reality by honoring the symbol. And we show disrespect for the reality by disrespecting the symbol.

With the Lord's Supper, then, we have a sacred symbol that serves as a frequent reminder—both a solemn and a joyful celebration—of who Jesus is and what He has done to save us. And in this symbol, more profound than a mere photo, Jesus gave us something we can not only see, but also touch, taste, smell, and hear. It's a confession and commemoration of the gospel that involves all five senses. What a powerful practice the Lord has left us! We would do well to honor Him by reverently, joyfully, and thankfully partaking of these meaningful elements in faith.

King, Israel's long-awaited Messiah, Judas descended into the depths of treachery, seeking to betray the King for a paltry reward.

APPLICATION: MATTHEW 26:17-30

Searching Our Hearts

In 1 Corinthians 11:27-28, Paul wrote, "Whoever eats the bread or drinks the cup of the Lord in an unworthy manner, shall be guilty of the body and the blood of the Lord. But a man must examine himself, and in so doing he is to eat of the bread and drink of the cup." I can't help but wonder if Paul had Judas Iscariot in the back of his mind when he penned those words. Like Judas, who went through the motions at that Passover meal but never let Jesus' words and actions penetrate his calloused heart, many who come to the Lord's Supper treat it similarly. Like Judas, they set themselves up in a place of rebellion against the Savior.

In gathering with fellow believers around the Lord's Table, we need to examine ourselves, letting His Word search our hearts. I don't mean for us to beat ourselves up for every little blemish in our lives. That would be a failure to remember that by unmerited love Christ's body was broken and His blood shed for the forgiveness of our sins. We must never forget that we are invited to the table by grace, just as we are invited into a saving relationship with Him by grace alone through faith alone. We don't earn a place at the table. But we also need to do some soul searching and life analyzing as we come to the table so the Spirit can banish from our midst any hints of treachery, betrayal, and hypocrisy.

Along these lines, take some time to meditate on Psalm 139:23-24. Do it now, and do it next time you are preparing to meet the Lord at the Supper table. Reflect on who He is and what He has done for us—*for you and for me!* Make these words your heartfelt prayer as well as the constant attitude of your life:

> Search me, O God, and know my heart;
> Try me and know my anxious thoughts;
> And see if there be any hurtful way in me,
> And lead me in the everlasting way.

Denial, Distress, Deception, Desertion
MATTHEW 26:31-56

NASB

31 Then Jesus said to them, "You will all ªfall away because of Me this night, for it is written, 'I WILL STRIKE DOWN THE SHEPHERD, AND THE SHEEP OF THE FLOCK SHALL BE SCATTERED.' 32 But after I have been raised, I will go ahead of you to Galilee." 33 But Peter said to Him, "*Even* though all may ªfall away because of You, I will never fall away." 34 Jesus said to him, "Truly I say to you that this *very* night, before a rooster crows, you will deny Me three times." 35 Peter said to Him, "Even if I have to die with You, I will not deny You." All the disciples said the same thing too.

36 Then Jesus came with them to a place called Gethsemane, and said to His disciples, "Sit here while I go over there and pray." 37 And He took with Him Peter and the two sons of Zebedee, and began to be grieved and distressed. 38 Then He said to them, "My soul is deeply grieved, to the point of death; remain here and keep watch with Me."

39 And He went a little beyond *them*, and fell on His face and prayed, saying, "My Father, if it is possible, let this cup pass from Me; yet not as I will, but as You will." 40 And He came to the disciples and found them sleeping, and said to Peter, "So, you *men* could not keep watch with Me for one hour? 41 Keep watching and praying that you may not enter into temptation; the spirit is willing, but the flesh is weak."

NLT

31 On the way, Jesus told them, "Tonight all of you will desert me. For the Scriptures say,

'God will strike* the Shepherd,
    and the sheep of the flock will
        be scattered.'

32 But after I have been raised from the dead, I will go ahead of you to Galilee and meet you there."

33 Peter declared, "Even if everyone else deserts you, I will never desert you."

34 Jesus replied, "I tell you the truth, Peter—this very night, before the rooster crows, you will deny three times that you even know me."

35 "No!" Peter insisted. "Even if I have to die with you, I will never deny you!" And all the other disciples vowed the same.

36 Then Jesus went with them to the olive grove called Gethsemane, and he said, "Sit here while I go over there to pray." 37 He took Peter and Zebedee's two sons, James and John, and he became anguished and distressed. 38 He told them, "My soul is crushed with grief to the point of death. Stay here and keep watch with me."

39 He went on a little farther and bowed with his face to the ground, praying, "My Father! If it is possible, let this cup of suffering be taken away from me. Yet I want your will to be done, not mine."

40 Then he returned to the disciples and found them asleep. He said to Peter, "Couldn't you watch with me even one hour? 41 Keep watch and pray, so that you will not give in to temptation. For the spirit is willing, but the body is weak!"

NASB

⁴²He went away again a second time and prayed, saying, "My Father, if this cannot pass away unless I drink it, Your will be done." ⁴³Again He came and found them sleeping, for their eyes were heavy. ⁴⁴And He left them again, and went away and prayed a third time, saying the same thing once more. ⁴⁵Then He came to the disciples and said to them, "ᵃAre you still sleeping and resting? Behold, the hour is at hand and the Son of Man is being betrayed into the hands of sinners. ⁴⁶Get up, let us be going; behold, the one who betrays Me is at hand!"

⁴⁷While He was still speaking, behold, Judas, one of the twelve, came up ᵃaccompanied by a large crowd with swords and clubs, *who came* from the chief priests and elders of the people. ⁴⁸Now he who was betraying Him gave them a sign, saying, "Whomever I kiss, He is the one; seize Him." ⁴⁹Immediately Judas went to Jesus and said, "Hail, Rabbi!" and kissed Him. ⁵⁰And Jesus said to him, "Friend, *do* what you have come for." Then they came and laid hands on Jesus and seized Him.

⁵¹And behold, one of those who were with Jesus ᵃreached and drew out his sword, and struck the slave of the high priest and ᵇcut off his ear. ⁵²Then Jesus said to him, "Put your sword back into its place; for all those who take up the sword shall perish by the sword. ⁵³Or do you think that I cannot appeal to My Father, and He will at once put at My disposal more than twelve ᵃlegions of angels? ⁵⁴How then will the Scriptures be fulfilled, *which say* that it must happen this way?"

⁵⁵At that time Jesus said to the crowds, "Have you come out with swords and clubs to arrest Me as *you would* against a robber? Every day I used to sit in the temple teaching and you did not seize Me. ⁵⁶But all

NLT

⁴²Then Jesus left them a second time and prayed, "My Father! If this cup cannot be taken away* unless I drink it, your will be done." ⁴³When he returned to them again, he found them sleeping, for they couldn't keep their eyes open.

⁴⁴So he went to pray a third time, saying the same things again. ⁴⁵Then he came to the disciples and said, "Go ahead and sleep. Have your rest. But look—the time has come. The Son of Man is betrayed into the hands of sinners. ⁴⁶Up, let's be going. Look, my betrayer is here!"

⁴⁷And even as Jesus said this, Judas, one of the twelve disciples, arrived with a crowd of men armed with swords and clubs. They had been sent by the leading priests and elders of the people. ⁴⁸The traitor, Judas, had given them a prearranged signal: "You will know which one to arrest when I greet him with a kiss." ⁴⁹So Judas came straight to Jesus. "Greetings, Rabbi!" he exclaimed and gave him the kiss.

⁵⁰Jesus said, "My friend, go ahead and do what you have come for."

Then the others grabbed Jesus and arrested him. ⁵¹But one of the men with Jesus pulled out his sword and struck the high priest's slave, slashing off his ear.

⁵²"Put away your sword," Jesus told him. "Those who use the sword will die by the sword. ⁵³Don't you realize that I could ask my Father for thousands* of angels to protect us, and he would send them instantly? ⁵⁴But if I did, how would the Scriptures be fulfilled that describe what must happen now?"

⁵⁵Then Jesus said to the crowd, "Am I some dangerous revolutionary, that you come with swords and clubs to arrest me? Why didn't you arrest me in the Temple? I was there teaching every day. ⁵⁶But this is all happening to fulfill the words

this has taken place to fulfill the Scriptures of the prophets." Then all the disciples left Him and fled.

of the prophets as recorded in the Scriptures." At that point, all the disciples deserted him and fled.

26:31 ªOr *stumble* **26:33** ªOr *stumble* **26:45** ªOr *Keep on sleeping therefore* **26:47** ªLit *and with him* **26:51** ªLit *extended the hand* ᵇLit *took off* **26:53** ªA legion equaled 6,000 troops

26:31 Greek *I will strike.* Zech 13:7. **26:42** Greek *If this cannot pass.* **26:53** Greek *twelve legions.*

At some point in every person's educational program, the teaching time is over and the time of testing begins. At the end of a college school year, it's final exam week. A doctoral program is punctuated with comprehensive exams and a dissertation defense. Law school culminates in the grueling state bar exam. Pastoral training usually concludes with a grilling before an ordination council. And let's not even talk about medical school!

Like a long period of intense training coming to its conclusion, the earthly ministry of Jesus was wrapping up. From this point on, there would be no more extensive teaching sessions, no more discourses, no more lectures or sermons, no more practice runs at preaching, no more question-and-answer exercises. The crowds would no longer gather to hear the Master's words or witness His magnificent miracles. There would be no more debates with the religious left or right, and no more challenges to the political zealots. All those events were over. The Messiah's hour had finally come, and there was no turning back.

In only a brief period, Jesus would experience trials and tribulations of heart and mind. He would spend hours in anguished prayer followed by hours of brutal beatings. Then His foes would serve up the ultimate injustice, finding Him guilty in spite of His purity, and executing Him for nothing. Parallel to this, His once faithful disciples would disappoint Him, betray Him, deny Him, and desert Him. Not a single one of them would make it unscathed through the time of testing.

— 26:31-35 —

Following the Last Supper, Jesus and the eleven faithful disciples got up from the table, sang together, and began making their way to a small, walled grove along the western slope of the Mount of Olives. Luke's account tells us that this "was His custom" (Luke 22:39). It also refers to the olive grove as "the place" (Luke 22:40), indicating a specific—that is, not random—location. It would have been extremely odd if Jesus and His disciples had been in the habit of trespassing in a stranger's olive

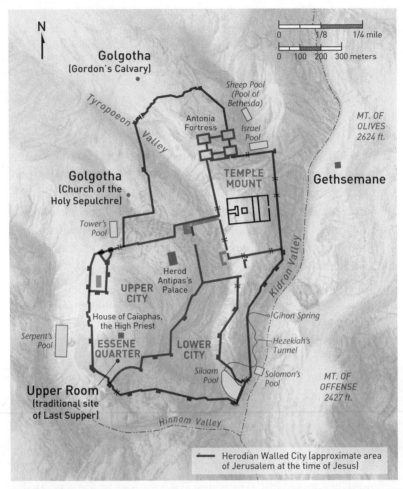

After the Passover meal, Jesus and the disciples crossed the Kidron Valley and ascended the western slope of the Mount of Olives to their private retreat, the olive grove known as the garden of Gethsemane.

garden, so we can be sure that the walled grove was owned by someone associated with Jesus or His disciples.

Early Christian tradition ties both the home where Jesus and the disciples celebrated the Passover and the garden of Gethsemane to the family of the young John Mark, who later became a close associate of Peter and wrote the Gospel of Mark.[14] If this is the case, it explains why Mark's Gospel mentions a "young man" (presumably Mark himself) who fled the scene of Jesus' arrest naked (Mark 14:51-52).[15] If the garden belonged to his family, he may have held the keys and been present among the disciples, perhaps with a few other family guests who were around during the Passover feast.

It's important to recognize that the place to which Jesus and the disciples were headed that night was a known location. John even says, "Jesus had often met there with His disciples" (John 18:2). It was, so to speak, Jesus' hideout, or secret base, while in Jerusalem. In the first century, as today, the Mount of Olives had numerous walled gardens side by side, their doors or gates virtually indistinguishable from one another. The only way to track Jesus down once He and the disciples ducked into that private fortress of solitude would have been if somebody "in the know" gave away the information. Of course, that somebody was Judas Iscariot (John 18:2).

As they were heading toward the Mount of Olives, Jesus stated matter-of-factly that every one of them without exception would "fall away" because of what was about to happen to Him (Matt. 26:31). To underscore His point, He quoted from Zechariah 13:7: "Strike the Shepherd that the sheep may be scattered." It would have been clear that in this illustration from Zechariah, Jesus was the Shepherd and the disciples were the scattered sheep. But immediately after this discouraging word, Jesus repeated the hopeful promise of His resurrection (Matt. 26:32)—a point the disciples seem to have missed entirely as they emphatically rejected Jesus' prophecy that they would fall away.

Speaking for himself—with the hearty agreement of the rest—Peter insisted that even if everybody else fell away, he would stay true (26:33). In the Greek text, the "I" of Peter is emphatic. We can imagine Peter pounding his chest in a dramatic, self-centered moment as he ups the ante and distinguishes himself from the rest of his companions. It's as if Peter were saying, "Even if all these spineless losers head for the hills, *I* will stick with you till the end!"

I can picture Jesus slowly shaking His head. Two wills collided that night: the sovereign will of the God-man who knew the future even more clearly than we know the past and the impetuous and presumptuous will of Peter, who didn't grasp his own weakness. Jesus refused to let Peter get away with that unchallenged statement, so He drove home the ugly truth with a very specific prophecy directed toward Peter himself: Before the rooster crowed at dawn, Peter would deny Him not once, not twice, but *three times* (26:34). In response to this embarrassing prediction, Peter doubled down, going all in with a promise that, even if it came to dying with Jesus, he would stay true to his Master (26:35). Then, not wanting to be outbid by Peter, the ten other disciples chimed in and made the same bold promise to stay at Jesus' side till the very end.

How foolish to directly contradict the words of the God-man! Yet, to these hasty and extravagant oaths of the eleven, Jesus responded with silence. What could He say that would convince them of their weaknesses? The facts of the matter would be clear soon enough, because these men were just hours away from turning on their Master and fleeing into the night. Before dawn, every one of them would have broken their dogmatic, unconditional, strongly worded promises. Though they were marching up the Mount of Olives looking like a loyal band of brothers, humming the first-century equivalent of "Onward, Christian Soldiers," it wouldn't last through the night.

— 26:36-46 —

Eventually they reached Gethsemane. The word *gethsemane* literally means "oil press." This means that the walled olive-tree grove was probably more cultivated and developed than just an average cluster of trees. John Peter Lange notes that the location was probably "a piece of land at the foot of the Mount of Olives, which was provided with a press, and perhaps also with a dwelling-house, or at least the usual garden-tower."[16] This further reinforces the fact that Jesus and the disciples were retiring to a well-known place, though inconspicuously hidden from the authorities. Perhaps laborers or relatives of the family to whom the olive grove belonged—possibly John Mark's family—would

© Todd Bolen/BiblePlaces.com

This ancient olive grove at the foot of the Mount of Olives is the traditional site of Gethsemane, where Jesus and His disciples retired on the night of the betrayal. Though we cannot be certain whether this is the original location, Gethsemane would have looked similar to this orchard.

Drops of Blood in Oil and Canvas

MATTHEW 26:36-46

My maternal grandparents' home had a number of framed oil paintings hanging in various rooms that had been painted by my Aunt Ernestine, who was an accomplished artist, though she lacked formal training. She had pure talent combined with many years of discipline. Growing up, I was always intrigued by her artwork, but one painting in the living room held my attention, especially when I was about three or four years old.

We had gone to my grandparents' house down in the little town of El Campo, Texas, for a holiday. In their living room hung one of Aunt Ernestine's grand paintings. I recall standing at the front of the fireplace and staring at the man portrayed in the painting, outside somewhere at night, kneeling, arms rested on a large boulder, hands folded in prayer. The man looked upward into the sky where dark, ominous clouds hung in the silver moonlight. As I looked more closely, I noticed it appeared that big drops of blood were running down the man's face.

I pulled a chair over so I could get up closer to the painting. Sure enough, there was blood on that person's forehead! I had no idea why. At first, I thought it was a story of a man who was lost in a forest, whose face had been battered by some low-hanging branches he had encountered while trying to find a way through. Or maybe some enemy had struck him. But here he was, all alone, praying for help while blood ran down his face.

A little later that afternoon, I asked my grandfather, "Who is that man in the painting?"

Always having time for me, he picked me up in his arms and held me shoulder high so I could be right about at the height of the painting. He said, "This is a picture your Aunt Ernestine painted of Jesus in the garden of Gethsemane. It's just before He was arrested and nailed to the cross for our sins. Here, let me show you." And we sat down on the sofa. He opened his well-worn Bible to Luke 22:44, and read, "And being in an agony he prayed more earnestly: and his sweat was as it were great drops of blood falling down to the ground" (KJV). Then my grandfather, wanting to be absolutely accurate, said,

(continued on next page)

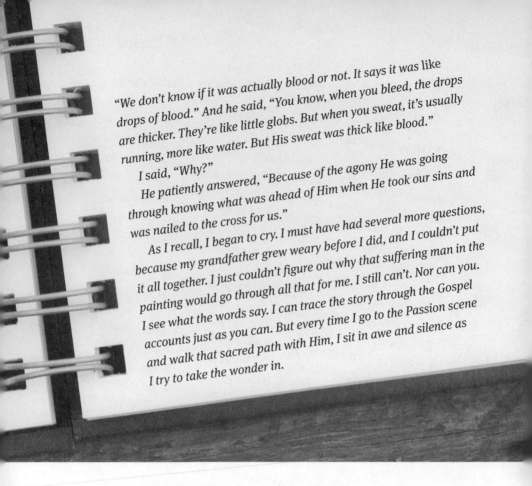

"We don't know if it was actually blood or not. It says it was like drops of blood." And he said, "You know, when you bleed, the drops are thicker. They're like little globs. But when you sweat, it's usually running, more like water. But His sweat was thick like blood."

I said, "Why?"

He patiently answered, "Because of the agony He was going through knowing what was ahead of Him when He took our sins and was nailed to the cross for us."

As I recall, I began to cry. I must have had several more questions, because my grandfather grew weary before I did, and I couldn't put it all together. I just couldn't figure out why that suffering man in the painting would go through all that for me. I still can't. Nor can you. I see what the words say. I can trace the story through the Gospel accounts just as you can. But every time I go to the Passion scene and walk that sacred path with Him, I sit in awe and silence as I try to take the wonder in.

have been present to guard the property from intruders. But Jesus and His disciples would have been known and welcomed through the gate without question.

Once they were inside, a scene began to unfold that is probably all too familiar to us. Most of us have heard this account read or preached on over and over again. We've seen it in paintings and movies of the life of Jesus. Such familiarity can sometimes lead to indifference, an inability to ponder the profundity of what happened. The reality is that here, in Gethsemane, Jesus' anguish reached its maximum level. Like an engine running in the red, Christ felt such strain that He was brought just to the point of blowing a gasket. Here His wrestling with anguish led to accepting the cup of suffering that was required for paying for the sins of the world. Here, heaven and earth, deity and humanity, locked horns, and the very human will of the God-man submitted unconditionally to the divine will.

After separating Peter, James, and John from the rest of the disciples, Jesus took them to a corner of the olive grove to pray. Surely, Jesus had insightful reasons for selecting these particular men to keep watch and pray with Him (see the feature "The Three Witnesses" starting on page 256). But this was no quiet prayer meeting with a few close friends. Immediately Jesus became "grieved and distressed" (26:37), burdened "to the point of death" (26:38). Falling on His face, He pleaded with His Father, wrestling, struggling, and coming to terms with the torturous suffering in mind, emotion, body, and soul that was about to occur the following day.

Jesus didn't quietly kneel in prayer, speaking softly to the Father with calm, serene tones. He repeatedly stood, then knelt, then fell to the ground on His face. Those three disciples watching Him would have seen a man struck with terror and crying out to God in anguish. A. T. Robertson surmises,

> The Master is about to taste the bitter dregs in the cup of death for the sin of the world. . . . He instinctively shrank from the cup, but instantly surrendered his will to the Father's will and drank it to the full. Evidently Satan tempted Christ now to draw back from the Cross. Here Jesus won the power to go on to Calvary.[17]

In this alarming scene, the true humanity of Jesus is on full display. A surprisingly powerful but understandable desire for preservation—compounded by satanic attack—took hold of Jesus' very human heart and mind, urging His human will to seek some way of escaping the pain. Just as he had done to Adam in the first garden, the serpent offered the second Adam, Jesus, an alleged alternative to obedience and a feigned fast track to glory. As always, Satan made self-preservation more appealing than self-sacrifice. Yet unlike Adam, Jesus cried out to the Father and submitted His human will to the divine will through agonizing hours of extreme spiritual warfare (26:39). So distressed was Jesus that His sweat fell to the ground like drops of blood (Luke 22:44).

Three times Jesus cast Himself upon the mercy of God (Matt. 26:39, 42, 44). Punctuating each excruciating battle of the wills, Jesus returned to see if the disciples were praying with Him as He had asked (26:40-41, 43, 45; see 26:38). But instead of standing or kneeling with Him in prayer, the disciples were sound asleep! How disappointing, and yet how predictable. Earlier they'd had such gallant and grand words, swearing unconditional allegiance even unto death. Now, during Jesus' most distressing moments of life, they couldn't endure even for a little while.

In the midst of all this anguish, the divine will prevailed when Jesus,

THE THREE WITNESSES

MATTHEW 26:37

Peter, James, and John. Only these three among the disciples accompanied Jesus when He resurrected Jairus's daughter (Mark 5:37; Luke 8:51). These three alone witnessed the Transfiguration of Jesus on the mountain, the appearance of Moses and Elijah, and the voice of God the Father from the cloud (Matt. 17:1-8; Mark 9:2-8; Luke 9:28-36). This same trio—along with Andrew—privately questioned Jesus on the Mount of Olives about the destruction of Jerusalem and the end times (Mark 13:3-4). And Jesus invited only these three to pray with Him in Gethsemane on the night of His arrest (Matt. 26:37; Mark 14:33).

Why these three men? Lukyn Williams suggests some reasons why they were each selected to be part of this inner triangle of witnesses:

> Peter, for his energy, zeal, and love, and the part he was to play in the founding of the Church; John, because he was beloved by Christ, and was to be the recipient of Divine revelation; James . . . [who was] soon to drink of Christ's cup and war a good warfare. The James here named is the son of Zebedee, and brother of John, and was put to death by Herod Agrippa (Acts 12).[18]

I also find it interesting that James died very early in the history of the church (probably around AD 44), Peter lived until about AD 67, and John survived until around the end of the first century. Thus, throughout the apostolic era, the church had access to eyewitnesses of these profound events and teachings in the life of Christ. The first two of this inner circle sealed their testimonies with martyrdom. James, the first of the Twelve to be martyred, suffered at the hands of Herod, likely under the instigation of the Jewish leaders (Acts 12:1-3). Peter, after writing two epistles (1 and 2 Peter) and serving as the source for one of the synoptic Gospels (Mark), was executed in Rome. And John, after writing the unique fourth Gospel, three letters, and the book of Revelation, died around AD 98, probably one of the only original disciples to die of old age.

Yet there was also one more immediately practical reason why Jesus pulled Peter, James, and John away from the other eight disciples that night in the olive grove. Jesus knew that in a matter of hours, Judas would arrive at the gate, and because he was known to the keepers of the garden, he would gain easy entrance to the private property. But instead of entering alone, he would lead in a crowd of armed soldiers to arrest Jesus. Who else, besides Jesus, knew of Judas's imminent treachery? Jesus had identified Judas as the traitor directly to John and indirectly to Peter (John 13:23-26). And it's quite possible that John had informed his brother, James, that something treacherous was afoot. With that knowledge, had those three witnesses stayed with the rest of the disciples near the entrance to the garden, it's possible they would have tried to prevent Judas's entry and delayed Jesus' arrest. But Jesus' time had come to be betrayed into the hands of sinners, and nothing in heaven or on earth would stop it (Matt. 26:45-46).

the God-man, surrendered unconditionally to the good and perfect plan of God the Father: "Not as I will, but as You will. . . . Your will be done" (26:39, 42). His divine will and human will perfectly aligned, and Jesus resolved to face the journey to the Cross. He was ready. But the disciples were not. He warned them, "Keep watching and praying that you may not enter into temptation; the spirit is willing, but the flesh is weak" (26:41). Their eagerness to stay faithful would be no match for their flesh. Within minutes they would become the very deserters and traitors they had vowed never to become.

Rising to His feet after those moments of prayer and having resisted the devil's greatest onslaught, Jesus gathered the three woozy disciples, saying: "Behold, the hour is at hand and the Son of Man is being betrayed into the hands of sinners. Get up, let us be going; behold, the one who betrays Me is at hand!" (26:45-46).

— 26:47-56 —

Immediately after Jesus roused Peter, James, and John from their sleep, the traitor, Judas, emerged through the garden gate with a crowd of armed men sent by the chief priests and elders (26:47). We can't be certain how many soldiers arrived on the scene to take Jesus into custody. The language used in John 18:3 suggests a large number—a "cohort" could be up to six hundred soldiers.[19] It's evident that the crowd armed with swords and clubs was taking no chances. If we suppose the entire cohort of soldiers arrived, they would have been ready to subdue any resistance with odds of about 50 to 1!

To help the arresting soldiers distinguish Jesus from the disciples, Judas had arranged a sign: The one he kissed was the one they were looking for (Matt. 26:48). Perhaps Judas had slipped in through the gate and quickly sought out Jesus while the front line of soldiers held back in the shadows, watching his movements. In any case, with snake-like subtlety and cruel irony, Judas walked up to Jesus, hailed Him as "Rabbi," and kissed Him (26:49)—a customary greeting in the ancient

Near East. If the soldiers were indeed hanging back, then nothing would have seemed awry to the eleven disciples at this point.

Jesus, of course, saw right through it. Luke tells us He responded, "Judas, are you betraying the Son of Man with a kiss?" (Luke 22:48). Then, fully resolved to face the trials set before Him, Jesus said, "Friend, do what you have come for" (Matt. 26:50). With that, the soldiers slipped out of the darkness and laid their hands on Jesus.

Chaos erupted.

On impulse, Peter grabbed his sword and stepped forward to make good on his promise to stand by Jesus no matter what (John 18:10; see Matt. 26:33, 35). He swung wildly, striking the slave of the high priest and cutting off his ear (26:51). Jesus immediately rebuked Peter, ordering him to put his sword away, because "all those who take up the sword shall perish by the sword" (26:52). He then reminded His disciples—and those arresting Him—that in a moment He could call down heavenly fury upon the soldiers in the form of more than twelve legions of angels (26:53), which would number over seventy-two thousand.[20] Just as the cohort of arresting soldiers outnumbered the disciples about 50 to 1, the heavenly army at Jesus' disposal could have outnumbered them about 120 to 1! Yet Jesus would summon no army that night. Rather, defusing the situation, He stepped forward and voluntarily surrendered to His enemies to fulfill the Scriptures (26:54-56).

Instead of surrendering themselves and marching with Jesus into the custody of the soldiers, as they had sworn to do, Jesus' disciples "left Him and fled" (26:56). Not a single one remained. Not even Peter, who a moment earlier was willing to kill for Jesus. As the soldiers bound Jesus and led Him out of the garden of Gethsemane, He was utterly forsaken by all His followers and friends.

APPLICATION: MATTHEW 26:31-56

From a Window to a Mirror

When we walk through a section of Scripture like this, it's easy to detach ourselves from the drama and observe the action from a comfortable distance. Like a member of an audience watching a film or a spectator sitting in the stands at a sporting event, we often want to retain mental objectivity while protecting our hearts from getting too deeply involved.

But if we step into the scene and ponder the question *Where am I in all of this?* then we open ourselves up to the potential for deep conviction and transformation. Let's take a moment to turn the window that looks into those profound events at Gethsemane into a mirror, so as to find ourselves reflected in the story.

Are you among the self-assured? Are you like those disciples who insisted, "That will never be me"? Do you think you would never turn away and deny the Lord? Sometimes self-assurance slides into arrogance: "Even if all others fall away, not me!" Consider the words of Paul: "Let him who thinks he stands take heed that he does not fall" (1 Cor. 10:12). Let the disciples' rapid descent from oath to desertion remind us that even those who are closest to Jesus can find themselves heading for the hills when danger arrives.

Or maybe you find yourself, like Jesus, in the midst of the struggle—a grand battle against the flesh, the world, and the devil. You know the will of God, but the temptation is so great you're not sure you can declare, "Not my will, but Yours be done." Well, *you can't*—at least not in your own power. Only through the power of Christ, by the indwelling presence of the Holy Spirit, can you hope to face the trials and temptations of this life. Call out to the Father, in the name of the Son, by the power of the Holy Spirit. He can deliver you just as Jesus was delivered from the temptation in Gethsemane.

Or perhaps you see yourself in the dozing, drowsy disciples, half asleep with indifference and passivity. Failing to carry out simple requests. Dipping into deep slumber instead of praying. Engaging in luxurious leisure instead of ministering. Letting others do all the work while you sit back and watch. Maybe you've forgotten that Christ calls His disciples to be awake and alert lest we fall into temptation. And then, when crisis hits, you lash out like Peter—thoughtlessly, impulsively, and disobediently. Because you didn't prepare spiritually, you respond carnally to circumstances around you.

As you ponder where you are now and where you need to be, take this opportunity to turn to God in repentance, relying on Him alone to restore you to close, intimate fellowship with Himself. We've seen what can happen if we don't attend to that most important of relationships: We could flee into the darkness like the eleven, with a legacy of regret and shame following close behind.

Who's Really on Trial?
MATTHEW 26:57-75

57 Those who had seized Jesus led Him away to Caiaphas, the high priest, where the scribes and the elders were gathered together. 58 But Peter was following Him at a distance as far as the courtyard of the high priest, and entered in, and sat down with the ᵃofficers to see the outcome.

59 Now the chief priests and the whole ᵃCouncil kept trying to obtain false testimony against Jesus, so that they might put Him to death. 60 They did not find *any*, even though many false witnesses came forward. But later on two came forward, 61 and said, "This man stated, 'I am able to destroy the ᵃtemple of God and to rebuild it ᵇin three days.'" 62 The high priest stood up and said to Him, "Do You not answer? What is it that these men are testifying against You?" 63 But Jesus kept silent. And the high priest said to Him, "I ᵃadjure You by the living God, that You tell us whether You are ᵇthe Christ, the Son of God." 64 Jesus said to him, "You have said it *yourself*; nevertheless I tell you, ᵃhereafter you will see THE SON OF MAN SITTING AT THE RIGHT HAND OF POWER, and COMING ON THE CLOUDS OF HEAVEN."

65 Then the high priest tore his ᵃrobes and said, "He has blasphemed! What further need do we have of witnesses? Behold, you have now heard the blasphemy; 66 what do you think?" They answered, "He deserves death!"

67 Then they spat in His face and beat Him with their fists; and others ᵃslapped Him, 68 and said, "Prophesy to us, You ᵃChrist; who is the one who hit You?"

57 Then the people who had arrested Jesus led him to the home of Caiaphas, the high priest, where the teachers of religious law and the elders had gathered. 58 Meanwhile, Peter followed him at a distance and came to the high priest's courtyard. He went in and sat with the guards and waited to see how it would all end.

59 Inside, the leading priests and the entire high council* were trying to find witnesses who would lie about Jesus, so they could put him to death. 60 But even though they found many who agreed to give false witness, they could not use anyone's testimony. Finally, two men came forward 61 who declared, "This man said, 'I am able to destroy the Temple of God and rebuild it in three days.'"

62 Then the high priest stood up and said to Jesus, "Well, aren't you going to answer these charges? What do you have to say for yourself?" 63 But Jesus remained silent. Then the high priest said to him, "I demand in the name of the living God—tell us if you are the Messiah, the Son of God."

64 Jesus replied, "You have said it. And in the future you will see the Son of Man seated in the place of power at God's right hand* and coming on the clouds of heaven."*

65 Then the high priest tore his clothing to show his horror and said, "Blasphemy! Why do we need other witnesses? You have all heard his blasphemy. 66 What is your verdict?"

"Guilty!" they shouted. "He deserves to die!"

67 Then they began to spit in Jesus' face and beat him with their fists. And some slapped him, 68 jeering, "Prophesy to us, you Messiah! Who hit you that time?"

⁶⁹Now Peter was sitting outside in the courtyard, and a servant-girl came to him and said, "You too were with Jesus the Galilean." ⁷⁰But he denied *it* before them all, saying, "I do not know what you are talking about." ⁷¹When he had gone out to the gateway, another *servant-girl* saw him and said to those who were there, "This man was with Jesus of Nazareth." ⁷²And again he denied *it* with an oath, "I do not know the man." ⁷³A little later the bystanders came up and said to Peter, "Surely you too are *one* of them; for even the way you talk ᵃgives you away." ⁷⁴Then he began to curse and swear, "I do not know the man!" And immediately a rooster crowed. ⁷⁵And Peter remembered the word which Jesus had said, "Before a rooster crows, you will deny Me three times." And he went out and wept bitterly.

26:58 ᵃOr *servants*   26:59 ᵃOr *Sanhedrin*
26:61 ᵃOr *sanctuary* ᵇOr *after*   26:63 ᵃOr *charge*
You under oath ᵇI.e. the Messiah   26:64 ᵃOr *from
now on*   26:65 ᵃOr *outer garments*   26:67 ᵃOr
beat Him with rods   26:68 ᵃI.e. the Messiah
26:73 ᵃLit *makes you evident*

⁶⁹Meanwhile, Peter was sitting outside in the courtyard. A servant girl came over and said to him, "You were one of those with Jesus the Galilean."

⁷⁰But Peter denied it in front of everyone. "I don't know what you're talking about," he said.

⁷¹Later, out by the gate, another servant girl noticed him and said to those standing around, "This man was with Jesus of Nazareth.*"

⁷²Again Peter denied it, this time with an oath. "I don't even know the man," he said.

⁷³A little later some of the other bystanders came over to Peter and said, "You must be one of them; we can tell by your Galilean accent."

⁷⁴Peter swore, "A curse on me if I'm lying—I don't know the man!" And immediately the rooster crowed.

⁷⁵Suddenly, Jesus' words flashed through Peter's mind: "Before the rooster crows, you will deny three times that you even know me." And he went away, weeping bitterly.

26:59 Greek *the Sanhedrin*.   26:64a Greek
seated at the right hand of the power. See Ps
110:1.   26:64b See Dan 7:13.   26:71 Or *Jesus
the Nazarene.*

From the perspective of the Jewish authorities, the foxhunt was over. They had finally apprehended the rabble-rousing rabbi of Nazareth, thanks to the cunning and conniving of one of His close associates, Judas Iscariot. But there was no time for celebrating. They had apprehended Jesus behind closed doors in the garden of Gethsemane under the cover of deep darkness. The crowds of Passover pilgrims in Jerusalem had all been asleep after the feast, so there had been no throng of curious onlookers to worry about. With the exception of Peter's striking Malchus, the servant of the high priest (John 18:10), none of the disciples put up a fight. Instead, they all fled. And as it turned out, even Malchus didn't end up with permanent damage after all. Jesus healed him (Luke 22:51). Thanks to Judas, Jesus had been identified, confronted, and captured, essentially without incident.

All that was needed now was a swift and silent legal proceeding to make official what was obvious to the Jewish authorities: Jesus of Nazareth was a false messiah, a charlatan whose words and actions were leading many people astray. If He wasn't dealt with expeditiously, He would rile up the common folk and likely cause a revolt, bringing Roman wrath upon the land, upon the people, and—God forbid—upon the cozy, established leadership of the priests and elders of Israel.

To prevent this worst-case scenario, then, everything had to be done quickly and quietly. The Sanhedrin needed to find Jesus guilty of blasphemy according to the Jewish Law. Then the Roman authorities would have to approve a sentence of death in order for the flame of that false prophet and false messiah to be extinguished once and for all. Sure, some corners would need to be cut and some charges trumped up. But weighing the needs of the many against the needs of the few, the end justified the means.

The result of this reasoning was a series of unjust and illegal trials intended only to bump off the falsely accused. Though Jesus was innocent from start to finish—never once proven guilty of anything punishable by even a slap on the hand—the rush to judgment couldn't be stopped. Diabolical forces greater than power-hungry priests and a corrupt council were at work behind the scenes.

Meanwhile, the drama returns again and again to another person "on trial" throughout this ordeal: Peter—the "rock" stuck in a hard place—who was desperately trying to make it look like he was keeping his word. But Peter's desperate attempts ended up fulfilling the very prophecy he had promised to avoid.

— 26:57-58 —

Though Matthew, Mark, and Luke all begin the account of the sham legal proceedings with Caiaphas, who was the actual high priest that year, the Gospel of John zooms in a little closer and tells us that Jesus' first trial took place immediately after His arrest in Gethsemane at the court of Annas, the "Godfather" of the high priestly family (John 18:12-24). (See the chart "The Trials of Jesus" on the next page.) Perhaps wanting to parade their catch before the revered Annas, the cohort marched to his home in the wee hours of the morning. Annas questioned Jesus about His teachings and about His disciples (John 18:19)—queries Jesus refused to answer on the spot, resulting in the first of many blows at the hands of His captors (John 18:22).

Meanwhile, John points out that Simon Peter had doubled back after fleeing Gethsemane (John 18:15). With the help of another

THE TRIALS OF JESUS

Trial	Officiating Authority	Scripture	Accusations	Legality	Type	Result
1	Annas, former high priest from AD 6–15	John 18:12-23	No specific charges brought.	Illegal: • No jurisdiction • Held at night • No charges • No witnesses • Abused during trial	Jewish and religious	Found "guilty" of irreverance and sent to Caiaphas.
2	Caiaphas, high priest from AD 18–36, and the Sanhedrin	Matthew 26:57-68; Mark 14:53-65; John 18:24	Claimed to be the Messiah, the Son of God, which they deemed blasphemy.	Illegal: • Held at night • False witnesses • No formal charge • Abused during trial	Jewish and religious	Declared "guilty" of blasphemy and held for sentencing until morning.
3	Sanhedrin	Mark 15:1; Luke 22:66-71	As a continuation of the earlier trial before the Sanhedrin, the charges remained the same.	Illegal: • Accusation changed • No witnesses • Improper vote	Jewish and religious	Sentenced to be turned over to Romans for execution.
4	Pilate, governor of Judea from AD 26–36	Matthew 27:11-14; Mark 15:2-5; Luke 23:1-7; John 18:28-38	Charged with treason and sedition against Rome.	Illegal: • Found "not guilty," yet kept in custody • No defense representation • Abused during trial	Roman and civil	Declared "not guilty" and pawned off on Herod Antipas to find a loophole.
5	Herod Antipas, governor of Galilee from 4 BC–AD 39	Luke 23:8-12	No specific charges brought. Questioned at length by Herod.	Illegal: • No jurisdiction • No specific charges • Abused during trial	Roman and civil	Mistreated, mocked, falsely accused, and returned to Pilate without a decision made.
6	Pilate	Matthew 27:15-26; Mark 15:6-15; Luke 23:13-25; John 18:39–19:16	As a continuation of the earlier trial before Pilate, the charges remained the same.	Illegal: • Declared "not guilty," yet condemned.	Roman and civil	Declared "not guilty" but sentenced to be crucified to mollify the angry mob. Simultaneously, a man guilty of murder, treason, and sedition was released.

disciple—probably John—known by the high priest's family, Peter gained entrance to the outer court to observe the proceedings of Jesus from afar. It was at this time that Peter denied being one of Jesus' disciples (John 18:17). But think about it. If he had admitted the truth, his cover would be blown, and he would have had to flee again. In order to make good on his promise to stick with Jesus—even though from a distance—he had to deny Him. Just this once.

Frustrated with Jesus and likely wanting to go back to sleep (it was probably around three in the morning), Annas sent Him to Caiaphas (John 18:24; cf. Matt. 26:57). The scribes and elders of Jerusalem were already gathered, perhaps having been roused from sleep and called to this emergency meeting while Jesus was at Annas's house. Now Jesus was brought into the presence of the most powerful men in Israel. Meanwhile, Peter had caught up with the crowd, worked his way into the courtyard, and sat down among the officers to observe the outcome (26:58). Peter likely stayed far enough away so as not to draw attention to himself . . . but close enough so Jesus would notice he was keeping his promise to remain loyal to the end.

— 26:59-68 —

While Jesus stood before the high priest (Caiaphas), and the Sanhedrin, His accusers bombarded Him with one false accusation after another. Their sole purpose was to find some quasi-credible crime worthy of execution (26:59). The entire "legal" proceeding was itself, from start to finish, illegal. The rulers of Israel blatantly disregarded numerous requirements prescribed by the Jewish code governing procedures of the Sanhedrin. According to the Mishnah, no trials were supposed to occur during the night hours or during feasts (*Sanhedrin* 4:1). Trials were to be public, not secret, and were to occur in the Hall of Judgment in the temple area (*Sanhedrin* 1:6; 11:2). Capital cases required a quorum of twenty-three judges and were to follow a strict order of arguments from both the defense and the prosecution (*Sanhedrin* 4:1). Like in today's justice system, accused persons were to have an advocate to speak on their behalf, and they could not be forced to testify against themselves (*Sanhedrin* 3:3-4). Conviction required the agreement of two or three independent witnesses, who would be examined and cross-examined individually (*Sanhedrin* 3:6; 4:1; cf. Deut. 17:6-7; 19:15-20). Contradictory testimonies were to be thrown out (*Sanhedrin* 5:2). And when the trial was over, members of the Sanhedrin were to adjourn for lengthy discussion to weigh the evidence, and the voting for or against conviction was to be done in orderly fashion, from the youngest members of the council to the oldest (*Sanhedrin* 4:1-2).[21]

It's clear that none of these procedures were followed. Instead, Jesus stood trial before Annas, Caiaphas, and the Sanhedrin at night during the Passover festival, likely before a handpicked group of bleary-eyed council members already prejudiced against Him. Nobody spoke on Jesus' behalf in any official capacity, and when He objected to the unjust treatment, they punched Him in the face (John 18:20-23)!

Witnesses were sought for the purpose of concocting a case against Him (Matt. 26:59-60). Eventually they found two colluding witnesses who ripped Jesus' words out of context. They testified that they had heard Jesus threaten to destroy the temple in Jerusalem and then miraculously rebuild it in three days (26:61). John's Gospel presents these words of Jesus in context (John 2:13-22), noting that Jesus had been speaking figuratively: "But He was speaking of the temple of His body" (John 2:21).

When Jesus reacted with silence before the insane ravings of the illegal council, the high priest insisted that He answer plainly—for Himself—whether He was the Messiah (Matt. 26:63). Finally breaking His silence, Jesus confessed the truth that He was the rightful King, their long-awaited Messiah (26:64). He quoted snippets of Psalm 110:1 and Daniel 7:13—both regarded as messianic prophecies by Jewish rabbis. In response, the high priest instantly convicted Him of blasphemy (Matt. 26:65). There was no dismissal for deliberation, no one standing as a witness for the defense, no request for the production of evidence. Just a declaration of the verdict from one man. Then, just as quickly, the Sanhedrin summarily sentenced Jesus to death (26:66). And upon His conviction, they immediately began abusing and humiliating Him (26:67-68).

The trial was a travesty of justice from beginning to end. And Peter observed the whole thing from outside, unwilling to stick his neck out to come to his Master's aid as a witness for the defense.

— 26:69-75 —

Panning away from Jesus' horrific suffering of brutality and public humiliation at the hands of angry, sneering, violent men, Matthew's narrative turns to Peter, outside in the courtyard, having separated himself from the jeering and cheering mob. We can picture him doing his best to hide, his face tucked away in the dark shadow of his robe. The last thing he wanted was to be detected. But maybe, just maybe, he could find a way to extricate Jesus from this mess. Suddenly, an unnamed servant-girl walked over, pointed her finger at him, and called him out. She'd seen him with Jesus (26:69).

Peter's cover was abruptly blown. What would he do? If he jumped up and fled through the gate, he could probably escape, but then he would be guilty of doing exactly what he had promised he would *not* do—abandon Jesus like the rest. So, he did the first thing that came to mind. He denied his association with Jesus loudly and clearly: "I do not know what you are talking about" (26:70). Peter backed away from the girl, inching toward the gate just in case he needed to run for it (26:71). But I'm guessing he also tried to stay close enough to the building's entrance to keep Jesus within view. But then another servant-girl recognized Peter and snitched: "This man was with Jesus!" (26:71).

Again, the "rock" was stuck in a hard place. Should he flee (and thus break his promise to Jesus), or should he lie and stay (and thus break his promise to Jesus)? In the very act of trying to keep his boastful promise, Peter was falling into a fulfillment of Jesus' prophecy. But what could he do? How many times had he denied? Once? Twice? How many did he have left before Jesus' words came to pass? Without thinking, Peter blurted out—this time with an oath—"I do not know the man" (26:72). Another lie, another denial.

Perhaps he listened for a rooster at that moment. But he heard nothing but his own heartbeat, his chest ready to explode. I can imagine he burst into a cold sweat at this point. Staggering around the courtyard, keeping his distance from the rest of the laborers and bystanders, Peter found another vantage point where he could see Jesus. According to Luke, he was able to linger for about an hour after that last denial (Luke 22:59). Perhaps he began to calm down, thinking he was out of the woods and had pulled off the ruse. Maybe he even exchanged small talk with some of the servants in an attempt to maintain his cover. By this time, he had been able to situate himself in a direct line of sight with Jesus, as if to show that he had not abandoned the Master after all, as the others had done. But at that moment, another voice came: "Surely you too are one of them; for even the way you talk gives you away" (Matt. 26:73).

Without a second thought, Peter cursed and swore, insisting again, "I do not know the man!" (26:74). At that precise moment, Peter heard the rooster crow loudly and clearly, as the morning sun began to peek over the horizon (26:74). It was done. While trying desperately to maintain his anonymity among the enemies, Peter had denied Jesus three times before dawn, thus breaking his promise to Jesus. Luke fills in a poignant detail: "The Lord turned and looked at Peter" (Luke 22:61). Their eyes met. Seeing the utter sadness in Jesus' bruised and bloodied face, Peter lost it. He recalled the Lord's prophecy: "Before a rooster crows, you will deny Me three times" (Matt. 26:75; see 26:34).

Overwhelming guilt and shame seized Peter. He had hit rock bottom. The chapter ends with a haunting statement: "And he went out and wept bitterly" (26:75). A. T. Robertson aptly describes the scene and its significance: "The tears were bitter, all the more so by reason of that look of understanding pity that Jesus gave him. One of the tragedies of the Cross is the bleeding heart of Peter."[22]

APPLICATION: MATTHEW 26:57-75

The Trial of Peter

It's easy to sit here and flay Peter, skinning him alive for his denials, his failures in this hour of trial. But I don't think that's all that helpful. God didn't preserve this account merely to give generations of people like us a basis for trying, convicting, and sentencing Simon Peter. That's what Pharisees do with those who fail. Rather, I think we're supposed to see our own plight before the Lord Jesus in this account of Peter. If you were in Peter's place—be honest now—how would you have responded?

Thankfully, Peter was gripped in his inner being as his conscience suffered the grief of a man who had backslidden to the brink. Two things prompted this reaction of total sorrow for his sin: Jesus' look and his own memory. In his moment of rebellion, he looked at Jesus, and Jesus didn't scowl or shake His fist. He simply looked back at Peter. At that moment, the words of Jesus' prophecy were fulfilled, and Jesus understood the truth that Peter, just like the rest of the disciples—just like the rest of humanity—was a rebellious sinner in need of a Savior. He needed not only forgiveness and strength but also repentance and restoration.

Peter went away and wept bitterly. Perhaps he returned to the place where he had earlier spoken with such self-assurance and puffed-up pride. Maybe he stood at the very spot and poured out his confession, acknowledging his total failure and utter weakness. In any case, he undoubtedly pondered the folly of his own boasting and the absolute power and providence of the God-man, who knew his heart better than he knew it himself.

Who was really on trial here? Jesus' experience—which still wasn't over at this point—could hardly be called a fair trial. He was innocent. In fact, He alone is the rightful Judge. Peter, meanwhile, was guilty, having failed one test after another.

Like Peter, all of us are, in a sense, on trial. We can see ourselves intertwined in this story of pride and self-assurance, of boasting and self-confidence, of comparison with others and zealous ambition to show ourselves to be better than the rest. Let's be honest: Left to ourselves, every one of us would follow Peter in his denials. In fact, many of us have already done so numerous times in our lives. Just linger in that thought for a moment. Admit your own weakness. Weep if you must. This is the first, essential step to full recovery and restoration. Without it, we're just one more denial away from rock bottom.

Thoroughly Guilty . . . Totally Innocent
MATTHEW 27:1-26

NASB

¹Now when morning came, all the chief priests and the elders of the people conferred together against Jesus to put Him to death; ²and they bound Him, and led Him away and delivered Him to Pilate the governor.

³Then when Judas, who had betrayed Him, saw that He had been condemned, he felt remorse, and returned the thirty ªpieces of silver to the chief priests and elders, ⁴saying, "I have sinned by betraying innocent blood." But they said, "What is that to us? See *to that* yourself!" ⁵And he threw the pieces of silver into the temple sanctuary and departed; and he went away and hanged himself. ⁶The chief priests took the pieces of silver and said, "It is not lawful to

NLT

¹Very early in the morning the leading priests and the elders of the people met again to lay plans for putting Jesus to death. ²Then they bound him, led him away, and took him to Pilate, the Roman governor.

³When Judas, who had betrayed him, realized that Jesus had been condemned to die, he was filled with remorse. So he took the thirty pieces of silver back to the leading priests and the elders. ⁴"I have sinned," he declared, "for I have betrayed an innocent man."

"What do we care?" they retorted. "That's your problem."

⁵Then Judas threw the silver coins down in the Temple and went out and hanged himself.

⁶The leading priests picked up the coins. "It wouldn't be right to put

put them into the temple treasury, since it is the price of blood." 7And they conferred together and ªwith the money bought the Potter's Field as a burial place for strangers. 8For this reason that field has been called the Field of Blood to this day. 9Then that which was spoken through Jeremiah the prophet was fulfilled: "AND ªTHEY TOOK THE THIRTY PIECES OF SILVER, THE PRICE OF THE ONE WHOSE PRICE HAD BEEN SET by the sons of Israel; 10AND ªTHEY GAVE THEM FOR THE POTTER'S FIELD, AS THE LORD DIRECTED ME."

11Now Jesus stood before the governor, and the governor questioned Him, saying, "Are You the King of the Jews?" And Jesus said to him, "*It is as* you say." 12And while He was being accused by the chief priests and elders, He did not answer. 13Then Pilate said to Him, "Do You not hear how many things they testify against You?" 14And He did not answer him with regard to even a *single* ªcharge, so the governor was quite amazed.

15Now at *the* feast the governor was accustomed to release for the ªpeople *any* one prisoner whom they wanted. 16At that time they were holding a notorious prisoner, called Barabbas. 17So when the people gathered together, Pilate said to them, "Whom do you want me to release for you? Barabbas, or Jesus who is called Christ?" 18For he knew that because of envy they had handed Him over.

19While he was sitting on the judgment seat, his wife sent him *a message,* saying, "Have nothing to do with that righteous Man; for ªlast night I suffered greatly in a dream because of Him." 20But the chief priests and the elders persuaded the

this money in the Temple treasury," they said, "since it was payment for murder."* 7After some discussion they finally decided to buy the potter's field, and they made it into a cemetery for foreigners. 8That is why the field is still called the Field of Blood. 9This fulfilled the prophecy of Jeremiah that says,

"They took* the thirty pieces of silver—
the price at which he was valued by the people of Israel,
10 and purchased the potter's field, as the LORD directed.*"

11Now Jesus was standing before Pilate, the Roman governor. "Are you the king of the Jews?" the governor asked him.

Jesus replied, "You have said it."

12But when the leading priests and the elders made their accusations against him, Jesus remained silent. 13"Don't you hear all these charges they are bringing against you?" Pilate demanded. 14But Jesus made no response to any of the charges, much to the governor's surprise.

15Now it was the governor's custom each year during the Passover celebration to release one prisoner to the crowd—anyone they wanted. 16This year there was a notorious prisoner, a man named Barabbas.* 17As the crowds gathered before Pilate's house that morning, he asked them, "Which one do you want me to release to you—Barabbas, or Jesus who is called the Messiah?" 18(He knew very well that the religious leaders had arrested Jesus out of envy.)

19Just then, as Pilate was sitting on the judgment seat, his wife sent him this message: "Leave that innocent man alone. I suffered through a terrible nightmare about him last night."

20Meanwhile, the leading priests and the elders persuaded the crowd

NASB

crowds to ask for Barabbas and to put Jesus to death. 21 But the governor ᵃsaid to them, "Which of the two do you want me to release for you?" And they said, "Barabbas." 22 Pilate said to them, "Then what shall I do with Jesus who is called Christ?" They all said, "ᵃCrucify Him!" 23 And he said, "Why, what evil has He done?" But they kept shouting all the more, saying, "ᵃCrucify Him!"

24 When Pilate saw that he was accomplishing nothing, but rather that a riot was starting, he took water and washed his hands in front of the crowd, saying, "I am innocent of this Man's blood; see *to that* yourselves." 25 And all the people said, "His blood shall be on us and on our children!" 26 Then he released Barabbas ᵃfor them; but after having Jesus scourged, he handed Him over to be crucified.

27:3 ᵃOr *silver shekels*   27:7 ᵃLit *from them*
27:9 ᵃOr *I took;* cf Zech 11:13   27:10 ᵃSome early
mss read *I gave*   27:14 ᵃLit *word*   27:15 ᵃLit
crowd   27:19 ᵃLit *today*   27:21 ᵃLit *answered
and said to them*   27:22 ᵃLit *Let Him be crucified*
27:23 ᵃLit *Let Him be crucified*   27:26 ᵃOr *to them*

NLT

to ask for Barabbas to be released and for Jesus to be put to death. 21 So the governor asked again, "Which of these two do you want me to release to you?"

The crowd shouted back, "Barabbas!"

22 Pilate responded, "Then what should I do with Jesus who is called the Messiah?"

They shouted back, "Crucify him!"

23 "Why?" Pilate demanded. "What crime has he committed?"

But the mob roared even louder, "Crucify him!"

24 Pilate saw that he wasn't getting anywhere and that a riot was developing. So he sent for a bowl of water and washed his hands before the crowd, saying, "I am innocent of this man's blood. The responsibility is yours!"

25 And all the people yelled back, "We will take responsibility for his death—we and our children!"*

26 So Pilate released Barabbas to them. He ordered Jesus flogged with a lead-tipped whip, then turned him over to the Roman soldiers to be crucified.

27:6 Greek *since it is the price for blood.*   27:9 Or
I took.   27:9-10 Greek *as the LORD directed
me.* Zech 11:12-13; Jer 32:6-9.   27:16 Some
manuscripts read *Jesus Barabbas;* also in 27:17.
27:25 Greek *"His blood be on us and on our
children."*

Like a film in which a fast-paced action sequence suddenly shifts into slow motion, Matthew's account of the life of Christ seems to slow to a crawl as Matthew—like the rest of the Gospel writers—provides scene-by-scene detail of the final hours of Jesus' life. The first thirty years of the life of Jesus of Nazareth occupied just two chapters (Matt. 1–2). His three-year public ministry spanned eighteen chapters (Matt. 3–20). His final week of ministry filled five chapters (Matt. 21–25). Then, the period from the Passover meal to the Crucifixion, a span of about twenty-four hours, is relayed by Matthew in two lengthy chapters (Matt. 26–27). Matthew dials down the pace of his narrative to provide a frame-by-frame, blow-by-blow analysis of these final twenty-four hours of Jesus' life.

CHRONOLOGY FROM GETHSEMANE TO GOLGOTHA

Event	Scriptures	Approx. Time
Prayer and agony in Gethsemane	Matthew 26:36-46 Mark 14:32-42 Luke 22:39-46 John 18:1	1:00 a.m.
Betrayal by Judas and arrest of Jesus	Matthew 26:47-56 Mark 14:43-46 Luke 22:47-53 John 18:2-12	1:30 a.m.
Irregular, unauthorized interrogation at Annas's residence	John 18:12-23	2:00 a.m.
Illegal trial at Caiaphas's residence	Matthew 26:57-68 Mark 14:53-65 Luke 22:54, 63-65 John 18:24	3:00 a.m.
Formal but illegal meeting of the Sanhedrin to confirm capital sentence	Mark 15:1 Luke 22:66-71	6:00 a.m.
First interrogation by Pilate at his residence	Matthew 27:1-2, 11-14 Mark 15:1-5 Luke 23:1-7 John 18:28-32	6:30 a.m.
Audience before Herod	Luke 23:8-12	7:00 a.m.
Final judgment of Pilate	Matthew 27:15-26 Mark 15:6-15 Luke 23:13-25 John 18:33-40	7:30 a.m.
Scourging in Praetorium, mocking by soldiers, and public condemnation	Matthew 27:26-31 Mark 15:15-20 John 19:1-16	8:00 a.m.
Walk to Golgotha and nailing to the cross	Matthew 27:32-35 Mark 15:21-24 Luke 23:26-33 John 19:17-18	9:00 a.m.
Events at the cross, climaxing in darkness over the land	Matthew 27:36-45 Mark 15:25-33 Luke 23:34-44 John 19:19-27	9:00 a.m.–12:00 p.m.
Jesus' final words, death, and earthquake	Matthew 27:46-56 Mark 15:34-41 Luke 23:45-49 John 19:28-30	3:00 p.m.

In the same amount of space in which he dealt with Christ's birth and the first thirty years of His life, Matthew covers the events of Christ's suffering and death. Clearly, these final hours are vital to Matthew's presentation of Jesus as the rightful but rejected King, Israel's long-awaited but cruelly scorned Messiah.

Where are we now in this slow, deliberate telling of the final hours of Jesus' life? After the late-night arrest in the garden of Gethsemane, the soldiers took Jesus to the home of Annas (John 18:12-23), then to the home of Caiaphas, the high priest (Matt. 26:57-68). There, Peter denied Jesus three times, just as the Lord had predicted. During the disjointed proceedings of the illegal hearings, half-witted witnesses brought half-truth allegations against Jesus, weaving together a case out of straw. And nobody was present to stand against the diabolical groupthink taking place at the instigation of the high priest and a hand-ful of wicked but powerful Jewish rulers. As they finalized their plans for having the Messiah executed and wiping His message off the face of the earth, these enemies of the Truth had to come up with a capital offense that would discredit Him before both the Roman governor (who alone could permit execution) and the general population of Jews (who could riot if they felt a gross injustice had occurred).

They needed permission from the governor, Pontius Pilate, to put their "false messiah" to death. And they needed a charge that would convince him to do so.

— 27:1-2 —

As the sun rose that Friday morning, the Sanhedrin—the Jewish council—met once again to come up with a game plan (27:1-2; Mark 15:1; Luke 22:66-71). Perhaps the frenzied and frantic decisions of the illegal mid-night trial a few hours earlier didn't sit well with some of the members of the Sanhedrin in the light of day. So, they questioned Jesus once again, this time extracting an even more direct confession from His own lips that He was the Messiah (Luke 22:67-70). It was, in their minds, a "gotcha!" moment. It satisfied the doubters and solidified Jesus' fate.

None of the cruel conspirators bothered to consider whether Jesus was actually telling the truth when He claimed to be the Messiah and Son of God. They already assumed the answer to their question. And His response was enough for them: "What further need do we have of testimony? For we have heard it ourselves from His own mouth" (Luke 22:71).

Why not call a few witnesses to testify on behalf of the accused?

PONTIUS PILATE

MATTHEW 27:2

The Jewish historian Philo of Alexandria relays an account concerning Pontius Pilate from the pen of Herod Agrippa, who described the governor as "a man of a very inflexible disposition, and very merciless as well as very obstinate."[23] Yet Philo also records an instance in which Pilate waffled and flipped a decision under the mounting pressure from Jewish leaders. In AD 27, the Jews protested against the inscribed shields Pilate had placed in Jerusalem in honor of the Roman emperor Tiberius. Philo again quotes Agrippa, who wrote that Pilate

> feared lest they might in reality go on an embassy to the emperor, and might impeach him with respect to other particulars of his government, in respect of his corruption, and his acts of insolence, and his rapine, and his habit of insulting people, and his cruelty, and his continual murders of people untried and uncondemned, and his never ending, and gratuitous, and most grievous inhumanity.[24]

When the Jewish leaders saw that Pilate operated politically on the basis of fear and personal self-preservation, they took advantage of it and put great pressure on him.

For Pilate to remove the shields would be a humiliating show of weakness to his own people and to the population under his jurisdiction. He would gain a reputation as a pushover. Yet, keeping peace and order in Judea was his primary responsibility. The Jewish leaders protested at Pilate's palace in Caesarea, refusing to return to Jerusalem until the inscribed shields were removed. Another Jewish historian, Josephus, described the governor's failed plan to break the backs of the Jewish leaders and establish his will:

> He ordered his soldiers to have their weapons privately, while he came and sat upon his judgment-seat, which seat was so prepared in the open place of the city, that it concealed the army that lay ready to oppress them. And when the Jews petitioned him again, he gave a signal to the soldiers to encompass them round; and threatened that their punishment should be no less than immediate death, unless they would leave off disturbing him, and go to their respective homes. But they threw themselves upon the ground, and laid their necks bare, and said they would take their death very willingly, rather than the wisdom of their laws should be transgressed. Upon which Pilate was deeply affected with their firm resolution to keep their laws inviolable: and commanded the images to be carried back from Jerusalem to Caesarea.[25]

This event proved to the Jewish leaders that Pilate could buckle under pressure. His obstinacy and resolve were façades that could be punctured given enough force from enough people. This knowledge would prove invaluable to the high priest and the Sanhedrin as they brought Jesus before Pilate to extract from him the license to carry out an unjust execution.

Maybe some recipients of Jesus' healings? Or Lazarus, who had been raised from the dead? Where was Malchus, the servant of the high priest, who just a few hours earlier had had his ear sliced off but then been instantly healed by Jesus' touch?

Jesus stood alone, totally innocent, yet surrounded by people who were thoroughly guilty. Having forced a consensus in a kangaroo court, the high priest and rulers of the Sanhedrin now had to march Jesus over to Pontius Pilate to gain permission to execute Him.

— 27:3-10 —

Matthew informs us that, in addition to Peter, who was lurking in the shadows of the first few hearings, another of the Twelve had witnessed at least some of the proceedings. Slithering like a snake on the margins of the crowds, trying to glean whatever information he could about what was taking place, was none other than Judas Iscariot (27:3). As Matthew's camera zooms in on the traitor, we find him in a no-man's-land. Having betrayed Jesus, he could never return to that familiar circle of disciples that had been his family for the past three years. And since he had fulfilled his usefulness to the Jewish leaders by leading the soldiers to Jesus, they wanted nothing more to do with him. Judas stood in the place of an outcast. To make matters worse, as the sun rose over Jerusalem, it suddenly dawned on him what he had done: He had betrayed the Messiah into the hands of sinners. One expositor envisions that the sight of Jesus being brutalized and hauled away "was devastating to Judas, more than even his money-hungry mind, his sordid soul, and his seared conscience could deal with. He felt remorse as he began to experience the intense, excruciating pain that is unique to profound guilt."[26]

Judas didn't start out as a disciple with thoughts of betraying Jesus. He began just like the other eleven—walking alongside Him, listening to His teachings, watching Him treat others with dignity and humility, witnessing one evidence after another that He really was the King, Israel's long-expected Messiah. Yet, he evidently did not fully commit himself to Jesus Christ in faith. Judas was fully informed but not truly transformed. His devotion to Jesus was always situational, always conditional, always subject to reevaluation.

Judas's actions in this scene can only be understood in terms of the darkness of total despair and utter hopelessness. Due to his resistance to the truth and rejection of the Savior's faithful and grace-filled offers of forgiveness, salvation, and new life, Judas presumably became increasingly more convinced that it was all a hoax. As Jesus failed to fulfill what Judas and others felt were the bare-minimum requirements of a warrior-king messiah, Judas probably began wondering if the critics had it right: His miracles were the works of a charlatan or a demoniac and were not the works of God.

After the deed of betrayal was over, a dark cloud of brokenness, confusion, disillusionment, and guilt overtook him. Having retreated from the loving grip of Jesus, Judas fell into the welcoming arms of Satan, who has been "a murderer from the beginning" (John 8:44). After casting the blood money to the indifferent and uninterested priests and elders and admitting that he had betrayed an innocent man (Matt. 27:3-4), Judas "went away and hanged himself" (27:5). Matthew doesn't fill in any of the gory details of the hanging. But he does note that the Jewish leaders used the thirty pieces of silver to purchase the "Potter's Field" as a kind of charitable burial place for strangers (27:6-7)—that is, as the location of a public-use common grave, which would also become known as the "Field of Blood" (27:8).

In the first chapter of the book of Acts, Luke fills in a few more details regarding Judas's self-inflicted fate. Though some commentators have noted that the facts of Luke's account and those offered in Matthew 27:3-10 contain apparent contradictions, a reasonable explanation emerges when we read these two accounts as complementary. Putting all the information together, I suggest the following sequence of ghastly events.

In his fit of remorse, Judas cast the thirty pieces of silver onto the temple floor and then hanged himself in a remote field (27:3-8). There his body remained, dangling between tree limb and ground until it decayed, became bloated, and eventually fell from the noose. Having landed on the rocky ground, it burst open, and his organs spilled out onto the earth (Acts 1:18-19). Ancient people would have considered this gruesome event as the most shameful way to die and an unthinkable way for a body to decay. In the Jewish mind, a hanged man was "accursed of God," and if the corpse was not buried the same day, the land was considered defiled (Deut. 21:22-23). Moreover, Jews avoided cadavers at all costs. This was cursed ground.

The priests didn't want the money, and no one wanted the land, so the landowner was compensated for his loss, and the field was reviled as "the Field of Blood." In a twist of irony, the money that had been paid to Judas became the money used to buy the land where he hanged himself. What a tragic legacy for a tragic life!

MATTHEW'S USE OF *GEZERAH SHAWAH*

MATTHEW 27:9-10

In a final comment before leaving the story of Judas behind, Matthew draws together several Old Testament passages in a Jewish practice of drawing parallels between the Old Testament and related contemporary events. This principle is called *gezerah shawah*, that is, an "argument from analogy," in which "biblical passages containing synonyms or homonyms are subject, however much they differ in other respects, to identical definitions and applications."[27]

Frequently in his Gospel, Matthew embeds important theological truths in rhetorical devices that his fellow Jewish readers would have caught. It's as if Matthew is hiding Easter eggs in his narrative for Jews to find, if they will only take the time to look carefully and think deeply. Matthew repeatedly invites his readers to go beyond the surface level of the narrative to think about who Jesus is by examining Old Testament patterns and prophecies. In the case of his Old Testament paraphrase in 27:9-10, Matthew points out the high price for rejecting Jesus as the King, Israel's long-awaited Messiah.

Matthew's patchwork paraphrase actually strings together several words, images, and ideas, mostly from Jeremiah, but also from Zechariah. The careful researcher would realize that Matthew is pointing his readers back to Jeremiah 18:1-6; 19:1-11; 32:7-15; Lamentations 4:2; and Zechariah 11:4-14. Note the cumulative effect of the themes from these passages. Also think about the startling similarities between these words and images and the fate of Judas Iscariot in the Potter's Field, which would become known as the Field of Blood.

Jeremiah 18:1-6. The prophet goes to a potter's house to observe the crafting of a clay vessel. When the vessel is ruined in the potter's hands, it's reworked into a new vessel. The initial vessel represents the people of Israel, who faced coming judgment for their unfaithfulness.

Jeremiah 19:1-11. God tells Jeremiah to purchase a clay vessel from a potter, bring the leaders of Jerusalem to the Valley of Hinnom, and smash the vessel to pieces on the rocks. This would illustrate the destruction coming upon Jerusalem for their sinful rebellion.

Jeremiah 32:7-15. God tells Jeremiah to purchase a field for a specific amount of money. He has the deed for the land placed in a clay pot to be buried for a long time. This illustrates that God would restore Jerusalem after the coming judgment on the land.

Lamentations 4:2. Jeremiah describes the "precious sons of Zion" (residents of Jerusalem) as "weighed against fine gold" and as "earthen jars, the work of a potter's hands." This reminds the readers that the people of Israel are in the hands of God just as a clay vessel is in the hands of a potter.

Zechariah 11:4-14. In a passage itself probably pointing readers back to imagery from Jeremiah,[28] Zechariah symbolically acts as a shepherd of the people of Israel. He is paid thirty pieces of silver as his wages. He throws this money into the house of the Lord "to the potter" (Zech. 11:13) and breaks his staffs as a symbolic indication of judgment.

Though this whole pearl stringing of related images may seem bizarre to twenty-first-century readers, it would have provoked first-century Jewish readers to deep meditation on the Scriptures. As R. T. France notes, "If we are to do justice to Matthew we must recognize that this is not a collection of unconnected Old Testament ideas thrown together at random, but the result of a careful theological study which takes account not only of superficial verbal 'coincidences,' but of underlying themes of prophetic expectation."[29]

What, then, was Matthew trying to get across to the astute investigator regarding Judas and the relationship between Jeremiah's broken pottery, the field, and the other related images? What was the message he was trying to get across through careful reflection and meditation on the parallels between the Old Testament texts and the tragedy of Judas? It was simply this: Judas's betrayal of the Messiah was a *type* of the Jewish leaders' rejection of Jesus. Their disobedience at the time of Jeremiah, which resulted in judgment, is seen as parallel to Judas's (and the Jewish leaders') rebellion against Jesus, which would also result in judgment. In AD 70, this was fulfilled, as it was in the Old Testament, in the invasion and destruction of the city and the temple.

— 27:11-14 —

After Jesus was dragged before Pontius Pilate (27:2, 11)—already beaten and bruised from the illegal mistreatment He had received at the hand of His captors—He experienced the fourth of six trials He would endure in the course of just a few hours. He had already appeared before Annas, Caiaphas, and the Sanhedrin, where He had been declared guilty of blasphemy for telling the truth that He was the Messiah, the Son of God. It would have been obvious to Pilate that the bloodied and beleaguered man before him was hated by the Jewish leaders.

Pilate was likely awakened early, which probably perturbed him. Nevertheless, he conducted a superficial interrogation, reviewing the same kinds of questions that had been posed to Jesus by the chief priests and elders all morning. The one that stuck out, though, which Jesus answered directly, would have reeked of sedition and treason: "Are You the King of the Jews?" To this direct question, Jesus gave a direct answer: "It is as you say" (27:11). At that point, the Jewish leaders stepped in and accused Jesus of various crimes, to which Jesus responded with silence, much to the amazement of Pilate (27:12-14).

Of course, Pilate was fully aware that the Jewish leaders had arrested and handed Jesus over because of envy (27:18). He knew that the case against Him had been prejudiced from the start and that Jesus was not guilty of a capital offense. The Gospel of John tells us that when Pilate eventually probed into Jesus' claims of kingship more closely, he found Jesus' claims of a kingdom "not of this world" to be mere religious superstition, not an offense deserving of death under Roman law (John 18:33-38). Nevertheless, the Jewish leaders pushed hard for Jesus to be executed for blasphemy according to their own Law (John 19:7). They even tightened the screws on Pilate by suggesting that any finding he might give in favor of Jesus would involve implicit disloyalty to Caesar: "If you release this Man, you are no friend of Caesar; everyone who makes himself out to be a king opposes Caesar" (John 19:12).

— 27:15-18 —

Finding himself in a precarious political situation, Pilate was seeking some way to free Jesus from the trumped-up charges of the Jewish leaders without breaking either their laws or those of Rome. He knew Jesus was innocent of everything except, perhaps, religious lunacy. Yet his experience with the stubborn rulers of the Jews in Jerusalem told Pilate that they would not be satisfied with a simple dismissal of all charges against Jesus. That could cause a riot or, worse, a report sent to Caesar saying that Pilate was providing a safe haven for treasonous claimants to the throne of Israel.

In the midst of his personal turmoil, Pilate recalled an annual custom that might just provide a way of escape from that political quagmire. Each year at Passover, the governor of Judea would release one convicted prisoner back to the people—an act of unconditional clemency as a sign of benevolence and mercy (27:15). One of the men awaiting execution that morning was a man named Barabbas, described as a "notorious prisoner" (27:16), guilty of insurrection and murder (Luke 23:25). Surely, Pilate reasoned, if the crowd was presented with a choice between freeing Barabbas or freeing Jesus, their sense of justice would prevail and Jesus would go free. Pilate also seemed to be aware of Jesus' popularity with the people, for "he knew that because of envy [the Jewish leaders] had handed Him over" (Matt. 27:17-18).

— 27:19-26 —

With the Jews' decision between Barabbas and Jesus hanging in the air—and while the chief priests and elders worked the crowd to drum up support for the release of Barabbas instead of Jesus (27:20)—Matthew provides an aside. He zooms in on Pilate, seated on his judgment seat, as a messenger emerges from the shadows, slipping Pilate a note from his wife. She informed her husband that the night before she had a nightmare revealing that Jesus was innocent and that Pilate should "have nothing to do with that righteous Man" (27:19).

Talk about being impaled on the horns of a dilemma! In one ear he started to hear murmurs of "Crucify Him" from the crowd as the religious leaders stirred them up, while in the other his wife was imploring him to show mercy. Like the corrupt politician he was, Pilate chose neutrality when he should have followed his conscience, the laws of justice, and the advice of his wife by letting Jesus free. Instead, he turned to the riled-up crowd and asked them to answer his question: "Which of the two do you want me to release for you?" (27:21).

Pilate clearly underestimated the seething, satanic hatred that had infected the mob that morning. When he gave them the choice between Barabbas and Jesus, they chose Barabbas. But what to do with Jesus, the one called Christ? Their answer was equally clear: "Crucify Him!" (27:22). While Pilate wanted them to provide some kind of justification for such an extreme punishment, they simply responded with a chant that echoed throughout the open court: "Crucify Him! Crucify Him!" (27:23).

Recoiling at the irrational rage about to boil over into a riot, Pilate called for a bowl of water. In the presence of the mob, he washed his hands of the matter and conveyed the symbolism of this act: "I am innocent of this Man's blood; see to that yourselves" (27:24). In response, the people called down a curse upon themselves in the form of an oath: "His blood shall be on us and on our children!" (27:25).

With the emotional temperature of the crowd spiking, Pilate followed through with his ill-conceived plan and released Barabbas to them (27:26). The cross that had been prepared for Barabbas would be used for Jesus. The thoroughly guilty murderer would go free while the totally innocent Lord would suffer the punishment for the murderer's sin—and, as we now know, for the sins of the whole world. The man whose name, "Barabbas," meant "son of the father," was freed while the true Son of the Father, Jesus, took his place among the condemned.

Pilate proceeded to have Jesus scourged. According to Luke's Gospel,

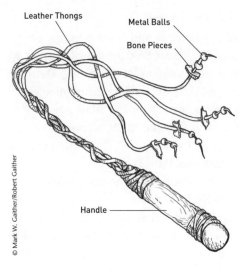

Leather Thongs

Metal Balls

Bone Pieces

Handle

© Mark W. Gaither/Robert Gaither

A *flagrum*, the brutal whip used by Roman torturers in scourging

he did this in an attempt to punish Jesus and then release Him, hoping the bloodlust of the crowd would be satisfied by the brutality of the whipping (Luke 23:16). Maybe Pilate even hoped it would knock some sense into this Jesus of Nazareth and convince Him to stop claiming He was King of the Jews. So, Jesus was led to a Roman garrison called the Antonia Fortress, which was adjacent to the temple. A soldier tied Him to a low post and stripped off His outer garments. To inflict the most damage, the *lictor*—the one responsible for the scourging—would typically select a whip with small weights or bits of sheep bone braided into the straps. Because this kind of whip caused so much physical harm so quickly, the victim often passed out or went into shock within just a few lashes. Yet even this torturous flogging did nothing to move the crowd from their one intention: "After having Jesus scourged," Pilate "handed Him over to be crucified" (Matt. 27:26).

APPLICATION: MATTHEW 27:1-26

The Strangest of Foursomes

At the trial before Pontius Pilate, we see on stage the strangest of foursomes. These characters in the drama present four very different pictures and prompt us to four very different reflections on our own place in the story of Jesus' final hour before His crucifixion. As we look at a description of each person in the scene, consider where you stand.

First, we have Jesus, the innocent captive. Though on trial, He says very little; but everything He says is the truth. It's unpopular truth. People disbelieve it. They hate Him for it. But He stands His ground, knowing that every word pushes Him closer to the Cross. For followers of Christ who have sworn to abide in Him even in the face of persecution, His actions serve as reminders that we must stand firm in the truth without wavering, regardless of the opposition we face.

Second, we see Pilate, playing the role of the vacillating judge. He waffles and wavers back and forth on the right course of action regarding Jesus. But there's nothing gray about the matter. It's a black-and-white issue. Jesus is innocent. He should be let off. But how easily the fear of the crowd can make us believe that doing the right thing is impossible in certain circumstances. When we face similar dilemmas, we should be prepared to listen to the clear voice of integrity, not to the shout of the immoral majority.

Third, we meet Barabbas, the notorious prisoner. He is no innocent scapegoat but a hardened criminal. Guilty of sedition, robbery, and murder, Barabbas is pulled into the scene as a clear opposite to the innocent Jesus. Perhaps, on the surface, we see no similarities between ourselves and that wretched sinner set free by no merit of his own. But upon closer reflection, we realize the sobering truth that *we are all Barabbas.* All who have been set free from sin and guilt by the substitutionary death of Christ experience spiritually what Barabbas experienced physically.

Finally, we have the wife of Pilate, the conscience of the scene. She has tossed and turned throughout the night, tormented by a dream of Jesus of Nazareth. By a supernatural stirring, she knows Jesus is innocent and that her husband should have nothing to do with His demise. Her knowledge of the truth prompts her to prod her husband toward doing what's right. Similarly, we are called to be the "conscience of the crowd," even when our small voices will likely go unheeded.

Those Final, Dreadful Hours
MATTHEW 27:27-50

NASB

27 Then the soldiers of the governor took Jesus into the ªPraetorium and gathered the whole *Roman* ᵇcohort around Him. 28 They stripped Him and put a scarlet robe on Him. 29 And after twisting together a crown of

NLT

27 Some of the governor's soldiers took Jesus into their headquarters* and called out the entire regiment. 28 They stripped him and put a scarlet robe on him. 29 They wove thorn branches into a crown and put it

NASB

thorns, they put it on His head, and a ªreed in His right hand; and they knelt down before Him and mocked Him, saying, "Hail, King of the Jews!" 30 They spat on Him, and took the reed and *began* to beat Him on the head. 31 After they had mocked Him, they took the *scarlet* robe off Him and put His *own* garments back on Him, and led Him away to crucify Him.

32 As they were coming out, they found a man of Cyrene named Simon, ªwhom they pressed into service to bear His cross.

33 And when they came to a place called Golgotha, which means Place of a Skull, 34 they gave Him wine to drink mixed with gall; and after tasting *it*, He was unwilling to drink.

35 And when they had crucified Him, they divided up His garments among themselves by casting ªlots. 36 And sitting down, they *began* to keep watch over Him there. 37 And above His head they put up the charge against Him ªwhich read, "THIS IS JESUS THE KING OF THE JEWS."

38 At that time two robbers were crucified with Him, one on the right and one on the left. 39 And those passing by were ªhurling abuse at Him, wagging their heads 40 and saying, "You who *are going to* destroy the temple and rebuild it in three days, save Yourself! If You are the Son of God, come down from the cross." 41 In the same way the chief priests also, along with the scribes and elders, were mocking *Him* and saying, 42 "He saved others; ªHe cannot save Himself. He is the King of Israel; let Him now come down from the cross, and we will believe in Him. 43 HE TRUSTS IN GOD; LET GOD RESCUE *Him* now, IF HE ªDELIGHTS IN HIM; for He said, 'I am the Son of God.'" 44 The robbers who had been crucified with

NLT

on his head, and they placed a reed stick in his right hand as a scepter. Then they knelt before him in mockery and taunted, "Hail! King of the Jews!" 30 And they spit on him and grabbed the stick and struck him on the head with it. 31 When they were finally tired of mocking him, they took off the robe and put his own clothes on him again. Then they led him away to be crucified.

32 Along the way, they came across a man named Simon, who was from Cyrene,* and the soldiers forced him to carry Jesus' cross. 33 And they went out to a place called Golgotha (which means "Place of the Skull"). 34 The soldiers gave Jesus wine mixed with bitter gall, but when he had tasted it, he refused to drink it.

35 After they had nailed him to the cross, the soldiers gambled for his clothes by throwing dice.* 36 Then they sat around and kept guard as he hung there. 37 A sign was fastened above Jesus' head, announcing the charge against him. It read: "This is Jesus, the King of the Jews." 38 Two revolutionaries* were crucified with him, one on his right and one on his left.

39 The people passing by shouted abuse, shaking their heads in mockery. 40 "Look at you now!" they yelled at him. "You said you were going to destroy the Temple and rebuild it in three days. Well then, if you are the Son of God, save yourself and come down from the cross!"

41 The leading priests, the teachers of religious law, and the elders also mocked Jesus. 42 "He saved others," they scoffed, "but he can't save himself! So he is the King of Israel, is he? Let him come down from the cross right now, and we will believe in him! 43 He trusted God, so let God rescue him now if he wants him! For he said, 'I am the Son of God.'" 44 Even the revolutionaries who were

Him were also insulting Him with the same words.

45 Now from the ªsixth hour darkness ᵇfell upon all the land until the ᶜninth hour. 46 About the ninth hour Jesus cried out with a loud voice, saying, "ELI, ELI, LAMA SA-BACHTHANI?" that is, "MY GOD, MY GOD, WHY HAVE YOU FORSAKEN ME?" 47 And some of those who were standing there, when they heard it, *began* saying, "This man is calling for Elijah." 48 Immediately one of them ran, and taking a sponge, he filled it with sour wine and put it on a reed, and gave Him a drink. 49 But the rest *of them* said, "ªLet us see whether Elijah will come to save Himᵇ." 50 And Jesus cried out again with a loud voice, and yielded up His spirit.

27:27 ªI.e. the governor's official residence ᵇOr *battalion* 27:29 ªOr *staff;* i.e. to mimic a king's scepter 27:32 ªLit *this one* 27:35 ªLit *a lot* 27:37 ªLit *written* 27:39 ªOr *blaspheming* 27:42 ªOr *can He not save Himself?* 27:43 ªOr *takes pleasure in;* or *cares for him* 27:45 ªI.e. 12 noon ᵇOr *occurred* ᶜI.e. 3 p.m. 27:49 ªLit *Permit that we see* ᵇSome early mss read *And another took a spear and pierced His side, and there came out water and blood* (cf John 19:34)

crucified with him ridiculed him in the same way.

45 At noon, darkness fell across the whole land until three o'clock. 46 At about three o'clock, Jesus called out with a loud voice, *"Eli, Eli,* lema sabachthani?"* which means "My God, my God, why have you abandoned me?"* 47 Some of the bystanders misunderstood and thought he was calling for the prophet Elijah. 48 One of them ran and filled a sponge with sour wine, holding it up to him on a reed stick so he could drink. 49 But the rest said, "Wait! Let's see whether Elijah comes to save him."* 50 Then Jesus shouted out again, and he released his spirit.

27:27 Or *into the Praetorium.* 27:32 *Cyrene* was a city in northern Africa. 27:35 Greek *by casting lots.* A few late manuscripts add *This fulfilled the word of the prophet: "They divided my garments among themselves and cast lots for my robe."* See Ps 22:18. 27:38 Or *criminals;* also in 27:44. 27:46a Some manuscripts read *Eloi, Eloi.* 27:46b Ps 22:1. 27:49 Some manuscripts add *And another took a spear and pierced his side, and out flowed water and blood.* Compare John 19:34.

History has no shortage of brutal methods of punishment and execution by cruel regimes who make a science of inflicting pain and suffering on guilty and innocent alike. Often, sadists, sociopaths, and psychopaths find their way into power, then transform the wheels of justice into gears of torture. Even in looking at recent history, we wince at accounts of soldiers, secret police, and other officials who have inflicted slow, humiliating pain on their captives, almost always with stone-cold disregard for human dignity, and often with insidious delight.

In reading the record of these events at the end of Jesus' life, it can be tempting to picture a scene of serenity and peace, like the portrayal in so many paintings and sculptures. Yet such images mislead and misinform. Even the most graphic of portrayals doesn't come close to the reality of first-century crucifixion. The grim details of the unjust trials, the vicious mocking, the brutal beatings, and, finally, the pitiless crucifixion of Jesus are more than our minds are able to comprehend. The anguishing ordeal was so dreadful and demeaning that most who lived in the era in which this extreme form of capital punishment was practiced refused to discuss it or even to think about it. The Roman orator and writer Cicero once wrote, "The idea of the cross should never come near the bodies of Roman citizens; it should never pass through their thoughts, eyes or ears."[30]

This method of execution used by the Romans in the first century was reserved for murderers, seditious slaves, and those who performed the worst kinds of heinous crimes in the colonies. It was always intended to send a message—a loud, clear, public message— that such crimes would not be treated lightly. Crucifixion was never used against Roman citizens, whose form of execution for capital offenses was a swift, comparatively merciful beheading. Jews shared the aversion to crucifixion particularly because of the prohibitions of Deuteronomy 21:22-23 and its association with being cursed: "If a man has committed a sin worthy of death and he is put to death, and you hang him on a tree, his corpse shall not hang all night on the tree, but you shall surely bury him on the same day (for he who is hanged is accursed of God)."

Because crucifixion was atrocious and generally avoided in conversation, and yet was also all too familiar in the first-century Roman world, the four Gospels don't spend an extensive amount of time with the details of Jesus' suffering and death on the cross. Those living in that era were well aware of the horror of crucifixion, and they neither needed nor desired an up-close-and-personal description. As such, Matthew records what occurred around the scene of the cross rather than describing all the details of the execution itself.

Today, most Christians are familiar only with the sanitized portrayals of crucifixion in G-rated Sunday school curricula or PG-rated movies on the life of Christ. To correct these mischaracterizations of the depths of Jesus' suffering, we'll need to provide a bit more detail about what came to mind when a Jew or Gentile living during the time of Jesus heard the word "crucifixion." But in doing so we don't want to lose sight of the things on which Matthew himself focuses, those things which are of "first importance" to our faith (1 Cor. 15:3).

— 27:27-31 —

Following His scourging, Jesus was placed in the custody of the soldiers who would carry out the sentence of crucifixion. Before the march to the place of crucifixion, however, Jesus was taken to the open courtyard of the Praetorium (27:27). This is probably another way of referring to the Antonia Fortress, named in honor of Mark Antony. It was strategically located just outside the northwest corner of the temple complex, having lookouts high enough for sentries to observe the activities in the temple court below and giving them clear views of the walled city of Jerusalem in every direction.[31] There, in the heart of Roman military strength, an entire battalion of about six hundred soldiers engaged in a parade in mock honor of the King of the Jews.[32]

The soldiers stripped Jesus of His already blood-soaked robe, ripping it from the deep wounds He had endured in the scourging a few minutes earlier. They replaced it with a robe of a reddish-purple color as a mock sign of His royalty (27:28). To match the robe, somebody twisted together a crown of Judean thorns and drove their 2- to 3-inch-long spikes into His already bloodied scalp. To complete the caricature, they placed a reed in His right hand as a taunting sign of power and authority. While crying out a sarcastic "Hail, King of the Jews!" they feigned homage to Him with exaggerated gestures of worship and honor (27:29). Amid their jeers, the Roman soldiers spat on Him, snatched the reed from His hand, and began beating Him with it in utter contempt (27:30).

After they had had enough "fun" with their condemned but innocent victim, they removed the robe and returned His garments. The time

A model of the **Fortress of Antonia,** which stood adjacent to the northwest corner of the temple complex. The courtyard in the center is the likely location of the mocking and beating of Christ at the hands of Roman soldiers.

had come. The preparations had been completed. During the seemingly endless ordeal of mocking and beating, two more criminals condemned to die had been retrieved from their cells and given crossbeams to carry. Taking the place of the freed Barabbas, the bloodied Jesus of Nazareth was led into the parade heading to the place of crucifixion (27:31).

— 27:32-34 —

The traditional route from the Antonia Fortress to Golgotha is known today as the Via Dolorosa (see the map on the next page). It winds through a noisy, bustling public marketplace along narrow stone streets sometimes barely wide enough for a donkey pulling a cart. If men and women lined the path two or three deep on both sides, it would be just possible for a person to slip through the center. It's quite likely that in the first century this road was similarly congested and chaotic, especially during the busy time of the Feast of Unleavened Bread.

Normally, the condemned would carry their own crossbeams to the place of execution. However, due to the vicious scourging and merciless beating Jesus had endured at the hands of the Romans, He was unable to carry His own cross. Matthew relays that the soldiers forced a man named Simon, from Cyrene—a city on the coast of present-day Libya—to carry the crossbeam for Jesus (27:32). The Gospel of Mark mentions that this Simon was "the father of Alexander and Rufus" (Mark 15:21), indicating that Simon and his family had become well known to Christians reading the Gospel of Mark. Thus, we can be fairly certain that sometime following the Crucifixion, Simon became a believer in Jesus as Lord and Savior, together with his family.

Regardless of the exact route followed by the soldiers as they led Jesus and the other two criminals, along with Simon of Cyrene, to the place outside the city walls where the three men were to be crucified, the parade would have descended into the Tyropoeon Valley before reascending at its western slope. They would have traversed through more ups and downs before passing through a gate in the wall and ending at a heavily trafficked intersection that wrapped around a high outcropping called "Golgotha," "Calvary," or "Place of a Skull" (Matt. 27:33).

Once the group arrived at the site, a crowd of passersby would have stopped to watch the soldiers carry out their gruesome detail. Those who tried to give Jesus "wine . . . mixed with gall" (27:34) were probably not the soldiers but were likely women who had made it their ministry of mercy to ease the suffering of those who were about to be crucified.

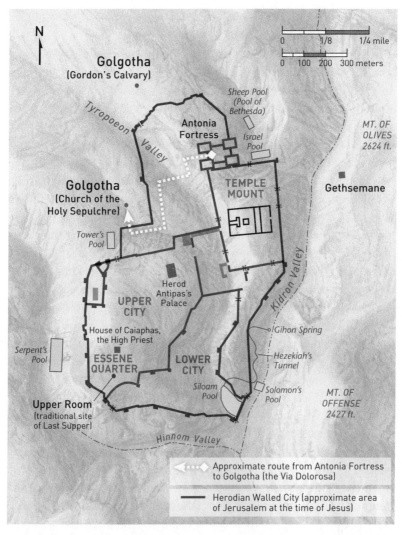

The actual route from the Antonia Fortress to Golgotha is uncertain, so the path indicated on this map is an approximation. Traditionally, it has been believed that the route wound up and down through a busy section of the city. This route is commemorated today by the Via Dolorosa.

A. T. Robertson explains, "The myrrh gave the sour wine a better flavor and like the bitter gall had a narcotic and stupefying effect. Both elements may have been in the drink which Jesus tasted and refused to drink. Women provided the drink to deaden the sense of pain."[33] R. V. G. Tasker suggests that Jesus refused to drink "because it was as a fully-conscious victim that He desired to make His supreme sacrifice. He offered Himself completely and with His faculties unimpaired."[34]

— 27:35-49 —

How simple the words appear in Matthew 27:35: "They . . . crucified Him." But as William Wilson writes, "Not only was the cross the most painful of deaths, it was also considered the most debasing. The condemned man was stripped naked and left exposed in his agony, and often the Romans even denied burial to the victim, allowing his body to hang on the cross until it disintegrated."[35] And though He could have taken an elixir to deaden the pain, instead, Jesus experienced the full force of the nails driven into His hands and feet.

Few plays, films, or artist's renditions of the Crucifixion portray the agonizing scene accurately. The soldiers responsible for crucifixion held Jesus down, pressing the flesh of His lacerated back against the rough wood of the cross. Others stretched His arms along the crossbeam and drove a 5-inch-long spike (not a nail) through the base of each palm, angled inward to exit the wrist. They bent His knees, placed His feet flat against the post, and drove a spike through each foot. The soldiers then tilted the cross up and guided the base into a hole on the hill, a hill called "Place of a Skull." By nine o'clock in the morning, the soldiers had finished driving wedges between the beam and the sides of the hole to keep the cross firmly upright. At the same time, another group of soldiers was doing the same to the two criminals being crucified with Jesus that day—one on His right, the other on His left (27:38). As terrifying as all of this was to the bystanders, for the Roman soldiers on crucifixion detail that day, it was all business as usual. In fact, they made a game of dividing His bloodied garments before sitting back to let the pain take its toll (27:35-36).

In crucifixion, a sign called a *titulus* indicating the name of the criminal and the crime was hung above the victim's head so everybody passing by on the road below could see the price that was paid for serious infractions of Roman law. Signs such as MURDER, PIRACY, INSURRECTION, TREASON, and ROBBERY would have been common. But when passersby saw the sign hanging above Jesus' head, written in Hebrew, Latin, and Greek, it undoubtedly would have caught their attention. Combining the information from all four Gospel accounts, Jesus' sign read: THIS IS JESUS THE NAZARENE, THE KING OF THE JEWS (27:37; Mark 15:26; Luke 23:38; John 19:19). The chief priests were so troubled by this public statement labeling Jesus as King of the Jews that they asked Pilate to clarify that Jesus had *claimed* that He was King of the Jews. To this request, Pilate simply responded, "What I have written I have written" (John 19:21-22).

EXCURSUS: CRUCIFIXION

MATTHEW 27:35

Various forms of crucifixion had been common in the ancient Near East for many centuries prior to the adoption of the practice by the Romans, who took advantage of this form of public execution to deter the residents of Roman provinces from insurrection. The idea was that anybody who took one glance at a person being crucified would think twice about participating in any kind of revolt against the emperor or his soldiers. Thus, crucifixion was made into a spectacularly horrific display of suffering, and it could often last for several days.

After a condemned person was handed over, the executioner and the other soldiers responsible for carrying out the sentence would place a crossbeam known as a *patibulum* on the person's shoulders. Contrary to many portrayals of Jesus' march to Calvary, the condemned did not carry the entire post and crossbeam. Such a weight would have been impossible to bear. The crossbeam, perhaps affixed to the victim by ropes, would have been taxing enough to carry to the place of execution.

When the prisoner arrived at the location where public crucifixions occurred, the *patibulum* was affixed to the top of a post (called a *stipes*) by means of a mortise and tenon joint—a hole in one piece in which a square peg in the other fit into place. This way, the implements of crucifixion could be used again for subsequent victims. The intersection of the post and crossbeam often resulted in what looked like a capital T, on which the crucified person was then tied or nailed, depending on how long the soldiers wanted the suffering to last. In most cases, the prisoner was stripped naked and exposed to public shame. The

specific crime of the condemned would be fastened to the cross so that all those passing by would know what offense(s) had gotten the person there. Having fastened the victim to the cross, the soldiers lifted it and then lowered it into a deep hole to keep it vertical while the victim suffered excruciating pain.

Even without the pain of the spikes that fastened the body to the post and crossbeam, a person hanging on a cross would experience insufferable pain as their forearms went numb and their shoulders felt like they were being pulled from their

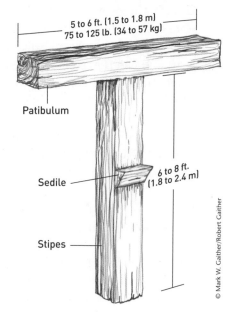

5 to 6 ft. (1.5 to 1.8 m)
75 to 125 lb. (34 to 57 kg)

Patibulum

6 to 8 ft. (1.8 to 2.4 m)

Sedile

Stipes

© Mark W. Gaither/Robert Gaither

Illustration of a Cross. The *patibulum* (crossbeam) was attached to the top of the *stipes* (post) with a mortise and tenon joint, which allowed a cross to be dismantled and used repeatedly for subsequent victims. Sometimes, to delay death and prolong suffering, the executioner attached a *sedile* (seat) between the victim's legs.

(continued on next page)

sockets. To relieve the numbness, victims would instinctively push themselves up with their legs. Then, after their legs would weaken, cramp, and tremble, they would arch their backs for relief. This constant shifting of positions was the only way to even remotely cope with the pain in their arms, chest, back, and legs.[36] All the while, the will to survive would keep the condemned writhing and crying out in pain until they finally grew too exhausted, too dehydrated, and too physically weak to pull in another breath. Death usually came by suffocation, not by loss of blood.

Perhaps to counter the clear—albeit mocking—written confession of His messiahship, the chief priests, scribes, elders, and other opponents and critics of Jesus made a point to mock and jeer loudly from the road (Matt. 27:39-43). Matthew indicates that one mockery involved the half-truth used against Jesus at His trial—that Jesus claimed He would tear down the temple and rebuild it in three days (27:40; cf. 26:61; John 2:18-19). This demonstrates that those blaspheming and hurling insults were not the simple common folk who happened by. The taunts and tormenting came from the religious elites who had conspired against Jesus and had Him crucified. They were at the foot of the cross to the bitter end in an attempt to spin the Crucifixion in a way that would make them out to be the righteous ones and Jesus the criminal.

These mockers also challenged Jesus to save Himself, come down from the cross, and thereby convince everybody to believe in Him (Matt. 27:41-42). Those self-righteous hypocrites even quoted a Scripture passage about God coming to rescue those in whom He delights (Ps. 22:8), insinuating that those who are not rescued are clearly rejected by God (Matt. 27:43). Even the two robbers, justly suffering for their crimes, joined in the jeering, until one had a miraculous change of heart and realized that Jesus was innocent and didn't deserve the punishment they were enduring (27:44; Luke 23:39-43).

Well beyond the torturous physical suffering and verbal abuse Jesus experienced on the cross, He also faced a deeper, more profound suffering as He bore the weight of the sins of the world. This was the darkest moment of His life as God the Father turned, as it were, His back on His Son, abandoning Him to utter despair, physical torment, emotional anguish, and the abyss of death. Think about this. The only one in the history of the world who, by His very nature and works, deserved deliverance, fellowship, and infinite favor from God, exchanged all that for the burden of our sin, guilt, and punishment. Instead of fellowship with God, He experienced isolation; instead of support, He experienced suffering; instead of rescue, He experienced death. In the midst of that deep, dark affliction, Jesus cried out in His native tongue, "Eli, Eli, lama sabachthani?" that is, "My God, My God, why have You forsaken Me?" (Matt. 27:46).

Had those at the foot of the cross been listening instead of heckling, perhaps they wouldn't have mistaken His words as a delirious cry for Elijah (27:47). Rather, they would have recognized the words as the opening line of Psalm 22. And if they had recalled the broader context of that psalm, they would have realized that everything happening to Jesus—from the mockery to the Crucifixion—had been prophesied about the Messiah. Psalm 22 says,

> My God, my God, why have You forsaken me?
> Far from my deliverance are the words of my groaning.
> O my God, I cry by day, but You do not answer;
> And by night, but I have no rest. . . .
> All who see me sneer at me;
> They separate with the lip, they wag the head, saying,
> "Commit yourself to the LORD; let Him deliver him;
> Let Him rescue him, because He delights in him." . . .
> I am poured out like water,
> And all my bones are out of joint;
> My heart is like wax;
> It is melted within me.
> My strength is dried up like a potsherd,
> And my tongue cleaves to my jaws;
> And You lay me in the dust of death.
> For dogs have surrounded me;
> A band of evildoers has encompassed me;
> They pierced my hands and my feet.
> I can count all my bones.
> They look, they stare at me;
> They divide my garments among them,
> And for my clothing they cast lots. (Ps. 22:1-2, 7-8, 14-18)

In this most pivotal moment in all of history, the most skilled interpreters of Scripture, the most well-trained scholars of theology, the most respected religious leaders in Israel, were blind. Instead of recognizing the Suffering Servant of Isaiah 53 and the pierced Messiah of Psalm 22, they tried to give Jesus another sip of sour wine, on a sponge at the end of a stick—a way of providing relief to a man who was, in their minds, suffering delirium (Matt. 27:48). Some folded their arms and continued to scoff: "Let us see whether Elijah will come to save Him" (27:49). Some in the crowd believed Jesus was a malicious charlatan, getting just what He deserved. Others thought He was a deluded lunatic, deserving of pity. Nobody recognized Him for who He really was and is: Lord and King, Israel's long-awaited Messiah.

— 27:50 —

At about three o'clock, after three hours of darkness (see 27:45), Jesus cried out with a loud voice and died (27:50). Matthew and Mark don't tell us what Jesus said with His last breath. However, Luke and John fill in a little detail here. After quoting from Psalm 31:5, "Father, into Your hands I commit My Spirit" (Luke 23:46), He took a deep breath and cried out, "It is finished!" (John 19:30). With that, Jesus breathed His last breath. At that moment, the atonement for fallen, sinful, depraved humanity was accomplished.

Jesus didn't die for His own sins. Though He was born into a fallen, broken world with a mortal body able to suffer, He had none of the stain of Adam's original sin and guilt. And though He was tempted by Satan and was bombarded with demonic attacks throughout His ministry, He never sinned in thought or in action. He was a perfect, unblemished Lamb who died not for His own sins but for the sins of humanity (John 1:29; 1 Cor. 15:3).

Without denying or diminishing the ugliness of the suffering, crucifixion, and death of Christ, the church has for centuries commemorated that day as "Good Friday." What appeared to be defeat was actually an unqualified victory over sin, death, and the devil himself. That ugly, rugged cross took its toll on the God-man, but it failed to have the final say. In the deepest darkness that the visible and invisible forces of this world had to offer, the victim became the Victor. And the instrument of punishment has become the symbol of salvation for countless believers ever since.

APPLICATION: MATTHEW 27:27-50

Jesus Paid It All

The suffering, crucifixion, and death of Jesus of Nazareth is a historical fact. At midafternoon that day, Jesus died. This is widely recognized. But to see behind that death to the profound theological truth of what it accomplished takes the eyes of faith. Jesus' death on the cross satisfied the righteous demands of the Father: "For Christ also died for sins once for all, the just for the unjust, so that He might bring us to God" (1 Pet. 3:18). This is the gospel (the good news). Had it not been for what He did for us on that cross, we would all perish in our countless sins. Our future would be filled with utter and absolute hopelessness. We'd die in our sins and never know the joy of forgiveness or eternal life.

As we consider Christ's death, which He underwent not for His own sins but for the sins of the world, let's think about our own part that we played in sending Him to the cross. Not one of us is innocent. Not one of us makes it very far without a sin of the mind, the heart, or the will. As Isaiah said, "All of us like sheep have gone astray, each of us has turned to his own way; but the LORD has caused the iniquity of us all to fall on Him" (Isa. 53:6). Reflect for a moment on your own sins—the attitudes and actions that compelled God the Son to come from heaven to earth in the Incarnation, and then drove the incarnate God-man from the earth to the cross in the Crucifixion: abuse, adultery, an argumentative spirit, arrogance, assault, backbiting, bitterness, blasphemy, boasting, bribery, coarse joking, complaining, contentiousness, coveting, deceit, defrauding, denying and despising the poor, dishonoring the aging, disrespecting parents, envy, evil motives, falsifying tax documents, fornication, fraud, giving grudgingly, not giving at all, gluttony, gossip, greed, harsh words, hatred, holding grudges, hypocrisy, idolatry, immodesty, spiritual indifference, ingratitude, jealousy, having a loose tongue, loss of temper, lust, lying, malice, manipulation, mistreatment of children and the defenseless, murderous thoughts, partiality, prayerlessness, prejudice, pride, racism, rage, rape, rebellion against authority, refusing to forgive, resisting the Holy Spirit, returning insult for insult, selfishness, sexual impropriety, slander, slothfulness, stealing, viewing pornography, violence, worldliness, not loving your neighbor, not loving your spouse, being unequally yoked with unbelievers, and on and on.

Over this list, which most of us find all too familiar, we can write in large, bold letters: JESUS PAID IT ALL. There is only one appropriate response to this truth: gratitude. Thank Him for enduring the scourging. Thank Him for taking your place on the cross. Thank Him for paying the complete price for your sins—past, present, and future. Thank Him for dying that day, that you might live forever. Jesus paid it all.

What Happened Next?
MATTHEW 27:51-66

NASB

⁵¹And behold, the ªveil of the temple was torn in two from top to bottom; and the earth shook and the rocks were split. ⁵²The tombs were opened, and many bodies of the ªsaints who had fallen asleep were raised; ⁵³and coming out of the tombs after His resurrection they entered the holy city and appeared to many. ⁵⁴Now the centurion, and those who were with him keeping guard over Jesus, when they saw the earthquake and the things that were happening, became very frightened and said, "Truly this was ªthe Son of God!"

⁵⁵Many women were there looking on from a distance, who had followed Jesus from Galilee while ªministering to Him. ⁵⁶Among them was Mary Magdalene, and Mary the mother of James and Joseph, and the mother of the sons of Zebedee.

⁵⁷When it was evening, there came a rich man from Arimathea, named Joseph, who himself had also become a disciple of Jesus. ⁵⁸This man went to Pilate and asked for the body of Jesus. Then Pilate ordered it to be given *to him.* ⁵⁹And Joseph took the body and wrapped it in a clean linen cloth, ⁶⁰and laid it in his own new tomb, which he had hewn out in the rock; and he rolled a large stone against the entrance of the tomb and went away. ⁶¹And Mary Magdalene was there, and the other Mary, sitting opposite the grave.

⁶²Now on the next day, ªthe day after the preparation, the chief priests and the Pharisees gathered together with Pilate, ⁶³and said, "Sir, we remember that when He was still alive that deceiver said, 'After three days I *am to* rise again.' ⁶⁴Therefore, give orders for the grave to be made

NLT

⁵¹At that moment the curtain in the sanctuary of the Temple was torn in two, from top to bottom. The earth shook, rocks split apart, ⁵²and tombs opened. The bodies of many godly men and women who had died were raised from the dead. ⁵³They left the cemetery after Jesus' resurrection, went into the holy city of Jerusalem, and appeared to many people.

⁵⁴The Roman officer* and the other soldiers at the crucifixion were terrified by the earthquake and all that had happened. They said, "This man truly was the Son of God!"

⁵⁵And many women who had come from Galilee with Jesus to care for him were watching from a distance. ⁵⁶Among them were Mary Magdalene, Mary (the mother of James and Joseph), and the mother of James and John, the sons of Zebedee.

⁵⁷As evening approached, Joseph, a rich man from Arimathea who had become a follower of Jesus, ⁵⁸went to Pilate and asked for Jesus' body. And Pilate issued an order to release it to him. ⁵⁹Joseph took the body and wrapped it in a long sheet of clean linen cloth. ⁶⁰He placed it in his own new tomb, which had been carved out of the rock. Then he rolled a great stone across the entrance and left. ⁶¹Both Mary Magdalene and the other Mary were sitting across from the tomb and watching.

⁶²The next day, on the Sabbath,* the leading priests and Pharisees went to see Pilate. ⁶³They told him, "Sir, we remember what that deceiver once said while he was still alive: 'After three days I will rise from the dead.' ⁶⁴So we request that you seal the tomb until the third day. This will prevent his disciples from

secure until the third day, otherwise His disciples may come and steal Him away and say to the people, 'He has risen from the dead,' and the last deception will be worse than the first." 65 Pilate said to them, "You have a guard; go, make it *as* secure as you know how." 66 And they went and made the grave secure, and along with the guard they set a seal on the stone.

27:51 ªOr *curtain* 27:52 ªOr *holy ones* 27:54 ªOr *a son of God* or *a son of a god* 27:55 ªOr *caring for Him* 27:62 ªLit *which is after*

coming and stealing his body and then telling everyone he was raised from the dead! If that happens, we'll be worse off than we were at first."

65 Pilate replied, "Take guards and secure it the best you can." 66 So they sealed the tomb and posted guards to protect it.

27:54 Greek *The centurion.* 27:62 Or *On the next day, which is after the Preparation.*

A married couple can remember the intricate details of their wedding day and the fond memories of their honeymoon. But it's doubtful they remember many details about the days that followed. Milestone birthdays like the big 4-0 and anniversaries like the twenty-fifth are often etched in people's minds. Photos and videos commemorate memorable events. But the days following those celebrations? There's probably not a picture or the slightest remembrance of what transpired. Nobody forgets his or her graduation from high school, college, or grad school—those memories are precious, never to be forgotten. But does anybody remember the day after? Not likely.

Our journey through Matthew's Gospel has brought us through the pivotal moment of the Cross—the passion of Jesus Christ. From His unforgettable arrest in the garden of Gethsemane, through the six illegal trials that led to the declaration of His guilt, and ultimately to the brutal scourging, crucifixion, and death—these faith-inspiring and soul-saving scenes are impossible to forget. At about 3:00 p.m. that Friday, Jesus shouted, "It is finished!" He bowed His head and released His spirit. He surrendered to death. Every Christian—and many non-Christians—could recount these events. But what happened at 3:30? Or 4:00? Most people, including most Christians, would have a hard time recalling the details of what occurred between Christ's death and resurrection. Some may wonder, *Does it even matter?*

Matthew records a handful of important—and even peculiar—scenes between Christ's death and His resurrection. As we compare the accounts of Matthew, Mark, Luke, and John related to Jesus' burial, the stage is set for us to get a complete picture of the dramatic, miraculous resurrection that occurred on Sunday morning. So, instead of jumping from the cross to the empty tomb, let's pause to take a closer look at what happened next.

— 27:51-53 —

After recording Jesus' last breath, all four Gospel writers immediately turn their attention to supernatural events that punctuated the Messiah's death. As an earthquake struck Jerusalem with enough power to split rocks, the veil in the inner sanctuary of the temple tore from top to bottom. A. T. Robertson describes the makeup of this sacred curtain: "This veil was a most elaborately woven fabric of seventy-two twisted plaits of twenty-four threads each and the veil was sixty feet long and thirty wide."[37] Like a massive theatre curtain separating the audience from the stage, this veil of blue, purple, and scarlet separated worshipers from the most holy place, the sacred space designated as the location of God's presence with His people. In the tabernacle and first temple, the most holy place, also separated by a curtain of blue, purple, and scarlet, was the resting place of the ark of the covenant (Exod. 26:31-33). Only the high priest passed behind the veil—and only once a year, on the Day of Atonement (Lev. 16; Heb. 9:6-7).

With the death of Christ, that veil of separation was torn asunder. As if slashed by an enormous invisible sword, the curtain split in two (Matt. 27:51). It was as if God were announcing through a powerful object lesson, "There is now immediate and total access into My holy presence—*for everyone.* Come!" As Hebrews 4:16 says, "Therefore let us draw near with confidence to the throne of grace, so that we may receive mercy and find grace to help in time of need." At the same time, the tearing of the veil was a sign to the high priests and religious elite who had conspired to crucify their Messiah. Their time was up. The rites and rituals of the old covenant that were merely a "shadow of the good things to come" could never "make perfect those who draw near" (Heb. 10:1).

The group of men and women hovering around Golgotha would not have known that the veil in the temple had torn. But they would have experienced the chilling, thick darkness that had blanketed the heavens for several hours and the sudden earthquake that rocked the land as if on cue the moment Jesus died. All these events announced, as a sort of wordless sermon, that the One who was crucified as King of the Jews was no charlatan or madman. Anybody with an eye to see or an ear to hear would have recognized that something extremely significant had just happened.

Another great sign—both peculiar and puzzling—accompanied the death of Christ. With the earthquake and the splitting of the rocks, tombs around Jerusalem were opened (Matt. 27:51-52). We must recall that in the first century, tombs were often caves in hillsides, in which the bodies of deceased persons were placed on slabs until they decomposed enough to be placed either in an ossuary (bone box) or in a pit of bones with the remains of their family members and ancestors. Matthew alone reports that when the earthquake struck Jerusalem, the large stones that enclosed many of the tombs in the area were opened to the light of day, exposing the bodies that had been placed in those sepulchres.

So far, there's nothing particularly strange about this. Earthquakes cause rocks to split. But beyond the tombs suddenly becoming opened, something miraculous occurred. The bodies of many "saints" (or "holy ones") who had died were raised from those very tombs that had been cracked open! After Jesus' resurrection, they came out of the tombs and appeared to many in Jerusalem (27:53). Who were these people? Why were they raised? What did they do afterward?

My simple answer to these questions is *I don't know.* If you turned to this page of this commentary looking for a definitive answer to this Bible mystery, you're going to be disappointed. And I would caution against believing any Bible scholar who thinks they have this one finally settled. Matthew gives us only one sentence on this matter. Mark, Luke, and John don't even mention the earthquake, much less the resurrections. So we don't have a lot to go by to help us land on a solution to this puzzling passage.

Let me give you a few of the typical answers and a cautious, tentative conclusion. I completely dismiss those who say this is just a myth, some kind of metaphorical fable intended to present a theological truth, not to be taken as historical fact. This is no mere illustration, no parable. Matthew intends to report actual events, not imaginary allegories. How tempting it is for some people to ignore the mystery of these saints being raised by writing it off as clever yarn spinning. The biggest problem I have with this dismissive approach is that *their* resurrection is mentioned in the same sentence as *His* resurrection. If theirs is a myth, why would we insist that *His* is a fact? And if His is a fact, why would theirs be a myth? I'm not going there.

One plausible interpretation pertaining to who was raised suggests that it was not *all* the dead saints who were raised, but just some who had died recently. The text implies that these "saints" were recognizable to many in Jerusalem, which suggests that they were not ancient ancestors whose identities were long forgotten. In line with this understanding, they may have been followers of Jesus who had died during His earthly ministry. Presumably, they would have been raised in restored mortal bodies, like Lazarus (John 11:43-44). As such, they would have eventually died again, with hopes of their future, glorious resurrection.[38]

Another possible view is that with Jesus' resurrection, some (or all) of the Old Testament saints (perhaps along with those people who had recently died during Jesus' ministry) were raised in glorious resurrection bodies just like Jesus'. Jesus was, indeed, the "first fruits" (1 Cor. 15:23), meaning that He was the first to be raised in such a glorified body—immortal, incorruptible, and fit for eternal, heavenly existence. If this is the case, then Christ brought with Him to heaven a select group of saints in their glorious bodies to be the first to participate in the resurrection harvest that will occur for others at the Second Coming.[39] A few of these were permitted to appear to people in Jerusalem as a sign of Jesus' resurrection power.

Those are two common views concerning who was raised and what happened to them. I tend to find the first view somewhat more plausible, but I haven't really landed. I may just keep circling the plane in a holding pattern until the Lord returns. I'd be in good company. My own revered Bible professor Dwight Pentecost once admitted to our Life of Christ class, "I'm stumped by all of this." If it were crucial to have a dogmatic view on this matter, Matthew would have made it clearer, and Mark, Luke, and John would have given us more detail.

— 27:54-56 —

Matthew is joined by Mark and Luke in providing complementary information on the reactions from the people at the cross to the observable phenomena associated with Christ's death: the heavenly darkness and the earthly quaking. First, the centurion in command of the soldiers responsible for carrying out Jesus' execution became "very frightened" at the events. He blurted out, "Truly this was the Son of God!" (27:54). That man had attentively overseen Jesus' scourging, mocking, beating, nailing, suffering, and death. He had closely observed Jesus' words, His righteous actions, and His holy disposition throughout the unjust treatment. And in contrast to Israel's religious elite, the centurion concluded that he had just crucified a righteous man (Luke 23:47).

Meanwhile, several women from Galilee who had been followers of Jesus were also present among the crowd of onlookers (Matt. 27:55-56). Matthew specifically mentions Mary Magdalene, Mary the mother of James and Joseph, and the mother of the sons of Zebedee (Salome; cf. Mark 15:40). John indicates that Mary the mother of Jesus was also present, along with Mary the wife of Clopas (who may be the same Mary as the "mother of James and Joseph" [or Joses]; see John 19:25; cf. Matt. 27:56; Mark 15:40).[40] Besides these, Mark mentions "many other women" who had followed Jesus to Jerusalem (Mark 15:41).

In response to the suffering and death of Jesus as well as the astonishing signs in heaven and on earth, the multitude of followers were beating their breasts and mourning greatly at the loss of their Master and Teacher (see Luke 23:48).

— 27:57-61 —

At this point in the sequence of events, John's Gospel fills in a detail not mentioned in Matthew, Mark, and Luke. Because it was the eve of the Sabbath, which would begin soon (at sundown), some observant Jews requested that the three men crucified at Golgotha have their legs broken to hasten their deaths so that their bodies could be buried before the Sabbath began. Pilate consented, but when the soldiers saw that Jesus was already dead, they left His legs unbroken and instead pierced His side with the end of a spear, releasing blood and watery bodily fluids. If there had been any question about whether Jesus had truly died on the cross, those suspicions were now removed (John 19:31-37).

With Jesus' death certain, and with the start of the Sabbath quickly approaching, the question of what to do with His body would have certainly arisen among the handful of women at the cross. Jesus was far from His hometown of Nazareth, the natural location for the family tomb and the place where Joseph was likely buried. They definitely would not have been able to make the multiday journey to Galilee before sunset. And letting a body as maimed and brutalized as Jesus' lie dormant in the home of one of the Jerusalem disciples was unthinkable. But if the body went unclaimed, it would have been thrown into a common grave with other disowned criminals—an undignified disposal for anybody, but especially for the revered Jesus of Nazareth.

As the women pondered what to do, two men stepped forward from their former place of anonymity and took charge. Matthew mentions only Joseph of Arimathea, a rich member of the Sanhedrin and secret disciple of Jesus. He requested permission from Pontius Pilate to take custody of the body of Jesus (Matt. 27:57-58; John 19:38). Perhaps emboldened by Joseph's willingness to reveal his devotion to Jesus before his fellow Jerusalem elites, Nicodemus—a Pharisee and also a member of the Sanhedrin—who had encountered Jesus earlier in His ministry (John 3:1-21), also stepped out of the shadows and assisted in what had to be a very hasty and incomplete burial before sundown (John 19:39-40).

A normal burial process would have involved a lengthy preparation of soaking strips of linen in a mixture of spiced resin and then carefully wrapping them around the body to counteract the stench of decomposition.[41] The full process, which usually took many family members working for several hours, would, in Jesus' case, have had to be done by a handful of servants working against the clock. After sundown, when the Sabbath began, no such work would be permissible.

As such, the burial of Jesus that Friday evening was surely intended to be temporary. It was just enough to get through the Sabbath. Most likely, the men and women at the cross discussed plans to return to the work early Sunday morning in order to complete the job of wrapping and spicing the body to prepare to transport it north to Nazareth. In any case, nobody seemed to recall (or take seriously) Jesus' repeated predictions of His own resurrection.

Due to the lateness of the hour, after hastily spicing the body with a mixture of myrrh and aloes generously provided by Nicodemus (John 19:39-40), Joseph of Arimathea permitted Jesus' body to be temporarily placed in "his own new tomb," which had been hewn into the side of a cliff (Matt. 27:60). John tells us that this new tomb, in which nobody had yet been laid, was in a garden (John 19:41). The Greek word translated "garden" is *kēpos* [2779], which can also refer to an orchard or plantation.[42] It's the same term used to refer to the "garden" of Gethsemane (John 18:1). In the ancient world, such a garden—especially one containing a tomb—would have undoubtedly been set off by a perimeter wall to mark it not only as private property but also as a sacred site for burial:

> So closely was the idea of the garden-orchard linked in antiquity with its enclosed perimeter that one could not speak of the first without invoking the second. The common linguistic associations among Latin, Greek, and Old Iranian in this instance reflect a shared conceptual model: in the ancient Mediterranean world a cultivated garden or orchard was unimaginable without the protective enclosure that surrounded it.[43]

Joseph of Arimathea's garden, though new, was a fully functioning one; later, John notes that Mary Magdalene mistook Jesus for "the gardener" (John 20:15), that is, a hired worker laboring in Joseph's walled garden. This garden was just outside the city walls, which we know had been constructed by the AD 30s. We know that the area north of the walled city of Jerusalem, in which the garden and tomb had been built, was in the process of being developed with new gardens and homes. Over the

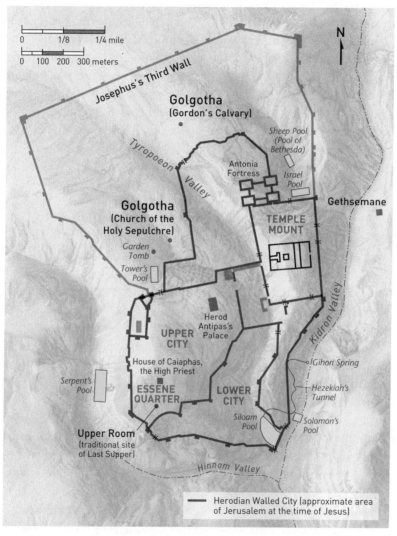

Though Golgotha and Joseph's garden tomb would have been located outside the walled city at the time of Jesus, a third, "north" wall, mentioned by Josephus, was subsequently constructed around the "New City" to protect the expansive developments of the first century.

next forty years, an additional wall would be constructed to enclose this "New City" (see the map on the previous page).

We often picture the tomb of Jesus as out in the middle of nowhere, surrounded by a wooded area off the beaten path. Instead, we should picture a walled garden within sight of Golgotha itself, perhaps just across the street, with a door or gate and a staff of gardeners working inside. In fact, Joseph himself may have been watching the goings-on at Golgotha from that garden all afternoon, waiting for his moment to step in and show an act of devotion to that mistreated rabbi from Nazareth.

In any case, with the rushed preparation of the body of Jesus completed and sunset quickly approaching, Joseph and Nicodemus—most likely with the help of the gardeners—rolled the stone over the front of the tomb and departed (Matt. 27:60). At least a couple of the women who had attended the Crucifixion watched closely to see where the body had been placed (27:61), no doubt planning on meeting at that very location around dawn on Sunday morning—after the Sabbath—to complete the preparation of the body for a proper, permanent burial later in the week (cf. Luke 23:55-56).

— 27:62-66 —

The last five verses in this chapter are unique to Matthew's account. In a sort of addendum to the description of the burial, Matthew cuts to the chief priests and Pharisees again trying to manipulate things behind the scenes by plotting and conniving. Matthew points out that they did all of this "on the next day, the day after the preparation" (27:62). That is, they were doing all this work on the Sabbath, which was forbidden by Jewish Law. Those hypocrites who had condemned Jesus and His disciples for "working" on the Sabbath were now hard at work against the so-called deceiver they had condemned!

Because the tomb in which Jesus' body had been laid was in a walled garden and was the private property of Joseph of Arimathea, the Jews would have had no right to access it without permission of the landowner or without some sort of warrant from the Roman government.[44] Certain they wouldn't get permission from Joseph of Arimathea, they had to go straight to Pontius Pilate. I imagine Pilate was in a bad mood since he had to go home and tell his wife that he had, in fact, sent to crucifixion the man she'd had a nightmare about. Now the same Jewish leaders who had brought Jesus to him were demanding that he send soldiers to secure the private property of another Jew who had just the day before asked Pilate for permission to have the body. By that point,

EXCURSUS: RESURRECTION ACCOUNTS HARMONIZED, PART 1—FROM THURSDAY TO SATURDAY

Through the course of this three-part excursus, we're going to track Jesus and His followers from the arrest in the garden of Gethsemane to the Resurrection . . . and beyond. In this way, we can see a plausible harmonization of the various accounts of the four Gospels, as well as a few other New Testament passages that mention the events of Christ's death, burial, and resurrection. In seeking to reconcile the biblical facts, it becomes important to keep tabs on the likely whereabouts of the various groups and individuals involved, because each New Testament author gives his account from a specific point of view. Sometimes this will require us to engage in some informed speculation and to draw on what we know of the geography of Jerusalem and its environment as well as early historical sources and traditions. With the biblical facts, a map, a little archaeology and history, and some common sense, we can seek to show how the various strands of the narrative can be woven into a coherent and compelling account. (Please consult the map of Jerusalem in part 2 of this excursus for the traditional locations mentioned in this reconstruction of events.)

MATTHEW 26–27

Before jumping into the various accounts of Jesus' miraculous, bodily resurrection (which we will do in the next commentary section), it's important to step back and survey the scene. The evening of Christ's arrest, the morning of His trials, and the day of His crucifixion sent many people scattering in a number of directions. If we're to make sense of Matthew's Resurrection account in comparison with those of the other New Testament writers, we need to make sure we're starting out on the same page. To do so, we need to recall who was where . . . and when.[45]

LATE THURSDAY/EARLY FRIDAY— GETHSEMANE

During Jesus' arrest in the garden of Gethsemane, the eleven disciples and any others who were present found their way out of the garden while Jesus was being taken into custody (26:56; Mark 14:50-52). Where did they all go? Scripture doesn't tell us, but we can make some good guesses based on sound reasoning. Initially, at the moment of their flight from Gethsemane, it would have been "each man for himself." Regrouping would have drawn too much attention. And we can be pretty sure that most of them would have avoided heading back through the Kidron Valley into Jerusalem. Remember, that's where the large mob of torch-carrying, club-wielding, sword-bearing soldiers had come from, and it was also where they were going. Instead, the disciples probably would have taken the most logical route away from Jerusalem and back toward Bethany, where they had been staying throughout the week (see Matt. 21:17; 26:6).[46] Likely, several of them had the same idea and would have ended up there, perhaps at the home of Lazarus, Mary, and Martha.

We know that two of the disciples, Peter and John, doubled back after initially fleeing the scene. Both of them began following Jesus from a distance, trying to inconspicuously mix into the crowd of soldiers, servants, and passersby (John 18:15-16). We aren't sure when—or even if—John slipped away from the series of trials as the night turned to dawn, but he

(continued on next page)

may have eventually returned to his home in or near Jerusalem or retrieved Jesus' mother, Mary, in the early morning.[47] Peter, on the other hand, denied Jesus in the courtyard of Caiaphas and fled into the night (Matt. 26:74-75). We can assume that Peter slinked off to the place where he was staying in Jerusalem (cf. Luke 24:12; John 20:10)—perhaps the home of John Mark's parents, where the Last Supper had been held.

Thus, while Jesus endured the trials alone, nine of the disciples were likely hiding out in or near Bethany, unaware of what was happening after Jesus' arrest. Peter fled during the trial before Caiaphas, presumably to a place in Jerusalem, also uncertain of Jesus' ultimate fate. John was probably the one most informed, having access to the court because he was known by the family of the high priest (John 18:15).

FRIDAY—GOLGOTHA

At the crucifixion of Jesus, John seems to have been the only one of the eleven disciples present, along with several women who had followed Jesus—Mary (the mother of Jesus); Salome (sister of Mary, aunt of Jesus, wife of Zebedee, and mother of James and John); Mary Magdalene; another Mary (the wife of Clopas, perhaps also the mother of James and Joseph [Joses])—and several other friends and followers (27:56; Mark 15:40-41; Luke 23:49; John 19:25). Perhaps Joanna (wife of Chuza, Herod's steward) and Susanna (a wealthy supporter of Jesus) were among the unnamed women at the cross (cf. Luke 8:1-3; 24:10). Besides all these individuals, Simon of Cyrene was also present for at least the beginning of the Crucifixion (Luke 23:26-27). By the end of the Crucifixion, somewhere in the vicinity were Joseph of Arimathea (a member of the Sanhedrin whose walled garden was likely within sight of the place of crucifixion) and Nicodemus (another member of the Sanhedrin).

Jesus died around the ninth hour of the day (about 3:00 in the afternoon). To prevent the body of Jesus from being thrown into a common grave, Joseph of Arimathea and Nicodemus gained custody of the body with the permission of Pontius Pilate (Mark 15:42-46; John 19:38-42). Nicodemus provided a large quantity of spices for a burial process that had to be hastily completed before sundown, the beginning of the Sabbath (Luke 23:54). No doubt the hired hands from Joseph's garden helped with the transport and preparation of the body. All the while, Mary Magdalene, Mary the wife of Clopas, and perhaps some others were also present and likely assisted in the partial preparation of the body (Matt. 27:61; Mark 15:47; Luke 23:55-56). Although the burial process was not completed, the Sabbath was upon them, so they quickly laid Jesus' wrapped body in Joseph's tomb and rolled the stone against the entrance (Matt. 27:59-60; Mark 15:46; Luke 23:53; John 19:41-42).

FRIDAY NIGHT— BEGINNING OF THE SABBATH

Though Scripture is silent on the matter, we can probably assume that the women would have discussed among themselves how, after the Sabbath, they would complete the work they had begun in preparing for the burial. Mary Magdalene and Mary the wife of Clopas would have consulted with Salome, and probably also with Joanna and Susanna. Because they lived in different parts of the city, they would have agreed to all rendezvous at the entrance to the garden of Joseph of Arimathea early Sunday morning to finish preparing Jesus' body for a proper, permanent burial.

After these verbal arrangements, they all returned to the places where they were staying for the Sabbath. Mary Magdalene

(continued on next page)

and Mary the wife of Clopas may have rejoined Mary the mother of Jesus at the home of Salome, the mother of John, somewhere in the southern part of the city. Joanna and Susanna likely returned to their quarters at or near the Hasmonean palace in the central part of the city. John would have been at his local home with Salome, watching over Mary, the mother of Jesus. And Peter may have been staying at the home of John Mark, possibly the same location where the Last Supper had taken place, in the southern part of the city in the vicinity of John's house.[48]

It would seem that, by this point, only John and the women knew the whole story of what had happened to Jesus. It's possible somebody informed Peter about what had transpired during the day. But the rest of the nine disciples, likely hiding out in Bethany during the Sabbath, probably had no idea what happened after Jesus' arrest. During the Sabbath, nobody could travel far enough to discover any news, and nobody would have been able to visit the tomb. Because the Jewish leaders were able to get Pilate's permission to post a guard at the tomb and to seal the stone on the Sabbath, none of Jesus' followers would have known that soldiers had been posted in Joseph's garden, likely with sentries at the entrance, along with the guards at the tomb itself (27:62-66).

Pilate must have felt like a rope in a frenzied tug-of-war between factions of Jews he cared nothing about.

When they gained an audience with Pilate, the Jewish leaders set forth their case: Jesus had said He would rise again after three days (27:63). Afraid that Jesus' disciples might abscond with the body under the cover of night so as to declare that He had risen from the dead, they petitioned Pilate for permission to secure the tomb (27:64). Weary of being nickel-and-dimed for the past two days by the Jewish leaders, Pilate's response was abrupt: "You have a guard; go, make it as secure as you know how" (27:65). It's probably best to understand Pilate's words not as "You have your own temple guards—use them," but as "Take a guard," meaning that their petition for a Roman guard was instantly granted (cf. 28:14).[49] However, the notion that these guards were at least initially assisted by the Jewish temple police is within the realm of plausibility (cf. 28:11); it would certainly fit within the Jewish leaders' obsessive desire to micromanage things in order to squash the Nazarene movement before it began.

Perhaps at the behest of the Jewish leaders, the small detail of soldiers assigned to the tomb sealed the massive stone with a Roman seal. Craig Blomberg explains this process: "The securing of the tomb would have involved the application to the stone of some kind of substance, perhaps a soft clay, impressed with the Roman imperial stamp. The seal would then be attached to the stone with a large rope or cord."[50] What a futile gesture! As if the resurrection of Jesus could be thwarted by an official decree of the Roman Empire!

APPLICATION: MATTHEW 27:51-66
Remembering the Easily Forgotten

It's easy to forget or overlook the details between Jesus' last breath before His death and the first breath of His new, resurrected life. We frequently talk about His death and resurrection as the saving works of Jesus Christ—and rightly so! But there are lessons to be learned and insights to be gained from the happenings of those rushed hours before sundown and the frantic scurrying of the Jewish leaders in the wee hours of the Sabbath, as they were trying to make sure their plot to defeat Jesus didn't unravel. Let me draw our attention to three reflections based on these scenes.

First, *when you come to the dead end of all hope, remember what happened right after Jesus died.* Most people who walked away from the body hanging on the cross walked away without hope. I don't read of anyone leaving the scene of death saying, "He'll be raised! It's just a matter of time. He'll be back!" All the disciples but John were scattered and hiding in fear. The women at the cross were wailing in despair. And the wicked rulers who had murdered their own Messiah were worrying that the body would be stolen. Nobody hoped for resurrection.

In your own life, when God seems to have let you down, look at what He did immediately after the death of Jesus, even before the Resurrection. He provided Joseph of Arimathea and Nicodemus to make sure Jesus wasn't dropped into a common grave. He provided curious women who would remember where Jesus was entombed so that they could be eyewitnesses of the empty tomb. God was working behind the scenes to bring about His purposes, even when none of His faithful ones could see it. When you lose a precious loved one and you feel hopeless and unable to go on, remember that when a person of God dies, nothing of God dies. The God who was powerful during the life of your loved one is still the powerful God of your life. He's still there for you to count on, rely on, and trust in.

Second, *when you think you know someone who is too far gone to believe in Christ, remember the centurion.* If that hardened, tough-minded Roman soldier could become aware of the truth, so can your lost loved one. And remember Joseph of Arimathea and Nicodemus—both wealthy members of elite Jewish society and members of the very council responsible for bringing about Jesus' death. God was working in their hearts behind the scenes. And when the time came to confess in words and actions, they stepped up. Think about that person you've been tempted to put on your "forever lost" list. Maybe a roommate from college, one of your sons or daughters, a parent, a close friend, or even a spouse (or former spouse). They seem so far from the Lord and so stone-cold to the gospel. Take time to remember him or her before the Lord. If God can speak to—and through—the centurion and can reach Joseph and Nicodemus, He can reach your loved ones, too. Don't give up on them.

Third, *when people concoct a scheme to thwart the plan of God, remember the Resurrection.* Like the soldiers who sealed the tomb to keep Jesus locked in forever, many try to work against God's plans through all sorts of human machinations. How foolish to think our silly logic, scientific facts, or well-financed movements could ever resist the hand of God. When He is ready and He makes His move, it trumps all human actions. It overcomes all barriers. God can split the temple veil in two from top to bottom. He can bring an earthquake or darkness over the earth. He can bring people out of the grave. In your own life, when you think everything is stacked against you and against your faith in Christ, never surrender. The followers of Jesus evidently did not take seriously Jesus' predictions that He would be raised from the dead. Otherwise, they would have behaved differently between that Friday and Sunday. When we are experiencing something difficult, we must keep in mind the reality of the Resurrection. The apparent finality of Friday may seem certain for a season, but Resurrection Sunday is coming.

Resurrection: What Happened . . . What Didn't?
MATTHEW 28:1-15

NASB

¹Now after the Sabbath, as it began to dawn toward the first *day* of the week, Mary Magdalene and the other

NLT

¹Early on Sunday morning,* as the new day was dawning, Mary Magdalene and the other Mary went out to visit the tomb.

Mary came to look at the grave. ²And behold, a severe earthquake had occurred, for an angel of the Lord descended from heaven and came and rolled away the stone and sat upon it. ³And his appearance was like lightning, and his clothing as white as snow. ⁴The guards shook for fear of him and became like dead men. ⁵The angel said to the women, "ᵃDo not be afraid; for I know that you are looking for Jesus who has been crucified. ⁶He is not here, for He has risen, just as He said. Come, see the place where He was lying. ⁷Go quickly and tell His disciples that He has risen from the dead; and behold, He is going ahead of you into Galilee, there you will see Him; behold, I have told you."

⁸And they left the tomb quickly with fear and great joy and ran to report it to His disciples. ⁹And behold, Jesus met them ᵃand greeted them. And they came up and took hold of His feet and worshiped Him. ¹⁰Then Jesus said to them, "ᵃDo not be afraid; go and take word to My brethren to leave for Galilee, and there they will see Me."

¹¹Now while they were on their way, some of the guard came into the city and reported to the chief priests all that had happened. ¹²And when they had assembled with the elders and consulted together, they gave a large sum of money to the soldiers, ¹³and said, "You are to say, 'His disciples came by night and stole Him away while we were asleep.' ¹⁴And if this should come to the governor's ears, we will win him over and ᵃkeep you out of trouble." ¹⁵And they took the money and did as they had been instructed; and this story was widely spread among the Jews, *and is* to this day.

28:5 ᵃOr *Stop being afraid*   **28:9** ᵃLit *saying hello*
28:10 ᵃOr *Stop being afraid*   **28:14** ᵃLit *make you free from care*

²Suddenly there was a great earthquake! For an angel of the Lord came down from heaven, rolled aside the stone, and sat on it. ³His face shone like lightning, and his clothing was as white as snow. ⁴The guards shook with fear when they saw him, and they fell into a dead faint.

⁵Then the angel spoke to the women. "Don't be afraid!" he said. "I know you are looking for Jesus, who was crucified. ⁶He isn't here! He is risen from the dead, just as he said would happen. Come, see where his body was lying. ⁷And now, go quickly and tell his disciples that he has risen from the dead, and he is going ahead of you to Galilee. You will see him there. Remember what I have told you."

⁸The women ran quickly from the tomb. They were very frightened but also filled with great joy, and they rushed to give the disciples the angel's message. ⁹And as they went, Jesus met them and greeted them. And they ran to him, grasped his feet, and worshiped him. ¹⁰Then Jesus said to them, "Don't be afraid! Go tell my brothers to leave for Galilee, and they will see me there."

¹¹As the women were on their way, some of the guards went into the city and told the leading priests what had happened. ¹²A meeting with the elders was called, and they decided to give the soldiers a large bribe. ¹³They told the soldiers, "You must say, 'Jesus' disciples came during the night while we were sleeping, and they stole his body.' ¹⁴If the governor hears about it, we'll stand up for you so you won't get in trouble." ¹⁵So the guards accepted the bribe and said what they were told to say. Their story spread widely among the Jews, and they still tell it today.

28:1 Greek *After the Sabbath, on the first day of the week.*

Cemeteries are silent and somber places, with row upon row of head-stones and mausoleums representing fading memories of once vibrant lives. Usually, when people visit cemeteries, they speak in hushed tones, even whispers. Occasionally we may hear children laughing, but that's often put down with a fierce "shush" by adults seeking to be reverent. The names, birth dates, and dates of death are etched in stone, not carved in wood, because they're permanent. For the deceased, the trip to the graveyard is a one-way journey.

Except for Jesus of Nazareth.

Though wrapped tightly in strips of linen cloth for the permanence of burial, He would soon slip out and never wear those cloths again. As a result of His miraculous, bodily resurrection, Jesus emerged from the sealed tomb fully and completely alive, raised to a new kind of life with a new kind of glorious body.

But just as His opponents and critics wanted Him dead when He was alive, they still wanted Him dead after He rose. They concocted *fake news* in an attempt to countermand the *great news* of the Resurrection. Then they paid a bribe to promote their story. Today, the motives and methods of many people are the same. To get out from under the miraculous truth of the full deity of Christ demonstrated by His glorious resurrection, critics continue to pull out all the stops to create alternate explanations, and they keep their propaganda machines going at full power to promote their fictions. As a result, there will always be those who believe what happened *and* those who believe what didn't.

— 28:1-4 —

Though two nights had passed, it would have been impossible for Mary Magdalene and Mary the mother of James to get the image of Jesus' limp, lifeless, bloody body out of their minds. No matter how many strips of linen had been used or how many pounds of myrrh and aloe, the stench of death would still be lingering in the air of the tomb. I imagine those thoughts crossed their minds more than once as they woke up early and started off toward the tomb together with Salome, the mother of James and John (Mark 16:1).

During their walk north through the city at the brink of dawn, the earth shook under them. Maybe it was an aftershock from the mighty quake a couple of days earlier—the one that had pounded the earth the moment Jesus died. Had the quake disturbed the garden and the tomb? What if another earthquake occurred while they were in the tomb itself? Could they be trapped? Surely these things worried them.

I can imagine that a little farther up the road, a handful of Roman soldiers made quite a ruckus as they charged past them in the opposite direction—pale faced, with the fear of death in their eyes. Where were the soldiers headed? Maybe instead of rushing *into* danger, they were running *from* it. Romans soldiers running from danger?

As the women passed through the Gennath Gate in the city wall, they approached the very mound of Golgotha where Jesus had been crucified. They had to pass that way to reach the garden of Joseph of Arimathea. There was no way around it. As they neared the garden, they were suddenly struck by a practical concern: Who would roll away the stone for them (Mark 16:3)? Maybe they could coax a few of Joseph's gardeners to open the tomb wide enough for them to slip in.

While such thoughts ran through the women's minds and across their lips as they headed for Jesus' tomb on the morning after the Sabbath, they had no idea what miraculous things had transpired at the garden tomb itself. During their walk, presumably from the home of Salome in the southern part of Jerusalem to the garden of Joseph outside the northern wall of the city, several things had happened at the tomb that were about to rock their world. An earthquake had occurred when a brilliant angel had descended from heaven and rolled away the stone of the tomb (Matt. 28:2-3). The Roman seal placed on the tomb had been broken, not by a disciple, not by a grave robber, but by a terrifying supernatural being. Then, as if to say to the armed soldiers, "I dare you to close it," the angel had sat on top of the stone. Heaven had claimed that place as holy ground.

The guards had trembled in absolute terror. They had fallen down to the ground like dead men (28:4). But then, apparently, as soon as they'd had the opportunity, they had picked themselves up off the ground, rushed out the garden gate, and hightailed it back to the city. It's possible that as they fled, they'd passed an unremarkable group of women of Galilee heading in the opposite direction—the two Marys and Salome.

In the meantime, at some point before the women cautiously creeped in to look at the tomb, the most astonishing miracle had occurred, which no human had been present to witness. Jesus of Nazareth had stepped out from the tomb, having been miraculously raised to life. His once broken, lifeless corpse had been transformed into an immortal body, infused with divine power, incorruptible and brilliant in its glorious perfection.

EXCURSUS: RESURRECTION ACCOUNTS HARMONIZED, PART 2—FROM SATURDAY NIGHT TO SUNDAY MORNING

MATTHEW 28

SATURDAY NIGHT— END OF THE SABBATH

Jews reckoned the end of a day—and the beginning of the next—with the setting of the sun. So, at sundown on Friday, the Sabbath began. With various groups of disciples in various places in Jerusalem and its vicinity, none could communicate with the others. Presumably, none of these scattered disciples knew that Roman soldiers had been placed at the garden tomb of Joseph of Arimathea. Everybody was lying low, observing the Sabbath, and hoping the crisis would blow over.

The women who were disciples of Jesus had likely helped with the hasty, incomplete preparation of the body for burial late Friday afternoon. Women could fly under the radar of the Jewish authorities, and they had arranged to go to the garden of Joseph, where Jesus' body was being held temporarily. Two of the women, Joanna and Susanna, being quite wealthy, would have had access to burial spices from the Hasmonean Palace, where Joanna's husband, Chuza, served as Herod's steward (Luke 8:1-3).[51] Mary Magdalene, Mary the wife of Clopas, and Salome, whose primary homes were in Galilee, would not have had such supplies ready at hand. When the shops reopened in Jerusalem upon the setting of the sun on Saturday night—the end of the Sabbath—these women could have purchased the spices necessary for preparing the body the next morning.

Though speculative, it is quite possible that Mary Magdalene, Mary the wife of Clopas, and Clopas himself—acting as a male guardian—departed Jerusalem at sundown on Saturday and traveled to Bethany to meet with Mary, Martha, and Lazarus. It would be reasonable to assume that the other nine disciples would be there after Jesus' arrest. If this reconstruction of events is accurate, then we have a pretty good picture of where Jesus' followers were gathered on

Jerusalem at the time of the crucifixion and resurrection of Jesus, with the traditional positions of major locations indicated

(continued on next page)

that Saturday night. Mary Magdalene, Mary the wife of Clopas, Clopas himself, and up to nine of the disciples were probably at Bethany. John, Salome, possibly Zebedee, and Mary the mother of Jesus were likely at John's home. Peter seems to have also joined them around this time if he had not already spent the Sabbath there (cf. John 20:2). And Joanna and Susanna would have been at or near the Hasmonean Palace.

As everybody retired for the evening, Mary Magdalene and Mary the wife of Clopas would have planned to get up very early—presumably having Clopas escort them to the home of Salome (where John lived) so all the women could head north to the garden together, meeting Joanna and Susanna. It is likely that at this point these disciples still did not know about the guards posted at the garden.

SUNDAY MORNING— RESURRECTION

Very early Sunday morning, while it was still dark (John 20:1), Mary Magdalene, Mary the wife of Clopas, and Salome met in Jerusalem and proceeded north through the center of the city, out one of the city gates (probably the Gennath Gate) to the garden of Joseph of Arimathea (Mark 16:1). They likely planned to meet Joanna and Susanna, who were probably coming from a different part of the city— the Hasmonean Palace.

While the women were still walking— around 6:00 a.m.—an earthquake occurred, and Jesus was miraculously raised from the dead (Matt. 28:2-3). The guards who had been stationed at the tomb since the previous day fled in fear through the garden gate, running back to the chief priests to report what had happened (28:11-15). Because the house of Caiaphas, the high priest, was located in the southern part of the city, it's quite likely that the soldiers would have run past the women who were headed north

toward the garden tomb. But the women wouldn't have had any idea why the soldiers were fleeing in such a hurry.

As the sun was rising, Mary Magdalene, Salome, and Mary the wife of Clopas passed through the city wall and headed toward the garden of Joseph of Arimathea (28:1; Mark 16:2; Luke 24:1). While they walked, they discussed how they might remove the large stone from the tomb to access Jesus' body (Mark 16:3). As they neared the garden, they likely found the gate flung open due to the flight of the soldiers and may have been able to see from a distance that the stone in front of the tomb had been rolled away (Mark 16:4; Luke 24:2; John 20:1).

At this point, a reconciliation of the various Gospel accounts requires us to assume that the group of women split up. Mary Magdalene, perhaps connecting the commotion of the soldiers with the open garden gate and the open tomb, assumed somebody had taken Jesus' body. She rushed back to John's house to inform the men there—John, Peter, and probably Clopas (John 20:2). Meanwhile, Mary the wife of Clopas and Salome apparently remained outside the garden gate cautiously awaiting the arrival of the male disciples.

Eventually Joanna and Susanna arrived at the garden gate with their supply of spices for burial preparations (see Luke 24:10). Being among Jerusalem's wealthy class and thus probably having a group of servants at her side, Joanna sallied forth with Susanna, Mary the wife of Clopas, and Salome to investigate the opened tomb instead of awaiting the arrival of the disciples. When they entered the tomb, they did not find the body (Luke 24:3). Instead, two brightly shining men—angels— appeared and announced the good news:

> Do not be afraid. I know whom you are seeking: Jesus of Nazareth, the crucified One (Matt. 28:5; Mark 16:6).

(continued on next page)

Why do you seek the living among the dead (Luke 24:5)? He is not here, but He has risen, just as He said. Come, see the place where they laid Him (Matt. 28:6; Mark 16:6; Luke 24:6). Remember how He talked to you when He was in Galilee, saying that the Son of Man must be betrayed into the hands of sinful men and be crucified and on the third day rise (Luke 24:6-7)? Go quickly, tell His disciples and Peter that He is raised from the dead and is going before you into Galilee. You will see Him there, just as He said. Behold, I have told you (Matt. 28:7; Mark 16:7).[52]

The four women rushed back to Jerusalem filled with astonishment and joy (Matt. 28:8). As they wove through the city streets—now beginning to bustle with morning commerce—they said nothing to anyone (Mark 16:8). If they had seen the guards earlier, then perhaps they now realized why they were running in the opposite direction, and may have now feared that the guards would be returning to the tomb. If so, the women would have had great motivation to take the long way to John's house through one of the gates farther east (such as the Ephraim Gate) rather than going back through the Gennath Gate to the south.

Little did the women know that, at the same time, the soldiers who had been guarding the tomb were reporting to the chief priests about the events that had occurred (Matt. 28:11). After consulting with other Jewish leaders, the priests bribed the soldiers to spread fake news—an untrue story about the disciples stealing the body of Jesus while the guards slept (28:12-13). They also promised to defend the soldiers before the governor and keep them out of trouble (28:14).

Meanwhile, Mary Magdalene made it to John's house in the southern part of the city to tell the news to John, Peter, and any others who were there (John 20:2).

Between her frantic breaths, she told them that somebody had taken the Lord out of the tomb, perhaps also relaying that Roman soldiers had been active in the area, that the gate to the garden was open, and that the stone had been rolled away.

Upon hearing this, Peter and John ran to the tomb (John 20:3-4), presumably heading straight north through the Gennath Gate. Meanwhile, the other women who had been at the garden gate had evidently already departed by another route. Upon arrival at the tomb, Peter and John found only the linen wrappings of Jesus' body; the body itself was gone. Confused, Peter and John returned to their own homes (John 20:5-10).

Mary Magdalene, no doubt already exhausted from all the back-and-forth movement of that morning, arrived back at the tomb after Peter and John had left. While there alone, weeping outside, she peered into the tomb and saw the same two angels the other women had seen (John 20:11-12). One of the angels asked, "Woman, why are you weeping?" Mary replied, "Because they have taken away my Lord, and I do not know where they have laid Him" (John 20:13). Then, as she turned to leave, Jesus stood before her, but she mistook Him for one of the gardeners arriving that morning to work (John 20:14-15). Thinking that perhaps the garden staff had moved the body to another location, she asked if the "gardener" could tell her where the body was so she could take care of it. In response, Jesus answered, "Mary!" In this moment, her eyes and ears were opened. She replied, "Rabboni!" ("Teacher") and grasped Him (John 20:16). Then Jesus said, "Stop clinging to Me, for I have not yet ascended to the Father; but go to My brethren and say to them, 'I ascend to My Father and your Father, and My God and your God'" (John 20:17). Mary rushed back to John's house and reported what she had seen (John 20:18; cf. Mark 16:9-11).

— 28:5-10 —

When the women approached the open, empty tomb in shock and awe, they found two brilliant angels keeping watch (cf. Luke 24:4). The one who had burst open the tomb immediately calmed their fears (Matt. 28:5). He informed them that although Jesus had been crucified, He had been raised from the dead, just as He Himself had promised.

Then, as the first tour guide at the "Holy Sepulchre"—centuries before it became a veritable tourist trap for pilgrims—the angel showed them that the tomb was, in fact, empty. He pointed to the place where Jesus' body had been lying (28:6). I can picture the women, hands over their mouths, eyes wide in astonishment, nodding in agreement. They had personally seen His wrapped body lying there just two nights before (27:61; Mark 15:47; Luke 23:55). The body was gone. *He* was gone. No doubt, their minds swirled with a cyclone of questions stirred by fear and excitement: *Did that angel say He was gone? Raised? What does it mean? Was He just taken away, or* really *raised from the dead? Wait—are those the linen strips He was wrapped in? Did somebody unwrap Him?*

As their minds raced, the angel's words snapped them to attention. He instructed them to rush off and tell the disciples that Jesus had risen from the dead. He *had* risen! This was no prank. No hoax. No religious metaphor. He was alive, out of the tomb, and on the move! The angel continued, "Behold, He is going ahead of you into Galilee, there you will see Him" (Matt. 28:7). *He is risen indeed!*

At the word "go," the women quickly filed out of the tomb with a mix of fear and joy to report to the disciples what they had seen and heard (28:8). The Gospels of Mark, Luke, and John relay similar stories of the women at the tomb on Resurrection morning. Some details are added, others omitted, but the accounts fit together to relay the same unified narrative of Jesus' miraculous, bodily resurrection. (See the three-part excursus "Resurrection Accounts Harmonized" for a possible reconciliation of the Resurrection narratives.)

Matthew's account follows the encounter with the angels at the tomb with yet another unexpected meeting—this time with the resurrected Jesus Himself! Though the order of events in Matthew's Gospel remains in line with the other Gospels, a comparison with the other accounts suggests that this encounter actually occurred a little later in the day. When Jesus met the women with a greeting, they immediately fell at His feet and worshiped Him (28:9). They had no confusion about who He was or what His resurrection meant. This was no mere man.

This wasn't just their King, Israel's long-expected Messiah. He was that, but much more. He was (and is) the God-man, worthy of honor and glory, praise and worship. The fact that they were able to "take hold of His feet" proved to them that He was no phantom, no ghost, no group hallucination. He had risen *bodily* from the grave!

— 28:11-15 —

Matthew pauses his account of the miraculous, bodily resurrection of Jesus in order to turn attention to the lie that gave birth to a counter-narrative. Having walked us through the eyewitness accounts of the women at the tomb and their encounter with angels as well as with Jesus Himself, the scene suddenly cuts away to drop in on Jesus' opponents as they tried to turn the good news into fake news. To the critics and enemies of Jesus, what really happened to the soldiers at the tomb was beside the point. The soldiers themselves reported to the chief priests the facts as they had witnessed them—the earthquake, the angel coming down from heaven, and the opening of the tomb (28:11; cf. 28:2-4).

This startling turn of events prompted yet another emergency ad hoc meeting of the elders. This was probably not an assembly of every member of the Sanhedrin, which would have included both Joseph of Arimathea and Nicodemus. Rather, the chief priests probably convened a "council within the council." This conspiratorial cabal had a double purpose: (1) to give off the appearance of legitimate deliberation and decision making and (2) to gather together enough deep pockets of Jerusalem's elites so they would have a large enough bribe to silence the soldiers (28:12).

A new version of the "truth" replaced the facts as they were: "His disciples came by night and stole Him away while we were asleep" (28:13). Along with the wad of cash lining their pockets, the guards also received assurances from the council that they would protect them from the governor if word of their dereliction of duty were to get out (28:14). The soldiers took the money and told the story, perhaps regarding it as less precarious than the truth. R. T. France explains,

> The story suggested by the chief priests was not only discreditable to the soldiers, but also dangerous, in that sleeping on guard duty was a serious offence, perhaps punishable by death. . . . But they may have been the more easily persuaded by the consideration that, even without the story of their sleep, their watch had been a failure. Either way they could expect little mercy from Pilate.[53]

In any case, the story's effectiveness as propaganda is proven by the fact that when Matthew published his Gospel around AD 65, the story was still being spread among the unbelieving Jews (28:15).

The inclusion of the details of the guards' experience at the tomb itself alongside the behind-closed-doors meeting of the high priests and elders has led many critical scholars to conclude that Matthew's account was made up. The problem is often presented this way: How would Matthew have known about the guards' experiences and the secret meeting? But there are several answers, all of which are plausible. The most straightforward explanation is that either the Holy Spirit revealed it to Matthew or Jesus Himself told him what transpired. Surely the resurrected God-man would know. But besides those supernatural means, more pedestrian sources quite reasonably could have conveyed this information. Perhaps one or more Jewish council members present at those meetings eventually repented and believed in Jesus, just as Joseph of Arimathea and Nicodemus had done much earlier. It would have taken only one convert from their ranks to blow the top on the whole conspiracy. Another possibility is that one of the soldiers at the tomb converted to Christ sometime in the thirty years following the Resurrection events and presented Matthew with the facts both from the tomb and from the scheming meeting of the council.

APPLICATION: MATTHEW 28:1-15

Good News vs. Fake News

Perhaps you've been told a narrative counter to the New Testament's testimony concerning the miraculous, bodily resurrection of Jesus. Maybe some well-educated teacher whom you admired did their best to convince you that the accounts of the Resurrection are irreconcilably self-contradictory. Perhaps somebody contended that all the Gospels should be dated late and placed their narratives in the category of myth or legend or even religious propaganda. Maybe you've even encountered the old, worn-out rag originally woven by the high priests—that the disciples stole Jesus' body in order to convince people He had been raised from the dead.

I'm convinced that all these alternate "facts" merely result in excessively desperate explanations that lack the compelling simplicity of the Gospels' presentation of Christ's resurrection. Regarding the fake news pushed by the Jewish leaders, closer analysis shows that its credibility is lacking. Consider these problems with the counternarrative fed to the soldiers by the Jewish rulers:

> All the disciples had forsaken Jesus in the garden of Gethsemane and had fled. It's hardly conceivable that, in their state of fear and confusion, they had taken the bold step to steal the body.

> Why would the disciples have even attempted to pull off a plan that required sneaking past guards at a walled garden gate and into a sealed tomb, which had to be opened noisily, followed by sneaking out again past those same guards? Who in their right mind would regard that as a plan that had even a remote chance of success?

> Assuming for the sake of argument that the disciples had managed to pull off the stealth overnight mission of sneaking past the guards and opening the tomb, why would they have taken the time to unwrap the burial cloths? Where would they have gone with a naked, bloody corpse?

> How could the disciples have possibly kept the conspiracy of the stolen body secret for decades? If most (or all) of them were in on the plot, which would have included making up stories of seeing Jesus raised from the dead, you'd think that at least one would have cracked under arrest, imprisonment, interrogation, torture, or execution. Yet all of them maintained their testimony of a miraculous, bodily resurrection to the end.

Despite the fact that it requires us to set aside our natural tendency to disbelieve the supernatural, the simplest explanation is the best. That is, contrary to the disciples' own expectations and contrary to the expectations of most people throughout history—including today—Jesus of Nazareth rose again on the third day, just as He had promised and just as the Scriptures themselves foretold (e.g., Isa. 53:10-12). The empty tomb is a fact of history. That the Jewish leaders alleged that the body was stolen is an implicit admission of the fact that Jesus was not there. The early, widespread, and numerous independent eyewitness accounts of encountering the resurrected Jesus are impossible to ignore (see 1 Cor. 15:1-8).

Ultimately, however, accepting the truth of the miracle of the resurrection of Jesus is an act of faith. And many people believe it, just as the disciples themselves did in the first century. Just as Christians have done in every generation since.

What Now?
MATTHEW 28:16-20

NASB

16 But the eleven disciples proceeded to Galilee, to the mountain which Jesus had designated. 17 When they saw Him, they worshiped *Him;* but some were doubtful. 18 And Jesus came up and spoke to them, saying, "All authority has been given to Me in heaven and on earth. 19 aGo therefore and make disciples of all the nations, baptizing them in the name of the Father and the Son and the Holy Spirit, 20 teaching them to observe all that I commanded you; and lo, I am with you aalways, even to the end of the age."

28:19 aOr *Having gone;* Gr aorist part. 28:20 aLit *all the days*

NLT

16 Then the eleven disciples left for Galilee, going to the mountain where Jesus had told them to go. 17 When they saw him, they worshiped him—but some of them doubted! 18 Jesus came and told his disciples, "I have been given all authority in heaven and on earth. 19 Therefore, go and make disciples of all the nations,* baptizing them in the name of the Father and the Son and the Holy Spirit. 20 Teach these new disciples to obey all the commands I have given you. And be sure of this: I am with you always, even to the end of the age."

28:19 Or *all peoples.*

After His miraculous, bodily resurrection from the grave, Jesus spent forty days on earth, mainly with His disciples (Acts 1:3). It must have been an incredible transition period for those men and women as they spent time with their resurrected Master, whom they had thought they would never see again. After He had died, they surely must have asked themselves, *What now? What do we do? Did we just waste three years of our lives on a fraud? Are we that blind? Are we that stupid?*

But with the resurrection of Christ, all the hope, all the confidence, and all the devotion and dedication were up and running again. No longer did they merely believe Jesus could be their King, Israel's long-awaited Messiah. Now His glorious resurrection made them certain of it! But as Jesus was presenting Himself alive "by many convincing proofs" and continuing to speak to them "concerning the kingdom of God" (Acts 1:3), the disciples were still asking similar questions: *What now? Is He going to set up His kingdom on earth? Are we going to be reigning with Him? Will He depose the corrupt leaders of Israel and liberate the nation from the Romans? Will He usher in the messianic age as prophesied by the Old Testament prophets?*

Jesus didn't leave them without an answer. During that forty-day period after His resurrection, He made it clear to them that although His own mission on earth was coming to an end, the message of salvation

EXCURSUS: RESURRECTION ACCOUNTS HARMONIZED, PART 3—SUNDAY AND BEYOND

MATTHEW 28

LATER THAT SUNDAY

Sometime on the morning of the Resurrection, while Peter wandered alone, perhaps returning to where he was staying (John 20:10), Jesus appeared to him (Luke 24:33-34; 1 Cor. 15:3-5). No details are given about this encounter.

By midmorning, a couple of the women likely traveled to Bethany to share the news with the disciples who seemingly had been gathered there since the Sabbath. Along the way, Jesus appeared to them, greeted them, and instructed them to tell the brethren to leave for Galilee to meet with Him there (Matt. 28:8-10). Upon retrieving the other nine disciples (Peter and John were already in Jerusalem), they all gathered together, presumably in Jerusalem. At this gathering, several of the women, including Mary Magdalene, Joanna, and Mary the wife of Clopas, reported everything they had seen, but the disciples wouldn't believe them (Luke 24:8-11).

Shortly thereafter, Cleopas (likely a variation of the name Clopas) and another male disciple headed toward Emmaus, perhaps to inform other followers of Jesus about what had been happening in Jerusalem (Luke 24:13). After their departure, Peter himself returned to the rest of the disciples, possibly now gathered at John's home, to relay his own experience (see Luke 24:33-34).

The two men on the way to Emmaus encountered Jesus, but they were mysteriously unable to identify Him. Jesus patiently explained to them the prophecies of the Old Testament that related to Him, and then revealed Himself to the two men as they sat to break bread. Immediately the two men rushed back to Jerusalem to tell their friends what had happened (Luke 24:13-35; cf. Mark 16:12-13).

By the time Cleopas and the other disciple arrived, everybody was stirred with excitement but confused by the events. Some still didn't believe, and for some reason, Thomas was not present. During the evening meal, Jesus Himself appeared to the disciples gathered there. He rebuked the doubters, ate with them to assure them He was not a ghost, and commissioned them as His representatives (Luke 24:36-49; John 20:19-25; cf. Mark 16:14-18).

A WEEK AFTER THE RESURRECTION

Eight days after Jesus had appeared to several women and to most of the disciples, the core group was again gathered indoors. This time, Thomas was with them (John 20:26). Jesus appeared to them once again and turned to Thomas specifically, challenging him for his stubborn unbelief (John 20:27; cf. John 20:25). Thomas responded, "My Lord and my God!" (John 20:28). Thus, all eleven disciples, as well as numerous other men and women, had become eyewitnesses of the risen Lord within a week of His resurrection (1 Cor. 15:3-7).

and of the coming of the kingdom must be communicated far and wide. In fact, that assignment was to be His followers' number-one commitment for the remainder of their years on earth. He declared this assignment in what has come to be known as the Great Commission, which is found in Matthew's final words. After hearing these words from their Lord, they would never again ask, *What now?* They had their perpetual marching orders—and so do we.

— 28:16-17 —

After His resurrection, Jesus appeared to individuals like Mary Magdalene (John 20:11-18), Peter (Luke 24:33-34; 1 Cor. 15:5), and His brother James (1 Cor. 15:7). In some cases, He appeared to two or three of His disciples at a time: to the women who had found the tomb empty (Matt. 28:9-10) and to Cleopas (presumably the same person referred to elsewhere as Clopas) and an unnamed disciple on the road to Emmaus (Luke 24:13-35; cf. Mark 16:12-13). And on a few occasions, He appeared to the larger group of most or all of the eleven disciples, usually behind closed doors (Luke 24:36-43; John 20:19-31; 21:1-25; 1 Cor. 15:5; cf. Mark 16:14). However, until this point, Jesus presumably had not revealed Himself alive to the larger circle of disciples in Galilee, where His followers likely numbered in the hundreds, if not the thousands.

Immediately after the Resurrection, the disciples were instructed to go to Galilee, where Jesus would meet with them (Matt. 28:7, 10; Mark 16:7). It seems that, for this gathering, Jesus had in mind a wider circle of disciples than just the eleven. If so, then during His brief appearances with the eleven to persuade them beyond all doubt that He was, in fact, alive, He probably instructed them to gather as many of the scattered disciples as they could and have them head for a particular mountain in Galilee. There He would appear to them for a special message (Matt. 28:16).

We don't know for sure at which mountain they held their planned rendezvous. The text doesn't give us any clues, but some have conjectured that Jesus selected Mount Arbel, on the western side of the Sea of Galilee, as the location for the solemn Great Commission. Wayne Stiles cautiously puts it this way:

I wonder in pure conjecture if "the mountain" to which Jesus brought His disciples for the Great Commission was Mount Arbel (Matt. 28:16). It really could have been. From here they could see the Sea of Galilee, where Jesus had commanded the wind and the waves, and Capernaum, where He had demonstrated His heavenly authority by teaching and performing miracles. They could see the place where Jesus had called them as disciples. And they could observe the highway that led to the nations.[54]

One plausible location in Galilee for the Great Commission is the majestic **Mount Arbel**, which overlooks both the Sea of Galilee and an international highway. This setting would have been quite appropriate for the commissioning of the disciples to "all the nations" (28:19).

It is quite possible that, at this gathering, the group numbered over five hundred. Recall that the apostle Paul mentioned that at some point "He appeared to more than five hundred brethren at one time" (1 Cor. 15:6). The meeting on the mountain in Galilee—arranged over the course of several weeks—is a quite plausible scenario for this appearance. If so, this would also mean that the Great Commission was meant not only for the small circle of eleven disciples but also for this larger group of His followers—and, by extension, for you and for me.

When they had all gathered on the mountain, Jesus appeared to them. If we assume that the larger group of followers was part of this meeting, then for many this probably would have been the first time they laid eyes on the risen Lord. Matthew tells us that the disciples "worshiped Him" but that "some were doubtful" (Matt. 28:17). How typical! They were torn between standing in awe of their risen Lord and struggling with feelings of uncertainty. What did it mean that He was here? And what now? They thought He was dead, but here He was—alive! And it probably got all the more confusing when they found out that He wasn't ready to do His ultimate work as Judge and King just yet. While the promises to restore the kingdom to Israel had not been abolished, they were being delayed (Acts 1:6-7). In the meantime, He had work for them to do.

— 28:18-20 —

The Great Commission is clear. Because of the absolute authority bestowed on Christ, both in heaven and on earth—that is, over all creation—His followers could go forth with confidence to "make disciples of all the nations" (28:18-19). And along with the commission came a reassuring promise: "I am with you always, even to the end of the age" (28:20). We know from other passages of Scripture that the power and presence of Christ would come to them by means of the baptism of the Holy Spirit, which they would receive at Pentecost in Jerusalem: "You will receive power," Jesus said, "when the Holy Spirit has come upon you; and you shall be My witnesses both in Jerusalem, and in all Judea and Samaria, and even to the remotest part of the earth" (Acts 1:8).

As we look at the brief, clear commission Jesus gave, we see that the plan included several things that would be a part of fulfilling it. The main verb of the commission, an imperative (command), is *matheteuo* [3100], meaning "make disciples" (Matt. 28:19). By "disciple," it suggests not simply somebody who has learned something, but somebody who is constantly learning.[55] It's not just someone who has *become* a member of a group, but someone who is an *active* member of a group. So, what does it take to make disciples in this sense and thus to fulfill Christ's Great Commission? Three participles that are dependent on the main verb describe the means by which disciples are made: going, baptizing, and teaching.

First, making disciples takes *going*. It will take reaching into hearts and communicating the good news that Jesus died for our sins and rose from the dead victorious. People need to know that there's nothing they can do to earn salvation. It is received by grace alone through faith alone in Christ alone. That's the proclamation we bear as those entrusted with the Great Commission. And we take that proclamation not just to family members, and not just to neighbors or people within our own country. We take it to the world—to the nations, as Jesus said.

There are no exceptions, no borders, and no boundaries to our disciple-making mission.

Second, making disciples takes *baptizing*—that is, initiating people into a conscious commitment to the triune God: the Father, the Son, and the Holy Spirit. This first stage in discipleship involves introducing new believers to God the Father, who created all things out of nothing and loves us unconditionally. It involves teaching them about God the Son, the incarnate God-man, who was born of a virgin, who died for our sins and rose again, who ascended into heaven, and who will come again as Judge and King. And it also involves informing them of God the Holy Spirit, who gives us new life, indwells us for sanctification, empowers us for service, unites us to Christ, and supplies us with gifts for ministry in His church. That's baptism in the name of the Father, Son, and Holy Spirit.

Finally, making disciples takes *teaching*—that is, building on the foundation of faith with instruction in living the Christian life. We teach that this is a life filled with good works, done not to earn salvation but rather because we have been saved. And we teach that it involves turning from lives of self-serving wickedness and sin to lives committed to the empowerment of the Spirit, marked by the fruit of the Spirit being increasingly manifested in our lives (Gal. 5:22-23).

Though Matthew's Gospel ends with the Great Commission, the other Gospels inform us that Jesus didn't immediately ascend to heaven from that mountain in Galilee. Jesus continued on with the disciples, returning with them to Bethany (Luke 24:44-53). It was in that vicinity that Jesus said His farewell after instructing them to remain in Jerusalem and await the Holy Spirit, who would come upon them soon (Acts 1:4-5). Luke completes his narrative about Jesus with a stunning account of His ascension and of the promise that one day, known only to God, He will return to take His throne and begin His earthly reign as the King, Israel's long-awaited Messiah:

> After He had said these things, He was lifted up while they were looking on, and a cloud received Him out of their sight. And as they were gazing intently into the sky while He was going, behold, two men in white clothing stood beside them. They also said, "Men of Galilee, why do you stand looking into the sky? This Jesus, who has been taken up from you into heaven, will come in just the same way as you have watched Him go into heaven." (Acts 1:9-11)

APPLICATION: MATTHEW 28:16-20

The Great Commission, Our Mission

Though we have completed our discussion of the life of Christ in this volume by bringing in an account of the Ascension from the book of Acts, Matthew ended his Gospel narrative with the Great Commission in Galilee for a reason. He wanted the Great Commission to be the last thing pulsating in the hearts of his readers. He hoped that those who were persuaded that Jesus is the King, Israel's long-awaited Messiah, would be moved and motivated by Jesus' command to make disciples of all the nations. As I read through Matthew's account of the Great Commission, four significant, practical observations emerge.

First, *Jesus spoke to very ordinary people who knew him personally.* Those who gathered on that mountain were just normal people, not super-spiritual celebrities. They had questions and struggled with doubts. They didn't understand how they could go on without Him or what they'd be doing once He left the earth. They had no "miracle kits" issued to them. None of them appeared with halos hovering over their heads. They wore no special uniforms and had probably not attended the first-century equivalent of a prestigious Bible college or seminary. They didn't have incredible strength on their own. In short, they were like most Christians.

Second, *Jesus presented a plan, and it was brief, simple, and clear.* He spoke calmly and deliberately. His words were self-explanatory. After making it clear that He had authority over everything anybody could imagine, He stated His plan for them in the form of a command. These would be their marching orders from here on out. They'd never have a reason to wonder, *What now?* The main verb of the commission states it plainly: "Make disciples" (28:19). There was also no room for doubt regarding the scope of the command: It was to extend to "all the nations."

Third, *Jesus was intense about the mission but relaxed regarding the method.* His repeated use of "all" reveals an intensity about the scope of everyone's involvement. He expected His disciples to be engaged in this work as active, energized, excited participants. And He expected their followers to do the same. And the next generation. And the next . . . all the way down to us. This world is dark, desperate, dangerous, hostile, and lost without Christ. That's true no matter where we go.

But as we reach out and encounter different nations and cultures, the working out of this commission requires the use of different methods. Notice that besides going, baptizing, and teaching, Jesus didn't give a detailed explanation—no step-one, step-two, step-three methodology universally binding in all situations. We use numerous methods to reach the lost and train disciples. Just think of the different kinds of people who must be reached through different means; sophisticated intellectuals can't be reached the same way we reach middle-school children. The methods we use to make disciples among prisoners on death row are going to be different from those we use to reach members of a small tribe in the Philippines.

Fourth, *Jesus expected obedient action from all His followers.* The Great Commission wasn't given so Sunday school kids could have another memory verse. Jesus didn't say these words so we'd have a short motto for our missions programs. And it wasn't just intended to be a passage for biblical scholars and theologians to analyze, dissect, discuss, and debate. Frankly, Jesus expects us to *do it!* In light of this, we are to trust in Christ, follow His teaching, and share the message of His salvation to everyone near and far. People of every nation need to hear the gospel and believe it so their lives can be transformed by Jesus Christ through the power of the Holy Spirit.

ENDNOTES

INTRODUCTION
[1] Josephus, *Antiquities of the Jews* 13.5.9.

OPPOSITION AND REJECTION OF THE KING (MATTHEW 16:1–25:46)
[1] Walter Bauer, William Arndt, et al., *A Greek-English Lexicon of the New Testament and Other Early Christian Literature*, rev. and ed. Frederick William Danker (Chicago: University of Chicago Press, 2000), 926.

[2] Bauer, et al., *Greek-English Lexicon*, 1049.

[3] F. F. Bruce, *New Testament History* (New York: Doubleday, 1969), 73.

[4] Josephus, *Antiquities* 13.5.9.

[5] See Merrill C. Tenney, *New Testament Times* (Grand Rapids: Eerdmans, 1965), 94–95.

[6] Elizabeth Barrett Browning, *Aurora Leigh*, 3rd ed. (London: Chapman and Hall, 1857), 275–76.

[7] See Josephus, *Antiquities* 15.10.3; 17.8.1.

[8] Stanley D. Toussaint, *Behold the King: A Study of Matthew* (Grand Rapids: Kregel, 1980), 200.

[9] R. T. France, *Matthew*, Tyndale New Testament Commentaries, ed. Leon Morris (Grand Rapids: Eerdmans, 1985), 253.

[10] A. T. Robertson, *Word Pictures in the New Testament*, vol. 1, *The Gospel according to Matthew; The Gospel according to Mark* (Nashville: Broadman, 1930), 133.

[11] Rienk B. Kuiper, *The Glorious Body of Christ* (Grand Rapids: Eerdmans, 1966), 21–22.

[12] D. Douglas Bannerman, *The Scripture Doctrine of the Church* (Edinburgh: T&T Clark, 1887), 5.

[13] Bauer, et al., *Greek-English Lexicon*, 384.

[14] John Peter Lange, *Commentary on the Holy Scriptures: Critical, Doctrinal and Homiletical*, vol. 8, *Matthew–Luke*, trans. Philip Schaff, new ed. (Grand Rapids: Zondervan, 1976), 199.

[15] R. Kent Hughes, *Mark: Jesus, Servant and Savior*, Preaching the Word (Wheaton, IL: Crossway, 1989), 1:202.

[16] Jim Elliot, *The Journals of Jim Elliot*, ed. Elisabeth Elliot (New York: Fleming H. Revell, 1989), 174.

[17] Leon Morris, *The Gospel according to Matthew*, The Pillar New Testament Commentary (Grand Rapids: Eerdmans, 1992), 438.

[18] See comments on Matthew 1:22-23 and the near/far fulfillments of Isaiah 7:14 in Charles R. Swindoll, *Matthew 1–15*, Swindoll's Living Insights New Testament Commentary (Carol Stream, IL: Tyndale House Publishers, 2020), 26–29.

[19] France, *Matthew*, 263.

[20] Bauer, et al., *Greek-English Lexicon*, 639.

[21] For a sampling of various viewpoints, see France, *Matthew*, 263.

[22] *The Merriam-Webster Dictionary*, new ed. (Springfield, MA: Merriam-Webster, 2016), 309.

[23] A. T. Robertson, *Commentary on the Gospel according to Matthew* (New York: Macmillan, 1911), 196.

[24] Richard B. Gardner, *Matthew*, Believers Church Bible Commentary (Scottdale, PA: Herald Press, 1991), 263.

[25] France, *Matthew*, 264.

[26] Toussaint, *Behold the King*, 211.

[27] Bauer, et al., *Greek-English Lexicon*, 919.

[28] Matthew 17:21 does not appear in the earliest Greek manuscripts of Matthew, and many scholars believe it was added to later manuscripts, based on Mark 9:29. See D. A. Carson, "Matthew," in *The Expositor's Bible Commentary*, vol. 9, *Matthew–Mark*, rev. ed., ed. Tremper Longman III and David E. Garland (Grand Rapids: Zondervan, 2010), 444.

[29] Bauer, et al., *Greek-English Lexicon*, 762.

[30] William Barclay, *The Gospel of Matthew*, The New Daily Study Bible, rev. and updated (Louisville: Westminster John Knox Press, 2001), 2:197.

[31] Carson, "Matthew," 446.

[32] See Toussaint, *Behold the King*, 214.

[33] Robertson, *Word Pictures*, 142.

[34] France, *Matthew*, 267.

[35] Josephus, *Jewish War* 7.218, in *The Works of Josephus: Complete and Unabridged*, ed. William Whiston (Peabody, MA: Hendrickson, 1987), 761.

[36] John G. Gammie, "Tax, Toll," in *The HarperCollins Bible Dictionary*, rev. and updated, ed. Mark Allan Powell (New York: HarperCollins, 2011), 1013.

[37] Morris, *Matthew*, 454.

[38] "Drachma," in Powell, *HarperCollins Bible Dictionary*, 203.

[39] Even if many of these traditions were developed around the more favorable depiction of the disciples in Acts (post-Pentecost) and in early church history, there can easily be a tendency within these traditions to downplay less-than-favorable portrayals of the disciples of the Gospel narratives and to see them only as venerable figures.

[40] Bauer, et al., *Greek-English Lexicon*, 749.

[41] France, *Matthew*, 270.

[42] See comments on Matthew 5:27-30 in Swindoll, *Matthew 1–15*, 100–101.

[43] Craig Blomberg, *Matthew*, The New American Commentary (Nashville: Broadman & Holman, 1992), 22:275.

[44] Some early manuscripts of Matthew do not contain 18:11, so many scholars believe it was added later and was not originally part of Matthew's Gospel. In any case, the verse mirrors Luke 19:10, so its truthfulness and authenticity as a saying of Jesus is not in question.

[45] Barclay, *Gospel of Matthew*, 219.

[46] See the discussion on the purpose and process of formal church discipline and dismissal as it relates to 1 Corinthians 5:1-13 in Charles R. Swindoll, *1 & 2 Corinthians*, Swindoll's Living Insights New Testament Commentary (Carol Stream, IL: Tyndale House Publishers, 2017), 75–86.

[47] John MacArthur, *Matthew 16–23*, The MacArthur New Testament Commentary (Chicago: Moody, 1988), 137.

[48] See the comments on Matthew 16:17-20.

[49] The same could be said with respect to the line of authority purportedly traced to Peter (i.e., the papacy of the Roman Catholic Church). See the feature "Was Peter the First Pope?" on pages 26–27 of the present volume.

[50] Alexander Balmain Bruce, "The Synoptic Gospels" in *The Expositor's Greek Testament*, ed. W. Robertson Nicoll (Grand Rapids: Eerdmans, 1951), 1:241.

51 Blomberg, *Matthew*, 283.

52 Anselm of Canterbury, *Cur Deus Homo* 2.7, in Sidney Norton Deane, trans., *St. Anselm: Proslogium; Monologium; An Appendix in Behalf of the Fool by Gaunilon; and Cur Deus Homo*, reprint ed. (Chicago: Open Court Publishing, 1926), 245–46.

53 Ray C. Stedman, "Breaking the Resentment Barrier," sermon preached at Peninsula Bible Church, Palo Alto, CA, July 13, 1969; transcript available at http://server.firefighters.org/stedman/stedmandvd/parables/pdf/0381.pdf.

54 Josephus, *Antiquities of the Jews* 4.8.23, in William Whiston, *The Works of Josephus*, 120.

55 *Gittin* 9.10, in Herbert Danby, trans., *The Mishnah* (Peabody, MA: Hendrickson, 2011), 321. (Italics in original.)

56 *Gittin* 9.3 (319).

57 Bauer, et al., *Greek-English Lexicon*, 555.

58 N. T. Wright, *Matthew for Everyone, Part 2: Chapters 16–28* (Louisville: Westminster John Knox Press, 2004), 42.

59 Francis Brown, Samuel Rolles Driver, and Charles Augustus Briggs, *Enhanced Brown-Driver-Briggs Hebrew and English Lexicon* (Oxford: Clarendon Press, 1977), 788–89.

60 Some have taken this statement in Matthew 19:11 as referring to the gift of singleness; however, it is more likely referring to the gift of marriage. See the comments in France, *Matthew*, 282–83.

61 Bauer et al., *Greek-English Lexicon*, 409.

62 Barclay, *Gospel of Matthew*, 247.

63 R. V. G. Tasker, *The Gospel According to St. Matthew: An Introduction and Commentary*, Tyndale New Testament Commentaries (Grand Rapids: Eerdmans, 1961), 188.

64 James Morier, *A Second Journey through Persia, Armenia, and Asia Minor, to Constantinople, between the Years 1810 and 1816* (London: Longman, Hurst, Rees, Orme, and Brown, 1818), 265.

65 Bauer, et al., *Greek-English Lexicon*, 247.

66 John Oxenham, "God's Handwriting," *All's Well!* (New York: George H. Doran, 1916), 85.

67 Robertson, *Word Pictures*, 161.

68 Lange, *Matthew–Luke*, 362.

69 Tasker, *The Gospel According to St. Matthew*, 193.

70 See Tertullian, *Prescription Against Heretics* 36.

71 Tasker, *The Gospel According to St. Matthew*, 195.

72 Ibid., 198.

73 Lange, *Matthew–Luke*, 372.

74 Sherman E. Johnson, "Exegesis of the Gospel According to St. Matthew," in *The Interpreter's Bible: A Commentary in Twelve Volumes*, vol. 7, *New Testament Articles, Matthew, Mark* (Nashville: Abingdon, 1951), 501.

75 See France, *Matthew*, 297.

76 William Barclay, *The Gospel of Luke*, The New Daily Study Bible, rev. and updated (Louisville: Westminster John Knox Press, 2001), 284.

77 Toussaint, *Behold the King*, 240.

78 Hughes, *Mark*, 273.

79 A. B. Bruce, "The Synoptic Gospels," 263.

80 France, *Matthew*, 305.

81 Myron S. Augsburger, *The Communicator's Commentary*, vol. 1, *Matthew*, ed. Lloyd J. Ogilvie (Waco, TX: Word Books, 1982), 252.

82 Nathan D. Holsteen and Michael J. Svigel, eds., *Exploring Christian Theology*, vol. 2, *Creation, Fall, and Salvation* (Minneapolis, MN: Bethany House, 2015), 253.

[83] *To Diognetus* 9.2–5, in Rick Brannan, trans., *The Apostolic Fathers in English* (Bellingham, WA: Lexham Press, 2012).

[84] Johannes P. Louw and Eugene A. Nida, eds., *Greek-English Lexicon of the New Testament: Based on Semantic Domains*, vol. 1, *Introduction and Domains*, 2nd ed. (New York: United Bible Societies, 1988), 693.

[85] Randy Alcorn, *Heaven* (Carol Stream, IL: Tyndale House Publishers, 2004), 337.

[86] Bauer, et al., *Greek-English Lexicon*, 1060.

[87] Robertson, *Word Pictures*, 177.

[88] France, *Matthew*, 319.

[89] Carson, "Matthew," 522.

[90] John Chrysostom, "Homily on Matthew 71," in Philip Schaff, ed., *A Select Library of Nicene and Post-Nicene Fathers of the Christian Church*, series 1, vol. 10, *Saint Chrysostom: Homilies on the Gospel of Saint Matthew* (New York: Christian Literature Publishing Company, 1888), 414.

[91] See rabbinical citations in Alfred Edersheim, *The Life and Times of Jesus the Messiah* (London: Longmans, Green, and Co., 1883), 2:717.

[92] Warren W. Wiersbe, *The Bible Exposition Commentary* (Wheaton, IL: Victor Books, 1996), 1:82.

[93] Barclay, *Gospel of Matthew*, 326–27.

[94] Tasker, *The Gospel According to St. Matthew*, 216.

[95] G. Frederick Owen and Steven Barabas, "Dress," in *The New International Dictionary of the Bible*, pictorial ed., ed. J. D. Douglas and Merrill C. Tenney (Grand Rapids: Zondervan, 1987), 286.

[96] Louis A. Barbieri, Jr., "Matthew," in *The Bible Knowledge Commentary: New Testament Edition*, ed. John F. Walvoord and Roy B. Zuck (Wheaton, IL: Victor Books, 1983), 74.

[97] Barclay, *Gospel of Matthew*, 336.

[98] Gerhard Kittel and Gerhard Friedrich, eds., *Theological Dictionary of the New Testament: Abridged in One Volume*, trans. and ed. Geoffrey W. Bromiley (Grand Rapids: Eerdmans, 1995), 1236.

[99] Some translations and commentators refer to eight woes rather than seven. However, 23:14 is not included in the earliest and most reliable Greek manuscripts of Matthew's Gospel. It seems to actually come from Mark 12:40 and may have been incorporated into this passage by later scribes because of its similarity to Matthew's series of "woes"; see France, *Matthew*, 327. In some translations, this inserted verse is numbered as 23:13; see A. B. Bruce, "The Synoptic Gospels," 280.

[100] John. B. Graybill, "Temple," in *New International Dictionary of the Bible*, 995.

[101] F. F. Bruce, *1 and 2 Thessalonians*, Word Biblical Commentary (Waco, TX: Word Books, 1982), 171.

[102] Tasker, *The Gospel According to St. Matthew*, 229.

[103] Robertson, *Word Pictures*, 190.

[104] For four different interpretations of this verse, see Lange, *Matthew–Luke*, 426–27.

[105] See Charles R. Swindoll, *Revelation*, Swindoll's Living Insights New Testament Commentary (Carol Stream, IL: Tyndale House Publishers, 2014).

[106] See France, *Matthew*, 348.

[107] See Toussaint, *Behold the King*, 281.

[108] Barbieri, "Matthew," 78.

[109] John F. Walvoord, "Revelation," in *The Bible Knowledge Commentary*, 975.

[110] Renald E. Showers, *Maranatha: Our Lord, Come! A Definitive Study of the Rapture of the Church* (Bellmawr, NJ: The Friends of Israel Gospel Ministry, 1995), 164–69.

PASSION AND TRIUMPH OF THE KING
(MATTHEW 26:1–28:20)

[1] Tenney, *New Testament Times*, 94.

[2] Barclay, *Gospel of Matthew*, 2:382.

[3] John L. Leedy, "Plants," in *New International Dictionary of the Bible*, 804.

[4] Three hundred denarii would have been close to a year's wages (cf. Matt. 20:2).

[5] Robert L. Thomas and Stanley N. Gundry, *A Harmony of the Gospels with Explanations and Essays* (San Francisco: HarperSanFrancisco, 1978), 206.

[6] F. F. Bruce, *New Testament History*, 139–40, 336.

[7] Details on the ancient Passover *seder* as observed in the first century are from Joseph Tabory, *JPS Commentary on the Haggadah: Historical Introduction, Translation, and Commentary* (Philadelphia: The Jewish Publication Society, 2008), 6–10.

[8] See Thomas C. Oden, *The African Memory of Mark: Reassessing Early Church Tradition* (Downers Grove, IL: InterVarsity Press, 2011), 91–98.

[9] Lange, *Matthew–Luke*, 468.

[10] William Barclay, *The Gospel of John*, The New Daily Study Bible (Louisville: Westminster John Knox Press, 1975), 2:145.

[11] D. A. Carson, *The Gospel according to John*, The Pillar New Testament Commentary (Grand Rapids: Eerdmans, 1991), 474.

[12] France, *Matthew*, 367–68.

[13] See M. C. de Boer, *Johannine Perspectives on the Death of Jesus*, Contributions to Biblical Exegesis and Theology (Kampen, Netherlands: Kok Pharos, 1996), 17:288.

[14] See Oden, *African Memory of Mark*, 83, 104–5.

[15] See Charles R. Swindoll, *Mark*, Swindoll's Living Insights New Testament Commentary (Carol Stream, IL: Tyndale House Publishers, 2016), 362.

[16] Lange, *Matthew–Luke*, 478.

[17] Robertson, *Word Pictures*, 212–13.

[18] A. Lukyn Williams, "The Gospel according to St. Matthew: Exposition," in H. D. M. Spence-Jones, ed., *St. Matthew*, The Pulpit Commentary, new ed. (New York: Funk & Wagnalls, 1909), 171.

[19] See Thomas and Gundry, *Harmony of the Gospels*, 2:223.

[20] Barbieri, "Matthew," 84–85.

[21] For more on the illegalities involved in Jesus' trial, see Laurna L. Berg, "The Illegalities of Jesus' Religious and Civil Trials," *Bibliotheca Sacra* 161.643 (July–September 2004): 330–42; see also Darrell L. Bock, "Jesus v. Sanhedrin: Why Jesus 'Lost' His Trial," *Christianity Today* 42.4 (April 6, 1998): 49.

[22] Robertson, *Word Pictures*, 221.

[23] Philo of Alexandria, *A Treatise on the Virtues and on the Office of Ambassadors* 38, in *The Works of Philo Judaeus, the Contemporary of Josephus*, trans. Charles Duke Yonge (London: Henry G. Bohn, 1855), 4:165.

[24] Ibid.

[25] Josephus, *Antiquities of the Jews* 18.3.1, in *The Genuine Works of Flavius Josephus, the Jewish Historian* (London: S. Walker, 1821), 2:73.

[26] John MacArthur, *Matthew 24–28*, The MacArthur New Testament Commentary (Chicago: Moody, 1989), 225.

[27] Wilhelm Bacher and Jacob Zellel Lauterback, "Rules of Hillel, the Seven," in *The Jewish Encyclopedia*, vol. 10, *Philipson—Samosz* (New York: Funk & Wagnalls, 1909), 511.

[28] France, *Matthew*, 387.

[29] France, *Matthew*, 387–88.

[30] Cicero, *Pro Rabirio* 5.16, as quoted in Walter Kasper, *Jesus the Christ*, new ed. (London: T & T Clark, 2011), 101.

[31] See Josephus, *Jewish War* 5.5.8.

[32] France, *Matthew*, 393–94.

[33] Robertson, *Word Pictures*, 231.

[34] Tasker, *The Gospel According to St. Matthew*, 264.

[35] William Riley Wilson, *The Execution of Jesus: A Judicial, Literary, and Historical Investigation* (New York: Scribner, 1970), 152.

[36] For a more detailed discussion of the effects of crucifixion, see Frederick T. Zugibe, *The Crucifixion of Jesus: A Forensic Inquiry,* 2nd ed. (New York: Evans, 2005).

[37] Robertson, *Word Pictures*, 235–36.

[38] Barbieri, "Matthew," 90.

[39] See John F. Walvoord, *Matthew: Thy Kingdom Come* (Chicago: Moody, 1974), 236.

[40] John D. Freeman, "Mary," in *New International Dictionary of the Bible*, 628.

[41] See a more detailed description of this in Charles R. Swindoll, *John*, Swindoll's Living Insights New Testament Commentary (Carol Stream, IL: Tyndale House Publishers, 2014), 377.

[42] Henry George Liddell, et al., *A Greek-English Lexicon* (Oxford: Clarendon Press, 1996), 947.

[43] John Bodel, "Roman Tomb Gardens," in *Gardens of the Roman Empire,* ed. Wilhelmina F. Jashemski, et al. (Cambridge: Cambridge University Press, 2018), 204.

[44] See W. W. Buckland and Arnold D. McNair, *Roman Law and Common Law: A Comparison in Outline,* 2nd rev. ed. (Cambridge: Cambridge University Press, 1952), 102.

[45] For further explanations of the details discussed in this harmony but not directly treated in Scripture, see John Wenham, *The Easter Enigma: Are the Resurrection Accounts in Conflict?* (Grand Rapids: Zondervan, 1984).

[46] See ibid., 57–61.

[47] That John had a home in the vicinity of Jerusalem is suggested by John 19:27, which says that after Jesus instructed John to take His mother, Mary, into his care, "from that hour the disciple took her into his own household." (In the Greek text, the term "household" is understood here rather than explicitly stated, but compare this to John 16:32, where the same phrase is used and seems to mean "to his own home.") Moreover, John 20:10 says that Peter and John returned "to their own homes" after inspecting the empty tomb. This suggests that they each had their own places to stay while in Jerusalem.

[48] On the traditional location of Mark's home (near that of John's family), see Oden, *African Memory of Mark*, 91–98.

[49] France, *Matthew*, 404–5; Lange, *Matthew–Luke*, 537.

[50] Blomberg, *Matthew*, 425.

[51] Note that Nicodemus had also had burial supplies at hand, indicating his wealthy status (John 19:39).

[52] The wording here isn't taken from any specific English translation but rather reflects my attempt to bring together the various parallel passages in a smooth manner.

[53] France, *Matthew*, 410.

[54] Wayne Stiles, *Walking in the Footsteps of Jesus: A Journey through the Lands and Lessons of Christ* (Ventura, CA: Regal, 2008), 164.

[55] Tasker, *The Gospel According to St. Matthew*, 277.